Praise for ꭧꞔꞔꞔꞔꞔ C-Suite ꞔꞔde

"In this compact book, Frangos focuses on the Holy Grail of the C-suite, which sits at the pinnacle of every professional career, and lays out not only a variety of reasons why people might want to achieve that goal, but also an assortment of methods for attaining it.... A lean and bracingly straightforward look at the core paths to the executive suite."
—*Kirkus Reviews*

"If you've ever wanted to really figure out how to ascend to the C-suite, this is your Rosetta Stone. Based on in-depth research and case studies, Frangos identifies and quickly brings to life the four key routes to the top. A must-read for all aspiring executives!"
—**James M. Citrin, Leader, Spencer Stuart CEO Practice, and Author,** *You're in Charge, Now What?*

"Frangos has created a roadmap for executives on the fast track. With concrete depth, she lays out the tactics that guarantee a spot on the top team."
—**Sylvia Ann Hewlett, Author,** *Forget a Mentor, Find a Sponsor* **and** *Executive Presence*

"Stories straight from CEOs combined with expert advice make this a true insider's guide. The framework provided by Frangos is clearly understood, practical and rooted in real-world insights, making this book a powerful tool for students and executives alike as they strategically map out the future of their careers."
—**Boris Groysberg, Professor of Business Administration, Harvard Business School**

"With insightful advice and input from scores of C-suite executives, Frangos creates a roadmap for professional success that is both compelling and entertaining."
—**David P. Norton, Co-founder, The Palladium Group, and Co-creator, Balanced Scorecard Collaborative**

CASSANDRA FRANGOS

CRACK THE C-SUITE CODE

HOW SUCCESSFUL LEADERS MAKE IT TO THE TOP

WHARTON
SCHOOL
PRESS
Philadelphia

© 2018 by Cassandra Frangos

Published by Wharton School Press
The Wharton School
University of Pennsylvania
3620 Locust Walk
2000 Steinberg Hall-Dietrich Hall
Philadelphia, PA 19104
Email: whartonschoolpress@wharton.upenn.edu
Website: http://wsp.wharton.upenn.edu

Ebook ISBN: 978-1-61363-085-3
Paperback ISBN: 978-1-61363-084-6

9 8 7 6 5 4 3 2

To all my friends (especially Laura Downing), family, mentors, and colleagues who helped me during the loss of my lovely mum, which coincided with the joy of writing this book.

Contents

Introduction
One Question, Four Answers

With so much changing in business, it is easy to recognize when something remains static.

That's what happened to me a few years ago when I was coaching a senior executive at Cisco. He had joined the organization two months prior and was already working through his first-90-days agenda and earning respect from his peers. As we wrapped up a conversation about his goals, he sprung the career question I hear most commonly from executives who are hovering two to three levels from the top: "So, what do you think I need to do to reach the C-suite?"

In this case, the executive's face became a little sheepish as he asked. Others inquire with intensity, in a deadly serious voice. Then there are those who lean in with a hushed, conspiratorial tone, as if entry into the C-suite requires some kind of secret code.

The question is common, though the circumstances in which it is asked vary widely. Executives want to reach the C-suite for different reasons. Some are extremely ambitious, and they see making the top team as the pinnacle of success. Others want to have greater impact and believe they can make a difference in the world working from the top. Neither of these reasons, nor any others I have heard, is wrong. They're just different.

In my role at Spencer Stuart, which entails collaborating with Fortune 500 leaders on executive assessments, succession planning, leadership development, and top-team effectiveness, I have had the chance to consider this question with great frequency. Previously, as former head of executive global talent and organizational development at Cisco, a company with 70,000 employees, I worked with the top team in numerous ways: successful executives planning their future, C-suite leaders orchestrating their succession, boards looking at the strength of the organization's leaders, executive recruiters looking for their next C-suite hire, and so on.

Most of my attention at Cisco, however, was spent interacting with two distinct groups. First, I worked with the top 500 leaders, conducting executive assessments, creating development plans, and attending to their coaching needs. They all wanted to succeed at Cisco, and my job was to help them advance or move on. Next, I partnered with the company's C-suite to help them develop leadership capabilities within their respective teams. Part of that involved putting succession plans into place. A few years ago, I worked with Cisco's board and our chief people officer to oversee the CEO succession process, when John Chambers handed the chief executive mantle to Chuck Robbins. That experience gave me a whole new lens through which to consider this question.

In my work at Spencer Stuart, as well as at Cisco, I have seen the race to the top team play out many times. Some years ago, I began to take notes and form my own conclusions about how to help people get there. Still, I needed to go deeper into the topic and get beyond my own experience. So my journey in exploration began. I talked to as many C-suite executives as I could, across industries over a multi-year period, at conferences and networking events, and over the course of my everyday job. I got in the habit of asking them to tell me their stories. Suddenly, I was the one asking the question, "So, what did you do to reach the C-suite?"

For this book, I formally interviewed dozens of CEOs and other C-suite executives from a broad range of companies and industries. After that, I surveyed 350 additional executives who are likely to be C-suite candidates in the future. I also interviewed the topmost experts in executive recruiting, leadership development, and management academia.

With this research and inquiry as the backdrop, I established a practical framework for how leaders make the leap into the C-suite. It helps that I have a keen interest in the intersection of psychology and business, which led me to pursue advanced degrees in education, psychology, and organizational development. My multidisciplinary background allowed me to piece together a coherent theory, despite the fact that the answer to the question at hand is somewhat different in every case.

When the executive I mentioned earlier asked his question, I answered it in the same way I always have: "I don't know how you'll reach the C-suite. It's different for everyone—you need to find the right path."

And this book, *Crack the C-Suite Code: How Successful Leaders Make It to the Top*, will help you find your own path. It reveals the Four Core Paths to the C-suite and explains what experiences and career strategies will hasten your journey. As you'll see, some of these paths entail introducing disruption into your career, while others require patience and tenacity. This combination of mastering the old and embracing the new mirrors business at large today, where leaders must remain ahead of change and complexity while they also steer everyday operations in a way that creates constancy.

Now, I would like to share these paths with you. Along each of them, you will encounter what is new about how to reach the C-suite, and you will also learn to master the things that may forever remain the same on this eventful, complex, and compelling journey.

Chapter 1

Four Core Paths to the C-Suite

When Chuck Robbins was named CEO of Cisco in May 2015, he was both a surprising successor *and* the obvious choice. His appointment was disruptive as well as clear and consistent. The passing of the baton in this race to the top was the result of a leapfrog succession, in which Robbins, Cisco's head of sales, advanced two levels in the organization to become chief executive. The board of directors bypassed two Cisco presidents to boost the 49-year-old Robbins up to the top slot,[1] and the announcement caught some external observers and analysts by surprise.

Yet, within Cisco, Robbins was acknowledged by many to be the ideal successor. His promotion was the product of an extensive succession planning approach that included an exhaustive search. As part of that, those of us on the team managing the succession process conducted qualitative and quantitative assessments on every serious candidate—detailing their strengths, development needs, strategic abilities, blind spots, followership profiles, and so on. The lengthy process was meticulous—so much so that the board's ultimate decision was unanimous. That unequivocal endorsement was a tremendous vote of confidence for Robbins, and it sent a positive message to the entire organization as well as the press and external stakeholders.

Robbins's story is as instructive as it is unique. The Leapfrog Leader Track, the one that helped him rise to the top, is one of the Four Core Paths that we will examine in detail throughout this book.

Over the course of my career, I've coached hundreds of executives at Cisco, Spencer Stuart, and elsewhere who aspired to serve on the top team. And many, like Robbins, have found their path and succeeded. One chief strategy officer (CSO) I know accepted the top strategy job after bringing his company back from the brink following the 2008 recession. Another, a banking chief financial officer (CFO), relinquished a coveted senior role at a Fortune 100 firm to accept the top finance job at a much smaller organization. Still another, now a young chief human resource officer (CHRO), managed to reinvent himself several times over until he was exactly what the CEO was looking for when she needed to unveil a new talent strategy that would radically decrease hierarchy in favor of a flat organization. Each of these successful executives was strategic. They expertly managed their careers while also remaining vigilant and scanning for emerging opportunities.

As I will demonstrate, there's more than one right way to reach the C-suite. Throughout this book, we will deconstruct the calculus of combining the right experience, a particular mindset, and 360-degree followership. These are the things that make the difference along each of the four paths.

I will offer guidance based on my experience, stories straight from dozens of successful C-suite executives, and specific advice designed to accelerate your chances of success along these paths. The fact is, C-suite opportunities are difficult to prepare for and harder to predict, in large part because the business landscape moves so quickly and the definition of leadership is shifting. Yet, by becoming familiar with the top four paths to the top and committing to continuous personal reinvention, you can vastly increase your chances for success.

The C-Suite Landscape: Managing and Embracing Career Change

Truth be told, the management literature is packed with advice on becoming the boss. Yet, the path narrows significantly as you ascend closer to the topmost executive spots. It is no fluke that so many of the C-suite executives I've interviewed are not only highly strategic in how they navigate their careers but also expert at responding to ongoing waves of change. The onus is on you as a leader to maintain consistent performance in your functional area while also adapting your leadership style to suit the times. That same pair of dynamic themes—maintaining consistency while enduring disruption—has come to dominate C-suite succession trends you will encounter today.

Looking at the C-suite team, for instance, you may notice that more seats have been added. At the same time, a few longtime members have stepped away. Its makeup varies by organization and industry, as always, but the overall C-suite rank has inched up "from about five [roles] in the mid-1980s to almost ten in the mid-2000s," according to published research.[2] This uptick, likely due to globalization and rising risk from disruption, signals the curation of new expertise and the elevation of roles in areas including technology (chief technology officer), risk and compliance (chief legal officer/security officer), and big data (chief data officer/privacy officer/digital officer). Similarly, as strategic priorities shift and organizations acknowledge that "businesses don't create value; people do,"[3] the CHRO has found a spot in the C-suite.

Conversely, as new functional roles gain prominence, others are waning in influence. Beginning in the aftermath of the 2008–9 recession, for instance, the chief operations officer (COO) position has notably dwindled. With just 30% of Fortune 500 companies employing a COO in 2016 (down from a high of 48% in 2000), their responsibilities in many companies have been absorbed by the CEO and the CFO.[4] Similarly, according to Spencer Stuart, the chief information officer (CIO) role is being "supplanted by the increasingly popular position of chief digital officer (CDO)."[5]

The age and tenure of top teams is another facet of the C-suite that remains familiar, while it is simultaneously being chipped away by constant change.

Research by noted Wharton School professor Peter Cappelli and his colleagues shows that less than a third of Fortune 100 leaders in

2011 started their careers with their current employers. That's down from 45% in 2001 and more than 50% in 1980. Even so, executives' age and length of tenure are both on the rise. These are unexpected trends that Cappelli believes are largely the result of the 2008–9 recession.[6] As they wrote in *Harvard Business Review*, "In such uncertain times, leaders have understandably been hesitant to leave their organizations for new opportunities."[7]

Despite the inconsistent data backdrop, a theme that I hear repeated by rising executives today is their desire to "reach the C-suite by age 45." People want to succeed at an earlier age. And some organizations are indeed appointing younger executives, including digital natives who have hastened their experience curve by rapidly rotating through a variety of roles and developing a strong organizational followership, and have built up their external brand on social media. Although this is particularly true of CIOs and chief marketing officers (CMOs), who are the youngest on average in the C-suite,[8] outliers can also be found leading established organizations: Ralph Lauren's former CEO, Stefan Larsson, and Ally Financial's CEO, Jeffrey Brown, among others, were elevated at age 41.

What all this tells us is that getting into the C-suite today requires checking many of the same boxes as before, while also bringing something radically new that organizations truly need. According to my research, boards and CEOs are searching for seasoned executives who possess a new type of mindset. Today, companies must course-correct fast, fend off insurgent competitors, and have an intense customer focus. These and other everyday realities require leaders to think on their feet. Increasingly, they need to be comfortable admitting that they don't have every answer. They must also be willing to self-correct and adapt to new leadership norms. For instance, as many management experts have noted, organizations are becoming just as focused on working in horizontal/connected teams as they are in developing individual leaders. More often, that requires leaders who think like entrepreneurs.

These changes, among others, are why I've written this book. You can't expect to foresee every shift in the external environment, but you can carefully steer your own career and professional development. The successful executives I've interviewed, and many others I've interacted with through Spencer Stuart and at Cisco, learned to act with limited information in a complex, unpredictable environment—and adapt quickly. Yet, each of them proceeded along one of four arguably predictable career paths that led them to where they are today. You'll see that several switched paths numerous times along the way, but simply knowing what paths exist made the change easier for them to manage. I hope that it will be the same for you.

The Four Core Paths to the C-Suite

My research revealed four primary paths to the C-suite. In accordance with my premise that executives require both old and new tools to succeed, two of these career paths are "traditional" and the other pair are "new" in a certain way. We will explore these Four Core Paths and the capabilities and experiences that define them. As part of a deeper discussion in the chapters that follow, I have woven in stories from the executives I've interviewed and worked with, in order to fully illustrate how these paths lead to the C-suite.

The Four Core Paths to the C-Suite

1. The Tenured Executive	2. The Free Agent
• Traditional path	• Traditional path
• Internal appointment	• Externally recruited
3. The Leapfrog Leader	4. The Founder
• Nontraditional path	• Nontraditional path
• Internal or external candidate	• New venture creator

The Tenured Executive

We will start with the most common path to the C-suite, if only to show that it is not always as clear-cut as it seems.

Promoting veteran executives has long been considered the most predictable path to the top team. (Data from 2012 show that 69% of Fortune 100 CFOs were promoted internally, with 31% recruited externally, for instance.[9]) And it's not for nothing. Promoting senior leaders on the inside track comes with significant perks. It is usually faster and less expensive to promote internally than to recruit externally. Research shows that internal hires are more likely to be considered "high performers" after the first year, and they have an elevated success rate in the first 18 months. In short, most companies promote their executives to the C-suite because doing so creates continuity and delivers less risk than the alternative.[10]

Yet, as we will see, this path to the C-suite arguably requires you, as an executive, to be more patient, achieve higher followership, and spend more time in your functional role compared with the other paths. It is neither as simple nor as predictable as it seems.

The Free Agent

The second path explores executives recruited externally. This includes outside appointees who move into the C-suite immediately, as well as individuals hired as "number twos" who ascend into a top spot. This path appears to be gaining steam of late, as 22% of CEOs between 2012 and 2015 were appointed from outside organizations.[11] That figure marks an increase in external hires compared with prior years, and the percentage is even higher in other C-suite roles. In fact, one 2013 study reported that the vast majority of CMOs are recruited externally.[12]

This path becomes ever more attractive as chief executives and boards look for leaders with skills that their organizations need right now, to compete and combat disruption. And this path has the added perk of positioning the wider organization for change, a factor that is often welcomed by investors. Securing a top spot from the outside requires you to not only demonstrate a flawless track record and reputation, but also develop your leadership brand in a more deliberate way compared with internal peers.

The Leapfrog Leader

In search of leaders who can respond to change and disruption, CEOs and boards are breaking with tradition and setting aside tenure to promote leaders who are a few levels down in the organization. In doing so, they bypass existing successors in favor of less likely candidates who can deliver the right mindset and set a new standard for the rest of the organization. I mentioned that Chuck Robbins was a Leapfrog Leader, and there have been numerous other noteworthy leaps as well, including Andrew Wilson at Electronic Arts, who skipped a level to become CEO at age 39, and Google's CEO, Sundar Pichai, who was elevated when Larry Page enacted a surprise restructuring. This path also includes fast-track leaders such as Aetna's Mark Bertolini and Microsoft's Satya Nadella, who were promoted rapidly through their respective organizations because of their ability to add value.[13]

On the Leapfrog Leader path, you need to be ready to confront ongoing industry disruption and present yourself as a strong champion of change for the organization. We will look at the full story of Leapfrog Leaders and how to think about the path in chapter 4.

The Founder

The Founder path encompasses not only entrepreneurial CEOs but also CFOs, CMOs, and any other founding C-suite leader who leaves an established organization to partner in a start-up or join a young or newly created company.

It's clear that the risk profile is different along this path, as is the mindset required to land the job and find success. As an entrepreneurial executive, you often need to satisfy venture capital investors as opposed to boards of directors, for instance, and you must be willing to own a wider range of responsibility in an environment that is lean and moving at lightning speed. Even more, the executives I interviewed made it clear that top-team chemistry is entirely different for Founders on the path to going public. Entrepreneurship is perhaps the oldest route to business building, but our focus will be on the current opportunities afforded by the digital economy and the specific challenges and opportunities it presents for becoming a top-team executive.

Getting There from Here: The Chapters Ahead

Chapters 2–5 drill down into the details of the Four Core Paths to the C-suite. As part of that, I propose a set of guiding questions to clarify the considerations associated with each path—that is, the basic tenets you should understand before proceeding. Next, I present a set of career agenda items and connect them to "accelerators and derailers" that either enhance or detract from your chances of success on the way to the C-suite.

1. *Actions and Experience.* We will look at career milestones through multiple lenses. As part of that, we will trace the crucibles that executives in my study told me were most important in their rise to the top team. In addition, we will look at the specific experiences that are relevant to each path. To make the C-suite short list as a Tenured Executive, for example, you need to go beyond success in your functional role and demonstrate a broad range of general leadership experience. Every organization has a slightly different framework for advancement, but I like to look at this through the lens of strategy and operations. You can be stronger at one of them, but you need to have experience in both.

2. *Followership and Brand.* This broad and consequential topic includes assessing your standing with the C-suite and/or board and elevating your reputation within your industry and among company colleagues. Regardless of path, you need multiple advocates and allies at all levels of an organization.

Admittedly, it's difficult to sustain *any* path without universal trust and support. Yet, Founders need a very different type of following compared with Leapfrog Leaders and Tenured Executives. Wendell Weeks, for example, a Tenured Executive, had numerous advocates at every level of Corning when he was named CEO. By contrast, several Founders I spoke with put far more of a premium on strategic industry networking and horizontal collaboration.

3. *Mindset and Perspective.* Finally, I hit on the suite of psychological assets that you need to have or develop to succeed in the C-suite. One such asset is an orientation toward lifelong learning and reinvention.

According to Michael Useem, professor of management and director of the Center for Leadership and Change Management at The Wharton School of the University of Pennsylvania, "Anybody heading into the C-suite must appreciate that they need to reinvent themselves." He went on to take the idea further, saying, "This applies not only when they are pushed by disaster, but even more, they've also got to reinvent themselves when things are going perfectly well."[14]

This is just one of the mindset aptitudes that can steer you toward the C-suite. Another is simple self-awareness. Do you know your strengths and what you will bring to the top team? Does your executive team need a change agent? Strategic thinker? Consensus builder? As we will see, an important part of the equation is what you add to the C-suite portfolio now and in the future.

After we explore the Four Core Paths to the C-suite, chapter 6 introduces hybrid paths to the top team and examines how and why executives change paths multiple times over the expanse of their careers. Finally, chapter 7 describes the process for executives who have landed on the C-suite short list, and offers observations on closing the deal and fitting in on the top team.

When Chuck Robbins accepted the CEO role at Cisco, fitting in was never going to be an issue. He was a fixture at Cisco and widely admired. Living up to lofty expectations, however, was another matter altogether.

He was well aware that he needed to fill the shoes of a giant: His predecessor, John Chambers, is widely considered to be one of the most esteemed organizational leaders anywhere. Still, Chambers was on hand to mentor Robbins as he proceeded along his leadership journey.

I hope that this book becomes part of your own journey of self-awareness and personal development. You can think of it as an executive briefing on reaching the C-suite or a trusted guide with advice and stories from your fellow executives. Then, it's entirely up to you to choose your path—no two stories are the same, and few leaders remain on a single path for the duration.

Chapter 2

The Tenured Executive

Jeffrey Immelt's successor at GE, John Flannery, has been a force at the company for over 30 years. IBM's Ginni Rometty started in 1981 as a systems engineer, long before ascending to CEO in 2012. Likewise, Mary Barra has worked at General Motors Company for her entire career—beginning as an electrical engineer at age 18 and steadily moving upward. And at Cisco? CSO Hilton Romanski originally joined the organization as an intern. They are all Tenured Executives.

The Tenured Executive Track is defined by executives who have remained at one organization for more than 15 years, steadily gaining experience and ascending ever higher. Examples of Tenured Executives are ubiquitous within hundreds of the world's most admired and enduring companies. In fact, the majority of CEOs and top leaders globally are elevated from within after working their way up, as opposed to on-boarding following an executive search.

The reasons vary: Executives with lengthy tenures are steeped in institutional knowledge and have a clear understanding of the organization's history and intricacies, and they know how to work with the sitting board and outside investors. For these reasons, CEOs appointed from within commonly edge out externally hired executives on performance measures in the first few years.[15]

Yet, as noted previously, the trend is decelerating, and the flow of outsider CEOs has increased from 15% in the 1970s to about 33% more recently.[16] Research tells us that companies today are more willing to look to outsiders in times of uncertainty or financial distress, and that shareholders react positively to the announcement of external leadership additions when an organization needs to reinvent itself.

In order to take the Tenured Executive Track to the C-suite, senior leaders must ace a complex combination of skills and abilities. And many have. GE's Flannery was chosen for his insider experience and inclusive leadership style, and yet he has also shown a willingness to break away from tradition and make surprising decisions.[17] Barra, meanwhile, used her hard-won insider credibility at GM to see the organization through multiple congressional hearings related to safety recalls and the industry bailout that marked the turbulent onset of her tenure as CEO.

As much as we may admire these and other Tenured Executives for their accomplishments and success, it is just as easy to admire them for finding the fortitude to stay in one place for the duration. In many cases, it would have been simpler to move on to new opportunities instead of remaining rooted and riding the ongoing cycles inherent in any organization.

But hitching your wagon to one organization also has a tremendous upside if you are looking up to the C-suite. Wendell Weeks, chair and CEO of Corning Incorporated, the materials developer that makes most of the glass for flat panel TVs, for instance, told me that the "culture of invention" at Corning has been a "perfect fit" with his passion for discovery ever since he joined Corning in 1983.[18] Beth Comstock, former vice chair at GE, said that GE's "fast pace and innovative vibe" gave her and other longtime leaders "permission to collaborate" and explore new ideas.[19]

Interestingly, this path to the C-suite, although the most traditional, is evolving as rapidly as the other core paths.

Core Questions for the Tenured Executive

The hastening pace of uncertainty across industries indicates that organizations need something different from their executives, regardless of tenure. In fact, I would argue that ongoing shifts in business make the Tenured Executive Track one of the trickiest paths to master. Amid new expectations, longtime leaders need to deliver the consistency that we anticipate from an insider, while also driving the disruptive innovation that taps into today's growth.

Let's start with the evolving core questions that you need to answer before you pursue the Tenured Executive Track to the C-suite.

Am I a Fit with the Culture?

Jim Citrin, leader of Spencer Stuart's North American CEO practice and author of *The Career Playbook*, told me that culture fit is "the most basic prerequisite that executives need to consider in order to succeed."[20] In fact, research by Spencer Stuart shows that approximately 65% of executives who fail do so because they come up short on cultural suitability, not because of capability gaps.

Edith Cooper, senior director at Goldman Sachs, agreed that understanding and embracing the culture is a basic success factor for Tenured Executives. In fact, Cooper herself joined Goldman in 1996 with culture in mind, and today she's a member of the firm's Management Committee.

After more than a decade working in financial services, Edith joined Goldman Sachs as global head of human capital management. The firm's culture of meritocracy, collaboration, and "delivering the best possible results for clients" enabled Cooper to envision an ongoing future for herself there.[21] Now, by virtue of her role, Cooper is a key arbiter of the firm's culture throughout the wider organization and externally.

It's clear that making it to the C-suite along this path without a culture fit is unlikely, and it is impossible to lead successfully in nearly any case without meeting this significant core requirement.

Am I Passionate about the Purpose?

Perhaps more nuanced than pure culture fit, shared purpose is nonetheless a Tenured Executive Track requirement. Shared purpose, or feeling passionate about "why we all work here," is important on every path to align goals, but even more so on the Tenured Executive path because it drives individual engagement on a C-suite journey that is *especially long and winding.*

Shared purpose is one of the things that Microsoft's Terry Myerson and I discussed. Myerson, executive vice president of the Windows and Devices Group, came to the computing giant when Microsoft, under Bill Gates, acquired Intersé Corporation, the software start-up founded by Myerson.

"I was part of the deal," Myerson said. "I never intended to be a corporate executive and I surely didn't join Microsoft thinking, 'Oh, I'm going to be here for a very long time.'"[22]

That was 1997, and today Myerson reports to Microsoft CEO Satya Nadella. He is responsible for Windows, Surface, Xbox, Minecraft, and all the software, applications, and games that are part of the Windows ecosystem.

Part of the shared purpose that Myerson has tapped into is the vision of Windows as a conduit into "ubiquitous computing," the idea that the internet is instant and everywhere as more devices and appliances become smart and networked. This evolving purpose, adopted first by Steve Ballmer and later Nadella, is what keeps Myerson looking to the future and "continuing to do what is right" in terms of "strategy and understanding of why we do things," from new product ideas and pricing plans for Windows products and service.[23]

Having a shared purpose fosters the resilience that Tenured Executives need to remain anchored along this path to the C-suite. When one product or strategy fails, shared purpose keeps executives aligned in their ongoing objectives.

Can I Change with the Organization?

Understanding how you tolerate change—embrace or avoid—is especially significant on the Tenured Executive Track, because it is easy to get stuck in your career when you remain at one organization for a lengthy period. Without the instant reset that occurs when changing companies, Tenured Executives need to embrace change actively and continuously.

Boris Groysberg, a professor of business administration in the Organizational Behavior unit at the Harvard Business School, told me that this imperative goes beyond simply learning new things. He said that it is just as important to "*unlearn* the things that are no longer relevant."[24]

"Today, executives need to remain ahead of disruptive technology, understand the role of social media and the cloud," Groysberg said. "But, tomorrow? It will be something different."

As part of that, you should create a series of experiences for yourself that enable personal and professional growth. In some organizations, mandatory role rotation and new assignments keep executives learning and developing, while other firms require leaders to be more proactive by looking for ways to disrupt themselves and their routine.

Comstock agreed with this idea, saying, "Leaders need to pursue experiences that get them comfortable with ambiguity so they can accelerate in their careers."

In Cooper's case, she cites a stint in London as an early transformative experience. She joined Goldman initially to help lead the firm's energy sales business in New York, and shortly after welcomed the opportunity to move to London to colead the firm's commodities division in Europe and Asia.

"At the time, it was a change that forced me out of my comfort zone," Cooper said. "I didn't feel especially ready for the responsibility, but I looked for support and took the leap." That was the beginning of many big changes and pivots along the Tenured Executive Track that led Cooper to the C-suite.

A related facet of change for Tenured Executives is organizational transformation. Leaders need to look beyond their current understanding of opportunities, make sense of industry change, and guide the organization accordingly. In other words, they need to remain ahead of change.

One way to achieve this is by practicing what MIT professor Deborah Ancona calls "sensemaking." Originally introduced by organizational theorist Karl Weick, sensemaking is a cognitive ability pertaining to "how we structure the unknown so as to be able to act on it . . . . [Sensemaking] enables leaders to have a better grasp of what is going on in their environments, thus facilitating activities such as visioning, relating and inventing."[25]

Beth Comstock, who thrives on leading change "because it offers the greatest opportunity to have an impact," said that GE underwent so much transformation and development in her time there that "it felt like I'd been at four or five different companies." She told me that her ability to see patterns and look across situations for commonalities and opportunities has served her extremely well as a Tenured Executive.

You won't be able to remain at one organization long enough to reach the C-suite unless you can reinvent yourself and lead others through change. Making sense of change, in all forms, is an active ingredient for avoiding inertia along this path to the C-suite.

Can I Create My Own Opportunities?

The successful Tenured Executives I've met, coached, or interviewed were focused and ambitious, yet many times they waited longer for their C-suite slot than peers on other paths. Instead of resigning when a "bigger" job title was open elsewhere, they found opportunities to pivot, do something new, and fully maximize where they were at any given time.

Instead of making fast advancement the immediate goal, Tenured Executives think differently to create opportunities. Comstock suggests taking on assignments that are not well developed, and owning them in a way that creates value and allows you to break out of your comfort zone.[26] I often coach executives to think about advancement in a nonlinear way and envision multiple scenarios for success on the way to the top team.

Interestingly, most Tenured Executives have been passed over for a C-suite role at least once, and they've needed to wait for their next opportunity.

As Myerson told me, "[As opposed to looking out only for myself], the point has always been to have the greatest impact year after year, and it's especially significant when you see your efforts are helping to drive the direction of the organization."

In other words, reaching the C-suite may be more circuitous on the Tenured Executive Track, but it's worth the wait.

Getting on the Fast Track: The Tenured Executive

The same three key agenda items apply differently to each path to the C-suite. In the case of the Tenured Executive, we will focus on the things that longtime leaders can bring that will set them apart by virtue of their deep knowledge of the organization and key relationships established over time.

✔ Actions and Experience	✔ Mindset and Perspective	✔ Followership and Brand
__Add value to the organization	__Exhibit tenacity, a combination of determination and patience	__Achieve wide followership
__Be versatile and look for opportunities to drive the organization forward	__Put the organization before yourself	__Attain executive sponsorship
__Lead transformations	__Develop an inside-outsider perspective: fit in, yet present a new vision	__Rely on personal supporters

✔ *Actions and Experience*

Microsoft's Myerson sums up experience on the Tenured Executive Track like this: "What you're really looking for is someone who can drive the business forward with a singular focus on trying to be the best . . . through every type of challenge."

Exactly. Tenured Executives need to demonstrate a vast range of functional and general leadership experiences on the way to the C-suite. To create focus, I coach executives to frame their experiences in three ways: *value*, *versatility*, and *change management*.

Add Value

First, demonstrate that your key accomplishments add value to the organization. Showing that your work has lasting impact sets you apart from even exceptional internal and external candidates for C-suite positions.

For Corning's Weeks, winning the Malcolm Baldrige National Quality Award in 1995, when he was leading external development in Corning's telecommunications business, was an accomplishment that put him over the top professionally prior to becoming CEO. Weeks said their business at the time was in a top position during the heady days of early fiber optics, and winning the Baldrige Award gave his team a valuable external lift that "truly validated the work we were doing for customers, and branded us as better than the rest in terms of quality and innovation." At the time, Weeks's division was the most profitable and forward-looking in the organization. All of the Tenured Executives I've interviewed can name multiple accomplishments that added significant value to the organization.

Be Versatile

Next, Tenured Executive leaders need to demonstrate that they have the versatility to drive the business forward—in both good times and bad. Chief executives and boards recognize that business cycles rise and fall, and your actions as a leader are relevant at both ends of the spectrum.

Like many Tenured Executives, Weeks has seen the business through spectacular highs and the lowest lows. Under his oversight in fiber optics, Corning's business in the mid-1990s soared.

"We rode the internet bubble and built advanced optical networks on the back of great inventions, some of which I'd helped shepherd into life," he said. "We became ever more successful."

Then, in 2001, the telecom bubble burst and it devastated the company. Almost all of its profitability disappeared. The organization went from being worth almost $120 billion to $1.5 billion in less than eighteen months.

Weeks stepped up to take ownership of the situation.

"Then-CEO Jamie Houghton basically said to me: 'You helped break this. Now go out there and fix it,'" Weeks told me.

It was an obvious inflection point. Weeks and Houghton decided that "a crisis is too good of an opportunity to waste." They took that moment to "decide what type of company [they] were going to be" and "embraced [their] core" of growth through innovation and making "keystone components" like liquid crystal displays.[27]

Weeks helped lead the company's restructuring and return to profitability. He became Corning's president and COO in April 2002 and was named CEO in April 2005.

Similarly, Myerson told me about Microsoft's memorable peaks and valleys and how he and others led the organization through them. Even as the organization hit $1 trillion in all-time cumulative revenue in 2016 (a very solid success that included Window's dominance in the desktop market), its challenges are publicly noted. The organization went up against Google with search engine Bing, for instance, and roundly failed to unseat Google as the consumer search default. And Myerson himself was charged with creating a Windows phone that could respond to the iPhone and Android. After significant initial investment, the initiative was ultimately not successful in the marketplace.

To Myerson, leading at the highest level as a Tenured Executive means "always holding a high standard and pushing for better products and better results all the time" and being a "let's go take that impossible hill" kind of person through ongoing success, challenges, and disruption.

Lead Change

Finally, Tenured Executives need to be able to lead through difficult change. Turnarounds, transformations, and restructurings are not only a core part of leadership but also a litmus test of your ability to proceed under intense, ongoing pressure.

Weeks said turning around the company following the fiber optics collapse shaped him as a leader more than any other single experience and most prepared him to become CEO.

"You can't be a leader without realizing that many people pay the price when you are wrong or things hit a decline," he said. "It forces you to think about not only how to make things right, but also how to *keep* them right and take that social contract people have signed seriously."

Cooper agreed, saying that one of the most difficult but necessary skills a top leader needs is the ability to make tough decisions that impact people's lives while also finding a way to illustrate and communicate the true values of the organization, "including a deep respect for people and their talent and worth." Cooper said leaders need to "be comfortable feeling uncomfortable" because "that is when you grow most as a leader."

By definition, Tenured Executives don't move on to the next opportunity when difficulties arise; instead, they stick around and respond to every market environment and fiscal outcome. As a leader along this path, you will most certainly be presented with chances to create value, illustrate versatility, and exercise change management. How you respond may earn you a spot on the C-suite short list or cause you to rethink your career path.

✔ Mindset and Perspective

There are dozens of personality tests and leadership models that isolate the emotional requirements executives need to lead. Ideal traits range from decisiveness and confidence to emotional intelligence and humility. All of these and others serve top leaders well, and a lack of any core characteristic, such as integrity, may be a deal breaker for getting into the C-suite.

That said, Tenured Executives need to surpass core characteristics and focus on nurturing additional traits that help them stand out.

Exhibit Tenacity

The initial characteristic on our short list relates to tenacity. Tenured Executive Track leaders need resolve to remain at one organization through feast or famine. A nuanced trait, tenacity manifests itself in a few very different ways: loyalty, focus, dedication, perseverance, and more. One uncommonly important manifestation of tenacity is simple patience. (Of course, most of us know that having patience or *waiting our turn* is far from simple.) Yet, patience provides payback along the Tenured Executive Track. It certainly did for Jay Galeota, president and COO of the pharmaceutical firm G&W Laboratories.

Prior to joining G&W in 2016, Galeota spent 28 years at Merck in a succession of increasingly high-level roles. In 2009, he interviewed for CSO, but the company selected an external candidate. Galeota was disappointed, but he managed to take it in stride.

Instead of the CSO job, Galeota was asked to run the hospital and specialty care unit of Merck. It turned out to be an extraordinary experience. He managed 27 products across seven therapeutic areas that made up the $11 billion global business. It was a line job and "an excellent alternative" to the C-suite role.

A few years later, when the CSO job opened up again, Galeota interviewed a second time for the role, and this time he got it.

"The decision sequence around the chief strategy role turned out to be a gift," he said. "I spent the time gaining a level of operating experience I never would have gotten if I had been put into a C-suite staff role years earlier."[28]

In Galeota's case, patience meant gaining additional experience while he waited for a succession situation to play out. Other times, it means pausing while restructuring realigns roles and opens up opportunities. Both Weeks and Myerson said organizational change played a role in their career advancement over time.

Put the Organization First

Another mindset characteristic that can accelerate executives on the Tenured Executive Track is a willingness to focus on the organization, putting it above your immediate career aspirations. As mentioned, getting to the C-suite can't always be your central objective on the Tenured Executive Track, as it can for those traveling the Founder and Free Agent paths, which we will discuss later.

Weeks insists that his journey to becoming CEO was never about putting his career trajectory out front, and far more about "following my passion and mastering what I was engaged in at the moment."

"I pretty much turned down every promotion that I got until they explained that they were only *asking* to be polite . . . . They would always say, 'Well, no, we'd actually like you to go and do this for a while,'" Weeks said. "Essentially, as long as I focused on my position with passion and intensity, the organization pulled me up."

Comstock agreed, saying, "I always just wanted to keep getting better at what I was doing, and as long as I did that and was looking for change and innovation the opportunities kept coming."

This is a common refrain for Tenured Executives—focus on being the best and advancement happens organically.

Be an Inside Outsider

A third mindset attribute that serves Tenured Executives particularly well is being an "inside outsider." This is all about fitting into the culture while you also stand out with ideas and insights that are disruptive. To be fair, the "insider" half of this is far easier to accomplish on the Tenured Executive Track than the "outsider" half.

Harvard Business School professor emeritus Joseph Bower literally wrote the book on inside outsiders, in 2007, with *The CEO Within:*

Why Inside Outsiders Are the Key to Succession. In it, he says that true inside outsiders "view their role through the lens of someone who just bought the company—unencumbered by the cognitive and emotional baggage that comes from a long tenure in the organization."[29]

This mindset needs to be actively cultivated—one must strive to have an open mind, remain objective, and keep an eye on how things are accomplished in adjacent industries and organizations.

Even after 28 years at Merck, Galeota described himself as an inside outsider. He said that he was always scanning with an "outside the walls" orientation to see how things were done elsewhere and what ideas he could bring back from other companies and industries he was interacting with. Comstock said that she, as well, always remains externally connected in order to pick up on "new trends that will matter to us."

"GE is a big place with so much leadership development that it might be easy to remain insular," she said. "But I kept close tabs on the outside world in order to take things in with an external lens."

Comstock also said being an inside outsider helped her find "white space opportunities."

The inside-outsider mindset, like the two other mindset traits mentioned, requires a talent for integration and balance. Tenured Executives need to be focused on success, yet willing to wait; pursue work that stokes their passion, yet put organizational success first; and thrive within the company while maintaining an outside perspective. Mastering both ends of the spectrum is a lot to ask. Yet, it comes naturally to Tenured Executives on the way to the C-suite, because their institutional knowledge, accumulated over time, serves to align their professional goals with what the organization needs most.

✔ Followership and Brand

Followership on the Tenured Executive Track is yet another both/and balance. All rising executives need to cultivate broad support and respect on the inside and outside. However, I would argue that it is impossible to rise above a certain level in an organization without senior executives who are willing to pull you up. More than anything else, gaining access to opportunities and advancement on the Tenured Executive Track requires securing internal support from above.

The conventional way of thinking about this is through the lens of sponsorship. In her book *(Forget a Mentor) Find a Sponsor: The New Way to Fast-Track Your Career*, Sylvia Ann Hewlett makes the case that mentors "support you from the sidelines" of your career by offering advice and encouragement, but sponsors are more powerful because they are "hands-on" advocates. They suggest you for major assignments, for instance, run interference when things go wrong, tell you when opportunities are opening up, and put you on the short list for promotions.[30] Hewlett, economist and founding president of the Center for Talent Innovation, is a strong advocate for advancing sponsorship for female executives in particular, but this is a tool suited for any Tenured Executive.

Cooper, one of two female executive officers at Goldman Sachs, benefited greatly from sponsorship throughout her career at Goldman.

"Time and again, when I found myself outside of my comfort zone, they never let me off the hook," she said. "In fact, they pushed and pointed me to accept bigger roles and assignments." She said that a few of her sponsors took an interest in her career from the beginning. "At times, they had more confidence in me than I had in myself," Cooper said.

Weeks, as well, had the guiding support of colleagues, including Corning's chair at the time, who "rallied behind [him], gave him the support [he] needed, and spoke up on [his] behalf."

What are the how-tos of gaining sponsorship? According to Hewlett, one way is through performance—overachievers are far more likely to gain sponsorship. Another way is through loyalty. Sponsors look for dedicated individuals they trust to be committed to the firm. Finally, sponsors look for people who have a personal brand that separates them from peers and exhibit qualities that add value to the firm.[31]

Galeota suggests getting started by going beyond the usual experiential résumé to thinking about your "relationship résumé."

"Early on, I was deliberate in seeking out people in the organization who I felt really had it together. I watched when they were presenting in meetings or when they worked with external partners or senior leaders. I tried to seek those people out, to be around them more and just learn from them," Galeota told me. "Many of them advanced within the organization and I learned more from them as they did."

Gaining support from executive sponsors is by far the single most important followership item Tenured Executives should attend to. But sponsorship it not the only guardrail for executives along this path. A close second is having ongoing personal support from family and friends. Why? As Dan Ciampa, advisor to boards and chief executives, and a former CEO himself, told me, "It's lonely at the top. Executives need to focus on their health and well-being in order to sustain their tenure and succeed as leaders in the long term."[32]

Family and friends will help you remain resilient and recharge when job stress impacts your well-being as well as your path to advancement. They also help you "keep things in perspective." As one C-suite leader told me, "Colleagues become a little bit like family after 20 years together, but then you go home and that's where you find the real support you need to succeed."

The Tenured Executive: Career Accelerators and Derailers

Accelerators	Derailers
• You are a natural fit within the organizational culture and know how to be successful operating within it.	• You feel like an outsider in the culture and can't make sense of internal organizational dynamics.
• You are motivated by a shared purpose that aligns your actions with the organization's objectives.	• You don't know the larger purpose and "why we all work here."
• You balance institutional knowledge with the ability to sense future industry trends.	• You thrive on quick wins and focus on short-term goals.
• Your key accomplishments add lasting value to the organization.	• Career advancement is what drives your decision making.
• You are focused on driving the business forward in all market conditions and you can lead transformational change.	• You can't envision remaining through "off years" and don't want to be part of working through organizational transformations.
• You put organizational needs above your short-term career aspirations.	• You have distinctive ideas but can't sell them to peers.
• You have an inside-outsider perspective, fitting into the culture while standing apart with ideas and insights that are distinctive.	• You have a difficult time making connections within the organization.
• You have multiple sponsors to pull you up in the organization.	• You feel out of sync with leadership and don't feel supported.
• Personal support from friends and family helps you remain resilient.	

Chapter 3

The Free Agent

D avid Simmons was a poster child for success at Pfizer when he left his job as president and general manager (focusing on emerging markets and established products) to lead a private organization, Pharmaceutical Product Development, Inc. (PPD), as chair and CEO.

Simmons called it "a remarkable opportunity to lead a world-class company through its next phase of expansion."[33] But he also admitted that it was a tremendously difficult career choice to walk away from a high-level job reporting directly to the CEO at a thriving brand-name organization.

His 15-year tenure at Pfizer began in 1996, when he migrated from the steel industry to lead Pfizer's IT infrastructure group in England. After a couple of years, "through serendipity," he moved from IT into his first general manager job in pharma, with full profit and loss responsibility, as country manager in Greece. It was about this time that Simmons went from what he calls an "accidental tourist" in his career to being a more deliberate strategist.

"I wasn't really thinking about my future for a time, I was just living the dream," he said. "Then, I looked around at the possibilities and realized, 'Hey, maybe I should be taking a longer-term view and have a plan.'"

Later, when Simmons was recruited to lead PPD, he was already a member of the C-suite at Pfizer. Despite feeling "a very high level of satisfaction" about his job, he made the strategic decision to leave. Simmons became a Free Agent in order to move to the corner office.

"I wanted to test myself," he said. "And the probability of that type of opportunity opening up, giving me the chance to reach the CEO level at Pfizer within five years . . . well, it was far from certain."

Like many of the executives I've interviewed, Simmons came in from the outside and landed the top spot over numerous internal candidates. Free Agents can also come in as "the No. 2" (COO or another senior position), with the clear understanding that they are next in line for a C-suite position. They spend a few years getting to know the organization (and vice versa) before the succession is formalized. These similar scenarios, which I refer to interchangeably as the Free Agent Track, are populated with executives who are recruited externally to join the C-suite.

In comparing Free Agents with Tenured Executives, it's easy to see that the risks are different for top-team executives coming in as outsiders. Several of the strategic imperatives for getting recruited and securing the job are distinctive as well. Becoming a Free Agent often comes down to the timing of a new opportunity, for example, but there are numerous distinct dynamics at play as well. Before we go further down this career path, we will examine some of the market forces that make acquiring top talent from the outside appealing to recruiters, CEOs, and boards. Keeping this context in mind will help you make the right professional choices to steer your career.

The Decision to Buy versus Build

It is notable that between 2012 and 2015, 22% of all CEOs appointed to the 2,500 largest companies in the world came from outside organizations.[34] This percentage marks an increase in external CEO hires compared with prior years, and the percentage is even higher in other C-suite roles. As noted earlier, a 2013 study indicates that the majority of CMOs are being recruited externally.[35] For CFOs, however, a Russell Reynolds study shows that internal promotions represent a clear majority, while external hires represent a "meaningful minority."[36]

Job titles aside, C-suite hiring trends are changing just as quickly as organizations themselves. In my work, and after consulting numerous colleagues and experts, I have found that companies turn to talent acquisition in several circumstances, beyond the obvious instance of a shallow pipeline of internal executive talent.

The most common reason organizations source top talent externally is to position themselves for change. According to one 2016 survey, 92% of business and HR executives identified "redesigning their organization" to meet global business demands as a critical need.[37] Similarly, the *Harvard Business Review* reported that "the industries facing the most disruption have brought in higher-than-average numbers of outsiders"[38] and noted that "38% of incoming CEOs in the telecommunications industry during the previous four years were recruited from outside the company."[39]

There is no shortage of evidence that the imperative for change and transformation fuels the Free Agent Track to the C-suite in several ways.

For instance, finance industry veteran Brian Duperreault was recruited to replace Peter D. Hancock as CEO of the insurance conglomerate AIG in 2017. Nine years after AIG's bailout by the Federal Reserve, Duperreault, an industry veteran known for his turnaround efforts, made it clear in interviews that he was recruited specifically to grow the insurer.[40] At Starbucks, Kevin Johnson was brought in from Juniper Networks to be COO, before being elevated to succeed the visionary founder Howard Schultz as chief executive. Johnson, a technology industry maven, was recruited in part to expand Starbucks's capabilities in mobile technology and create new products and technologies. Examples like these are universal—Free Agents are also change agents.

Another shift that impacts the Free Agent path to the C-suite is the onset of activist investors and shareholders who lobby for fresh thinking and new leadership when results or stock prices trend downward. Although this is a decidedly global trend, the most conspicuous case in the United States in recent memory occurred at the private ridesharing organization Uber in 2017, when investors pressured founder and CEO Travis Kalanick to resign and the board installed Dara Khosrowshahi, formerly of Expedia, to take over.

The Free Agent Track opens up when a strategic shift is required or when existing executives don't have the skills or experience to support the organization at a particular moment in time. It is also important to note that these needs for new top talent sometimes coexist with organizational challenges that may *not* be conducive to easily on-boarding new executives: Organizational culture, the depth of executive training capabilities, and the expectations among the existing top team, to name just a few, may not make it easy for a Free Agent to take the lead.

With this as the backdrop, it's clear that this path has a distinctive set of challenges and opportunities, and therefore, Free Agent leaders need to be more strategic than ever.

Core Questions for the Potential Free Agent

One executive I know runs an $8 billion business unit in the telecom sector. He'll be a CEO someday—everyone around him knows it. Yet, he doesn't want to be the chief executive at the company where he presently works. He envisions leading a smaller, more entrepreneurial organization. Similarly, one of my close friends is the lead executive recruiter for a large management consulting firm, but she wants to be a CHRO. She knows that she won't be happy until she's a CHRO, and she makes sure other people know it as well. Why hide it when her allies can help her get there?

Being a Free Agent requires self-reflection to decide when the time is right. There are trade-offs inherent in leaving one organization to join another, and knowing what you want (and being able to assess the risks) amounts to half the battle. You can begin the due diligence by considering some core questions to help determine whether the Free Agent Track will take you where you want to go.

Am I a Good Fit in My Present Company?

When fit becomes a negative factor it moves executives off the Tenured Executive Track and makes them Free Agents. In my work, I've seen that culture is the most meaningful variable of fit. Corporate cultures change when mergers, leadership transitions, turnarounds, business model change, or industry shifts realign the core values of an organization. These shifts can leave the company unrecognizable to longtime executives who are not on board with the change. Other variables that impact fit and make executives more likely to move around are skills and aspirations. When your defining skills and talents are no longer valued or your ideas and aspirations don't sync up with the organization, it's a signal to reposition yourself at a new place.

What Will I Do If I Am Passed Over?

When they fail to land the job they want in their organization, Tenured Executives often turn into Free Agents. The scenario looks like this: You've spent a decade or more rising to the top 5% of an organization and you're parked a level or two away from the top team. Then, a C-suite succession opportunity presents itself and you make it onto the short list. Ultimately, you aren't the chosen one. Now, you have a choice to make—stay or go?

When Chuck Robbins succeeded John Chambers at Cisco, we lost several top executives, not because they lacked talent—indeed, they were high performers—but because they felt they needed to move elsewhere to reach CEO sooner. The fact that they came so close at Cisco was a wake-up call: They were ready for the big role. Of the executives who exited, some are Free Agents on their way to a CEO role, and a few are CEOs at smaller organizations.

When Galeota did not receive the CSO job the first time, he remained at Merck and waited for his next chance—and the gamble paid off. What will you do when this happens to you?

How Fast Is My Career Clock Ticking?

Even if a succession or missed promotion hasn't left you the odd one out, it's important to acknowledge when you are open to becoming a Free Agent.

When Kelly Kramer got the call to join Cisco, in 2012, she was CFO of GE Healthcare Systems and a 20-year veteran at GE. In other words, she was an overachiever. Would Kramer have made it to the C-suite as overall CFO at GE? Possibly, but not soon enough for her. When she made the change, she was ready for the C-suite and Cisco offered her a clear path as a Free Agent. Kramer accepted a role at Cisco as a senior vice president, corporate finance, with the understanding that she was on a succession path; three years later she was elevated to CFO.

Timing is a common consideration for Free Agents. If you are ready, but there's no opportunity where you are, or you are not first or second in line, then it may be a signal to look elsewhere. Being a Free Agent might mean moving to a smaller organization, and it sometimes requires relocating.

Other timing issues come into play for the Free Agent as well: Is your organization in questionable health? Is it being acquired? Is your industry failing to transform fast enough? Situations such as these indicate that "the writing is on the wall," and it may be time to move in order to reach the top.

What Is My Strategic Career Plan?

Many executives find themselves on the Free Agent path because they are in pursuit of a specific situation or experience. A turnaround assignment. A general manager job with additional direct reports. An entrepreneurial leadership position. Whatever it is, if it is important to you, you may need to move around to check the box.

Patricia Fili-Krushel, for example, has covered vast ground as a broadcast media executive. She served as chair of NBCUniversal News Group, president of ABC Television, and CEO of WebMD, to name a few of her top jobs. She made her way around the notoriously male-dominant media universe as the right opportunities presented themselves, and she always managed to have a strategic perspective.

In 1999, Fili-Krushel left her position as president of ABC Daytime television to take on her first C-suite role, CEO of WebMD. At the time, most executives in her shoes would have been hesitant to abandon established media and entertainment to move online, but Fili-Krushel saw the upside.

"The higher you go, the more skill sets you need to call upon," she said. "At the time, I needed to get some digital experience and this was my chance to do exactly that."[41]

Fili-Krushel went from traditional broadcast media into digital and from establishment to entrepreneurship. And if that wasn't enough disruption, the dot-com bubble burst on her watch and Fili-Krushel spent a year cutting costs to get the company to the breakeven point as part of her first turnaround effort.[42] The experience served her well. That intense stint as CEO of WebMD is what subsequently brought her back to Time Warner, this time in a C-suite role reporting to CEO Dick Parsons. In the turbulent post-merger period at AOL Time Warner, her digital experience combined with the WebMD turnaround gave her the right profile—and chops—to win the Time Warner role and endure there for nearly a decade.

The Free Agent Track to the C-suite arguably entails a more strategic career perspective than the Tenured Executive, because deciding when and where to move means you need a plan.

Where Is My Next Growth Opportunity?

Numerous executives told me they moved from a longtime position at a large organization to accept a C-suite role at a smaller firm, specifically to grow and feel challenged.

Galeota spent 28 years at Merck before joining G&W Laboratories—a New Jersey–based maker and marketer of specialty pharmaceuticals. Galeota began his career at Merck in his 20s, as a sales rep, and exited as chief strategy and business development officer and president of emerging businesses in 2016. When Galeota was considering the chance to lead G&W, a highly respected senior leader at Merck gave him some sage advice.

"You know, you can stay here for the next five years and keep doing what you're doing, or you could go and do a whole bunch of things you've never done before," Galeota recounts an advisor within Merck told him. "You'll be worth more in five years if you do the latter."[43]

The advice resonated with Galeota and turned out to be accurate. Galeota described his move to G&W as a business "workout" that forced him to hone and retest many aspects of his business and leadership skills. Forcing himself out of a comfortable position demanded "a renewed level of learning and challenge" that wouldn't have happened in his prior role at Merck.

It's true that no one thing—growth, learning, timing—will be the factor that puts you on the Free Agent path. It's always a combination of factors. But in answering these questions, and using self-reflection, you will be in a position to consider the risks and remain open to the opportunities that this path presents.

Getting on the Fast Track: The Free Agent

The Free Agent option is arguably the most complex of the Four Core Paths to the C-suite. To follow it to the top, you need to be confident and strategic while also keeping an open mind and exhibiting a willingness to learn new tricks. On top of that, you are going up against internal candidates who know the culture and have people pulling them up. My advice? Start preparing well in advance. Here's where to begin.

✔ Actions and Experience	✔ Mindset and Perspective	✔ Followership and Brand
___Take on the tough jobs	___Be versatile and adaptable	___Cultivate external advisors
___Go for *growth* experiences	___Be confident and ready to take risks	___ Have a powerful, distinctive story to tell
___Deliver skills that are in high demand	___Be open and willing to listen and learn	___Develop strong customer followership and loyalty
___Demonstrate why you are worth the risk		

✔ *Actions and Experience*

Free Agents are lesser known to the CEO, board, or whoever is making the top-team hiring decision during the succession time frame. Executive recruiters and consultants make it their mission to get to know the rock stars and overachievers in each industry, but the burden is on you to position yourself and your accomplishments in a way that boosts you above internal candidates. In many ways, this circumstance is an opportunity as well as a challenge for Free Agents.

The experiences and abilities that give Free Agents the edge over other executives on the C-suite short list are ones that they accumulate over the entire course of their careers. Here is what you will need to demonstrate.

Take on the Tough Assignments

Eileen Drake is CEO and president of Aerojet Rocketdyne, a rocket engine and propulsion systems manufacturer for US defense and space applications. Drake was hired away from Pratt & Whitney in March 2015 to be Aerojet's COO, and two months later she was elevated to chief executive.

One glance at Drake's history and it's simple to see that she has the right stuff. Following an ROTC scholarship in college, Drake proceeded to flight school and spent eight years on active duty as an aviation officer.

"I went from a kid in college to being put in charge of a helicopter unit with guys who had been flying choppers since Vietnam," she said. "That's the type of environment where you need to use every ounce of grit and leadership ability that you have . . . and then some."[44]

After the military, Drake started as a supervisor on the production floor at Ford Motor Company and worked her way up to the executive level. From serving in the US Army to dealing with the United Auto Workers union, it's no surprise to learn that Drake steps right up for challenging assignments. When I spoke to her, she told me she likes the "tough jobs" the best because she learns the most from them.

When Drake was still new to Ford, management asked for a volunteer to go to Germany to represent the company at its plant for the new Ford Focus. Nobody wanted to go because the company had a major problem with the power steering system on the vehicle. Drake raised her hand and went.

"I got yelled at in German for two months straight," she said. "When I got back, the plant manager promoted me."

Drake is one of several Free Agents who told me they "opened up opportunities" for themselves as executives by taking the tough jobs and then "figuring out how to be successful in them."

Mary Petrovich, named one of the 100 Most Influential Women of 2016 by *Crain's Detroit Business*, was CEO of AxleTech International from 2000 to 2010. The Troy, Michigan, manufacturer and supplier of heavy-duty automotive components had no profits and $100 million in revenue when Petrovich was recruited by The Carlyle Group to take the helm. In five years, Petrovich grew AxleTech to $600 million in revenue and $120 million in profits.

Like Drake, Petrovich advises taking the "tough jobs." She herself accepted several tough assignments throughout her career: She worked in finance at Chrysler when Lee Iacocca was leading the company out of bankruptcy. She was recruited to be the director of cost management for AlliedSignal when GE alum Larry Bossidy was creating efficiencies and streamlining the organization during its transformation phase in the late 1990s.

"I was forever in the center of the challenging situation. I always found a way to say yes to it, always found a way to get it done," she said.[45]

Petrovich and other executives on the Free Agent Track take tough assignments to build valuable skill sets that lead them to the C-suite.

Go for Growth Experiences

Similar to taking the tough assignments, Free Agents target the positions that will offer them the greatest growth—even if that entails a step back. If a job gives them a strategic advantage, they use it to prove themselves.

When David Simmons was Pfizer's country manager in Greece, he asked the head of HR for Europe what it would take to get handed a bigger assignment—say, regional president for Eastern Europe, which included Greece and Turkey. He felt ready for more.

Essentially, he was told, "You can't get there from here," Simmons said. "Instead, they wanted to see how I performed running marketing in a larger region."

The role, which turned out to be in Canada, reported to a country manager, a position Simmons had already held. After some internal hand-wringing, Simmons accepted the step back, and it ultimately went better than anyone expected. "We did four product launches in a year and a half and they were all really good . . . a couple of them were high ranking relative to other countries."

Simmons's next assignment? Running the Eastern Europe business.

A tenacious focus on growth and a willingness to step up illustrates not only fierce competitiveness but also the Free Agent's belief in meritocracy. They prove themselves throughout their career and use their experience to locate their next chance to lead.

Bring Skills That Are in High Demand

Coming into an organization from the outside gives Free Agents the chance to position themselves to deliver what an organization needs most. As companies recruit leaders, they are also acquiring skills, industry intelligence, and sometimes even a business strategy.

One executive I know accepted a chief technology officer role at a British tech firm. He was appointed for several reasons: He had worked at top Silicon Valley companies for over a decade, he brought top engineering talent with him, and he was a great fit with the culture. But even more, he had a plan for cybersecurity at a time when the organization was desperately in need of one.

Knowing what an organization needs most—and showing that you can provide it—is a key way to reach the C-suite. Mary Petrovich came to AxleTech with a plan to turn it around. Pat Fili-Krushel brought digital leadership chops to Time Warner when the company was struggling to cement its merger with AOL. David Simmons brought extensive international pharma experience to PPD when it was planning to expand through global acquisitions. In my role at Spencer Stuart, I've found that when an organization doesn't have a skill it needs internally, orchestrating a key hire is an effective way to solve the problem at the leadership level.

Show You Are Worth the Risk

Organizations spend a great deal of money and mindshare developing their culture and cultivating a pipeline of leaders over a period of many years. Sourcing C-suite leaders externally is arguably risky, and Free Agents, therefore, need to show that they are worth the potential peril. The best way to do that is to demonstrate that you can deliver results.

Galeota put it this way: "I wanted anyone looking at my résumé to say, 'No matter where we put this guy he figures out how to succeed.'"

In Galeota's case, that meant early in his career helping to take Merck's cholesterol medicine Zocor from about $100 million in sales to over a billion; later leading the team that developed and launched Merck's highest-grossing products ever, the diabetes medicines Januvia and Janumet; and ultimately running Merck's $11 billion Hospital and Specialty Care business line.

The Free Agents I interviewed each had their own Januvia story, and it was part of what sealed the deal on their journey to the C-suite.

✔ Mindset and Perspective

Many of the C-suite executives I've coached and encountered have mindset assets in common, including a drive for results and the capability to lead at a very high level. Yet, the Free Agent path calls for a few special qualities that can serve to hasten your success.

Be Versatile and Adaptable

The Free Agent, or any other leader coming in from the outside, needs to know their way around the organization's culture and be adaptable enough to fit within the existing top team. This is true even for disrupters in full turnaround mode: Whether it is the board or CEO, there's always someone with whom you will need to develop chemistry or camaraderie.

Pat Fili-Krushel suggested that a static disposition is a classic derailer for top executives.

"My feeling is that you need to own your crisp perspective, but you also need to know when to adjust," she said. "I see so many people who can't or won't do that."

A nuanced way to take this best practice to the next level is by considering what Roger Martin, former dean of the University of Toronto's Rotman School of Business, calls "integrative thinking—the ability to face constructively the tension of opposing ideas and, instead of choosing one at the expense of the other, generate a creative resolution . . . that contains elements of the opposing ideas but is superior to each."[46]

Martin argues that this is how the world's best leaders think. As for the Free Agent, an important part of what they bring to organizations is fresh thinking and new ideas. Presenting fresh thinking in a way that fits within the context of an organization's values is the sweet spot Free Agents should aim for.

Be Ready to Take Risks

The next mindset feature of elevated importance to Free Agents is their appetite for risk. Every top executive needs to be confident, but coming in from the outside involves a higher degree of difficulty and potential for failure.[47] Mary Petrovich talked about "intestinal fortitude," and Simmons said, "there's no risk-averse way to reach the C-suite."

"If you want to break through, you've got to lean in and take chances with your career," he said. "There's just no 'safe' way to it."

Be Open to Knowledge and Newness

Kelly Kramer mentioned a mindset requirement that brings versatility and risk management together—a desire to continue learning. Kramer told me that her desire to learn led her to try new things and take on much more without looking back or second-guessing herself. That sounds a lot like a Free Agent credo.

"The only thing that matters is that you keep learning and get to know your space better than anybody else," she said. "That's what keeps you ahead of everything else and solves 99% of the other issues you'll encounter."[48]

✔ Followership and Brand

Getting into the C-suite as a Free Agent happens by virtue of cultivating strong industry followership and a prominent leadership brand. After all, externally sourced additions to the top team are often the result of relationships executives develop and maintain over a period of years—with other leaders, board members, industry colleagues, and executive recruiters.

Networking is natural at high levels of leadership, but taking the next steps, in the ways I will explain, is what will get you considered more seriously for C-suite slots.

Cultivate a Network of External Advisors

Mentors inspire you and act as career consultants, and sponsors actively promote you within an organization—but that's not enough. Top executives need a network of trusted advisors, including key individuals outside their current organization. This team of advisors extends your industry reach, offers valuable intelligence, and helps you steer your career. At the senior executive level, networks of trusted advisors have a reciprocal relationship—they help each other—even if some members are more powerful than others. In time, power dynamics and job titles realign and you might have the most to offer.

David Simmons told me about his "little cohort of advisors" and the big part they played as he was considering the CEO role at PPD.

"I started receiving regular calls from recruiters and private equity firms, and I was unsure how to respond," he said.

Satisfied with his place at Pfizer (a company president responsible for $19 billion in annual sales and approximately 20,000 employees), Simmons didn't want to get distracted. And yet, a part of him wanted to know what opportunities were out in the market and what they might mean for him. His first call was to his long-time trusted advisor (and Petrovich's previous leader when she was at Allied Signal), Larry Bossidy, who gave him some seasoned advice.

"Go back and write your own job: what are the elements that would tempt you to leave Pfizer? What are the automatic disqualifiers? Don't bother with anything that doesn't sync with that," Bossidy told him.

Always the analytical type, Simmons put some of his other advisors in the consulting sector to work on his behalf. They helped him crunch numbers and extrapolate to compare the PPD role with what Pfizer might have to offer him in the coming years based on possible successions. They also used what they knew to create a hypothesis about how many relevant industry opportunities might emerge for him externally over the next two or three years.

"They had all this data and we looked at it every which way," he said. "The net-net of that was this was a pretty scarce opportunity."

Simmons was satisfied that a "better" position wouldn't come along. He consulted his outside advisors and accepted the job.

The Free Agents I interviewed were all exceptional at relationship building: Galeota has the type of network that Simmons talked about, and he has also been active in more formal networks like the G100, "a private network of current and rising CEOs" and senior executives. Fili-Krushel's advisors cut across the entire media landscape. Petrovich has a powerful network based on her many positive Carlyle and Company affiliations. And they each act as trusted advisors for *other* executives—sharing their experience and offering guidance when peers call on them for advice.

Have a Powerful Story to Tell

Another way to boost your chances to rise above the rest as a Free Agent is to have a powerful story to tell. High performance and leadership ability are table stakes in the C-suite, so what is the one narrative you have that sets you apart?

Fili-Krushel talks about the crucibles she faced when she was the CEO of WebMD during the dot-com bust, as well as her tenure at Time Warner following the AOL merger. Galeota talks about beating a major pharmaceutical competitor to market and leading Merck's ultimately top-grossing product through clinical trials and onto the market.

Having a story to tell helps people see what you stand for. When you're making your case to come into the C-suite from the outside, people need to know what makes you a good leader and why you'll be able to get others to follow you. Get your story straight.

Develop Strong Customer Followership

When you are competing against a cadre of successful internal candidates for a C-suite position, think about the assets you have that will make you more appealing. What could be better than bringing close relationships with you to work?

Professional service and finance firms, sales organizations, and client-based companies have noncompete clauses, and executives are careful not to bankrupt their previous organization or make it worse when they walk out the door. That said, the recruiters, CEOs, and board members that I work with say that a candidate's external network is a big part of what sets them apart and makes them appealing.

Contacts that matter include strong vendor relationships, talented colleagues that might one day need a new home, and, yes, in some industries customers and clients also fit neatly into this equation.

What is perhaps the best relationship of all? Your previous employer. As one executive told me, "Networks aren't zero sum, quite the opposite." In many instances, when a top executive leaves one company for another, both companies find ways of working together in the future—with the executive as the common denominator.

The Free Agents I interviewed had a final thing in common. Nearly all said something to the effect: "Oh, I wasn't really looking for the next job or vying for a C-suite role. I just looked straight ahead and focused on being the very best at my job and generating more results." Then, they went right on to tell me how strategic they were in managing their career. It's clearly both—Free Agents need career savvy and excellence in performance.

Simmons put it this way: "If you want to be CEO, the first thing is that you need to be planful, because you need to build out your capabilities and have results that cast you in the best competitive light. But the second thing is, don't be too planful. You'll never get the call if you spend your time looking for it instead of doing the work."

The Free Agent: Career Accelerators and Derailers

Accelerators	Derailers
• I am very willing to take calculated risks in my career.	• I prefer a comfortable career path, defined by continuity rather than calculated risks. I don't want to transfer to a new location.
• I step up to accept the tough assignments and look for roles that allow me to grow my skills, abilities, and experiences.	• I don't like to "stand out" or sell myself or my accomplishments.
• I deliver specific capabilities and attributes that my industry needs most right now.	• My skills and contacts are highly specific to my particular organization or industry.
• I have a powerful narrative to tell about myself that illustrates what I stand for as a leader.	• My support network and advisors are largely internal to my organization.
• I bring new contacts, ideas, and insights, but can also connect with existing company leaders and work within the confines of an established organizational culture.	• I am well known mostly internal to my organization.
• I have a strong leadership brand, an industry following, and a network of external advisors.	

Chapter 4

The Leapfrog Leader

A few years ago, Cisco was searching for a successor to lead the Asia Pacific region, a high-growth area for the company. Traditionally, it would have looked to an expat at the senior vice president level to fill this kind of strategic role. And when the search began, the company originally set out to find a prototypical leader.

But then Cisco went in a different direction. Even with several exceptional, traditional candidates emerging, the organization chose to take a risk on a younger, less experienced local leader. He had a close connection to key Asia customers, smart ideas on how the region was developing, and a keen sense of the disruption that was needed in the market. He was also at least one level below the traditional vision for the position. Taking a bet on his potential, Cisco promoted him immediately, and the region has accelerated under his leadership.

More and more, CEOs and boards are disregarding hierarchy to fill key positions with savvy leaders one or two steps down in the organization. In a 2014 report, the Boston Consulting Group labeled the occurrence "leapfrog successions."[49] The shift is especially noteworthy when it occurs at the highest levels, with leaders skipping the usual steps to become C-suite successors. In 2013, for example, Burger King chose 33-year-old Daniel Schwartz to be CEO, despite having no fast-food experience prior to three years at Burger King.[50] That same year, Whole Foods hired 35-year-old Jason Buechel, who spent 12 years as a consulting partner at Accenture driving strategic transformations in retail, as its CIO.[51]

To be clear, this path to the C-suite has much less to do with age than with the qualities and characteristics these executives bring to their new positions. Steve Kandarian, for example, became president and CEO at MetLife in May 2011.[52] Previously MetLife's CIO, Kandarian had less operational experience than MetLife peers who were running large divisions of the insurer, but he had considerable experience analyzing complex risks and identifying emerging opportunities within the insurance sector. Neither Kandarian nor Schwartz were promoted based on longtime leadership or experience managing a large profit-and-loss statement (P&L).

As we saw with Cisco's Asia Pacific executive and Whole Foods's Buechel, this is an emerging trend that goes beyond the chief executive role to cover all members of the C-suite. Leapfrog Leaders can skip steps to land on the board of directors as well, which I view as an extension of the C-suite. They can leap from one industry into the C-suite of another, or from academia, consulting, or nonprofits into the C-suite of a traditional organization. Regardless of specific cases, the common denominator along this path to the top team is that leaders leap over levels in an organization or skip major milestones in the established succession process.

Core Questions for Prospective Leapfrog Leaders

Leapfrog leadership is a sign of the times. Organizational complexity has increased everywhere as companies navigate fast-changing global markets, fend off insurgent competitors, and rely ever more on social media and other disruptive and social technologies. These new realities require different ways of thinking. As a result, organizations are rewarding leaders who can find order in the chaos, understand emerging business models, and are wired for change and reinvention. Does this sound like you?

Tapping into this talent trend requires aspiring C-suite leaders to remain alert. After all, it is difficult to *plan* to leap levels, and it entails positioning yourself appropriately. As part of that, the following guiding questions will help you evaluate whether the conditions are favorable for you to skip steps and hop on this path to the C-suite.

Can I Fill a Gap in the Leadership Pipeline?

When the leadership cohort just below the C-suite isn't reinventing itself rapidly enough, keeping up with industry trends, or staying in tune with customers, the top team may look elsewhere to fill key roles. This gap signals a possible opening for a less likely candidate with fresh eyes and sharp instincts. Similarly, if the "obvious" successor isn't a match with the growth strategy of an organization, it paves the way for a more surprising choice. I've seen boards and CEOs make a nontraditional choice numerous times in this case. Do you have an alternative vision that can deliver your organization into the future?

Is the Culture Stuck . . . and Can I Help Get It Unstuck?

If management is gearing up to accelerate change, they may take a chance on a successful change agent who can be a role model for the rest of the organization. I've seen this dynamic occur more often in general leadership functions, including CEO, because culture shifts generally cascade from the top down. One notable example is Mary Barra, promoted directly from executive vice president of global product development at age 51. Barra skipped steps to become General Motor's first female CEO at a time when the car giant needed to break away from the shadow of the US government bailout of the auto industry and reinvent itself as a more customer-centric organization.

Is My Functional Area of Expertise in Flux?

As business models morph, expectations for C-suite roles change shape and can require a makeover. The CMO is an example of a job that is evolving fast, and CEOs may choose someone two levels down in the company who is more in tune with the fast-moving conventions of digital transformations in marketing. Similarly, boards and CEOs are looking for heads of HR (CHROs) who have strategic and operational experience, and are therefore going outside the function more often to find leaders. For example, Barra served a two-year stint as GM's global head of HR, after fulfilling a high-ranking manufacturing role.

Are the Hiring Managers Open-Minded?

When Cisco appointed Amy Chang to its board in 2016, it was a type of Leapfrog Leader maneuver. Chang is the founder of Accompany, a successful Silicon Valley start-up. She has a pedigree from Google but no large company board experience to speak of. She was appointed to Cisco's board by CEO Chuck Robbins, himself a Leapfrog Leader. The point is that senior leaders who are known to be open to fresh thinking are more likely to appoint people with nontraditional experience—that is, someone who hasn't already done the job twice in the past.

Is Organizational Change Imminent?

Widespread structural change—particularly promotions or disruption at the top—tends to create a chain reaction that sweeps people upward in the organization. When one or more executives are tapped to lead a new business, for instance, some of their peers might exit the organization while others are promoted, thereby creating a domino effect.

An acquaintance of mine at a Fortune 100 firm experienced exactly this. He went home one day as a midlevel manager and came into work the following morning as chief security officer. His boss and several other close colleagues were promoted rapidly, and it swiftly accelerated his own path to the C-suite.

A dramatic organizational change, similarly, is what brought Sundar Pichai into the executive suite at Google. In 2015, Larry Page, Google cofounder, stunned analysts by moving to be CEO of Google's newly organized holding company, Alphabet, and elevating Senior Vice President Pichai to become Google's CEO—restructuring the organization in the process.[53]

Instead of waiting to gain tenure or complete additional consecutive assignments to round out your executive portfolio, the Leapfrog Leader Track is one whereby you are catapulted up the ranks. Of the four paths to the C-suite, this path is by far the most difficult to orchestrate. It is unlikely that you can systematically plan to become a Leapfrog Leader. Yet, leaders can be prepared for the path to present itself by strategically managing their experience, reputation, and network in certain ways. With that in mind, we will take a closer look at the mix of elements that can help you position yourself as a leader who has the potential to rise above the rest and leap levels.

Getting on the Fast Track: The Leapfrog Leader

Leapfrog Leaders ascend rapidly through the ranks, skipping steps along the way. That leaves little time for strategic career planning. Instead, it requires a full focus on succeeding in a variety of key experiences, remaining open to feedback, and projecting a positive, future-focused vision for the organization.

✔ Actions and Experience	✔ Mindset and Perspective	✔ Followership and Brand
__Rotate rapidly through diverse experiences	__Love reinvention	__Attain 360-degree internal support
__Stand out in key roles	__Be comfortable with uncertainty	__Build internal and external followership
__Experience failure, recovery, and reinvention	__Be self-aware	

✔ Actions and Experience

"Do you have 20 years of experience or 20 years of the *same* experience?"

When I heard esteemed Wharton professor Peter Cappelli pose this question at a conference, it struck me as an exacting way to sum up the range of experiences that Leapfrog Leaders need to pursue. In most cases, this path to the C-suite involves accelerated exposure to diverse assignments, underscored by mastery in the areas that matter most in your organization. In addition, because Leapfrog Leaders may be younger, and by definition skip traditional steps, their exposure to opportunities must be focused for impact.

Rotate Rapidly through Diverse Assignments

Leapfrog Leaders such as Cisco's Chuck Robbins and GM's Mary Barra[54] were similarly oriented toward gaining the right array of experience before they were elevated to top teams in Leapfrog Leader successions.

Another executive I interviewed, Selma, a marketing executive working in London, was a senior vice president with 16 years' experience at the same bank. In 2017 she was recruited by a Swedish conglomerate to join its managing board—its version of the C-suite—thereby skipping a whopping three tiers.[55] Her experience is illustrative of many executives I've seen along this accelerated career path. Equal parts English and Swedish (she considers herself personally *and* professionally diverse), Selma rotated rapidly through numerous functions, moving upward steadily during her tenure at the investment bank.

"I managed P&Ls, ran the sales and marketing team and R&D, I was director of new product development, I worked in London, New York and France," she said. "Every three years I went to do something different."

Selma swiftly mastered multiple functions, moving up and over, which gave her the extraordinary experience base that is a hallmark of Leapfrog Leaders.

Stand Out in Key Roles

Leapfrog Leaders have less time to gain the experience they need, so they put themselves at the center of the assignments that matter most to the organization.

GM's Leapfrog Leader, Barra, is someone who held extremely diverse positions at the automaker (she joined the company in 1980 as an engineering student and became a plant manager, executive director of engineering, and head of human resources), but she also held what many said was the most *important* role at GM. Essentially, her job was guiding the automaker to design cars that people would want to buy while remaining on-cost.[56]

Likewise, Robbins's arc of experience was right on the mark to leap levels. Before catapulting past two presidents to become chief executive, the 49-year-old Robbins was senior vice president of worldwide field operations, leading both partner relations and Cisco's 16,000-strong sales force. Prior stints included running sales for the United States, Canada, and Latin America and running US commercial sales, which oversees Cisco's direct relationships with corporate customers. In other words, he was never idle at Cisco, consistently achieving and advancing. Perhaps more importantly, the partners and teams in Robbins's portfolio have always been *central to Cisco's growth*. For instance, Robbins helped build the company's direct commercial sales operation to generate 25% of Cisco's revenue. Robbins also helped oversee Cisco's pivotal computer-security and collaboration business, which includes its WebEx online conferencing service.

Pass the Success and Failure Test

Beyond accelerating through all the right career moves, Leapfrog Leaders must master additional interrelated experiences—failure and reinvention—to demonstrate resilience.

Selma told me about her experience in an early marketing role at the onset of her tenure in banking, when she failed to achieve her key performance goals by "a long shot." But she never skipped a beat:

She made a series of fast adjustments and exceeded her goal the following year. According to Selma, this experience was far from her only professional crucible, but it was highly significant because it taught her about grit and resilience. "It reinforced for me that I always needed to own up to failure, remain resilient and adapt myself and the business."

Likewise, both Robbins and Barra weathered numerous highs and lows. Before becoming CEO, Robbins reinvented himself numerous times and drove the successful transformation of Cisco's sales organization, "cementing its place as the envy of the industry," Cisco said in a news release announcing his appointment. Likewise, Barra spent her career in the center of the famously turbulent auto industry, deftly managing transition and corporate restructuring, and attempting turnarounds of arguably massive proportion.

Each of these Leapfrog Leaders had less seniority than their colleagues a level or two above them, but their targeted experiences put them on a path to skip career steps.

✔ Mindset and Perspective

Experience gaps may be built into this accelerated career path, but the bold, visionary thinking of Leapfrog Leaders more than makes up for the deficit. The executives I've seen who fit into this category have three components in their personal profile that define how they think and by extension how they act.

Love Reinvention

First, Leapfrog Leaders gravitate toward reinvention and are seldom stuck on tradition. As we saw by the way Barra, Robbins, and Selma rotated swiftly into new roles, this path was forged for explorers. In fact, Leapfrog Leaders are often elevated because they understand how to navigate nascent business models and have a bold vision to remain ahead of shifts that seem daunting to the rest of us.

Selma put it this way: "We [as leaders] have to embrace the power of difference every day in terms of the decisions we make about strategy, operations and even staffing." She said, "Challenging yourself to be brave and look past the obvious—to what is emerging—can be incredibly rewarding."

She went on to comment, "The willingness to take risks, even if they don't work out, is probably the biggest differentiator you will have in your career as a leader."

Be Comfortable with Uncertainty

Next, executives along this path operate decisively without having every answer. Again, this goes back to the operating environment so many industries find themselves facing today—they must change and transform constantly to survive. One COO who leaped into the C-suite of a retail giant told me: "If I wait for the signals to be clear before I act, it's too late. I need to have confidence in the vision I have today and be ready to turn on a dime tomorrow, even if that means plunging ahead and disrupting our own business."

Chuck Robbins spoke about this mindset trait at a *Fortune* magazine event in 2016, as Cisco was undergoing a "massive transformation," including a shift away from merely selling routers and switches to a software subscription model that involved selling data and security analytics services to companies. Robbins said: "You have to be incredibly honest with yourself about the things that made [your organization] great historically, and which ones of those will make you great in the future and which are going to hold you back."[57]

Without this comfort with uncertainty, it is highly unlikely that Barra would be in the position she is, leading General Motors.

Be Self-Aware

Lastly, Leapfrog Leaders are highly attuned to the gaps in their own skills and experiences. They listen to others and surround themselves with people who complement their strengths. John Chambers hinted at this crucial quality in Robbins, telling him: "What I like most of all is you're a fast learner. You know what you know, and you know what you don't know."[58]

Leapfrog Leaders are drawn to change, they thrive amid uncertainty, and they are open to admitting what they don't yet know.

✔ Followership and Brand

Achieving followership is a prerequisite for accelerating on any path to the C-suite, but 360-degree support networks epitomize the Leapfrog Leader more than any other.

By definition, Leapfrog Leaders are not "next in line" for the top team, which means they must gain support from colleagues across the spectrum. This includes winning over the board and CEO, who will make the ultimate decision. Both Barra and Robbins, for instance, were the unanimous choice of their respective boards for CEO, and both were mentored by the CEOs they succeeded.

Leapfrog Leaders also gain respect from other members of the current top team, who must accept them. They must be ready to hang with the executives one level below the C-suite, as well, whom they will be conspicuously elevated above. Finally, they must have strong relationships outside the organization—with vendors, partners, and investors—so their surprise appointment sends a positive message to the marketplace. All of this adds up to support from many different types of people and followership at all levels.

Having worked with Robbins at Cisco, and coached Selma informally for many years, I could clearly see that both were widely respected and admired across their respective organizations by multiple different factions. Robbins was active on social media platforms, where he established himself as approachable and authentic. Likewise, Selma was highly regarded inside the bank and far beyond. In fact, when she was recruited for the C-suite team in Sweden, a major factor was her followership there. Selma started her career as a marketing manager in Sweden before moving to the bank, so she returned with an inside-outsider reputation that served her well during the succession search and beyond.

The Leapfrog Leader: Career Accelerators and Derailers

Accelerators	Derailers
• You have a forward-looking vision for the organization.	• You have a traditional vision for the organization.
• You know what you don't know.	• You have excelled in one functional or technical role for many years.
• You have held diverse roles, including positions that were pivotal to the success of the organization.	• You favor custom and stability.
• You are unafraid of calculated risk and have an affinity for reinvention.	• You are unsure of your development needs.
• You are widely respected and have multilevel support.	• You surround yourself with others like you and have followership gaps.
	• You prefer to have all the answers and feel in control.

Chapter 5

The Founder

A my Chang, former head of analytics at Google, was just two levels removed from Larry Page and the C-suite when she stepped away from her role at the search giant to cofound Accompany, the venture-funded digital personal assistant start-up. This move epitomizes the experience of most executives on the Founder Track—when they are ready for a C-suite experience, they create one for themselves.

Accompany, which aggregates information to instantly arm professionals with the insights they need for prospecting, networking, or any type of business interaction, boasts "the largest database of senior decision makers in the world."[59] For instance, its relationship management product has an executive briefing feature that pulls together things like news and social updates, financial performance data, and staffing announcements, and then uses artificial intelligence to generate insights that are sent to users before important meetings.

Explains Chang: "It's the type of dossier a personal assistant might assemble to prepare you with everything you need." Ironically, that is exactly what Chang admits is one of the greatest challenges inherent in pivoting from the executive ranks to becoming a founding CEO: "There's so much you don't know every day, so much you can't plan for . . . it's impossible to be entirely prepared." As we will see, succeeding on this path to the C-suite has as much to do with mastering the mindset as achieving specific experience milestones.

Christopher Wu, the cofounder of Paper Culture and a self-described "stationery fanatic" who directs his business as much in areas such as environmental sustainability as materials and modern design, agrees with Chang's assessment of becoming a Founder.[60] Wu started his career in management consulting before going to Harvard Business School and subsequently embarking on successive executive positions at Yahoo, Snapfish, and Hewlett Packard before launching Paper Culture.

"As an entrepreneurial leader, you need to know your mission and what differentiates you, but everything else is in permanent flux," he admits. "Even if you have tons of skills and knowledge, they are pretty much obsolete in three years—there needs to be a commitment to a constant state of renewal."

That "state of renewal" applies across the board for executives on the Founder Track. Neither Chang nor Wu can be certain their businesses will still be thriving in 2020. Yet both put their finger on one of the most critical points about this distinctive path to the top: It's not for the faint of heart. And for exactly that reason many observers consider entrepreneurship to be an option that is entirely separate from the other C-suite career paths.

I would disagree, however. Although many of the original high-flying start-ups from the 1990s were founded in garages and college dorm rooms, the latest wave of new ventures is just as likely to spring from the more experienced minds of established executives. According to the Kauffman Foundation, the average and median age of US-born tech founders is 39, and twice as many are over 50 than under 25.[61] In addition, people 55 or older are twice as likely to launch a high-growth start-up compared with the under-35 crowd, according to *Forbes*.[62] Age aside, there are several reasons why becoming a Founder offers an accessible and promising path to the C-suite.

The first is the growth of the start-up diaspora. The original "new economy" trailblazers are today a training ground for future Founders. Nearly 30 years after Yahoo's stock price hit its 1999 peak of $110.39, many of the name-brand tech start-ups have become Fortune 500 organizations. Amazon was founded in 1994, Google in 1998, and Netflix in 1997. Since then, they have recruited and trained thousands of executives who, like Chang and Wu, learned the ropes, added considerable value, soaked up the entrepreneurial ethos, and eventually left to start their own organizations. In effect, the growth and success of innovative internet companies have created a workforce that is less reticent to leave traditional business behind to embrace entrepreneurship and become Founders.

The next reason entrepreneurship has become a mainstream path to a top team is the emergence of the so-called gig economy, also known as the sharing economy, an extension of traditional freelancing. We have seen an explosive increase in individuals who choose to work independently and remotely, moving directly from one assignment to the next and from company to company as independent contractors managing everything from creative design tasks to IT and consulting roles. A study by Intuit predicts that by 2020, 40% of American workers will be independent contractors, and many other studies put that percentage much higher.[63] Although mobile talent does not generally apply to the top team, the shift toward working in ways that you want, and building a career that suits your personal values, adds fuel to the fire for executives who would be Founders. Every one of the entrepreneurial executives I interviewed mentioned "greater control" and "a focus on personal values" as factors in their decision to become Founders and create their own top team.

The last overall trend I'll mention in regard to this entrepreneurial path is the rapidly changing shape of organizations. As companies continue to evolve, they are becoming flatter, less dependent on hierarchy, and organized around small, responsive teams that are better equipped to satisfy customer needs. In short, this means all executives must be disrupters. These and so many other shifts in business mark our need to use entrepreneurial tools to become faster and more responsive executives overall. This has caused the seeds of start-up culture to emerge within larger organizations. The mainstreaming of agile operations means that more executives are learning to think like entrepreneurs and are plotting their career course accordingly.

In fact, nearly 40% of start-up founders were corporate executives at one time, including many who had held CEO positions; and close to 29% were previously senior vice presidents, vice presidents, managers, or directors, according to Harvard Business School.[64]

Becoming a Founder can be seen as an expedited path to the C-suite, whereby leaders sacrifice a large measure of security to create something all their own with a team of like-minded partners. Some founders are in it for the long haul—to build a business and generate long-term value. Others are serial entrepreneurs, moving successively from launch to exit strategy multiple times over. Still others build their start-up and find themselves back in big business after their venture is acquired. The point is that this path to the C-suite is in many ways more versatile and less "zero sum" than the rest. Yet, that upside comes with considerable risk. One way to assess that risk for yourself is to consider how the founders I interviewed made it work for them and under what circumstances.

Core Questions for Would-Be Founders

Compared with the other career paths we've explored, those who follow the Founder Track stand apart because they actively create their own opportunities, and therefore have greater control over the timing of their advancement into the C-suite. But how will you know if (or when) this particular path applies to you? According to the executives I've worked with and interviewed, there are several questions to answer that help determine your fit as a Founder.

Am I Having the Impact I Want?

Entrepreneurs are an upbeat bunch. Few of the Founders I met left their executive positions because they were unhappy. In fact, most loved what they were doing and were extremely successful. In some cases, they would have reached the C-suite in their organization eventually. But in each instance, they wondered: Can I have a greater impact out on my own?

Erik Larson was a senior director at Adobe Systems before he launched Cloverpop, an online business software that uses behavioral economics to guide better and faster decision making. Larson said the idea of building a business had captivated him for years. "It was always something I knew I'd do," he said. "But even more, I found it amazing to think about creating a business that employed people and generated real value in the world. That's what was really interesting."[65]

Similarly, Wu left Snapfish to cofound Paper Culture with two goals in mind. "We wanted to build a great business, of course," he said. "But just as important, we wanted to make a difference across many different dimensions."

For Wu and his founding partners, that meant having a positive impact on the planet and raising awareness for climate change. As part of that purpose, Paper Culture plants a tree for each order fulfilled.

As these Founders illustrate, the rationale for this path goes beyond a desire to lead at a high level and nurture a successful business. Hopes for achieving greater impact further motivate Founders to choose this path and follow it to the C-suite.

What Problem Will I Solve?

For Founders, ideas are at the center of everything. Chang talked to me about ideas that kept her awake at night until she finally decided to "go for it." Larson said the idea of using behavioral economics and science to improve decision making was "an idea he couldn't let go of."

Yet, even beyond any specific idea or execution strategy, many of the Founders I interviewed said they were motivated to solve a particular problem.

Susan Marshall is a case in point. She was the senior director of product marketing at Salesforce before she became a Founder. The entrepreneurial light went on in Marshall's head one day when she was out on the road talking to customers and hearing about the same unsolved problems over and over.

"They all bought multiple tools from us, but it never seemed to amount to a solution that worked," she said. "I thought, 'There's got to be a way to pull this technology together in one place and give customers access to the system they need.'"[66]

Marshall surmised that if she could solve their problem and help them be successful, she would also be successful. With that in mind she launched Torchlite, a software and services solution that helps marketers get more done by connecting freelance talent, campaigns, and marketing technology into a single campaign management platform.

Marshall's story is not unique. Both Chang and Larson said their ventures sprung from a desire to improve how they and others around them worked and lived, and to solve a particular problem or fill a void. As for Wu, Paper Culture took shape in part with a directive from his pregnant wife.

"She said, 'Look, you have one job,'" Wu recalled. "That is to go out and get birth announcements." Wu launched Paper Culture, and his problem was solved.

Who Are My Cofounders?

Founders and their coconspirators go together like peas and carrots. Taking your potential cofounders and their skills into account can get you closer to deciding whether the entrepreneurial path to the C-suite is right for you.

Perhaps the most important assets cofounders deliver are experience and contacts that supplement your own. Like any top team, start-up cofounders need a full complement of technical expertise, executional experience, and leadership chops. Some Founders are engineers, others are finance gurus, and still others are generalists.

Chang founded Accompany with several partners, including the former CFO of Ning, Ryan McDonough, who moved over to become Accompany's CFO. She also brought on a best friend and fellow Googler with considerable technical chops to serve as her chief technology officer (CTO).

One of Wu's cofounders, Anurag Mendhekar, was a former colleague from his earlier stint at Yahoo and a start-up CEO at several previous ventures. Mendhekar assumed the CTO role at Paper Culture and is a mentor to Wu, who is the CEO.

Beyond a portfolio of contacts and experience, cofounders help you decide when this path to the C-suite is right for you. Several of the Founders I spoke with said their cofounders "served as sounding boards" and offered an "objective reality check" early on about the viability of the business and the likelihood for success.

Am I Staked Financially?

Funding and venture investment is a broad topic that goes beyond the scope of finding a path to the C-suite. The finances that come to the forefront for individual executives, however, pertain to their own personal livelihood. For most top executives, choosing the Founder Track requires the fiscal sacrifice associated with leaving a high-paying executive position to go out on their own. Cloverpop's Larson put it this way: "The financial question is probably the most important. No matter how long you think it'll take to be a viable business, you need to be ready for it to take five times longer."

Another Founder I interviewed told me: "I walked away from an annual million-dollar salary to make nothing at first and then pay myself maybe $90,000 annually." Yet, today, he's on his sixth start-up as CEO.

The Founders I interviewed all had some type of financial cushion when they were making their move: personal savings, a spouse who was gainfully employed, or financial liquidity following an exit from their previous position, for example. Even with an opportunity for a soft landing, however, executives and their families need to be okay with the inevitable financial trade-offs and personal risk that come with pursuing the Founder Track to the C-suite.

Do I Have the Personal Support I Need?

The importance of personal support can't be overstated along any path to the C-suite. Reaching the highest levels of leadership is difficult and stressful no matter how one arrives. That said, the lack of institutional infrastructure—benefits, training, salary—in start-up environments means an executive's personal support network must be especially strong. Personal support comes primarily from cofounders, friends, and family, and its uplifting impact is undeniable.

Chang said that without her husband's moral support she never would have had the courage to leave Google. Larson told me that his wife's encouragement and her own extremely successful career made it possible for him to take the leap. Wu, who left Snapfish, got married, welcomed his first child into the world, and bought a house all in the same year, said, "I wouldn't recommend doing it like that, and even under the best of circumstances it's a high-stress endeavor."

What Will I Do If I Fail?

One thing is certain if you choose the Founder's path: You will fail at some point. Maybe not initially, and maybe not ultimately, but there will be a time (and perhaps many times) when you fail in some significant way.

Unlike the other paths to the C-suite, the Founder's path involves frequent failure, which means you need to determine whether failure and reinvention is a realistic option for you. We will look at failure in more detail when we examine resilience and the Founder's mindset. At present, it is enough to search yourself and decide how you would fare if you fail. Will you reinvent yourself? Pivot? Recommit and forge ahead? Change paths? Regardless, ask yourself the question and envision what your next move would be.

These questions for future Founders queue up our discussion of experience, mindset, and followership, and illustrate that although this path is distinctive in many ways, some of the elements for success are common across all Four Core Paths.

Getting on the Fast Track: The Founder

Founders have such varied experiences and backgrounds. Yet, the entrepreneurial ecosystem has certain requirements for entry, as well as core capabilities that will accelerate your experience along this exciting, unpredictable path to the C-suite.

✔ Actions and Experience	✔ Mindset and Perspective	✔ Followership and Brand
__Progress through self-directed experiences and hands-on learning	__Have a tolerance for ambiguity and an affinity toward risk-taking	__Attract cofounders and leadership team members
__Develop extreme functional expertise	__Accept failure as part of the path	__Utilize the investor ecosystem
__Master specific skills: sales, communication, networking, team building	__Be resilient and have a plan for reinvention	__Gain support from the Founder network

✔ Actions and Experience

Experience accelerates career advancement along most paths to the C-suite. However, it's difficult to prepare to transition from a corporate setting to an entrepreneurial environment.

As Chang told me: "My organizational experience [at Google] helped me in some ways, but in many other ways it hurt. It's a mixed bag because the rules are so different when you're starting from scratch." She and other Founders admitted that moving from a relatively stable environment to one with far less predictability and institutional support is a challenge, and that the typical "tour of duty" that acclimates you for a spot in the corporate C-suite is not an apt simulation for the start-up experience.

Still, despite its peculiarities, there are certain types of experiences that will help steel you for the Founder's path.

Practice Self-Directed Learning

The first mode of experience Founders pursue is practice. Larson, for one, managed to put in some serious practice prior to Cloverpop. During his 12 years at Macromedia and Adobe, he "consciously focused on developing new products and testing different business models, and avoided working on large legacy products." He also "worked on acquiring businesses in order to see companies at all different stages."

This type of purposeful, self-directed learning is a common substitute for formal training by Founders. This explains why so many Founders come out of corporate settings that allow executives to experiment and innovate on their own, such as Google and 3M.

Cultivate Extreme Expertise

The Founders I observed also had deeply specialized functional and technical expertise and experience that served them well. Chang has an electrical engineering degree from Stanford and was the head of Google's analytics for years. All of that came in handy at Accompany, where she and her partners needed to build an entire data platform themselves. Susan Marshall had extensive product marketing and management experience at Apple, Adobe, and Salesforce, and was deeply involved in the rapid evolution of digital video, audio, mobile, social, and data management technologies. That gave her the know-how to try to disrupt digital marketing and "fix what's broken" in the industry. This type of extreme expertise gives executives the knowledge and credibility to go out on their own and forge the Founder's path.

Develop Sales and Communications Skills

Finally, the Founders I have encountered all possess a suite of interrelated abilities that allow them to evangelize their venture to multiple audiences. For example, basic sales skills are critical. As a Founder, you need to sell your ideas across your network to investors, partners, vendors, and customers.

"I was selling for the first time since I sold Girl Scout cookies and it was eye-opening," Chang told me. "A $150,000 sale is a very different level than what I was accustomed to—and I was learning it on the job."

Similarly, it's critical for Founders to use their communication abilities to attract the talent they need to fill asset gaps. Because they must do more with less, Founders need to think critically about the capabilities they have on hand, and then go out and acquire the rest. If you yourself are motivated and qualified to take on the CTO role at a start-up, for instance, you will likely need to attract or hire a finance and operations specialist or a marketing and sales expert.

Whether we are talking about selling or cyber-security, as a Founder you need to put your deep experience to work for you, surround yourself with a portfolio of experts, and hustle to learn everything else by doing it on the fly.

✔ Mindset and Perspective

Mindset considerations on the Founder's path are entirely defined by managing extreme risk and uncertainty. Moving from a corporate position to become a start-up leader requires an immense change in perspective. With that in mind, you will need to focus on a few overlapping themes to help you get off the ground as a Founder.

Have a Tolerance for Ambiguity

The idea of "not knowing" was a major theme in my conversations with founding executives. One experienced Founder summed it up like this: "On Mondays, I wake up with the realization that I don't know what I'm going to need to learn to do by Friday. By Wednesday, that notion bears out, and I'm scrambling to plug gaps and solve problems I never could have foreseen. By the end of the week, well, I'm simply figuring it all out as I go. In other words, hang on tight because it's a wild ride."

Success as a Founder means you need to make decisions with limited information, adapt fast, and cope with risk. When you can handle that trio of tough tasks, your mind will be primed for the ambiguity you will find on the Founder path.

Accept Failure as Part of the Path

Failure is another fact for Founding executives. How you deal with it will play a part in determining how far you get.

Before Larson launched Cloverpop, he prepared himself for future hardship, thanks in part to Macromedia's high tolerance for risk and a culture of learning through experimentation. "It didn't matter how many eggs you broke, the point was to make things happen and keep adjusting," he said. In fact, Larson "welcomed failing" so he could "get comfortable with the failure experience" and become more resilient. In other words, when failure happened, he embraced it to hone his instincts and persevere in the face of fear.

Chang agreed with the idea that failure can be constructive for Founders, saying that the fear is always there but that you can use it "as part of the driving force" that motivates you to innovate and get better every day.

Be Resilient and Have a Future Vision

The upside of all the uncertainty and risk is that this C-suite path is exciting—and in some ways forgiving. Successful Founders arguably have nine lives. As one start-up executive told me, "On the Internet you always get another chance the moment you can patch some code and redeploy it."

The orientation toward course correction is arguably the most important part of the Founder's mindset. Instead of focusing on erroneous assumptions or missed opportunities, Founders look to the next moves they need to make to get it right. You need to be willing to adjust your vision and pivot. Additionally, you must model resilient behavior to the rest of the organization and sell your "Plan B" to investors and partners. One of the start-up CEOs I studied told me that resilience is perhaps more important than big ideas, because even the best of plans are likely to be revisited and adjusted along the way.

What is apparent, based on these mindset imperatives, is that understanding one's self is a core capability for Founders. As bold and unbreakable as Founders need to be, they also need to be willing to practice self-reflection. According to Marshall, "You have to know yourself really well to decide if this is something you're prepared for and—even more—something you really want for yourself."

✔ Followership and Brand

The rationale for attracting followers as a Founder is different from that in the other paths. While followership for top-level leaders at established companies has a 360-degree emphasis, a uniquely important facet of followership for Founders is creating and maintaining a fully functioning top team of cofounders. As mentioned, Founders need to attract partners who complement them stylistically, believe in their ideas and mission, and are willing to take risks alongside them.

Chang asserts that achieving followership on top teams hinges on chemistry, trust, and mutual respect. "I tried to attract people with divergent points of view who would argue with me in a constructive way," she said. "[I wanted a culture] where we trust each other enough to debate openly without taking differences personally."

Followership, for Founders, also plays into attracting investors. In this case, the relationship is based in part on crafting a pitch, but also on the Founder's relationship and reputation within the investor's network. Again, it's about establishing mutual trust. After all, many times a Founder's investors may also serve as mentors.

When I spoke with Ken Coleman, tech industry pioneer and advisor to the venture capital firm Andreessen Horowitz, he admitted that most Founders are initially naive about what it takes and what's required to succeed.

"The responsibility, the challenges, and the sacrifices you will face are immense," he said. "Especially in the C-suite, where everyone is counting on you to get it right."[67]

Coleman's best advice? "Talk to plenty of people who have done what you are trying to do, have mentors, and above all . . . rely on your network to help you understand what you are stepping into."

A final distinctive element of achieving followership for Founders is gaining support from peers within the start-up ecosystem. In entrepreneurial havens like Silicon Valley and New York City, the infrastructure for business building is everywhere—whereas in places like Trenton, Cincinnati, or Detroit (and hundreds of other cities), Founders count on one another for everything from sharing resources and networking to moral support. I've seen Founders who share office space, back-office responsibilities, and even staff in order to keep costs in line.

Although leadership and followership are inextricably intertwined by definition, for Founders these ideas are sometimes interchangeable because of the small size of most teams and the lack of hierarchy.

If I could give executives eyeing this path to the C-suite only one piece of advice, it would be this: Know yourself and know what you are getting into. Most start-ups fail, and you will need to be prepared to turn that outcome into something positive, whether that is a different twist on your original idea or your next venture altogether. My impression is that most executives who select this path are entrepreneurial by nature, and once they make the leap they will never go back to leading an established organization.

The Founder: Career Accelerators and Derailers

Accelerators	Derailers
• You have an entrepreneurial vision of yourself, are mission driven, and want to have broad impact.	• You like the job security and compensation structure of a traditional business.
• Making money and personal enrichment are secondary to you.	• You strive to control outcomes and prefer predictability.
• You are self-aware—you know what skills you bring and what you need to source from partners.	• You are risk averse.
• You are motivated to solve problems.	• You don't like selling yourself or your ideas.
• You have deep functional expertise.	• You prefer to delegate.
• You have an affinity for reinvention and are unafraid of failure.	• You are happier as an individual contributor as opposed to a team leader/member.
• You are ready to pivot and rethink your vision.	• You surround yourself with others who are like you.

Chapter 6

Hybrid Paths to the C-Suite

The Four Core Paths represent the precedent for success set by a clear majority of today's top executives. They are the most widely traveled ways to reach the C-suite, and one obvious advantage of choosing a well-worn path, such as these, is the ease of following in another's footsteps. Many executives are also students of leadership: They learn by example and emulate their contemporary mentors and broader historical role models. Yet, even within these four archetypes, there is considerable variation. Every story is unique.

The demographic shifts within organizations and the structural evolution mentioned earlier are changing the shape of careers, from entry-level jobs to top-team positions. Tenure within companies is dropping, the need for entrepreneurial solutions is increasing, and organizations are adapting from hierarchies to matrixes and team-based units with fewer levels in the middle.

These changes open up alternate paths and hybrid opportunities for executive advancement. Lateral moves, skipping steps, varying experiences, and nonlinear career paths offer different ways to reach the C-suite. For instance, one study shows that individuals with "hybrid skills"—that is, core leadership experiences plus specialized technical expertise—are in high demand within top jobs.[68] Gary Pinkus, McKinsey & Company's managing partner for North America, put it this way in the *New York Times*: "Work has become incredibly cross-functional" whereby managers in areas such as marketing need to be able to understand engineers and engineers need to be able to communicate business outcomes.[69]

This means the strategies we use for attaining a top spot no longer require a consistently upward trajectory. Or, looking at it through the lens of three-dimensional chess, reaching the C-suite today can often occur with a knight's circuitous path as opposed to a queen's sweeping, linear swiftness.

For example, Sean Hinton, CEO of the Soros Economic Development Fund, reached the C-suite after studying in London to be a conductor. Later, he was also a McKinsey & Company consultant and a fellow at the Aspen Institute. In between all that, he served as Mongolia's first honorary consul-general in Australia.[70] Hinton's path to the top was decidedly nonlinear, and yet this type of circuity is arguably becoming more common in business.[71]

With that in mind, let's look at several alternate paths to the top, along with their accelerators and derailers, in the hope that these options demonstrate that you can use hybrid building blocks to blaze your own way.

Nontraditional Paths

We have seen throughout this book that there are multiple ways to reach the C-suite. The nontraditional paths that follow show that opportunities arise when executives are able to prove themselves in unusual ways.

Consulting → C-Suite

Like Hinton, Cisco's Ruba Borno landed on the executive leadership team by way of Big Three consulting. Currently chief of staff to CEO Chuck Robbins, Borno earned a master's degree and PhD in engineering (as opposed to an MBA), and her previous role was at Boston Consulting Group. As a consultant, Borno worked with technology and media companies, including Cisco, to manage digital transformation, postmerger integration, and strategy execution—all things that are central to Cisco's business. That knowledge base, combined with her firsthand familiarity with Cisco's operations and executives, made Borno an ideal C-suite candidate for the execution-focused role of chief of staff.

- *Accelerator*: The *consulting* path to the C-suite opens up when a consultant or advisor becomes so steeped in an industry and its main players that he or she secures deep-dive exposure to the type of problem solving and operational know-how that is instrumental to organizations.
- *Derailer*: This path is more commonly aimed at operationally focused and functional C-suite roles and may not provide the general management exposure and line leadership needed for some central C-suite positions.

Mergers and Acquisitions → C-Suite

Mergers and acquisitions drive structural changes in organizations that can carve openings for new roles. For instance, when a large company acquires a start-up, founding officers can be kept on to create continuity and help everyone make the most of the deal. Terry Myerson, for one, landed at Microsoft in 1997, when the software giant acquired his web software start-up. Likewise, Yoky Matsuoka was vice president of technology at Nest in 2014, when Google acquired the company. Matsuoka later left to be CEO of a health-data startup, but then she returned to Nest in 2017 as chief technology officer.

The rub is that postacquisition executives are seldom brought directly into the C-suite. They may land several levels down and need additional experience before getting in line for a top job.

- *Accelerator*: In an acquisition situation, start-up executives are most valuable to acquiring firms if they have institutional knowledge to share and (in the case of tech start-ups) technical familiarity with the product or business.

- *Derailer*: It takes time and patience to turn an acquisition into a legitimate path to the C-suite. Timing and culture differences can make on-boarding a challenge.

Spinoff→ C-Suite

Corporate restructurings, like spinoffs, generate leadership opportunities when a conglomerate divests part of itself to create a smaller, more focused entity. In an ideal situation, the move creates value for the spinoff as well as the parent company.

For example, NV "Tiger" Tyagarajan became president and CEO of Genpact, the global professional services firm, several years after he helped spin the business off from GE. Originally a service organization within GE Capital, Genpact (as a solo business) has grown to become a giant in digital transformation and outsourcing consulting.

Tiger, an industry leader and an architect of Genpact's pioneering delivery model, was initially reluctant to leave GE, but he recognized the spinoff as an entrepreneurial opportunity to "make a mark in the world."[72]

"It was a new business model at the time and I knew it was going to change the way services get delivered," Tiger said.

Although spinoffs are on the rise, with 35 in 2016 (worth about $100 billion in initial market value), this is a specific opportunity that is best suited to leaders with an extensive understanding of the spinoff organization and industry.[73]

- *Accelerator*: Spinoffs can be an action-packed opportunity for seasoned executives who are ready to go beyond business-as-usual in an entrepreneurial landscape that is basically built for growth.
- *Derailer*: Spinoffs can be a risky proposition for executives. Although many spinoffs have a solid track record for success, others are little more than opportunities for large companies to divest weak or low-margin divisions.

Moving from C-Suite to C-Suite

Executives who leap from one C-suite situation to the next might be moving into a different role, trading up, or simply looking to do something different. The most obvious C-suite switch is simply jumping from one organization to another in the same role, but there are other possibilities to consider along this path.

Board → CEO

As an extension of the C-suite, board members play a critical role in CEO successions. Less often, board members themselves move into traditional C-suite roles. Research from Stanford University Graduate School of Business shows that outside directors moved into CEO roles 58 times in Fortune 1000 companies between 2005 and 2016.[74] According to the study, directors can be an attractive option for the top team because of their inherent inside-outsider nature.

Yet, according to Groysberg, this path may signal dysfunction in the boardroom.[75] He told me that sourcing a CEO from the sitting board may signal a lack of readiness for the succession. In addition, the move is most prevalent (68% of the time) when a sitting CEO resigns suddenly, another sign of disarray at the top.[76]

- *Accelerator*: Outside board members stand out as candidates in CEO succession situations when they are "well versed in all aspects of the company, including strategy, business model, and risk-management practices . . . and [they have] personal relationships with the executive team."[77]
- *Derailer*: This is not a long-term position. Directors turned CEO don't stay in place long, with those named on an interim basis remaining less than 6 months and those named permanently staying an average of 3.3 years.[78]

Functional C-Suite → CEO

It is not unheard of to have a COO, CFO, or even a CSO become CEO—as long as they have experience beyond their particular functional roles. Indra Nooyi is one excellent example. Appointed CEO of Pepsico in 2006, Nooyi served as CFO for five years, during which time she restructured Pepsico and led multiple acquisitions. Although moving from CHRO to chief executive is less common, Euro Disney's onetime CEO, Philippe Gas, moved directly from the human resources lead at the organization to CEO, where he remained from 2008 to 2014. In all, Gas served at Disney in various capacities for over 20 years.

- *Accelerator*: Certain C-suite roles are on the CEO fast track. COO and CSO are sometimes considered chief executive "understudy" positions, meaning the role is created as part of the CEO succession process to give short-list candidates access to the right experiences as a way to pressure-test their instincts.
- *Derailer*: Not all C-suite executives are ready for the top spot. To become CEO, leaders in functional C-suite roles need to show more than just a successful tenure within their respective functions. They must also complete prior rotations in general leadership positions such as division president or product line director—jobs with people management and P&L responsibility.

Founder-CEO → Established C-Suite

A final "C-suite to C-suite" path I have seen up close occurs when start-up founders move into C-suite positions at established companies. When I spoke with Anthony Soohoo of Walmart, he told me that his status as an "occasional entrepreneur" is integral to what makes him effective in his current position as senior vice president and group general manager of Home e-commerce for Walmart.

Previously, Soohoo founded Dotspotter, a mobile entertainment news service acquired by CBS Corporation in 2007, and more recently cofounded Dot & Bo, an online home goods community aimed at millennials. Of his work as a corporate officer at the big-box retailer, Soohoo said: "Entrepreneurship is more of a mindset now . . . one that is sought after no matter the size of the company."[79]

Soohoo and other founders turned corporate executives know that core entrepreneurial skills, such as team building, idea development, and customer focus, are core capabilities for all senior leaders today.

- *Accelerator*: Entrepreneurial leaders get on the C-suite short list in established organizations when they can show that they are visionaries and evangelists who have benefited by experiencing key start-up experiences such as resilience and reinvention following failure.
- *Derailer*: Not all founders are cut out to be C-suite executives in traditional businesses. To be considered for the job, founders need to demonstrate that they can fit into the corporate culture and manage the political dynamics in a way that gets things done.

Choose Your Own Adventure

While top-team positions are admittedly scarce and highly competitive, one of the best ways to get yourself on the short list is to be proactive in making it happen.

New Role Creation

I have coached people who were elevated to the C-suite on the fast track when their specialty suddenly became central to the organization's needs: security experts who became chief security officers, and even one digital marketing maven who became chief experience officer. In part, these folks were in the right place at the right time.

They were Tenured Executives doing great work in a trending specialty. Yet, it was always much more than that. They proactively focused their efforts in new fields and made a name for themselves as top experts. In addition, they raised their hand to lead key projects and stepped up to interact with the C-suite team when their technical expertise was needed.

Beth Comstock suggests creating your own path by accepting assignments that are somewhat undefined—and expanding their scope. She advises finding and filling a key strategic need and turning it into a vehicle for advancement. Take human resources as an example. At one point, HR was not a common function within the C-suite. Then, HR executives proved their strategic worth and now they are part of the C-suite establishment.

- *Accelerator*: You stand the best chance of having your role bumped up to the top team if you can show that your specialty (security, data, innovation) is central to the CEO's agenda and can be a key lever for organizational success.
- *Derailer*: C-suite job titles come and go. Your specialty needs to be broad enough to withstand changing trends in order to be deemed worthwhile on the top team.

Moving Down to Move Up

Another proactive (and brave) way to forge a path to the top is by rotating laterally or even moving down the ladder to gain enough key experience to move you back up into a bigger position.

One HR leader I know aspires to become a CEO. He knows he "can't get there from here," but he has a plan to remedy the situation. First, he is actively looking for a new position running a division or business line. After that, he plans to volunteer for a global assignment to check that box. He has a handle on his experience gaps and is stepping down from the top team—until he has the right experience to lead it.

- *Accelerator*: Be strategic. Moving down to move back up is most effective when you choose positions that will help you grow professionally and *add value* to the organization.
- *Derailer*: Think about your career timeline. Making multiple moves is time-consuming, and finding the right roles requires patience. Once you move down, will there be enough time to move back up and reach your goal?

Crossing Paths to the C-Suite

These hybrid paths have something in common with the Four Core Paths explored in previous chapters: They might not be enough. In fact, you may need to try more than one to reach the C-suite. Mary Barra was a Tenured Executive as well as a Leapfrog Leader. Selma was a Free Agent and later a Leapfrog Leader. Terry Myerson was a Founder turned Tenured Executive.

Switching paths is common, and it demonstrates your tenacity as well as your strategic mindset. The ability to tolerate and embrace change appears in every chapter as a core capability that will help you accelerate your career trajectory.

How will you know when to change paths? Some executives change paths because the one they are on is not leading where they need. Perhaps a C-suite slot is not available on the Tenured Executive Track and you need to become a Free Agent. Other executives change paths because they find an opening for fast advancement.

Tiger was on the Tenured Executive Track at GE, and it was a path that he expected to remain on for the duration of his career. But the opportunity to spin off and be a leader at Genpact was too good to pass up. Jay Galeota left Merck to join G&W Labs for the same reason—it was an excellent opening.

If one path is not enough to reach your C-suite dream, your second or third might deliver. All the various experiences you need to reach the top are available along every path. Remember, if you switch paths you are not starting over. You bring your experiences, mindset, and followership with you.

Might Tiger or Galeota return to their past employers one day in C-suite roles? Quite possibly. I plan to stay tuned.

Chapter 7

Reaching the Top Team

R egardless of your path, the terrain changes when you are finally approaching the peak. Maybe you are considering an opportunity or have landed on the C-suite short list? Well, this is your chance to dig in, demonstrate resilience, and showcase your capabilities. The challenge is to elevate your game when the pressure is most intense. The CEO and board need to see that you can perform at the highest level.

What can help you achieve your goal? Know the process cold and be prepared to perform.

The Process

Some C-suite searches last a few months, while others take years to complete. In part, the duration depends on the complexity of the succession. Is the outgoing leader leaving "on schedule and as planned" or is the departure unexpected? Ready or not, there are certain staging areas you will need to pass through on the way to the C-suite.

1. The Executive Assessment

All major CEO successions, and many other top team searches (CFO, COO, CHRO, and so on), utilize formal executive assessments. Led by HR or a consulting/executive search firm (or more likely both), assessments are designed to deliver in-depth insight into your leadership style. They also reveal the specific conditions under which you thrive and struggle.

As Spencer Stuart's Citrin told me: "Well-designed executive assessments don't simply measure past performance, they help predict the potential for future performance of an executive."[80] As part of that, they appraise reputation, leadership capabilities, reactions under pressure, and many other intangible qualities that can be difficult to determine through interviews and traditional performance assessments alone.

Although the specifics vary, Cisco used a two-part assessment as part of the rigorous 2015 CEO succession process that swept in Chuck Robbins as CEO. Part one was a quantitative evaluation created by Spencer Stuart, designed to measure the candidates' business and functional capabilities against industry peers. The second part was more qualitative. Conducted by our internal executive talent team, it keyed in on leadership ability based on a multitude of in-depth interviews with peers, supervisors, and direct reports. The results blend qualitative and benchmarked data on outside C-suite executives to offer an objective indication of each individual's abilities, mindset, and followership.

Assessments also reveal development needs. For instance, if assessments indicate that an executive is failing to connect with direct reports or falls flat on communication skills, it draws a red flag. In addition, assessments take the current top team's makeup into account from a portfolio perspective. If they show that the C-suite is light on a specific technical or strategic capability, that would be dialed into the assessment process during the search to fill the open C-suite spot.

Although you can be practically and emotionally prepared for the assessment process, it's not a system you can game. I coach executives to be confident, take the assessment seriously, put their best self forward, and represent themselves accurately. (Need practice? See the following sample assessment questions.)

Sample Assessment Questions

1. I WORK BEST WHEN I AM:

   a. Leading a team of professionals.
   b. On my own, so I am not affected by the thinking of the crowd.
   c. Part of a diverse team of individual contributors.

Teams are integral to most organizations today. Even if the position in question is at the top, an organization will want to assess your ability as a team leader and member.

2. ONE OF MY TOP QUALITIES IS:

   a. Emotional intelligence.
   b. Undivided focus on results.
   c. Customer relationships.

In many cases there are no "wrong" answers. The objective is to get a clear sense of who you are and how you would fit within the organization.

3. IMAGINE YOU ARE ATTENDING A MEETING WHERE ONE OF YOUR PEERS IS PUBLICLY BERATING A DIRECT REPORT. YOU WOULD:

   a. Step up and defend the direct report.
   b. Find a way to defuse the situation and confront the leader later.
   a. Talk to HR after the meeting.

If none of the answers seem quite right, be honest and err on the side of common sense.

4. CORPORATE GOVERNANCE AND INTEGRITY ARE:

   a. Not a part of my direct job.
   b. Something every executive should be responsible for upholding.
   c. Qualities the board will oversee.

When integrity and honest business practices arise, always double down and demonstrate your eagerness to take responsibility.

5. VACATION TIME AND PTO ARE:

   a. Perks to avail myself of when I have the free time.
   b. Crucial to the health and well-being of all employees.
   c. Mandatory to use to set the example for other employees.

Some questions and answers must be considered with the organization's culture and norms in mind. Still, balance and outside interests are looked upon positively as a means for avoiding executive burnout.

6. WHEN I FAIL, I:

   a. Am devastated and take full responsibility.
   b. Decide what we can learn from the experience and move on to the next challenge.
   c. Unsure, I seldom fail.

All seasoned executives need to be able to talk about their experiences with failures. In addition, indications that you are resilient score high.

7. DIVERSITY MEANS:

   a. Hiring people of all races.
   b. Valuing different perspectives, experiences, backgrounds, and lifestyles.
   c. The organization will be better suited to meet the needs of a wide array of clients and customers.

Questions like this are geared to get a sense of your nuanced understanding of complex business issues. Answer (a.) may not be technically incorrect, but it might signal that your understanding of the topic is one-dimensional.

8. IN MY FREE TIME I LIKE TO

   a. Go hiking or otherwise spend time outdoors.
   b. Volunteer at local nonprofits.
   c. Spend time with my family.
   d. Other.

Again, no wrong answers here. Viewed together, your response will help the organization put together an accurate picture of who you are and how you would fit within the culture.

Given their in-depth nature, not everyone makes it through the assessment process entirely unscathed. It can be grueling when development areas are put in the spotlight. Still, if you are ready for something bigger and better, it is right there on the page. If not, you can consider the results of the assessment and make adjustments for next time.

Another upside? An astute candidate can learn as much about the organization (its values and what it is looking for) as the organization learns about them.

2. The Interviews

You will almost certainly be subject to multiple rounds of interviews, either one-on-one or in front of a panel. It pays to know what each interview setting entails.

A common interview venue you will likely encounter as a C-suite candidate is the executive lunch or coffee. This informal event can seem low key, but don't underplay its importance. In addition to your experience, your host will be assessing your social skills and executive intelligence and considering the chemistry you would bring to the top team. Commonsense rules apply here. Take your cues from your host, and follow their lead even though you might feel tempted to take over the discussion.

Early-stage conversations like this, over a meal or coffee, can help you decide whether the opportunity is a fit. The research you conduct on your own, prior to the meeting, can give you some of the answers: How is the organization performing? Are current executives engaged or are they heading for the exits? Beyond that, ask your host about the culture and strategy of the organization and what they are hoping to achieve as they fill the open role.

The next C-suite interview format to consider is the formal discussions you will have with executives, C-suite peers, and recruiters. These can occur in a small group setting or individually. In this case, be prepared to tell your story and describe your successes and failures. Your interviewer will be looking at everything from your qualifications to your leadership brand and how talented you are as a communicator. Regardless, the best advice that I have is to be prepared and know who you're meeting with. During the discussion, find ways to connect and focus on areas of commonality. Conversely, also be ready to set yourself apart from your peers, with ideas, accomplishments, and the specific vision you convey.

The final interview type I will mention is the meeting with board members. Although this won't happen in every case, CEOs of public companies and other key hires are sure to meet with some board members. When we interviewed for John Chambers's successor, for instance, all of Cisco's board members (with the exception of Chambers himself) interviewed each internal candidate individually. In this case, the board was provided with a set of guiding questions, but the process allowed each member to draw on their expertise and develop their own questions. In general, interviews allow board members to build a rapport with each candidate and get to know their individual capabilities, leadership style, and future potential. Remember that board members are outside insiders. They will be as interested in your thoughts on the industry as they are on your fit with the organization.

Throughout every consecutive stage of the interview process, ask questions that will help you position yourself as a strong candidate. Use the time and access to learn as much as you can about the job, the executive team, and your possible fit within the organization.

Sample Interview Questions

1. TELL ME WHAT YOU KNOW ABOUT THE ORGANIZATION AND THE JOB.

Meaning: Have you done your research? Do you have a clear understanding of the organization?

2. WHAT PROFESSIONAL VALUES MEAN THE MOST TO YOU?

Meaning: Are your values a good fit with ours?

3. WHO ARE YOUR ROLE MODELS OR MENTORS IN BUSINESS AND HISTORY?

Meaning: Are you a student of leadership and do you have a grasp of the wider context of business?

4. WHAT IS YOUR LEADERSHIP STYLE?

Meaning: How do you treat people and manage power?

5. WHAT ARE YOU MOST PROUD OF IN YOUR CAREER?

Meaning: What are your successes and where have you added the most value?

6. WHERE DO YOU NEED DEVELOPMENT OR WHAT ARE YOUR WEAKNESSES? HOW WOULD YOU COMPENSATE FOR THEM?

Don't fall into the trap of avoiding this question or providing a transparent or false answer. Demonstrate that you are introspective, honest, and self-aware.

7. TALK ABOUT A TIME WHEN YOU FAILED—WHAT HAPPENED AND WHAT DID YOU DO?

Meaning: Are you resilient? How do you approach the inevitable failure?

8. TELL ME A STORY THAT DEMONSTRATES WHO YOU ARE AS A LEADER.

Meaning: Are you a good communicator? Do you have a good story to tell?

9. BASED ON WHAT YOU KNOW, WHAT CAN WE AS A BUSINESS BE DOING BETTER?

Meaning: What ideas do you have and are you strategic?

10. IS THIS A JOB YOU WANT, AND WHY?

Meaning: Are you serious about the position?

11. WHAT QUESTIONS DO YOU HAVE FOR US?

Meaning: Are you curious and inquisitive?

---

3. Scenarios That Test Your Mettle

Organizations test and try out internal C-suite candidates by rotating them through a succession of difficult assignments to see how they respond and react. At Cisco, as succession planning progressed in 2015, we gave internal candidates increasingly bigger jobs and devised detailed development plans. Once we were confident about which executives belonged in the CEO pipeline, we provided them with coaching, gave them roles with greater scope and accountability, delivered exposure to the board and external investors, and provided speaking opportunities that put them out on the world stage.

If you are a Tenured Executive or a possible Leapfrog Leader, be ready to pass these real-time tests. Outside candidates, including Free Agents, won't generally have this chance to prove themselves, but the onus is on them to make the case that they can handle these situations, and that they are equal or superior to internal candidates. No matter what path you are on, you should ask for these types of opportunities to gain experience, expand your comfort zone, and demonstrate that you have excelled in complex assignments.

A Checklist for the Eleventh Hour

The skills, mindset, and followership assets described throughout this book will help you stand out as a candidate during an active C-suite succession.

But before closing, let's return to some of the most relevant capabilities that CEOs, boards, and executive recruiters will look for as they make their final selection for the top team. Keeping these in mind will help you impress and rise above the rest.

Manage Your Executive Temperament

Landing on the C-suite short list requires the bold moves and displays of dominance that arguably typify some aspects of executive temperament. Yet, once you are under imminent consideration, it will be just as important to demonstrate that your ego is in check.

"Knowing when to wield power is one part of serving as a leader—but it is just one of many facets. In fact, leaders get selected out when their need for power gets too high,"[81] Ciampa said.

With collaborative competencies like persuasion and influence becoming ever more important for leaders, arrogance and power plays are common derailers during the final climb to the top team and beyond.

Focus on Change and Reinvention

A focus on change and reinvention was a common theme across all Four Core Paths, and it will be a decisive topic as you interview for a specific role. On one hand, you need to show that you value the current corporate culture; on the other hand, you must have a vision to drive change, growth, and transformation. Similarly, you need to show that you have a lifelong love of learning and the ability to unlearn the things that no longer apply.

Have a Knack for Communication

You will need to convey authenticity and persuasively communicate the values and vision of the organization.

Model Resilience

Modeling resilience is a requisite requirement for the C-suite. You should be able to share stories that illustrate how you have turned failure and adversity into something positive.

Be Strategic in Ideas and Execution

You will need to show that you can make the critical turn from being a functional expert to managing strategy in a global sense.

Wharton School professor Michael Useem put it this way: "Executives need to think holistically about the entire division or operation, and ultimately the entire enterprise." He admits that this is easier said than done. "You're representing your particular 'C' in the C-suite—chief of marketing, or whatever it may be—but then unequivocally you also must have the big picture and think strategically about the enterprise."[82]

This means having "strategic foresight"[83] and translating ideas into actions that impact your organization and C-suite area.

Convey Emotional Intelligence

Emotional intelligence has always been a key leadership trait, but it has grown in prominence as leaders need to engage people of different demographics who want to work in new ways and find more meaning in the workplace.

Master Team Building

Loners seldom reach the C-suite. As hierarchy becomes less relevant and organizational structures become flat or more matrixed, top-team candidates are judged based on their ability to integrate multiple perspectives as opposed to acting solely on their own beliefs. Similarly, consider your impending slot on the top team and be able to articulate what you bring that will make the C-suite stronger.

Understand Servant Leadership

Several of the above ideas (teamwork, temperament, communication, emotional intelligence) culminate in what Robert K. Greenleaf called "servant leadership" in 1970.[84] That is, he introduced the idea of *leadership as a means to serve employees and society*. Although it may be a classic concept, it is at the center of a common question posed during many modern succession discussions: *Is he/she a servant leader?* Get to know this idea and how you exhibit leadership in a way that fulfills the needs of others. This is but one piece of the leadership equation, but it remains an important ideal embodied by the best C-suite leaders.

Conclusion
Four Paths, One Last Question

In the introduction, I mentioned the finance executive I coached a few years back at Cisco. At the time, he was considering his career path and searching for a fast track to the C-suite. More recently, I checked in with him to see if he had cracked the C-suite code and found his path. He did—but it didn't lead where he expected.

For a number of years, he ascended swiftly as a Tenured Executive. He accepted global assignments and continued to expand his experience portfolio. Then, he hit a career inflection point and made the decision to reinvent himself. He left traditional business altogether to join a nonprofit—running its endowment. He told me that everything he accomplished in his career up until that moment pointed him to this current job, and he couldn't be happier.

Will he lead that nonprofit or another one someday? He might. But his decision to change direction leads into the final question on our C-suite checklist: *Is this the right plan for you?*

Bar none, the executives I interviewed told me that being on the top team was exhilarating, rewarding, and far more complex and difficult than they had ever anticipated. It's clear that you need sponsors to champion your rise to the top team. But there's more. Personal support is equally important. CEOs and other C-suite job discussions frequently include spouses and explicit questions about your personal support system.

Why? Because the stress of being at the top can take its toll.

Many CEOs will tell you that accepting a spot in the C-suite is a family decision. Do you have the support you need? If so, you may decide that the top team is exactly what you want. Go after it. You might be ready for the stress, excitement, and ongoing exhilaration that come with serving on the top team. Even more, you might someday find yourself leaping levels on the way to that job. No matter how you get there, I hope that everything learned on the way up makes your leadership tenure long and rewarding.

Appendix: Contributing Executives and Expert Advisors

Peter Cappelli is the George W. Taylor Professor of Management at The Wharton School, director of Wharton's Center for Human Resources, and author of numerous books, including *Why Good People Can't Get Jobs*.

Amy Chang is CEO and founder of Accompany, Inc., and previously was global head of product, Google Ads Measurement and Reporting.

Dan Ciampa is one of the world's leading authorities on CEO and senior leadership transitions and author of five books, including *Transitions at the Top: What Organizations Must Do to Make Sure New Leaders Succeed* and *Right from the Start: Taking Charge in a New Leadership Role* (with Michael Watkins).

James Citrin is leader, CEO Practice at Spencer Stuart, and one of the world's foremost executive recruiters and author of six books, including *The Career Playbook: Essential Advice for Today's Aspiring Young Professional*.

Kenneth Coleman is chair of Saama Technologies, Inc., a long-term veteran of Silicon Valley, and special advisor to Andreessen Horowitz Venture Capital Firm.

Beth Comstock was the first woman to serve as vice chair at GE, leading the company's efforts to accelerate new growth, develop new markets and service models, drive brand value, and enhance GE's inventive culture.

Edith Cooper is senior director at Goldman Sachs, and formerly the global head of human capital management responsible for the recruitment, development, promotion, and well-being of the firm's global workforce.

Courtney della Cava is a senior director at Bain & Company and global leader of Bain Executive Network.

Eileen P. Drake is CEO and president and director of Aerojet Rocketdyne Holdings Inc.

Patricia Fili-Krushel is a veteran media industry executive who served as chair of the NBCUniversal News Group; executive vice president, administration, at Time Warner Inc.; CEO of WebMD; president of the ABC Television Network; and president of ABC Daytime.

Jay Galeota is president and COO at G&W Labs, and past chief strategy and business development officer and president, emerging businesses, at Merck.

Taylor M. Griffin is the COO of The Miles Group (TMG).

Boris Groysberg is a professor of business administration in the Organizational Behavior unit at the Harvard Business School and author of *Chasing Stars: The Myth of Talent and the Portability of Performance*.

Sylvia Ann Hewlett is the founder and CEO of the Center for Talent Innovation, the founder of Hewlett Consulting Partners, LLC, and author of *(Forget a Mentor) Find a Sponsor: The New Way to Fast-Track Your Career*.

Kelly Kramer is executive vice president and CFO at Cisco and past CFO of GE Healthcare's Healthcare Systems business.

Erik Larson is founder and CEO of Cloverpop, a cloud app for better and faster business decision making, and writer on both entrepreneurial leadership and the business impact of behavioral science.

Susan Marshall is founder and CEO of Torchlite and a 20-plus-year technology veteran deeply involved in the rapid evolution of digital video, audio, mobile, social, and data management technologies.

Yoky Matsuoka is chief technology officer at Nest, a onetime semi-professional tennis player in her native Japan, and a MacArthur Fellow "genius award" recipient.

Terry Myerson is executive vice president, Windows and Devices Group at Microsoft. He leads the team responsible for the software platform and devices within Microsoft's workplace, gaming, and cloud solutions.

Mary Petrovich is an operating executive at The Carlyle Group and executive chair of AxleTech International.

Joseph Ryan is president and founder of True North Advisory Group, and he teaches extensively in Wharton's executive education programs.

Duncan Simester is a professor at the MIT Sloan School of Management, where he holds the NTU Chair in Marketing and is also head of the marketing group.

David Simmons is chair and CEO, PPD, and former president and general manager of the emerging markets and established products business units for Pfizer.

Anthony Soohoo is senior vice president and group general manager of Home eCommerce at Walmart and was cofounder and CEO of online furniture store Dot & Bo.

NV "Tiger" Tyagarajan is president and CEO of Genpact.

Michael Useem is a professor of management, director of the Center for Leadership and Change Management at The Wharton School of the University of Pennsylvania, and author of several books, including *The Leader's Checklist: 15 Mission-Critical Principles.*

Wendell P. Weeks is chair and CEO of Corning Incorporated.

Patrick Wright is Thomas C. Vandiver Bicentennial Chair and founder and faculty director of the Center for Executive Succession in the Darla Moore School of Business at the University of South Carolina.

Christopher Wu is CEO and founder of Paper Culture.

Acknowledgments

This book could not have been written without the help of so many talented advisors, mentors, colleagues, and friends.

The idea of becoming an author goes back to earlier in my career when I worked for Bob Kaplan and Dave Norton, founders of the most influential management concept—the Balanced Scorecard. They inspired me to pursue thought leadership, and without their encouragement I wouldn't be where I am today. During my time working for them I had one especially fabulous leader who has grown to be one of my closest friends, Laura Downing. She encouraged (and sometimes pushed) me to write a book. Without Bob, Dave, and Laura I would not have taken this journey.

Bob Kaplan connected me with Boris Groysberg at Harvard Business School. To my delight, Boris became a mentor and friend. He later wrote a Harvard Business School case on work that I and others did as part of the 2015 CEO succession at Cisco. Boris was a wonderful advisor on this book project, and he also helped me think through important career decisions of my own.

My doctorate work at the University of Pennsylvania offered me the gift of having Joe Ryan as my dissertation advisor. He took an interest in me, inspired me, and encouraged me to pursue my passion for research and thought leadership. He has been a sounding board and friend throughout this project.

Erica Dhawan, who is fearless in putting her excellent ideas out into the world, encouraged me to do the same. She served as a role model, and I am thankful for her influence and lucky to call her a friend.

I have had the tremendous fortune at Cisco of being part of the Center for Talent Innovation, where I met its founder, Sylvia Ann

Hewlett—for whom I have great admiration. She supported me and generously shared her connections and contacts. Duncan Simester, from MIT, is a close friend and esteemed colleague. He worked with me to put together world-class leadership programs at Cisco, the participants from which were an inspiration for this book. Jim Citrin is someone I have admired and followed for many years. Cisco's CEO succession gave me my first chance to work with Jim and learn from him. He has shared his knowledge and network with me, for which I am extremely grateful.

Numerous other great thought leaders played a role in this book: Sandra Horbach from Carlyle helped me understand private equity, David Reimer of Merryck allowed me to see trends in leadership, Dan Ciampa inspired me with his wisdom on leadership, Bill Catucci taught me much that I needed to know, the team at G100 helped me learn future trends, Courtney della Cava from Bain encouraged me and shared her knowledge, Matt Cutler helped me understand entrepreneurship from a founder's perspective and introduced me to many of his colleagues, Kate O'Keeffe has been my kindred spirit on innovation and helped me develop ideas, and Patrick Wright from the Center of Succession generously shared his thought leadership. Michael Useem and Peter Cappelli, my former professors at The Wharton School of the University of Pennsylvania, have been an inspiration to me. I benefited greatly from the knowledge they have shared for this project.

The idea for this book would not have come about without the amazing talent and curiosity of the many Cisco executives I have worked with over the years. They were open with me and shared their career aspirations, often asking, "How do I get into the C-suite?" It's been a joy to help many of them achieve their personal and career ambitions. The colleagues from my former executive talent team are amazing people. I learned from them and enjoyed every minute of working together. I am also extremely thankful for having John Chambers and Chuck Robbins as inspirational role models for leadership.

My trusted advisors for the book have been incredibly important to me and have made the process truly enjoyable. Cathy Benko was instrumental as a sounding board on how to put thought leadership together. She introduced me to Carolyn Monaco and Jacque Murphy—and the journey began. Carolyn has been a wonderful advisor, encouraging me to be courageous and put my ideas out into the world. Jacque has been the best collaborator, writing partner, and friend I could have ever dreamed of. I am in awe of her talent. Jill Totenberg pushed me outside my comfort zone and taught me how to "market" ideas in a meaningful way. Jill, Carolyn, and Jacque supported me not only through this process but also as I lost my mother while writing this book.

Karen Yankovich helped me learn social media and strategy in a way I could have never done on my own. I have also been very fortunate to work with an innovative and talented publishing company, Wharton School Press. Shannon Berning, Steve Kobrin, and Teresa Kocudak have been incredible to work with and have taught me how to be an effective author.

Finally, the many executives and thought leaders I interviewed for this book were not only enlightening but also amazingly generous in sharing their career stories. I thank them for their ongoing leadership and for serving as role models to so many young and aspiring executives.

Notes

1   Boris Groysberg, J. Yo-Jud Cheng, and Annelena Lobb, "CEO Succession at Cisco (A): From John Chambers to Chuck Robbins," Harvard Business School Case 417-031, August 2016.

2   Gary L. Neilson and Julie Wukf, "How Many Direct Reports?," *Harvard Business Review*, April 2012, https://hbr.org/2012/04/how-many-direct-reports.

3   Ram Charan, Dominic Barton, and Dennis Carey, "People before Strategy: A New Role for the CHRO," *Harvard Business Review*, July–August 2015, https://hbr.org /2015/07/people-before-strategy-a-new-role-for-the-chro.

4   Richard Oldfield, "Who's at the Table?: The C-Suite and 20 Years of Change," PwC, accessed October 10, 2017, http://www.pwc.com/gx/en/ceo-agenda/ceosurvey /2017/gx/20th-anniversary/the-evolution-of-the-c-suite.html.

5   Lars A. Gollenia, "Digital Leadership: Will the Chief Information Officer Role Disappear?," Spencer Stuart, January 2017, accessed October 10, 2017, https://www .spencerstuart.com/research-and-insight/digital-leadership-will-the-chief -information-officer-role-disappear.

6   Peter Cappelli, Monika Hamorid, and Rocio Bonet, "Who's Got Those Top Jobs?," *Harvard Business Review*, March 2014, 43.

7   Ibid.

8   "Age and Tenure in the C-Suite: Korn Ferry Institute Study Reveals Trends by Title and Industry," Korn Ferry, February 14, 2017, accessed October 10, 2017, https:// www.kornferry.com/press/age-and-tenure-in-the-c-suite-korn-ferry-institute -study-reveals-trends-by-title-and-industry/.

9   Russell Reynolds Associates, "Where Do CFOs Come From?," 2012, http://www .russellreynolds.com/insights/thought-leadership/where-do-cfos-come-from.

10 Jean Martin, "For Senior Leaders, Fit Matters More Than Skill," *Harvard Business Review*, January 17, 2014, https://hbr.org/2014/01/for-senior-leaders-fit-matters -more-than-skill.

11 "CEO Turnover at a Record High Globally, With More Companies Planning for New Chiefs from outside the Company," PwC Strategy&, April 19, 2016, https:// www.strategyand.pwc.com/global/home/press/displays/ceo-success-study-2015.

12 Ron Torch, "What to Look for in Your Next CMO or Senior Marketing Leader," Torch Group, November 2016, http://www.torchgroup.com/torch-light-newsletter /newsletter-3.

13 Roselinde Torres, Gerry Hansell, Kaye Foster, and David Baron, "Leapfrog Succession: A New Trend in Appointing CEOs?," BCG Perspectives, November 6, 2014, https://www.bcgperspectives.com/content/articles/talent _leadership_human_resources_leapfrog_succession_new_trend_appointing _ceos/.

14 Michael Useem, interview by the author, May 18, 2017. Unless noted, all other quotes from Useem in this chapter are from the same author interview.

15 Joseph L. Bower, "More Insiders Are Becoming CEOs, and That's a Good Thing," *Harvard Business Review*, March 18, 2016, https://hbr.org/2016/03/more-insiders -are-becoming-ceos-and-thats-a-good-thing.

16 Kevin J. Murphy and Jan Zabojnik, *Managerial Capital and the Market for CEOs*, April 2007, https://ssrn.com/abstract=984376.

17 Joann S. Lublin and Kate Linebaugh, "Meet the Next CEO of General Electric: John Flannery," *Time*, June 12, 2017, https://www.wsj.com/articles/meet-the-new -ceo-of-general-electric-john-flannery-1497281807?mg=prod/accounts-wsj.

18 Wendell Weeks, interview by the author, June 30, 2017. Unless noted, all other quotes from Weeks in this chapter are from the same author interview.

19 Beth Comstock, interview by the author, June 28, 2017. Unless noted, all other quotes from Comstock in this chapter are from the same author interview.

20 James Citrin, interview by the author, April 21, 2017. Unless noted, all other quotes from Citrin in this chapter are from the same author interview.

21 Edith Cooper, interview by the author, June 23, 2017. Unless noted, all other quotes from Cooper in this chapter are from the same author interview.

22 Terry Myerson, interview by the author, June 12, 2017. Unless noted, all other quotes from Myerson in this chapter are from the same author interview.

23 Lisa Eadicicco, "Microsoft's Windows Chief on the Surface, Virtual Reality and More," *Time*, May 9, 2017, http://time.com/4772078/microsoft-windows-10 -surface-terry-myerson/.

24 Boris Groysberg, interview by the author, May 18, 2017. Unless noted, all other quotes from Groysberg in this chapter are from the same author interview.

25 Deborah Ancona, "Sensemaking," in *The Handbook for Teaching Leadership: Knowing, Doing and Being*, ed. Scott Snook, Nitin Nohria, and Rakesh Khurana (Thousand Oaks, CA: Sage Publications, 2011), 3.

26 Michelle King, "GE's Beth Comstock on How Women Can Thrive in the Emergent Era," *Forbes*, June 6, 2017, https://www.forbes.com/sites/michelleking/2017/06/06 /ges-beth-comstock-on-how-women-can-thrive-in-the-emergent-era/3 /#6d744cf46392.

27 Sara D. Davis, "CEO Brought Corning back from Death's Door," *USAToday*, February 9, 2007, http://usatoday30.usatoday.com/tech/news/2007-02-19-weeks -ceo-forum_x.htm#.WaMd-YMky0M.email.

28 Jay Galeota, interview by the author, July 5, 2013. Unless noted, all other quotes from Galeota in this chapter are from the same author interview.

29 Joseph Bower, *The CEO Within: Why Inside Outsiders Are the Key to Succession* (Boston: Harvard Business School Press, 2007), 272.

30 Sylvia Ann Hewlett, *(Forget a Mentor) Find a Sponsor: The New Way to Fast-Track Your Career* (Boston: Harvard Business Review Press, 2013), 23.

31 Sylvia Ann Hewlett, "Make Yourself Sponsor-Worthy," *Harvard Business Review*, February 6, 2014, https://hbr.org/2014/02/make-yourself-sponsor-worthy.

32 Dan Ciampa, interview by the author, June 6, 2017. Unless noted, all other quotes from Ciampa in this chapter are from the same author interview.

33 David Simmons, interview by the author, June 20, 2017. Unless noted, all other quotes from Simmons in this chapter are from the same author interview.

34 "CEO Turnover at a Record High Globally."

35 Torch, "What to Look for in Your Next CMO or Senior Marketing Leader."

36 Russell Reynolds Associates, "Where Do CFOs Come From?"

37 Tiffany McDowell, Dimple Agarwal, Don Miller, Tsutomu Okamoto, and Trevor Page, "Global Human Capital Trends 2016: The New Organization, Different by Design," https://www2.deloitte.com/ru/en/pages/about-deloitte/press-releases /2016/change-organizational-structure-and-talent-strategies.html.

38 Curt Nickisch, "Outsider CEOs Are on the Rise at the World's Biggest Companies," *Harvard Business Review*, April 19, 2016, accessed July 24, 2016, https://hbr.org /2016/04/outsider-ceos-are-on-the-rise-at-the-worlds-biggest-companies.

39 "CEO Turnover at a Record High Globally."

40 Chad Bray, "'I Am Here to Grow A.I.G.,' Its New C.E.O., Brian Duperreault, Pledges," *Dealbook* (blog), *New York Times*, May 15, 2017, https://www.nytimes .com/2017/05/15/business/dealbook/aig-brian-duperreault-ceo.html?_r=0.

41 Patricia Fili-Krushel, interview by the author, June 15, 2017. Unless noted, all other quotes from Fili-Krushel in this chapter are from the same author interview.

42 Kathleen L. McGinn, Deborah M. Kolb, and Cailin B. Hammer, *Traversing a Career Path: Fili-Krushel (A)*, Case Study (Boston: Harvard Business Publishing, 2008).

43 Jay Galeota, interview by the author, July 5, 2013.

44 Eileen Drake, interview by the author, June 12, 2017. Unless noted, all other quotes from Drake in this chapter are from the same author interview.

45 Mary Petrovich, interview by the author, May 1, 2017. Unless noted, all other quotes from Petrovich in this chapter are from the same author interview.

46 Roger Martin, *The Opposable Mind: How Successful Leaders Win through Integrative Thinking* (Boston: Harvard Business School Press, 2009), 12.

47 Martin, "For Senior Leaders, Fit Matters More Than Skill."

48   Kelly Kramer, interview by the author, June 12, 2017. Unless noted, all other quotes from Kramer in this chapter are from the same author interview.

49   Torres, Hansell, Foster, and Baron, "Leapfrog Succession."

50   Devin Leonard, "Burger King Is Run by Children," *Bloomberg BusinessWeek*, June 24, 2014, http://www.bloomberg.com/news/articles/2014-07-24/burger-king -is-run-by-children.

51   Whole Foods Market, "Whole Foods Market Names Jason J. Buechel as Global Vice President and Chief Information Officer," January 7, 2013, http://media .wholefoodsmarket.com/news/whole-foods-market-names-jason-j.-buechel-as -global-vice-president-and-chie.

52   MetLife, "MetLife Board Names Steven A. Kandarian to Succeed C. Robert Henrikson as President & CEO," March 21, 2011, http://investor.metlife.com /phoenix.zhtml?c=121171&p=irol-newsArticle&ID=1541277.

53   Abhishek Narendra Singh Jadav, "Google Reorganises, IIT Topper Sundar Pichai Appointed CEO," TheQuint, November 8, 2015, https://www.thequint.com /technology/2015/08/10/iit-topper-sundar-pichai-appointed-ceo-google -reorganises.

54   Leapfrog Leaders including Barra and Robbins, who skipped steps to reach the C-suite, can also be Tenured Executives. Other Leapfrogs are Free Agents. We will examine how these paths overlap in chapter 6.

55   Selma's story, based on interviews, is a composite of two executives who asked not to be named. All other executives in my study are named and speaking on the record.

56   Associated Press, "GM Names Mary Barra CEO, 1st Woman to Head Car Company," Politico, December 10, 2013, http://www.politico.com/story/2013/12 /general-motor-ceo-mary-barra-100943.

57   Jonathan Vanian, "Cisco CEO Chuck Robbins Has Had a Very Busy Year," *Fortune*, July 13, 2013, http://fortune.com/2016/07/13/cisco-chuck-robbins-busy-year/.

58   Robert Hackett, "Why Cisco's Board Chose Chuck Robbins to Lead as CEO," *Fortune*, May 5, 2015, http://fortune.com/2015/05/05/cisco-ceo-chuck-robbins/.

59   Amy Chang, interview by the author, May 22, 2017. Unless noted, all other quotes from Chang in this chapter are from the same author interview.

60   Christopher Wu, interview by the author, May 25, 2017. Unless noted, all other quotes from Wu in this chapter are from the same author interview.

61   Neil Petch, "Age Is Not a Barrier in Startup Success," *Entrepreneur*, January 24, 2017, https://www.entrepreneur.com/article/269930.

62   George Deeb, "Does Age Matter for Entrepreneurial Success?," *Forbes*, April 16, 2015, https://www.forbes.com/sites/georgedeeb/2015/04/16/does-age-matter-for -entrepreneurial-success/#1228c3b530f1.

63 Intuit, "Intuit 2020 Report: Twenty Trends that Will Shape the Next Decade," October 2010, accessed November 13, 2017, http://http-download.intuit.com/http .intuit/CMO/intuit/futureofsmallbusiness/intuit_2020_report.pdf.

64 Glen Tullman, "From CEO to Startup: It's More Than Giving Up the Corner Office," *Forbes*, February 6, 2016, https://www.forbes.com/sites/glentullman/2016/02/06 /from-ceo-to-startup-its-more-than-giving-up-the-corner-office/#49129d177518.

65 Erik Larson, interview by the author, May 11, 2017. Unless noted, all other quotes from Larson in this chapter are from the same author interview.

66 Susan Marshall, interview by the author, May 25, 2017. Unless noted, all other quotes from Marshall in this chapter are from the same author interview.

67 Ken Coleman, interview by the author, June 30, 2017. Unless noted, all other quotes from Coleman in this chapter are from the same author interview.

68 Burning Glass Technologies, "Blurring Lines: How Business and Technology Skills Are Merging to Create High Opportunity Hybrid Jobs," Burningglass, http://burning-glass.com/research/hybrid-jobs/. Last accessed on November 2, 2017.

69 Neil Irwin, "How to Become a CEO? The Quickest Path Is the Winding One," *New York Times*, September 9, 2016, https://www.nytimes.com/2016/09/11/upshot/how -to-become-a-ceo-the-quickest-path-is-a-winding-one.html.

70 "Sean Hinton," Open Society Foundations, accessed November 2, 2017, https:// www.opensocietyfoundations.org/people/sean-hinton.

71 Bill Snyder, "Sean Hinton: Consider the Nonlinear Path," Insights by Stanford Business, July 11, 2017, https://www.gsb.stanford.edu/insights/sean-hinton -consider-nonlinear-career-path.

72 Tiger Tyagarajan, interview by the author, June 23, 2017. Unless noted, all other quotes from Tiger in this chapter are from the same author interview.

73 Joe Cornell, "The Top 15 Spinoffs," *Forbes*, January 5, 2017, https://www.forbes .com/sites/joecornell/2017/01/05/the-top-15-spin-offs-of-2016/#18d1e316204d.

74 David F. Larcker and Brian Tayan, "From Boardroom to C-Suite: Why Would a Company Pick a Current Director as CEO?" Rock Center for Corporate Governance at Stanford University Closer Look Series: Topics, Issues and Controversies in Corporate Governance No. 64; Stanford University Graduate School of Business Research Paper No. 17-27, March 28, 2017, https://ssrn.com/abstract=2940524.

75 Boris Groysberg and Deborah Bell, "Dysfunction in the Boardroom," *Harvard Business Review*, June 2013, https://hbr.org/2013/06/dysfunction-in-the -boardroom.

76 Larcker and Tayan, "From Boardroom to C-Suite," 2.

77 Ibid., 1.

78 Ibid., 2.

79   Anthony Soohoo, interview by the author, June 14, 2017. Unless noted, all other quotes from Soohoo in this chapter are from the same author interview.

80   James Citrin, interview by the author, April 21, 2017.

81   Dan Ciampa, interview by the author, June 6, 2017.

82   Michael Useem, interview by the author, May 18, 2017.

83   Boris Groysberg, "The Seven Skills You Need to Succeed in the C-Suite," *Harvard Business Review*, March 18, 2014, https://hbr.org/2014/03/the-seven-skills-you-need-to-thrive-in-the-c-suite.

84   Greenleaf Center for Servant Leadership, "What Is Servant Leadership?," https://www.greenleaf.org/what-is-servant-leadership/.

Index

About the Author

Cassandra Frangos, EdD, is a consultant at Spencer Stuart, focusing on collaborating with Fortune 500 leadership teams on executive assessments, succession planning, leadership development, and top team effectiveness.

Previously, Cassandra was the head of global executive talent practice at Cisco, where she was responsible for accelerating the readiness of the talent portfolio to transform the business and culture. Through trusted partnerships with executives, she deployed innovative solutions for organization design, succession planning, assessment, coaching, and development programs that drive business results and innovation. She also played an integral role in the 2015 succession planning for Cisco's CEO, one of the most respected and longest-tenured CEOs in the tech industry.

Prior to Cisco, Cassandra was head of organization development and learning at a biotechnology company. During her prior management consulting career at Wyatt Worldwide, she was an effective business partner with leadership teams of Fortune 500 companies to facilitate organizational change efforts and develop talent and organizational strategies that delivered results. Cassandra was also the human capital practice leader at a management consulting firm led by thought leaders Drs. Bob Kaplan and Dave Norton, founders of the Balanced Scorecard.

Cassandra earned a doctorate degree from the University of Pennsylvania in a joint program with The Wharton School and the Graduate School of Education. Her research focus was on innovation and organizational practices. She received a dual master's degree in organizational development and positive psychology in a joint degree program with Case Western Reserve University and Ashridge Business School. Her undergraduate degree is in business administration and psychology from Northeastern University. She has authored several publications with Harvard Business School Publishing and with leading industry journals.

WHARTON
SCHOOL
PRESS

About Wharton School Press

Wharton School Press, the book publishing arm of The Wharton School of the University of Pennsylvania, was established to inspire bold, insightful thinking within the global business community.

Wharton School Press publishes a select list of award-winning, bestselling, and thought-leading books that offer trusted business knowledge to help leaders at all levels meet the challenges of today and the opportunities of tomorrow. Led by a spirit of innovation and experimentation, Wharton School Press leverages groundbreaking digital technologies and has pioneered a fast-reading business book format that fits readers' busy lives, allowing them to swiftly emerge with the tools and information needed to make an impact. Wharton School Press books offer guidance and inspiration on a variety of topics, including leadership, management, strategy, innovation, entrepreneurship, finance, marketing, social impact, public policy, and more.

Wharton School Press also operates an online bookstore featuring a curated selection of influential books by Wharton School faculty and Press authors published by a wide range of leading publishers.

To find books that will inspire and empower you to increase your impact and expand your personal and professional horizons, visit *wsp.wharton.upenn.edu.*

Wharton
UNIVERSITY *of* PENNSYLVANIA

About The Wharton School

Founded in 1881 as the world's first collegiate business school, the Wharton School of the University of Pennsylvania is shaping the future of business by incubating ideas, driving insights, and creating leaders who change the world. With a faculty of more than 235 renowned professors, Wharton has 5,000 undergraduate, MBA, Executive MBA, and doctoral students. Each year 18,000 professionals from around the world advance their careers through Wharton Executive Education's individual, company-customized, and online programs. More than 99,000 Wharton alumni form a powerful global network of leaders who transform business every day.

For more information, visit *www.wharton.upenn.edu.*

Printed in the USA
CPSIA information can be obtained
at www.ICGtesting.com
JSHW02215525O324
59878JS00006B/439

FORGING A
DESIRE LINE

Visit us at www.boldstrokesbooks.com

FORGING A
DESIRE LINE

by

Mary P. Burns

2020

CREDITS
EDITORS: VICTORIA VILLASENOR AND CINDY CRESAP
PRODUCTION DESIGN: SUSAN RAMUNDO
COVER DESIGN BY TAMMY SEIDICK

Acknowledgments

Novels are never really written alone, so I want to thank all the people who helped this one come to fruition.

It was borne of a challenge from Shawn N., a longtime personal friend, when he found out I'd broken a twenty-year writer's block. I was working on a coming-of-age story, and he invited me to the Rainbow Book Fair. I was amazed by what I learned there, and studied the genre by reading novels for three years. Then, I took him up on his challenge. Many of the authors/books I chose to read happened to be Bold Strokes authors, and they were good, so I knew where I wanted to send this manuscript first.

My beta readers were of paramount importance. Debbie Duncalf, Anne Stoddard, Linda Doll, Jon Fried, Suzanne Schuckel Heath, and Gary Reed patiently slogged through first and second drafts, pulling no punches in their criticisms. I can't thank them enough.

My editors (and family) at Bold Strokes Books, Victoria Villasenor and Cindy Cresap, took such good care of my vision and my words (as well as my punctuation and grammar!) while Sandy Lowe and Carsen Taite took care of so many other things marketing and otherwise. And to Radclyffe, thank you for asking me to step up to the task of rethinking and remolding the story. Your notes were a master class.

I owe an enormous debt of gratitude to the Monday Night Brilliant Writers Group for their love and support, as I wrote nothing for years, and for their unerring guidance and constructive criticism when I finally did. I often felt like Sisyphus as they urged me on through the many edits of this novel before I sent it out, but their advice paid off.

My siblings have been my cheerleading squad since I wrote my first short story when I was eight. I remember my older sister Alice sitting down at the dining room table in our apartment the first summer I moved to New York and was typing my first script, waiting to read the pages as they came off the typewriter. We lost her this year, but I know she's pulling for me from above.

To my partner, Andrea, who has stood by me through thick and a lot of thin as I chased this dream, "thank you" doesn't even come close.

Finally, to Ronni McCaffrey, thank you for telling me I have a touch of the poet.

Dedication

For Andrea.
It's been a long road getting me here.
Thank you for walking it with me.

Desire lines
are the dirt trails
that hikers forge off the beaten path.
Desire lines can also be found in cities,
formed as a result of economic development
and evolving travel patterns.

And they can be created in the heart
as we find our way toward falling in love
with someone.

Chapter One

Morning sun streamed in the open windows, but the warmth of the quilt pulled at Charley Owens to stay put on this cool September Saturday morning. Bing and Bob had woken her early for breakfast, curling up beside her on the bed afterward and breathing Purina's Ocean Whitefish on her, the sounds of a relatively quiet New York City, like a faraway gentle tide, lulling them all back to sleep. Now she gently ran a finger down the white blaze in Bing's black face and tapped his little nose. He squeaked at her and buried his face in white-mittened paws, wrapping his tail around his head until all she could see were two small ears.

Finally giving in and leaving the coziness of her bed, Charley went out to the living room to retrieve the notepad and folder she'd left on her desk, then trotted back to nestle under the comforter. Settling back in against the pillows, she went over her to-do list. The fall cleaning was a top priority. She had to finish it by the second weekend of November, when it would be her turn to host the Sunday night NFL dinner for her coterie of football friends. The folder held the manuscript pages she'd agonized over last night. As she began reading, she reached for her small, flat talisman stone on the end table, and idly ran her thumb over the word *balance* etched into its smooth surface. Then, she picked up the pencil on her nightstand, and began editing.

She'd finished this novel years ago when it was her final project in graduate school. It was good. Her thesis mentor had given her an A-plus and an introduction to an agent who never saw it. Days after she hung her MFA degree on the wall, writer's block hit and closed everything down. Or maybe it was the dog that she and Brooke had nearly killed on the road trip they'd taken to Maine to celebrate Charley getting her degree. They'd found a vet in the next town and the dog had lived, but the novel was stillborn in the aftermath.

She hadn't meant to retrieve the manuscript from the back of the filing cabinet last January. After a week off from work so she could have some much-needed downtime before moving from the A&R department to Legal to assist a newly-arriving executive vice president, she'd been on a cleaning binge and was going to throw it out. What was the point of keeping it? *It takes up room and I'm not that person anymore.* She read the first page, and then the second, and the third page. The next morning, she sat down again in front of page one, the fear that her gift and her voice, silent for so long, were gone sitting down with her. But she sharpened a pencil anyway. The person she'd become had a lot of work to do. Six months later, a phoenix had begun to rise from the ashes. At least, that's what she hoped it was.

The phone rang, startling her. Her first thought went to her boss, Emily, who had been in London for the last week, but she rarely called when she was on a business trip because Charley was a master at anticipating her needs whether she was in the office or halfway around the world. She waited for the robotic caller ID to tell her who was calling.

"Call from...Brooke West."

Charley grabbed the receiver. "Good morning, sunshine."

"Hey, babe. What are you up to?"

"My fall cleaning." She certainly couldn't admit that she was still in bed. And she would never confide that she was writing again. What if she failed again?

"You're the only person I know who still does that."

"You don't? It's cathartic. And maybe I should take a closer look at your moldings and underneath your couch pillows if you don't. Maybe I'd find that remote you lost last month."

"Hey, my cleaning lady takes care of that...I think she does, anyway."

"You never check?" Bob, looking like an errant fluffy gray dust bunny that had wafted up onto the pillow next to her, rose and stretched, pushing all her papers aside. She delicately knocked him over and he glared at her.

"Who looks underneath their couch pillows, for Christ's sake? And don't you do that tonight. You are still coming, aren't you?"

"Of course. Why? Who have you invited as the Miss September temptress?"

There was a moment's hesitation on Brooke's part. "I don't know what you mean."

"Liar. You guys are like Harry & David's Fruit-of-the-Month Club with the single women at our dinners. Did you think I didn't know?"

"Crap. Listen, it was Jamie's idea from the get-go. And we all agreed you should be back in the dating pool."

Charley cringed. It wasn't a pool she'd wanted to wade into for a while now. "Maybe I don't want that."

"How much longer are you going to hide? You're cheating some woman out of a really good wife."

"I think I'm still bitter, darling. Have you *all* been in on it, even Lindsay?"

Charley heard Brooke's sigh of defeat. "She said you didn't want anything to do with dating again."

"Good. I'm glad I have one friend who understands."

"Yeah, not really. Tonight's bachelorette is courtesy of her tennis club. I actually met the woman last week. She's very nice. And pretty hot, I might add."

"You met her?" Somehow, that seemed a step too far. Or maybe it was good they were vetting the women they were parading in front of her. Although they were batting zero.

"Lindsay wasn't sure about introducing you to Karen, so she wanted Jamie and me to pass muster first."

"Why? What's wrong with her?" The last one had a voice reminiscent of Minnie Mouse, and the one before that spent the evening talking about all her exes. Charley had wanted to run before the bread was passed.

"Absolutely nothing. She's smart, and funny, and gorgeous, and built. And she's thirty-seven. Perfect age for a trophy wife."

"I can't go out with anyone that young. We won't have anything to talk about. Plus, if she's built, she won't be interested in me. I'm a long way off from getting rid of this 'I quit smoking twenty years ago' weight gain." She didn't like admitting that truth, but she trusted Brooke with almost all her vulnerabilities.

"You're getting there. Slowly."

"Ho! Thanks for the vote of confidence."

"What? I said you're looking good. And Jamie and I certainly didn't have any trouble talking with Karen."

"Then maybe you should date her."

"Not thinkin' Annie would appreciate that."

"Fine. I'll take Annie off your hands, you take Karen out."

"Oh, no you don't. You had a shot at her but you chose Tricia."

Charley laughed, even as she winced at the mention of Tricia. She was always grateful Brooke understood that her fling with Annie had been just that, a short-lived affair right before Annie moved to San Francisco. When she came back to New York a few years later, Charley and Brooke ran into her in a movie theater, she'd introduced them and that was that. She was never sure who swung the first lasso, but within weeks, they were a couple.

"Why is this woman single if she's such a catch?"

"Recently ended a relationship. You know, we've gone out of our way to find some of the nicest women for you."

"Maybe I don't want nice."

"Oh, now there's a challenge. Why didn't you say so?"

She sighed. "Brooke, I don't want anything."

"Karen's a redhead. Your kryptonite."

A wisp of annoyance rose up. "Fine. I'll meet her, we'll see what happens."

"What happens is that you always leave without giving the woman your phone number."

"I'm not ready." There was more to it than that, but she didn't want to examine things that would only open old wounds.

"You *are* still hiding."

In the silence that followed, Charley knew Brooke was waiting for her defense, but she didn't have one. At least, not one Brooke would be willing to accept. "I don't want another relationship. Not so soon, anyway."

"Soon? Three years is not soon! And who said anything about a relationship? Ain't nobody else gonna be Tricia, honey," Brooke said. "You need to change your expectations. Or maybe see what else you want. There's lots of candy in the store, Charley, and you can try more than one kind. You used to be good at that."

"Thank you, Dr. Ruth." *I don't want to try anyone else. Tricia was enough for one lifetime.* "I don't think I like candy anymore."

"I'm serious. Take Karen out once. You might be pleasantly surprised."

"And *I'm* serious. I like my independence, I like having my time to myself, and I really like *not* having to worry about anyone else's needs but my own."

"What about the intimacy of someone caring about you, about where you are and what you're doing and when you're coming home to her?" Brooke asked.

"Sometimes I really hate you," Charley said without any conviction.

Brooke laughed. "As always, the pleasure is all mine. See you at six thirty?"

Charley welcomed the hot water in the shower after hanging up with Brooke. She bent her knee up into the stinging heat. It still gave her trouble three years after the surgery for the ACL tear, despite all the physical therapy exercises she'd continued doing to combat the pain and immobility that had never really gone away. A knee replacement really wasn't on her list of "things to do later in life." She didn't want to contemplate it now, either, not while she was busy being irritated by the call with Brooke. She tried to let the water calm her while she thought about how to ask her friends to stop setting her up. They'd been doing it for nearly two years now because they loved her and wanted to see her happy again. *So maybe I'll tell them I met someone.* The white lie would serve a dual purpose. It would get them off her back and force her to talk to the woman in the locker room whose privacy she'd unintentionally invaded last night when she'd sought refuge from the after-work crowds in the back section she rarely used. The woman was changing into a swimsuit, her lean body and muscled shoulders those of a swimmer. She was striking, a tomboy-next-door-handsome type hitting middle age with grace and beauty.

The woman had turned briefly at the intrusion, mildly annoyed. Charley was struck by the brilliance and color of her green eyes, like a forest after a thunderstorm, all the leaves glittering with raindrops. She wasn't sure why those eyes simultaneously scared and delighted her, but she wanted to find out. She'd seen something unusual in that flash of emerald, and it jarred a feeling long dormant within her. Charley's gaydar had also pinged when the woman glanced at her a moment later, a hint of curiosity playing across her features. *I need to see her again.* Reflexively, she reached between her legs and stroked her fingers back and forth, the hot water acting as a lubricant. She leaned against the tile wall, let the water cascade over her, and eased two fingers inside, beginning a slow rhythmic pump, her thumb riding the spot where her soft clit hardened. Anticipation spread in the pit of her stomach, its heat flooding her body. A moment later, her hips moved faster in answer to the demand for release. But she didn't want faster. She wanted slow and sensual, imagining the woman beneath her in bed, those rich green eyes locked on hers while Charley moved in and out of her, warm and wet, teasing her with her thumb. She fantasized slowly skimming the woman's breasts, taking in one nipple and then the other, provoking them with her tongue, gently sucking and rolling them between her lips until they stood at attention, and then softly pulling at the hard peaks as the woman begged her for more. She wanted to know how the woman's body would tense against hers, where she would touch Charley, if her thighs would squeeze her hips as she climaxed, as she bucked up against her and grabbed her shoulders, letting Charley ride her until they both collapsed against the pillows, completely spent. She wanted to know.

Charley's orgasm erupted and she grabbed the showerhead, hanging on until the spasms slowed. When she could stand again, she turned up the hot water. Most mornings, she needed the ten minutes of steam room conditions to get everything in her body moving in sync again. The family arthritis gene had finally manifested itself and she could sympathize with her older brothers and the aggravating pain they'd been complaining about for nearly a decade. Now, however, she simply wanted to come down from her reverie in a blast of hot spray. Obviously, everything was working just fine if she could handle herself standing up against the shower wall for ten minutes. But the phone rang, so she shut off the water and opened the bathroom door farther so she could hear the caller ID.

"Call from…Vivian Owens."

The audible voice mail from her fifteen-year-old phone kicked in. "Good morning, darling. You're probably on your way to Long Beach. Or are you on the ferry? It's a beautiful day for a hike; did you decide to go out to the Greenbelt? Either way, I want to invite you."

Charley grabbed the receiver. "No, I'm here. I was in the bathroom." Dripping on the rug, she toweled off with her free hand. Bing jumped down from the bed to help her by licking her ankles dry. "What's up?"

"Well, some of the girls are having tea tomorrow at Sally Simmons's apartment, and I'd really like to go. Can I count on you? Four o'clock tomorrow?"

"Of course." *Well, there goes the Broncos-Giants game…* "Can I bring anything?"

"I'll ask Sally, but chances are no. And yes, you can sneak away and check the scores on the football games. Jim will have them on, I'm sure."

They discussed a few other odds and ends, and when Charley hung up, she was smiling. Conversations with her mother had changed over the last year. *Or maybe I have.* Until recently, her mother would never have asked her to spend an afternoon this way. She would've called Robert, the oldest sibling, leaving Charley relieved, yet feeling derelict in the Daughter Department. But turning fifty last December had changed her outlook on so many fronts. It had also shifted her relationship with her mother onto another plane, since she no longer worried as much about how her mother saw her, either. And that seemed to have brought a new rapprochement to them, her mother reaching out more often, and Charley reciprocating each time.

After pulling on a pair of shorts and a polo shirt, Charley opened the cupboard beneath her kitchen sink and began pulling out cleaning supplies. *Down a quart on the Murphy's Oil. Figures.* She cut an apple into her yogurt and made a shopping list. This would require a trip to the hardware store. Still, it couldn't be helped. *Who am I kidding? I love the hardware store.* Bob stalked by, climbed into the cupboard, and wedged himself between the Tide and the box of garbage bags. She rubbed between his ears and he pulled back, rumbling loudly. Settling on the couch with her bowl of yogurt, she looked around the small living room, assessing the job at hand. Seasonal cleaning always made her feel good, in command and in control of her life. It had been the one thing she and her mother had done together when she was a child. Everything else had been shared with her dad, from tinkering with car engines to learning about home repairs with her brothers.

Back in the kitchen, she shooed the cat out of the cupboard. After cleaning, she'd spend time writing. The chapters she worked on once the apartment was clean always felt so much sharper. She picked up the book she'd started reading a few nights ago, tossed it into her canvas marketing bag, and headed out to find a spot in the morning sun on one of the benches in the little park across the street. Sometimes she felt guilty about stealing this kind of time, but reading was like breathing air. They were never going to carve *diligent assistant, dutiful daughter, and loving wife* on her headstone. So, as Dorothy Parker advised, she might as well live.

Halfway down the hall, she turned back for the pages she'd been editing, and her pencil box. It wouldn't hurt to read them over again.

CHAPTER TWO

By four thirty, Charley was stretched out on the couch, exhausted. *I shouldn't be so tired...God, I'm getting old if I can't maintain this level of activity.* She checked the college football games on TV. *What am I going to do in ten years? Will I have to hire someone to clean?* Bing jumped up and planted himself on her chest, facing the TV and flicking her ear with his tail. Propping the to-do list against his haunch, she dismissed the worry and crossed out each task that had been completed, pleased that she had emptied all the bookcases on the wall, washed them down, moved them away from the wall to vacuum behind them, dusted the books, cleaned the corner of the room where her stereo and CDs lived, and put everything back. It had taken her five hours. She closed her eyes and drifted off. The clock on the mantelpiece above the fireplace chiming five woke her. She sat up, took a moment to shake off the fog, and headed to the shower.

Standing in front of her open closet door didn't make the choices grow exponentially. For once, she didn't want to be her casual khaki self. But she did want to know if she still had the power to attract another woman, especially a younger one. Even if she no longer wanted the chase, she still liked that thrill. The closet was small, so Charley pushed her office clothes to one side and stepped partway in to pull a pair of black dress slacks and a nearly sheer white tank top from the back. She reached farther in and found her silk Mandarin-collar jacket. Braced against the wall, she lifted the clear dry cleaner bag to appraise the delicately embroidered black, spring green, and white bird designs on the sky blue background. It was quite a daring piece with a deeply cut décolletage that revealed more than Charley was usually comfortable showing. One strategically placed frog button held it together at the tapered waist. She'd bought it to entice Tricia, and whenever she'd worn it, that jacket had turned heads, delighting Tricia, and guaranteeing a night of play in bed when they got home. That was the kind of control she wanted to exert tonight.

Back in the bathroom, Charley retrieved the eye makeup she rarely wore anymore and set to work, achieving the look she wanted in record time. She popped in her contact lenses and stepped back to check herself in the bathroom mirror. Her hair needed cutting, but she'd hide that by putting it up in a loose chignon with a couple of the strands escaping on either side, an effect that always had women reaching to capture those strands and tuck them back behind her ear.

The color of the silk jacket intensified her eyes, and the mascara and eyeliner echoed the black outlines of the birds, creating an enticing effect, exactly what she'd intended. Wanting to add the advantage of height to her five-and-a-half-foot frame, she slipped on the three-inch black heels, wrapped the white pashmina shawl around her shoulders, slid the *balance* talisman into a pocket, and headed out.

The doorman in Brooke's building didn't recognize Charley at first, which pleased her. And when Brooke opened her door, she did a double take.

"Holy shit."

"I'll take that as a compliment." Charley leaned against the doorframe.

"Way to go, blond bombshell. I don't think I can let Annie see you. She might have second thoughts."

"Annie's yours. I'm after something else tonight." Charley pushed Brooke aside in mock-diva fashion and walked into the apartment. Across the room, a woman sitting with Lindsay turned to look at her, and her dark chocolate eyes took Charley in and stayed trained on her. It had to be Karen.

"Seriously? You're going to step up to our challenge?"

Charley was momentarily distracted. Brooke had been right. Karen was quite attractive. Her face, with its sprinkling of freckles, was classic Katherine Hepburn. High, sharp cheekbones accented an aquiline nose, and ginger brows arched perfectly over intelligent eyes. Red curls cascaded over her shoulders. And she *was* built. Charley dropped her gaze to the full breasts the unbuttoned black Henley didn't hide, the snug blue jeans hugging slim hips, and the hand-tooled black cowboy boots that completed the outfit. When she looked back up, Karen met her with the hint of a smile. She put her hand on Brooke's arm, all bluster gone. "I don't know...I thought I'd at least make the effort," she stammered, brushing a piece on nonexistent lint off her jacket. "You know, just because I haven't taken the bait here all these months doesn't mean that I'm not meeting and considering women."

"You are not."

"Actually, yes, I am. I've met someone at the Y..."

"Really? And you've been holding out on us?"

"No, I only met her recently. I don't know enough yet to make a judgment." Lying had never come naturally. She should have had a better cover story at the ready.

"You haven't worked up the courage to speak to her."

"I didn't say that. I'm assuming that's Karen?"

"Yes, let's go meet her. We'll get back to Gym Woman later." Brooke rolled her eyes. "As if."

"No, wait. I don't want to start the evening so awkwardly. Is Annie in the kitchen?" Charley took her *balance* stone out of her pocket and played it through her fingers.

"We've established that she's mine, Owens. You're stalling."

"I want to say hi." Charley turned the stone over and over in her hand.

"Oh, my God, you still have the stone I gave you?"

"Of course I do," Charley said, looking at it in her palm. "You made a promise with it that the world would right itself again after Tricia, and it did. Now this keeps me centered whenever I feel off."

"C'mon." Brooke put her arm around Charley's shoulder, squeezed it reassuringly, and walked toward the living room. "I don't think Karen has any idea we invited her to meet you."

The new pain that resonated with that squeeze reminded Charley of the day's efforts. And her age, as she considered Karen's youth and beauty. "She's the only other single woman in the room, you idiot. I'm sure she can do the math. Did Lindsay meet her during a tournament?"

"No, she's giving her tennis lessons."

"Oh, my God!" Jamie stood to hug Charley. "Look at you!"

Charley was always amazed that the skinny little baby dyke who'd roomed with Brooke their freshman year of college had grown into such a handsome rough-and-tumble butch and was now crushing her in a bear hug. Out of the corner of her eye, Charley saw Karen lean over to say something to Lindsay, taking her hand. Lindsay hesitated a moment, then she replied in earnest and at length. She knew in that moment that coming tonight had been a mistake.

"Hey, I know we were supposed to go out for dinner right after Labor Day," Jamie said, "but you know Lindsay, the social bee who has to pollinate every flower. I don't even remember the last night we were home for dinner." She grimaced. "I hate goin' out. How did I end up with her? Anyway, I owe you. And you…" Jamie held Charley at arm's length. "Wow."

Charley turned to Lindsay, a tiny dynamo who'd reminded her of Sally Field's Gidget the day they'd met in freshman English class so long ago. She still had that rosy air about her as she touched her elbow and enfolded her in a hug.

"Oh, how are you? You look spectacular!" Lindsay reached for Karen, who'd been studying Charley. "I want you to meet Karen Hughes, one of my students. Karen, this is Charley Owens."

"A pleasure." Karen shook Charley's hand. "I've been looking forward to meeting you tonight. Can I get you a drink?" Karen indicated the sideboard where Brooke had set up a bar.

"Already got it." Brooke handed Charley a highball glass with an orange slice on the side and three cherry stems riding the froth. "Jim Beam sour. For future reference." She winked at Karen, who stepped closer to Charley.

"They're trying to fix us up, you know that, I'm sure," Karen said quietly.

Charley bent her head conspiratorially close to Karen's. "Yes, I know. I should tell you they've been trying to match-make me for two years." She heard Karen's intake of breath.

"Really? Lindsay tells me you're quite a catch. That's why I came tonight. But, still single despite their efforts?"

"And what do you do for a living?"

Karen smiled. "Right. Not the smoothest opening on my part, was it? I'm an attorney."

"Oh? A firm I'd recognize?" Charley frowned at Jamie and Brooke eavesdropping, and they returned to their conversation.

"No. Small outfit representing Broadway producers. Which means I get tickets to everything on or Off Broadway. I'd love to take you to see whatever your heart desires."

Charley heard the teasing edge in Karen's voice. "Oh. Well, I might take you up on that some time." They'd been talking for all of two minutes and Karen was already dangling future dates in front of her.

"I also get to attend the Tonys. With a plus-one."

"Okay, now you're just showing off."

"I have to flag your attention somehow. Who doesn't love a Broadway show?"

"I've already seen a lot of them."

"Fair enough, but two years and your friends can't find a match for you? Now I'm beyond intrigued."

"Don't be, and don't get your hopes up. I'm not interested in dating." It was blunt, but Charley wasn't a game player.

"Ouch. That's the fastest rejection I've ever gotten."

"I'm sorry. It's not you. I was in a relationship for a long time and I don't want…" Charley hesitated. Karen *was* attractive. "I don't think I want that again." She didn't want to entertain the idea of that kind of emotional investment again, not if there was another chance she'd be left on the other side with nothing.

"I see… Can I be direct and ask what happened, or should we save that discussion for dinner next week?"

Charley cocked her head. "That is direct. Now you're intriguing me." She allowed herself a reappraisal. At least they both had their cards on the table.

"Good. Set point, Karen Hughes."

Charley laughed. "I'm sure Lindsay told you why I'm divorced."

"I got a little bit of the background, but I'd much rather hear the story from you over dinner and a good bottle of wine. We can trade barbs about cheating wives because that's also what happened to me."

"That's tough," Charley said, softening. "I'm sorry."

"So that's a yes to dinner?"

"Oh, I didn't say that."

"You know, I only came tonight to mollify Lindsay. She's been after me for months. Probably because our situations are so parallel. But when you walked through the door, well, everything changed."

Indignation mixed with surprise hit Charley. "Lindsay's been after you for months? Really?"

"Six at least." Karen sighed. "I told her my friends don't want to talk about my breakup anymore. They think I need to get over it. But it's still painful, which I'm sure you understand. Have dinner with me. I'd like the chance to get to know you."

Charley hesitated. *Is she where I was two years ago? Does she need a friend or is she looking for more?*

Before her resolve disappeared, Annie's squeal interrupted the moment, the wine glasses clinking in her hand as she juggled a bottle in the crook of her arm. "Why didn't anyone tell me you were here!"

"Your wife didn't trust that you wouldn't run off with me tonight," Charley said, hugging the lissome blonde who could've passed for her younger sister.

"She knows whereof she speaks," Annie said, stepping back to take Charley's measure. "Does Anna Wintour know you escaped?"

"Flattery will get you everywhere. Does Mario Batali know you're on the loose? What's for dinner?"

"Ha. Nothing exciting tonight, I'm afraid. Lasagna and a salad. Here." She handed the glasses and bottle to Charley. "I need to co-opt Brooke to help me in the kitchen. Isn't it odd, though," Annie asked, pointing between Brooke and Karen, "to have two redheads under the same roof? This never happens."

"We're a rare breed," Karen admitted.

"Brooke is really more strawberry blond," Jamie said, angling her chair to sit down.

"She's still trouble," Charley said, "always has been."

"Well, you know what they say about redheads." Karen looked at Charley. "The deeper the shade, the more trouble they are. But very worth it."

Charley blushed under Karen's deliberate gaze.

"C'mon, Trouble." Annie pulled Brooke into the kitchen, and moments later, they emerged with platters of lasagna, a large bowl of salad, and a basket of garlic bread.

"Who's sommeliering tonight?" Annie asked, pulling a corkscrew from her pocket and tossing it next to the bottle of wine.

"Not a verb yet, Annie," Brooke ribbed her.

"It will be by the end of the decade," Charley said, picking up the corkscrew and plunging it dead center into the cork.

Discussions flowed around the table for several hours, touching on everything from politics to the *Times* best seller list, the new fall TV shows, bitching about work, and finally settling on the age-old topic of who among their friends was sleeping with someone they shouldn't.

"Are you enjoying this back-fence talk or can we clear the table so we can escape to the kitchen?" Karen asked Charley, sotto voce.

Brooke and Jamie rose to help when they began collecting plates and silverware, but Charley asked them to stay put, shooting Brooke an admonitory look.

"We'll talk about you," Jamie warned her.

"Of course you will. Knock yourselves out." Charley stuck her tongue out at them as she left the room with a pile of dishes.

"Boy," Karen said, once they were in the kitchen, "you all can be a little harsh with each other. I'd hate to see how you treat the people you *don't* like!"

"You must have friends you've known forever that you can throw down with."

"How long have you all known each other?"

"Over thirty years now. We went to college together." Charley set her armload of dishes in the sink and took Karen's out of her hands.

"Hmm. I don't think I still know anyone I knew when I was seven…"

"Oh…that's right. I almost forgot how much younger than us you are." Charley let the arrow fly on purpose.

"Wait," Karen said, flustered. "You're not going to let the age difference between us interfere with what we've spent all evening building, are you?" Karen reached for an errant lock of Charley's hair and tucked it behind her ear.

Charley smiled to herself. *Game point, Charley Owens.* "Have we built something?"

Annie came into the kitchen, more dishes piled halfway up her arm.

"That age difference thing is a myth once you hit your late twenties, don't you think?" Karen asked a little too eagerly. "And if you're going to turn on the water, you'd better take that jacket off. It's silk, isn't it?"

"She's right. You'll ruin it otherwise. And lucky for us you wore something under it so you *can* take it off," Annie noted. Charley unbuttoned the jacket and hung it over a chair.

Karen glanced from Annie to Charley. "You wear that jacket without that top?"

"Usually," Charley said.

Karen stared at Charley for a moment as she began washing dishes. "Well, then, when we go out next week, you can wear it that way for me."

Charley smirked at her teasingly. "You haven't earned that right yet."

"Fine. The sixth date."

Charley turned to Annie. "Go on with you. Make your report back to the table. I know that's why they sent you in."

Annie chuckled as she left the kitchen.

"Why the sixth date?" Charley asked.

Karen pulled a dishtowel from a rack hanging next to the sink. "Because that's the night you'll sleep with me."

Charley caught her breath. "You're awfully confident."

"All right, the seventh date, then. You can't deny we've had a good time tonight."

"That doesn't mean we'll end up in bed." For an instant, though, Charley pictured Karen in her bed before shutting the image out, and for the first time in a long time, it occurred to her that she might be lonely…physically and intimately lonely.

Karen had leaned around her at the sink. "You think I can't win you over?"

"Can you?" Charley felt Karen's hand on the small of her back and shivered.

"Let me try?"

Charley dried her hands on the towel in Karen's other hand, picked up the forks and dessert plates sitting on the counter, and handed them to her. "Take these out to Annie." The moment the door swung shut behind her, Charley put on her jacket and let herself out the door that led from the kitchen to the service elevator. She knew if she didn't leave now, she'd be sorry. She'd never done anything this blatantly rude in her life, and everyone would be angry with her when they realized she'd simply left, but there was no other way to handle it. Putting everything on the line again wasn't an option now that she was emotionally where she wanted to be, and she was even annoyed in this moment that her friends hadn't been able to see that while they busily tried to fix her up. The elevator door opened, and Charley stepped in, pulling her phone from her pocket to text an apology to Brooke.

CHAPTER THREE

Charley awoke early on Sunday morning. The first thing that hit her was her rather insolent exit strategy from Brooke's dinner party. She rolled onto her side and punched the pillow, then reached for Bing, curled up inches from her, and hugged him close. He snuggled against her and she wondered if it shouldn't have been Karen snuggling into her instead. She heard the loud thump of the thick *New York Times* hitting the doormat in the Sunday silence. A lifetime ago, Tricia would've brought it to her from the hallway where the delivery boy dropped it each morning. *I miss Tricia. No, I don't miss her. I miss being treated with love. I miss a woman who can do that.*

The cat stretched, yawned, and turned, regarding her dubiously, as only a cat can, and she knew she'd made the right decision, despite Brooke's response to her apology as she'd stepped into the cab outside her building. It had been in all caps, which was never good.

Her phone emitted the buoy clangs that signaled an incoming text. That sound had been part of her life since childhood vacations on Cape Cod's shores, so when she'd stumbled upon it online, she'd immediately downloaded the comforting sound. Imagining it was Brooke with one of her "Furthermore!" soapbox follow-ups, she plucked the offending phone from the nightstand.

Brooke: *Annie says I need to apologize, that we were wrong.*

Charley lay back on the pillows. She and Brooke had their share of face-offs in the BFF department, but Charley found it painful when they did. *You don't. I was rude.*

Brooke: *No doubt. But I got nasty.*

I deserved it. There was a long pause, but she knew Brooke would never leave an apology there.

Brooke: *Annie says no one ever deserves that.*
She there?
Brooke: *Yes.*
Tell her I love her.
Brooke: *Goes without saying. You left yr pashmina.*

Charley knew that was as close as Brooke could come to saying, "I'm sorry."

I know. I'll get it next time.
Brooke: *What about me?*

Charley sent a question mark, not sure she understood the question.

Brooke: *You still love me?*

Always. Charley laughed at Brooke's response, the dancing baby with his shades on and a pacifier in his mouth, and she sent back the red kiss lips. Then, hearing the cats' supper dish scraping across the kitchen floor, and knowing Bob was the protester behind it, she got up to retrieve the paper and feed the boys.

By two, with the NFL game on as she worked, Charley had nearly finished cleaning off her desk. She'd decided to purge her files, too, and now she needed a break. Her tendons ached from tearing up old bank statements and doctors' reports. *I really need to get a shredder.* And she was hungry. She stood by the window looking out at the park across the street. Dead brown leaves scuttled everywhere in the afternoon breeze. Some of the trees still hung on to whole branches of brilliant green ones, though, and in the depth of their last blaze of summer, Charley saw the emerald eyes of the woman from the locker room. She wondered if there was anyone in her life, and what she might be doing right now, trying to imagine her someplace as mundane as the supermarket. *No, she'd be at one of the farmers markets. Or at the Guggenheim.* As she imbued the woman with life, the phone rang, pulling Charley from her reverie.

"Call from…Vivian Owens," came the muffled robo-voice. Charley looked around for the receiver. "Call from…Vivian Owens." Bing jumped off the couch, and she saw the light blinking on the handset. He'd been lying on it. But she didn't move, listening instead for a message.

"Hello, dear, just Mother reminding you to pick me up at four. See you later."

For an instant, as Charley stared at the game on TV, she almost wished she'd said no to her mother and let Robert pick up the slack after all.

After lunch and a shower, her back still aching from all the bending and lifting, Charley did some stretches. In front of the closet once again, she contemplated what in her wardrobe would be sharp enough and comfortable enough for this afternoon's outing. The navy blue chinos with a white button-down seemed just the ticket. She threaded a Vineyard Vines ribbon belt with the pink martini-drinking elephants through the belt loops and grabbed the navy pumps with the gold buckles. While the belt wouldn't amuse her mother, a staunch Republican, Sally Simmons's son Jim, a friend since high school who was now a Democratic councilman, would notice it right away when she sat down to watch the game with him, and he'd appreciate the humor. She tied a pink sweater around her shoulders. *That should work.*

Looking at her reflection in the mirror, an aging (and if she was being polite, voluptuous) ex-jock stared back at her, and she wondered for possibly the millionth time if her mother had felt cheated, not having the "standard issue" daughter. She sensed her mother had finally made peace with her only daughter being gay, but Charley knew she had keenly missed some of the things mothers look forward to sharing with daughters: the first serious boyfriend, prom nights, a wedding, grandchildren, the advice she would've given with each of those events. She sighed. *There was nothing I could've done. I am who I am.*

Her mother was waiting in the lobby when Charley's cab pulled up to the building; the doorman helped her out to the taxi. Charley didn't need to ask her how she was. The cane she wielded told her it wasn't a good day, even though she was in a blue suit, heels, and full makeup ("my armor," she called it). Small talk during the ride covered a myriad of topics from the PBS news shows her mother loved, to the bursitis that had been acting up lately. When they got to Sally's, Charley mentally squared her shoulders and helped her mother from the cab.

Sally Simmons's palatial West End Avenue apartment always left Charley envious. The sunny living room where the women gathered was furnished in wingback chairs, sofas upholstered in dark leather, Oriental rugs, and oval walnut tables, all set off by floor-to-ceiling bookcases. It looked like it had popped right off the movie screen, the gentlemen's club from *Around the World in Eighty Days*, and Charley found it thoroughly charming. Despite her advanced years, Sally still hosted these events for her diminishing circle of friends, so many of them long widowed like she was. Charley got her mother settled on a sofa with a cup of tea and some cookies and searched for Margaret McNabb, her mother's best friend. After spotting her across the room with her bridge group, she made her way over to them and asked Margaret to join her mother.

"My public calls," Margaret joked, primping her platinum hair. "Why don't you girls come with me? Let's cheer Viv up—she's been so glum lately with the knee."

Several women joined Margaret on the trek across the room, Charley serving as an impromptu cane for Abigail Morgan, one of her mother's neighbors. She surveyed the room, wives and widows of the Greatest Generation dressed in their Sunday best, which for some of them, Charley could tell, was a Herculean effort. They seemed at home in this environment, like tropical birds settled in the trees of their native rain forest, all chatting at one another about aches, pains, home health aides, the bad economy, and how handsome the newscaster Brian Williams was. The afternoon progressed quietly enough. Charley spent time in the den with Jim watching football and trading stories on the difficulties of looking after elderly parents. By six o'clock, her mother was ready to leave. Charley got her coat and was walking around the room with her as her mother said her good-byes when she happened to glance toward the foyer of the apartment and to her astonishment, saw the handsome woman from the Y tucking a blanket around the legs of Irene Palmer, a friend of her mother's who was now wheelchair-bound. "Excuse me, Mother," Charley said, interrupting her mother's conversation, much to her annoyance. "Who is that at the door?"

"Why, you know Irene Palmer."

"No, I mean the woman with her."

"That's one of her private duty nurses. Irene has round-the-clock care now. Let me just say good-bye to Judy and we can go."

Charley silently cursed Judy as she watched Irene's nurse push her out the door.

Chapter Four

C harley was certain she'd only been asleep for five minutes when Michael Bublé's "It's a Beautiful Day" crashed her dream at five o'clock Monday morning. Opening one eye, she grabbed her phone from the nightstand and silenced the musical alarm. Her other eye felt like it was glued shut. Rubbing at the grit, she shuffled into the bathroom. *Oh my God, why did I stay up so late? The game wasn't even that good.* Bob came in behind her and complained before she'd reached for her toothbrush, so she picked him up and carried him to the kitchen. Bing trotted in when she opened the bag of food.

The buoy tone echoed in the quiet of the apartment and she checked her text messages.

Busy day here already, just warning u. Need u on deck ASAP.

Charley texted back an icon of a speeding cab and ducked into the shower. Twenty minutes later, the phone rang. It would be the car service. "I'll be right down," she said, hung up, and rushed to finish dressing.

In the office, she settled at her desk and opened her email. There were already twenty in her inbox from her boss, who was six hours ahead of her in London. Scanning the subject titles, she could see it would be a long day. Emily's first request was for Charley to work her magic on the PowerPoint she'd attached. The log Charley used to keep track of things was sitting in its usual place on her desk, and she opened it and began working her way through each message, prioritizing what else her boss wanted. She hated wasting time on a project if its relevance had taken back seat to something else, and

Emily's Road Runner personality sometimes left Charley hanging midair off a cliff like Wile E. Coyote if she didn't wrangle her properly. She sent the edited list back to her to make sure they were on the same wavelength.

An hour later, deep into Emily's presentation, Charley stopped and sat back, surprised. Then she fast-forwarded through the rest of it, realizing this was a merger proposal with a new Middle Eastern music streaming entity. Why hadn't Emily told her about this? Before she could answer her own question, Harry, the department's second-in-command, appeared at her desk, interrupting her. "Hey, I have a huge meeting today and Robin won't be in for maybe three more hours. Could you help me with a report?"

"Oh, Harry, I can't right now. I'm working on something for Emily."

"Shit. How long will that take you?" Harry came around her desk to look at her screen just as she switched it to the Monday music streaming report she did each week for the Legal and Marketing Departments. She had no idea if he knew what was going on, and if he didn't, she couldn't chance his finding out by seeing the presentation.

"Best guess, another hour. I can help you when I'm done."

"Shit."

"Maybe you could call Robin, ask her to come in now?"

"Yeah, could you do that? Thanks."

Charley sighed, dialed Robin's number, left a terse message, and weighed the merits of finally coming clean to Emily about Harry's dependence on her when Robin wasn't around, which seemed to be more often lately. When the document was ready to send, so was a rough draft of how she wanted to present the problem, and her solution, to Emily. She opened an email, polished the draft, and sent them both off. Five minutes later, Charley's Instant Message pinged.

Hand Harry's report to Zoë when she comes in. I need u today. I'll call him and tell him. He can be such a pain.

Poor Zoë. Hired four months ago as the third assistant to the growing group, she was the complete team player, performing admirably and never complaining. Charley had already sung her praises to Emily a number of times.

The phone rang a moment later, and Charley glanced at it, her console holding almost everyone's line in her department. Emily's cell number appeared on Harry's Caller ID, and Charley knew he knew who it was, yet after three rings, she had to answer.

"Wait…he's not even picking up?" Emily asked. "He had to see it was me."

"You're not his wife or his son."

"Whoa. I should've been on that list from day one."

"Want me to say something to him? You know he'll have an excuse as to why he couldn't even look up to see that it was you, but we both know he did."

"I'll speak to him," Emily said quietly. "I need to give him new sheet music if I want him to sing a different tune."

Charley could almost see that telltale vein of anger coming to life on Emily's forehead as she buzzed Harry's intercom. Seconds later, she heard him apologizing profusely, his office back-to-back with the thin wall behind her desk. Emily had allowed a fairly lengthy honeymoon period after joining the firm mid-January, but now she was putting both her team and the other departments she'd been charged with revamping under her thumb, and Charley was enjoying the show. She smiled as she put Harry's report into a folder for Zoë. It might not be such a bad day after all.

Hours later, Charley sent the final PowerPoint to Emily and decided it was time for lunch, and that she'd call it a day and have it at home since she'd been there seven hours. The merger was still on her mind, but she trusted that Emily would tell her about it when the time was right. When she passed Robin's desk, Charley reminded her she was scheduled to cover the receptionist's lunch hour now and delighted in watching her panic.

"Wait, I have a lunch date!"

"Really? Cancel it."

"But I can't."

I could only hope it's a job interview. "You'll have to. It's your rotation. Besides, you know what my policy is about lunch dates. If you'd told me earlier, I'd have covered you," Charley said. "Did you ask Zoë?"

"She can't do it."

"Okay, then." Charley heard Robin slamming cupboard doors as she walked away and laughed to herself. It had taken her a long time to get here, but she loved being the top assistant, and she ran a tight, efficient ship. Assistants like Robin who shirked their duties pissed her off.

On the walk home, Charley finally let herself think about the woman from the Y, and she hoped she'd see her again tonight. She tried to think of the best, or at least a somewhat clever way, to break the ice and tell her she'd seen her at Sally's tea yesterday, but everything she thought of fell short. Bing and Bob greeted her at the door. Bob stood over a beat-up catnip mouse, swaying back and forth, daring Charley to pick it up. "Mouse," she growled as she tossed the mail onto the butcher-block table, knelt on the floor, pinched the mouse's tail, and slowly slid him around, Bob hunkering down in response. *How would I open the conversation with her?* Bob swatted at the mouse and Charley pulled it back. *What can I safely say?* Ears back, Bing pounced, grabbing the grubby felt toy in his teeth. *Will she wonder why I didn't approach her at Sally's?* Bob jumped on Bing and both cats tore down the hall. Getting up off the floor proved a challenge. *I clearly need to ramp up my core exercises.* She pulled herself up using the back of the couch. In the bedroom, a low thrum of anticipation began vibrating in her chest as she changed into her swimsuit, shorts, and a polo shirt, grabbed a jacket and her canvas gym bag, and headed to the pool.

Lost in Lady Gaga's "Bad Romance" on her iPod as she swung through the Y's front door, Charley didn't see that Neely Robinson, the pretty young security guard she enjoyed flirting with every morning on the way in to aquatics class, was sitting behind the security desk until she handed over her ID. She pulled out her ear buds. "Hey, what are you doing here? Did they change your shift?"

"Marcus called in sick. And where have you been the last week? I almost had the front desk call your apartment to make sure you were all right." She swiped Charley's card through the digital reader.

"Oh, that's so sweet of you. My boss is in London so I'm already at work at six. I can't come to David's classes until week after next."

"Well, you're way early for the evening class. Gonna be crowded in that locker room now."

"I know." *That's exactly why I'm here.*

"So…how was your weekend? Spend it in your usual cocoon of privacy hiding from the world?"

"No." The hint of Neely's cocoa butter fragrance wafted over the counter. Charley breathed it in. It reminded her of the beach, and she loved that Neely wore it year-round. "Another painful dinner with my friends trying to fix me up yet again."

"Ah…and was Miss September a tempting piece of fruit or can I continue asking you out for that drink you keep refusing?"

Charley enjoyed this teasing banter, which had begun not long after Neely showed up on the front desk a year ago, and Charley revealed in one of their morning conversations that she was gay.

"Of course, you can ask. I count on it." She winked at Neely and headed for the stairs. Keeping the charming young woman at bay had turned into a game of flirtation that Charley looked forward to every morning. She couldn't imagine why Neely, who was probably half her age, was attracted to her, although she did occasionally daydream about what a liaison between them might be like. *I can't fool around with anyone's heart like that. Or allow anyone to gamble with mine again.* So she played with her every chance she got, which she hadn't done with any woman in a long time, and let Neely continue her subtle pursuit. It was harmless fun.

The locker room *was* swarming, and for half a second, she found it almost ludicrous that she was ecstatic. When she got to her usual row, the women from the yoga class were ensconced there again, one of them using her favorite locker. Charley gladly turned to the back row. And there was the handsome tomboy, stepping out of a pair of navy blue slacks. Charley's heart rate spiked and she slipped by her, opened the last locker in the row, and hung her bag on the open door. The hint of lemon that Charley had detected the other night pervaded the area again, and she wondered if it was the woman's perfume. She liked the way it lightly diffused into the air.

"Busy in here again tonight. No space in my usual row," Charley said, cocking her head toward the next row when the woman looked at her, that momentary irritation chased by the curiosity again. The crinkles at the corners of her emerald eyes, evidence of that certain age just past a woman's youthful desirability but before that last blaze of mature beauty, made Charley weak in the knees. But she took in a deep breath and launched her first offense. "You were at Sally Simmons's tea party yesterday, weren't you, picking up Irene Palmer?"

The woman turned to face Charley, surprised. "You know Irene?"

Her voice was soft and smooth, honeyed, and a little deeper than Charley thought it would be. "My mother does. Vivian Owens. They've been friends for years. Although these days, it's all correspondence and phone calls since my mother doesn't go out much anymore." Charley watched the woman's eyes melt into warmth as she spoke.

"Of course. I've mailed many notes to your mother for Irene. And read her responses to her. She's quite a pistol."

Charley held out her hand. "That she is. I'm Charley Owens."

The woman shook her hand with a firm grip.

"Joanna Caden."

"Have you been with Irene long?" As Charley began to undress, Joanna turned her attention to her earrings, removing the diamond studs and dropping them into a small felt drawstring bag on the locker shelf.

"Almost a decade now, yes."

Joanna bent her head to unclasp her necklace, and Charley's breath caught at the sight of the elegant curve of her neck. Afraid she might give herself away, if she hadn't already, Charley grabbed her cap and towel, jammed her feet into her flip-flops, and hurriedly slapped her red lock onto her locker.

"I'm sorry, I've got to dash to my class. Anita doesn't allow late-comers into the pool." Charley almost ran out of the locker room, mentally berating herself. She'd had physical reactions to women before, all of them completely controllable. But this one was visceral, triggering the need to run, and it had caught her short. And she knew why.

She hadn't been interested in any woman since the breakup with Tricia. Window-shopping, yes; there were a lot of beautiful women in this city, from runway types to the androgynous "bois," some of whom could turn Charley's head even though she didn't always care for the look. But experiencing the shot of adrenaline that only hit her when she came across something, or someone, she instinctively knew she wanted but who was possibly just out of her reach? That hadn't happened in a long time. It had proved worth it the first time, with Tricia. If she still had the range to grasp that far, would it be worth it a second time? She wouldn't have considered it in the aftermath of Tricia. But now, she wondered if maybe her friends *were* right to push her...

Charley hit the pool shower and delicately picked her way over the wet tiles to the shallow end where Styrofoam weights sat at intervals along the pool's edge.

"All right," Anita called out, snapping her cap over an abundance of light brown hair wound into a bun and lowering her chubby body into the shallow end of the pool. "Let's warm up by gliding from wall to wall." Anita's reputation was well known at the Y. The only teacher who got into the pool with her classes, she ran them with an iron fist. No talking was allowed; she demanded total attention and expected full compliance with the paces she put them through. David, the morning instructor, had, on the other hand, perfected a routine that Charley had memorized by the third week; nor did he seem to care that the dozen or so people in the pool every morning treated the time like a big coffee klatch as he called out the exercises from the side of the pool. While she loved the camaraderie of David's class, she lived for the drive of Anita's regimented boot camp.

Charley slid into a spot in the second row and let her body sink into the warm water, hoping to forget the opportunity she'd just blown as Anita led them through stretches, balancing movements, and resistance exercises with the weights. But when the woman to her right bumped into her, she realized she was so focused on Joanna that she had no idea what the class was doing. Anita was staring at her with one eyebrow cocked.

"We've moved on to another exercise. You might want to keep up."

Charley could feel the flame creep up her neck and focused on the class.

Afterward, Charley approached the locker room with trepidation, trying to formulate a breezy remark to cover for her quick exit if Joanna happened to be there. She walked through the door, and as she turned the corner, Joanna was walking toward her, already dressed and on her way out.

"Hey, I'll see you again sometime," she said, her green eyes seeming to sparkle as she smiled at her.

"Sure…" Charley said, watching her disappear up the stairs, her resolve not to get involved with anyone again floundering in her wake.

Chapter Five

The bartender set a gin martini and a Johnnie Walker Black in front of Brooke. She handed him several bills and turned to Charley, her glass raised. "Peace offering?"

Charley raised hers back, took a sip, and glanced around the noisy bar, annoyed. "Annie made you do this, didn't she?"

"I was going to call you next week, make you sweat a little." The bartender put Brooke's change on the bar, and she tucked it under her coaster.

"How badly did Karen take it?" Charley asked.

"She got over it, seemed to understand that it was you, not her. Lindsay took it worse."

"Aww, crap." Charley closed her eyes in frustration, and then took a big gulp of her scotch. "I didn't mean to do that to her."

"She can be a sensitive little flower. Plus, now she feels she's put her student in a compromising position. Maybe you should call her."

"Yes, Mother." Charley spotted a couple across the bar taking turns intimately talking into each other's ear. Watching them seemed an act of trespassing and she immediately pictured herself and Joanna in their places.

"Charley?"

"Hmmm?"

"Where the hell did you just go? I was talking to you and you checked out."

"Sorry. I'm looking around this bar and it's date night special. On a Tuesday?"

"That's why I brought you here."

Charley looked at her, confused.

"Look, we had a long discussion after Karen left the other night, and I think we realized that if you thought your only option was to leave without telling us…well, that spoke volumes."

"Oh, my God, hallelujah!"

"No, this does not in any way absolve you or otherwise let you off the hook."

"But you just said—"

"I said that you leaving us holding the bag was a sign that we need to let you—"

"Alone, you need to let me alone, Brooke."

"You need a woman, Charley, even if it's only for one night."

"I don't do one-night stands."

"You used to. You were Queen of the Love 'Em and Leave 'Em Brigade in college. People joked about installing a toll booth in your doorway."

"I was nineteen. I was young and free. And stupid."

"Well, now you're old and jaded. And apparently still stupid."

"Excuse me?"

"Don't get on your high horse, Lady Godiva. Look, it's been three years, and quite frankly, we all know that what went wrong between you and Tricia didn't happen overnight. In fact, it was coming for a long time, so it's more like six years. I mean, how long are you going to carry this emotional baggage around? You do realize it's stopping you, don't you?"

Charley looked at the young couple once more, hating Brooke for being right. "What would you really know about it, Brooke? If Annie cheated on you tomorrow, what would you do? If one day, everything that was perfect disappeared the next day because you weren't enough for her. What do you think you would do?"

Brooke swirled the last of her drink in her glass. "It would kill me." She drank the dregs, set the glass down, and signaled the bartender for another round. "But we've been here before, you and me. And I've told you I would eventually pick myself up and dust myself off because I need someone in my life. And I think you do, too."

The bartender set the drinks down in front of them and extracted two bills from the pile beneath Brooke's coaster.

"I think the possibility of Karen scared you."

"The possibility of anyone scares me."

"And that's what we were trying to get you through by setting you up with all these women. That's all, just to get you over that hump."

Charley turned to face Brooke on her barstool. "Why is this so important to you?"

"Because..." Brooke clasped Charley by the shoulders and she saw the concern in her eyes, noticed for the first time the delicate "worry" lines beginning to appear on Brooke's forehead and around her mouth. "I don't want you to be that woman we all read about in the *Times* article last year who'd been dead for weeks among her nineteen cats before the smell signaled her neighbors."

"Oh, for God's sakes!" Charley swatted Brooke's arms away.

"Charley, they ate her face!"

"I will never be that cat lady, you idiot!"

"What I really want is to know that you're having fun again. I want to know you're eating cheese and crackers in bed with some woman after having wild sex."

"I will never eat crackers in bed, either!"

"You're not hearing me, Charley."

"What!"

"You're stagnating. You go to work, you go to the pool, you go home. We haven't even been on a hike since April...I miss that."

"I know. We should go out to Pelham Bay before the weather turns. But I like my life the way it is. I like being single. It's very orderly. And stress-free."

"And emotion-free," Brooke added. "And, frankly, boring. You're boring, sweetie."

Charley was stunned. "Are you saying that without a woman in my life, I'm of no value? That is so post-feminist, post-lesbian sexist!"

"It's post nothing. It is a word of advice from your friends who think you're shriveling like a raisin. You need to walk on the wild side again, babe. There's nothing wrong with being single if you're living it up, but you're just hiding."

Charley glanced at the young couple again. Their foreheads were touching; the man leaned in to kiss the girl, and Charley could picture the curve of Joanna's neck as she unclasped her necklace, her emerald eyes as they'd talked about Irene yesterday evening…

"Dare I ask…has anything transpired between you and Gym Woman? If she actually exists?"

Charley was surprised. Had something shown on her face? She searched Brooke's countenance for any trace that she'd been caught out. And then she did something that she hadn't done in a long time. "No. Nothing," she lied.

"Well, I'm just going to keep asking until my questioning drives you to make it happen."

"Then I'll have to begin dodging your phone calls, won't I?"

"Honestly, Charley," Brooke said, the exasperation evident, "if you're not going to put yourself out there to meet anyone, how is it going to happen? What fairy tale has her showing up in your life without you opening the door?"

"Maybe it doesn't. You know I really don't want anyone in my life again. It's a lot of work. And I'm sorry if that doesn't sit well with you." Charley watched beads of sweat trickle down her nearly empty glass. "Or…maybe she's already in my life. Maybe she's a friend and we haven't connected those dots yet." The ice left in the glass succumbed to the heat of Charley's hand, plopping over into the centimeter of water that had pooled, and she sucked it into her mouth. "If I already know her, the hard part is done. That's how I've envisioned her."

Brooke sighed. "If."

Charley was too tired to go to Anita's Wednesday evening class. She and Brooke had stayed out far later than either of them had intended, drinks turning into dinner as they analyzed all their friends' lives, laughing at their own gossipy arrogance. But she hated the slippery slope of laziness she felt came with skipping a workout, so she fed the cats, shouldered her gym bag, and walked to the Y.

Excitement hit her on the way over at the thought she might see Joanna. In the locker room, her favorite row was empty. She went right to the last row, though, closed her eyes for a second, and turned the corner. Joanna was there.

"Hey," Charley said. "Nice to see you tonight."

"Oh, hi there." Joanna worked her way out of sweat-soaked shorts and a T-shirt. "I'm a little bit of a mess here. They chose today to turn off the air conditioning in the weight room."

"Well, that's no fun." Charley opened a locker, stowed her bag, and unbuttoned her shirt.

Anita appeared around the corner. "Charley, good, I caught you, I wasn't sure you were coming tonight. We have to hold class in the slow lane of the east pool. The west pool is closed, there was some kind of accident there this afternoon."

"Oh, crap," Charley groaned. "I hate that pool. It's so cold."

"Don't worry," Anita said as she walked away. "I'll make you guys work so hard you'll sweat."

Joanna chuckled. "That pool you hold class in is a warm bathtub."

"And your east pool is cold enough for ice fishing!"

Joanna had wrapped a towel around herself and picked up her soap and shampoo. "You'll be fine, lightweight." She headed toward the shower.

Charley was sure she'd picked up a slight tease in Joanna's voice.

In the lap pool, Anita drove them like a Marine drill sergeant in the slow lane. Fifteen minutes in, just when Charley thought the muscles in her bad knee might seize up from the cold, Joanna walked in in her blue Speedo. Charley immediately forgot her knee as she watched Joanna slip into the lane marked "Fastest" at the far end, and she did, indeed, slice through the water with speed. She was grace personified. And a total distraction, as she thought of other places where Joanna would move with equal athletic flexibility. Anita caught her attention with a look of disapproval several times.

Joanna was still doing laps when Charley's class was over. She wondered how awkward it would be if she waited for her, decided she'd figure out something to say that would make it feel utterly normal, and took a seat on the low white tile wall. The workout Anita had just put them through began hitting her in places she'd forgotten could hurt. She was going to have to sit in the sauna before she changed and went home.

Rubbing her knee while she concentrated on a good line that would sound breezy and possibly "new friend hanging out and waiting for you," Charley didn't see Joanna get out of the pool until she was standing right in front of her, a half-smile on her face, one eyebrow raised.

"Need a pool buddy to walk you back to the locker room?"

There was that barely perceptible tease again, and Charley could feel the heat and color rising right out the top of her suit and up her neck as she looked up at Joanna. And then came the answering surprise in Joanna's glittering green eyes. Charley picked up her towel. "I had a couple of cramps from Anita's class I needed to work out. But I'm going that way, yes."

They walked in silence, Charley feeling more than a little foolish. She'd never been able to control that blush, and she couldn't help wondering what Joanna must be thinking. But if ever there was a time to capitalize on it, it was now. "So…as my new pool buddy, would you be interested in going out for a coffee some time?"

Joanna stopped in the middle of the hallway. "Are you asking me out?"

The question caught Charley by surprise. It was exactly what she was doing, but Joanna's reaction told her she might've stepped on a land mine. "Uh…coffee…would only be a date if you wanted it to be."

"No, I don't. Want it to be. Charley, I'm toxic right now. You should really only think of me as an acquaintance."

Charley nodded slowly. "Okay."

They continued to the locker room, the silence seeming heavier, and when they reached the sauna, she opened the door. "I have to sit in here for fifteen minutes or so or I'll turn into a pretzel before midnight." Charley watched Joanna walk down the hall, all graceful athleticism, and was struck with a pang of desire. Minutes later, the dry heat was soothing every ache in her body, but not the one in her mind. She leaned back and closed her eyes. When she opened them again, Joanna was coming down the hall, dressed to leave. She stopped and pulled the door open. Cool air rushed in.

"So, as your new pool buddy, I sort of screwed up back there. Coffee's a really nice idea. As long as it's not a date. If you're even half as funny as your mother is in her letters, I have to get to know you. But I don't think I can manage it until Monday. I'm on duty the rest of this week."

Charley nodded. "Monday it is."

"And listen, you've been in here almost twenty minutes. You're going to dehydrate if you're not careful." Joanna handed her a bottle of water and left.

Charley looked at the clock hanging on the wall outside the sauna, smiled, and drank down half the bottle. Joanna had been paying attention to how long she'd been in here. That was promising.

With Emily in the air on her way back to the States, Charley went to the Y Thursday for David's seven a.m. class. Her boss's incommunicado state meant a quiet day. Tomorrow would be much the same with Emily working from home. Turning onto Forty-Seventh Street, she spotted Neely standing outside the Y. It was unusual to see her away from her post. "Hey," Charley said as she drew near. "What are you doing out here? Everything okay?"

"Collecting myself. We had an incident in the men's locker room. Ambulance left a minute ago."

"What happened?"

"Heart attack. EMS thinks he'll be okay, but I'm a little shaken."

Charley put her hand on Neely's shoulder. "Anything I can do?"

Neely's gaze, when she looked at Charley, was serious. "Are you busy Friday night?"

Charley knew immediately what was happening, but she wasn't sure which direction she should take, knowing that her answer this time would define their relationship one way or the other. For good. "I…I don't know."

"Of course you know. Everyone knows their schedule. Guy that left here in that ambulance, his schedule just got blown out of the water. I didn't used to when I was younger, but now I see these things as signs."

Internally, Charley agreed. Her father's death when she was twelve had taught her all too well the fleeting nature of life, but she had chosen to live it from the second row since then, not wanting to be touched too deeply by it, not wanting much to be expected of her. For a moment, she looked at the ground, Brooke's rebuke Tuesday night about her life being emotion-free chasing around in her head, her further advice to walk on the wild side nipping at her careful core.

"Please…come dancing with me and my friends. It's a club downtown that plays some seriously good music. I'd really like to spend time with you."

"I, uh…"

Neely stepped closer. "It's a couple hours, Charley," she said softly. "It could be fun. We'd be with other people, and I promise if you're not having a good time, I'll get you home right away. I just feel like…I need something more than flirting after watching someone's life change in an instant like that. I don't want to be on the platform watching the train leave without me."

Charley inhaled, the cocoa butter fragrance hitting her. *Maybe I do need to walk on the wild side for a minute. Or at least lean over the railing and look at it.* "Okay," she said.

Neely's smile was a mix of relief and joy. "Why don't you let me pick you up, or meet you somewhere before, and take you to the club."

"Why? Where is this place?"

"It's a little hard to find for the uninitiated."

Charley blinked.

"It's a storefront on Franklin near Hudson. You wouldn't know it was anything. You'd walk right by it."

"Okay…well, what time do you want to pick me up?"

"About ten o'clock."

"Ten!"

"I know it's late, but you could come to dinner with us, too. We get together at a restaurant way downtown at eight. I would love it if you came to dinner. I just didn't want to press my luck by asking you for the whole night."

"Well, if I'm coming dancing, I'll come to dinner."

"You will?" Neely's expression of delight made Charley smile. "Okay, I'll pick you up at seven. Do you like Jamaican?"

"Yes."

"You're gonna love this place, then," Neely said, opening the door to go back inside.

On her way out after class, Neely stopped Charley at the desk.

"Give me your phone for a minute?" she asked, pointing to Charley's hip pocket.

"What for?" Charley was baffled.

"C'mon." Neely flicked her fingers.

Charley handed it over.

Neely pressed her phone's screen to Charley's. It emitted a beep. "Now you have me in your contacts in case you need to call me before we meet tomorrow night. You can get me by pressing one button. But..." Neely smiled mischievously. "I suspect you already knew that."

"You must be feeling better," Charley said, taking her phone back and heading out the door, "because you have the devil in you again."

Chapter Six

Taking Neely's advice that the dance floor could get warm, Charley decided to wear jeans and a vintage Creedence Clearwater Revival T-shirt. Would Neely's friends even know who CCR was? She put her most comfortable cowboy boots on, slung a windbreaker over her shoulder, and went downstairs to wait for her. At the front desk, Frankie nodded in the direction of the lobby reception area as Charley headed for the front door.

"You have a visitor."

A single red rose in her hand, Neely stood there. Charley almost didn't recognize her. Neely's dark hair with cherry stripes was always caught up in a loose bun at her security post, but it now rippled down the back of a black leather biker jacket, giving her the kind of bad girl appeal Charley had always been attracted to but never had the nerve to chase. Black dress slacks hinted at muscular thighs. Neely's skin color contrasted sharply with the white dress shirt that was fashionably cut to reveal the plane between her breasts, which drew Charley's undivided attention. She realized she'd lingered there when she looked up and saw the shy smile. The cocoa butter scent, barely perceptible at the Y, now cloaked her as Neely hugged her. The leather of her jacket warmed up immediately under Charley's hands; she leaned into the softness.

"I'm going to feel underdressed next to you tonight," Charley said.

"You look perfect. I...wanted you to have this," Neely said, giving her a rose, "but I realize it's not very convenient to carry. Can we leave it with your doorman?"

Handing the flower over the counter, Charley told Frankie she'd pick it up later. As they walked toward the subway, Neely took Charley's hand.

"My friends know you're coming. I hope you like them."

"Is there anything I need to know?"

As the train made its way downtown, Neely told Charley about the people in her life. Most of them had gone to Hunter College with her. Charley was momentarily embarrassed that she'd assumed Neely hadn't attended college because she worked as a security guard, and then she wondered why Neely held the job if she had a degree, but she couldn't figure out a way to ask her without sounding condescending. And possibly out of step, considering the kind of necessary "gig" economy her generation was adapting. After getting off at Fulton Street, they strolled toward the South Street Seaport's waterfront.

"We're early," Neely said, sitting on the concrete steps of the pedestrian plaza at Pearl and Water Streets. "Tell me about *your* friends." She patted the step next to her. "What kind of person does Charley Owens hang out with?"

"Friends from college, just like you, and people I worked with and became close to over the years." In the middle of telling Neely about them, her phone vibrated in her pocket, tickling her thigh. Afraid it could be Emily, she pulled the phone out, apologizing to Neely. It was Brooke.

Brooke: *Hope yr watching the Penn State game. It's a corker*

She didn't reply, figuring she could text her after dinner. Returning to the conversation, Charley began telling Neely more about the women her friends had tried to fix her up with recently, and had her laughing at some of the absurdities. They both heard the rowdy group of people turn onto Water Street and make its way toward them. Charley glanced up. Her defense system kicked in, her unblinking "New York mask" descending, but then Neely rose and waded right into the crowd, and after several hugs, put her arm around Charley's shoulder.

"Everybody, this is Charley."

"You didn't tell us she's white, Neely," a voice from the crowd intoned.

Neely paid it no attention. "This is my crew. I'll introduce you."

Charley hesitated, counting heads. Her system for coding names to colors or objects was pretty good, but not for a group this big. She crossed her fingers and hoped something would stick as Neely pointed everyone out, and she shook as many hands as she could reach.

They continued down the block to Vanessa's Jerk Joint, which appeared to be closed until Bertie rang a bell, and in the dim light, Charley saw a tall, regal woman making her way to the door followed by a man in chef's whites. The woman turned on several lights. Charley recognized Vanessa from her website—she'd researched the restaurant to find out it was considered one of the jerk jewels of the city, its Jamaican owner celebrated for her savvy marketing acumen as well as for the unique spice combination she'd brought with her when she'd emigrated. Charley was immediately taken by how the canary yellow of the shirt she wore highlighted her face and echoed the yellow pinstripes of her black suit. And when Vanessa unlocked and opened the door, Charley saw the yellow sling-back heels and smiled: the woman's savoir faire obviously extended well beyond marketing and cooking. Everyone filed in behind Bertie.

"Thank you for opening for us, Aunt Vanessa. You're so good to us," Bertie said from the depths of Vanessa's arms.

"You children are so good for my cash register," she replied and glanced at Charley. "You have a guest tonight."

Neely took Charley's hand and stepped forward. "Vanessa, this is my friend Charley Owens. She comes to the Y every morning."

"A pleasure to meet you," Vanessa said, the numerous delicate gold and enamel bracelets on her wrist tinkling as she shook Charley's hand. "A friend? Unusual for you." She turned back to Charley. "Please know that any friend of my flock is welcome here. Just see you don't keep Neely from her studies." Vanessa winked at Charley, who turned to Neely, surprised.

"Your studies?" Charley said when they'd finished jockeying for seats at a table out of view in the back of the restaurant and she found herself on one side of Neely with Stacey on the other side. Neely had introduced Stacey as her best friend, but Charley immediately sensed something was off with this young woman, who was so dismissive that she'd pretended not to see Charley's extended hand.

Vanessa had shut off the lights in the front of the restaurant and now stood at the head of the table. "Donald is working his magic in the kitchen. What is everyone drinking?" No pad or pen in sight, she nodded as each person ordered.

Neely leaned against Charley. "What perfume do you wear?"

"State secret. And you're dodging my question."

"I'm getting my master's in creative writing at Hunter," Neely said matter-of-factly, sitting up again.

"You're kidding me." Charley didn't know whether to be relieved that Neely might be closer to thirty or exhilarated that there was much more to her than she had imagined. "I wish I'd known this about you when you first started at the Y."

"My education would've made a difference to you?"

Charley heard the disappointment in Neely's voice, and an edge to it that she'd never heard before. Looking at her, she was caught by both the pain and the question in her eyes. And then she was trapped by the deep black of them, and Neely's handsomeness.

"Would you have said yes to me sooner if you'd known?"

"It would have made no difference." Charley sat back, somewhat defeated. "I would love to have known. Twenty years ago, I went through the creative writing program at Columbia."

"Seriously? So, pot calling the kettle black, you never shared that."

"Well, I can't really stake a claim to writing anymore." The pages sitting on her desk flashed through Charley's mind. "I had writer's block for a very long time."

"That sucks. How long and how did it happen?"

Charley related the burnout following graduate school, and then the month she'd spent at a writers' colony in Vermont that was supposed to be restorative. "It was cold and damp even for late May," Charley told her. "And then when Brooke came to pick me up and take me to Maine so we could celebrate my MFA, this dog…" Charley looked down at her empty charger plate. "We were on this little country road and he came out of nowhere chasing the car. Brooke misjudged where he was and we hit him." Charley saw the look of alarm on Neely's face. "We stopped, obviously. And the owner came running, and we got him to a vet in time, but it was like something stopped ticking inside."

"You fixed it with the dog and made it right. When you have something to say that you can't keep inside anymore, when it needs to come out because it's burning and keeping you up nights, that block is gonna be a map dot in your rearview."

Charley played with her napkin. "Actually, it might be…no, it is. Months ago, I took out that novel I wrote in graduate school, to throw it out, actually, but then I read it, and something *did* ignite inside, and I had to get back to it. But not the way it was. So, I'm reconstructing."

"I'd love to look at it."

Vanessa had been making her way around the table, putting a drink in front of each customer, exchanging questions and small talk with each of them. When she got to Neely, she said, "You been holdin' out, haven't you?"

Neely smiled, contritely at first, but it blossomed under Vanessa's kind study. Charley dissolved inside, knowing that smile so well. Under the muted lighting, the smile cast Neely in a moment of susceptibility and she radiated an allure Charley had never seen before.

"Don't hide that light under a bushel, I keep telling you."

"She was hiding *her* light," Neely protested, gently knocking her shoulder into Charley's.

"Oh, well, two wrongs make a right, isn't that what they say?" Vanessa moved down the table.

"And what about you? Do you have anything I can read?" Charley asked.

Neely laughed.

"No, seriously. What are you working on for school?"

"A short story, a novel, and some poems. My ass is tired, and my pencils are worn down to little nubs."

"Anything published?"

Neely pulled out her phone and after a quick internet search, she showed Charley the screen.

"I know this literary review."

Donald came to the table with three platters of food, Vanessa right behind him carrying several more, and the aromas of curry, plantains, and jerk spices swept over the table. The dishes began threading their way through many hands. Charley gave the phone back to Neely.

"Why do you work as a security guard? There must be something else you could be doing," Charley said, holding a platter of jerk chicken stew as Neely spooned some onto her plate.

"You mean something literary? In publishing? No. I need to keep my writing life separate from my real life. For now. Plus, with classes, I had to take something where the hours worked for me. The Y is perfect. And, I don't have to pay for a gym."

Charley nodded. "Smart."

"Tell me something…if you thought I was a low-level security guard, maybe without much education," Neely asked with a side-long glance, "why did you finally say yes?"

"Because you were right the other morning. Life can be surprisingly short." Charley looked directly into her dark eyes, and what she saw reflecting back made everything around her disappear for a moment. She really wanted to admit she'd been attracted to her but decided caution was warranted, despite Brooke's advice. "And I already knew I liked you. To us," she said, picking up her glass.

"To Jack Hersh," Neely replied, "for showing us the really hard way that we needed to take a chance."

As their glasses touched, Charley saw Stacey turn away in disdain. Just then, her phone vibrated in her pocket again. *Oh, shit, Brooke!* She pulled it out, saw that it was, indeed, Brooke again asking where she was, so she shot her a quick, *Out w/the girls from work.*

"Let's ask Charley…" Bertie called down the table. "Who's better, Jay Z or Young Jeezy?"

Charley searched the expectant faces, hoping they weren't making fun of her, and slipped her phone back into her pocket. "I'll be honest, I don't know Young Jeezy's work. And I find Jay Z too commercial. For my money, if you want the truth of pain in someone's lyrics, Eminem."

"Huh," Stacey said. "Didn't think you knew the genre."

"Mostly, I don't," Charley said. "But I listen from time to time, I check the Billboard charts and some blogs, so I stay on top of what's going on, and my nieces and nephews play things for me. Here's one for you," Charley addressed the table, wondering if they'd understand the cliché she was about to drop on them. "Who was better—the Beatles or the Rolling Stones?"

The table erupted in both laughter and debate.

"We weren't born then." Stacey's snide tone was unmistakable.

"Doesn't mean you don't know their stuff." Neely pointed her fork at her. "It's historic."

"Historic," Stacey sneered. "Like Charley."

She decided to ignore the remark and waded into the debate from a firsthand perspective. Half the table was amazed she'd been to a Stones concert in 1978. "That's before I was even born, y'all!" Jesus noted. And half the table wasn't sure they could ever recall hearing a Beatles song on the radio; all they'd ever known was hip-hop and rap. Rusty admitted she listened to classical music, too, and Bertie made fun of her. A moment later, Handel's "Water Music" began permeating the restaurant through the sound system. Everyone became quiet.

"Well, I guess we know where Vanessa stands," Jesus said. "Who'd'a thunk a jerk joint had classical in their sound system? Charley, Democrat or Republican?"

"Oh, no," Bertie sighed. "Now we're in for it."

When Vanessa gave them the tally for dinner and Neely added cash to the tray for Charley, Stacey turned to Bertie. "See that," she said, hooking her thumb at Charley, "she isn't even reaching for her wallet."

Neely immediately turned to Stacey. "She won't be reaching for it at all tonight. She's my guest."

"Well, lucky you," Stacey said, leaning around Neely for all the table to see and hear. "And you must make ten times what she does."

The remark burned. "I don't know about that," Charley replied as politely as she could, although she was seething underneath. "But she asked me out, and even though I thought we should go Dutch, she insisted, so I'm respecting her wishes."

Neely threw her napkin on the table and excused herself. Stacey leveled Charley with a hard gaze and followed Neely. Jesus slid over into the empty seat.

"Don't let her rattle you. She's been at you all night. I'm sorry I didn't see it coming or I would've sat here in the first place."

Charley sighed and sat back. "Thank you." She put her hand on Jesus's. "It's been a long time since I dealt with so much lesbian drama."

Jesus shook his head, chuckling. "Oh, these girls all about that. They make us queens look positively regal."

"I'm not sure I have the patience for it anymore. But, is there a history here I should know about? With Stacey?"

"They've been friends since they were five," Jesus explained. "Grew up together in the Wagner Houses. Stacey's always had it bad for Neely. We can't figure out why Neely hasn't ever been interested in Stacey that way."

Maybe because she's a bitch. Charley reached into her pocket for her *balance* stone.

As they left the restaurant, Charley turned to Neely. "I'm sorry if what I said about not expecting you to pay upset you. I didn't mean it to."

"It did, I'll be honest, but actually Stacey put it into perspective for me in the ladies' room."

"Oh?" Charley was warily surprised.

"Yes. She thought you were right not to expect me to pay, although I asked you out, because you're both older and make more than I do. And before you interrupt, she was being practical and wondering if I'd hurt your sense of responsibility."

"Not at all. As long as the next time, I pay."

"Really?" Neely's face lit up.

"Yes. What?"

"'Next time?'"

Charley took Neely's arm. "I'm having a good time. I'd love to go out with you again." The leather of Neely's biker jacket warmed up under her hands and she pulled her closer, enjoying the sensuality, breathing in the cocoa butter, now less a reminder of the beach than the reality of Neely. She had surprised herself with the admission to Neely; she hadn't expected the evening to turn out like this, or for Neely to be so engaging that she already knew she wanted more with her, more time, more fun, more…she didn't allow herself to finish the thought.

The subway was crowded at eleven o'clock on a Friday, everyone heading for clubs or coming home from dinners with friends. She and Neely stood facing each other, and the swaying of the train moved Neely right up against Charley.

"You smell so good," she whispered.

"And your perfume reminds me of the beach. I love the beach."

"I'm glad I remind you of something you love."

Charley eyed Neely with a provocative half-smile. Neely touched her forehead to Charley's, then dipped in for a kiss. It was just long enough for Charley to be struck by the audacious act and to know she wanted to feel those lips again later tonight.

Back on street level, Jesus and Stacey led the way toward the club. There was no sign outside the door, but a short velvet rope attached to two stanchions held several dozen people in line. The doorman moved the rope aside for them.

"Wow," Charley said to Neely. "Who in your group rates this kind of treatment?"

"Stacey. She works with the bouncer during the day. He always makes sure we have the table with service near the dance floor."

"You come every week?"

"I don't, but almost everyone else does."

Charley felt the bass under her feet before she heard the music. As they filtered down the hall toward the inner sanctum, she could make out Rihanna blasting the dance floor and Jesus swung into action, cake-walking the length of the hall, and holding the heavy vinyl flaps open so everybody could enter. Neely pulled Charley right onto the dance floor and they stayed there as the DJ mixed her way through several songs. When a rap poured from the speakers, Neely pointed to their table. Stacey had seen to it that there was no room in the banquette for them, so Jesus pulled over some chairs, Charley rolling her eyes at him as he shrugged. Before they could sit down, Stacey and Bertie headed for the floor. Stacey leaned in close to Charley.

"This is Young Jeezy's 'R.I.P.' Listen good."

As Stacey melted into the crowd, Charley laughed to herself, knowing exactly what she would hear.

"Okay, what did she say? Nothing bad, I hope?" Neely asked.

"This is a Young Jeezy rap. I think she thinks there's a message for me."

Neely shook her head.

"And listen, you can't protect me all night, you know."

"I'm sorry. I don't know why she's doing this. I talked to her, but I'm not sure it had an effect."

"You really don't know why she's doing this?"

"All right, yes, I do, but she knows there's nothing there."

In her peripheral vision, Charley caught Stacey heading up to the DJ booth. A moment later, another rap faded up. She still had

Stacey in her crosshairs when the lyrics broke through, something about dating outside your race. She could've laughed at Stacey's ploy if it wasn't so immature. Deciding she needed to level the playing field right away, she surreptitiously took Stacey by her wrist when she reached the banquette, leaving her no choice but to sit next to her.

"You know," she said, leaning close to Stacey, "Neely's not the first black woman I've been with."

Stacey regarded her cagily.

"Neely, the DJ's playing Stacey's request." Charley pointed toward the speaker.

Neely listened for a moment and then glared at Stacey.

"Am I your first white girl? Because I was telling Stacey," Charley gesticulated between the two of them, "I dated black girls in the early eighties. When people still stared at us. I thought that era was past."

Stacey said nothing, but Charley could see that she was smoldering and leaned toward her again. "You know who I've never dated?" Charley looked her up and down, then spoke into her ear. "I never dated any smokin' Latina women like you. I understand you're incredibly sweet tasting. Is that true?"

Stacey reached for her drink, but Charley beat her to the throw, putting her hand on the glass at the same time.

"You know if you do that, Neely won't speak to you for quite some time. So why don't I save face for both of us, since you saved it for me in the ladies' room at Vanessa's—oh, yes, she told me," Charley offered when Stacey registered shock. "Leave the drink in the glass and let's play nice the rest of the night."

"I don't have to care about you," Stacey snarled.

Charley moved in for the kill. "I didn't say you did. You want to stay in her orbit, though, you better pretend to be okay with whoever she pursues. Undermine that and she finds out? You'll be done. That's a little wisdom from someone *historic* who's lived through it a time or two with *my* friends," Charley said, moving closer to Stacey's ear as some heavy bass shook the dance floor. "You do whatever you want to but understand that there are consequences. And if she'd wanted you, it would've happened when you were teenagers. That's a lotta years to be carrying a torch."

Stacey bolted from the banquette, dragging Jesus onto the floor with her.

Neely slid over next to her. "I suppose I shouldn't ask because I know curiosity killed the cat, but what did you say that made her want to throw her drink at you?"

"That's between Stacey and me."

Neely took Charley's hands in hers and ran her thumbs over them. She reached for the back of Charley's neck and pulled her in for a kiss, catching Charley off-guard. "Please don't hurt her."

Charley traced Neely's lips with her index finger. "Can I ask why the two of you never got together?"

Neely caught her hand again. "You see how she is. I can't have that near me. I guess I've remained her friend because we have so much history."

Charley sized her up. "Then you're a very loyal friend. Come on," she said, pushing Neely out of her chair as "Blurred Lines" brought the crowd to its feet for the line dance.

"You know this?" Neely asked, amazed.

"I'm full of surprises." Charley sighed at one more reminder of her age, and then maneuvered Neely into a row as Robin Thicke's falsetto signaled the first move.

With the next song, the DJ shifted gears, floating a slow song down, dispersing the crowd and filling the floor with linked couples. Neely caught Charley around the waist. "Stay."

Charley hesitated, and Neely spun her around so that her back was against Neely's front. She took Charley's right hand, crossed it over to her left hip, and pulled her closer. The cocoa butter fragrance washed over her, and she inhaled it as deeply as she could. Neely entwined the fingers of Charley's left hand in hers and tucked their hands against Charley's right breast. Rolling her hips to the music, she began to circle the dance floor with Charley locked in her arms. The music built. Neely cupped Charley's breast, rubbed it gently, catching her nipple between two fingers and rhythmically coaxing it to the music's languid beat. The move elicited an unexpected reaction between her legs, causing her back to arch, her head tilting toward Neely's shoulder. She felt Neely hug her tighter and brush her lips across the side of her neck. Charley tensed and turned her head until her mouth touched Neely's ear.

"What are you doing?" she protested, even as she began to abandon herself to the security of Neely's arms, the seduction of her scent. The phone vibrated in Charley's pocket again, but she didn't care.

"Something I've wanted to do for a long time." Neely kissed the side of her neck down to her shoulder, her palm rubbing light circles again over Charley's breast. Confounding herself, she closed her eyes and surrendered to Neely's embrace, pressing against her when Neely again found Charley's nipple through the shirt fabric and teased it to attention, keeping it there, keeping Charley on edge until the song merged into the electronic beat of the next number. They broke apart and Charley took Neely's hand to lead her back to their table. She knew Neely's friends had been watching what was happening on the dance floor. Some of them were amused. Stacey bristled with barely concealed anger.

As she dabbed sweat from her neck and forehead with a cocktail napkin, Charley was aware that Neely had moved as close to her as she could.

"That was a slow dance. How did you get so hot?" Neely asked, fanning Charley.

"You know what made me hot." Charley turned to face her. "What are we doing, Neely?"

"Having fun…letting go a little…enjoying each other." Neely ran her hand up Charley's thigh, pushing her fingers deep between her crossed legs. "I like you a lot, I have since the first day I saw you, but I have no expectations of a relationship, if that's what you're worried about." Neely caressed Charley's cheek. "I just want to be with you. And judging by the way you melted into me on that dance floor, you want that on some level, too."

Charley didn't know what that level was, but she knew Neely was right as she watched her kiss the palm of her hand. Charley caught a handful of Neely's hair intending to pull her in for a kiss, but instead she let her go. "I don't mean to be Cinderella, but I need to leave. I have a busy day tomorrow…well, now it's today. I'm sorry."

"Let me take you home."

"No. Not tonight. I want you to stay here with your friends." Charley pulled her phone out of her pocket and hit her Arrow cab app. There was a taxi three blocks away, and Neely grabbed her coat to walk Charley out.

On the sidewalk, Neely pulled her in for a kiss as she held the cab door open. "Next Friday?"

"I could be talked into doing this again." She wasn't sure that was true, but with the cab waiting, she didn't want to try to convince Neely that there were better options.

On the ride home, Charley reveled in the night with Neely and wondered what primal urge had allowed her to drop so many physical guards at once. She also wondered if she really wanted to get involved with a group so much younger, especially one that still had its own lesbian drama going on. Her phone vibrated again, intruding on her thoughts. She looked at it.

Brooke: *U home? U safe? U drunk? Lie on yr side, one foot on the floor.*

Charley chuckled at the reference to the night she'd gotten so drunk freshman year that Brooke had sat at her desk waiting to see if she threw up so she could turn her over and keep her from choking to death. Which had probably saved Charley's life, something Brooke never let her forget.

Too old and too sophisticated to get drunk anymore.

Brooke: *Just snorted my beer up my nose at that one! Sophisticated!*

Charley laughed out loud. At least she hadn't pointed out *old.* She paid the cab driver, walked into the building, and took Neely's rose back from Frank, who'd put it in a glass of water.

For the first time in over twenty years, Charley left everything in a heap on the floor, set her clock, and got under the covers without a second thought. After a few minutes, she got up again and took four Advil. She didn't want to be a sore mess in the morning. Looking at herself in the bathroom mirror, she bet Neely wasn't popping any ibuprofen. She sighed and headed back to bed.

CHAPTER SEVEN

Charley and Brooke stood in silence at the railing of the Staten Island Ferry as the orange hulk's horn blasted and it backed away from the pier. Charley knew she needed to apologize. Again. She'd been apologizing all week since admitting to Brooke on Saturday morning that she hadn't been "out with the girls" on Friday night but at a club with Neely. It was unusual for Brooke to hang up on her. When Charley had called right back, it was Annie who answered and said, "Give her a minute. She's more hurt that you shut her out than that you lied." So, she waited a day. Sunday, she texted an apology. Nothing. Two days later, she dropped off a handwritten note. That had prompted a text from Annie.

Annie: *Staten Island Ferry tom'w morning, 8:30. She needs a day off, playing hooky, and agreed to a hike to Lake Ohrbach w/you.*

Charley thanked Annie for mediating and emailed Emily to say she was taking a personal day, which wasn't an issue since Emily was home sick.

"The note was a nice touch," Brooke said, sipping her coffee, her eyes never leaving the shore of the island in the near distance. The morning sun barely warmed them before the ferry turned into the westerly breezes sweeping the Hudson River.

"I figured you'd be a captive audience to my plaintive cry of apology."

"I could've ripped it up without opening it."

Charley looked at her and saw she was serious. "Yes. You could've." She waited the appropriate number of seconds she knew

Brooke would need to preen her feathers. "But then you'd have missed me totally abasing myself. Because I was devastated. Which gave me a taste of what I did to you, shutting you out, and I didn't like it."

Brooke looked at her. "Then don't do it again."

"I won't. I was being…selfish and protective."

"Of what?"

"Myself. Under the scrutiny of your judgment. Which can be, at times, harsh."

Brooke nodded. "I know." She finished her coffee and tossed the cup into the trash. "Okay, so you talk, I won't judge. Who or what is a Neely?"

Charley laid out the entire scope of the relationship since meeting Neely. And then she waited, her hands folded on the rail.

"A whole year of flirting with a hot young babe and not a word to me or Annie."

"It was harmless fun. It was never supposed to culminate in Friday night."

"And yet it did. So, what happened to change the dynamic?"

Charley sighed. "Karen. And Joanna. And Jack Hersh's heart attack." Had she been a blobby green Martian with a horn rising from her forehead, Charley would've understood the utterly dumbfounded look on Brooke's face. But as well as the two of them could read each other, she realized now just how much she'd shut Brooke out. "A member at the Y had a heart attack last week on Neely's watch and it galvanized her. I think it led her to decide she's not living her best life." Charley checked Brooke's face for a new reaction. Seeing the same surprised look firmly in place, she continued. "So, she asked me out, for real, and it was right after you urged me to walk on the wild side."

"I didn't mean for you to swing for the fences!"

"No judging! *You* said I needed a woman. I got one."

"I meant a one-night stand."

"I chickened out, but that was my initial thought."

"Oh, my God, you were going to sleep with…with a…how old is she?"

"I don't know. She could be thirty, maybe. And I wasn't going to sleep with her. I was just tempted."

"Thirty? And you were worried about Karen at nearly forty…"

"Neely isn't a contender."

"What does that even mean?"

"She's way too young. I could never build a relationship with someone that much younger than me. But it was nice to feel attractive. Wanted."

"Wait, you said you don't want a relationship."

The ferry had docked, and they were making their way off in the crowd reverse-commuting to work.

"I don't. She's fun, Brooke. And she takes me at face value, she doesn't judge."

"Okay, I get the message."

"And she's very sensual. When she touched me on the dance floor, I…well, if we'd been in bed, I probably would've come." Charley thought she'd said that quietly enough to Brooke, but several people near them looked at her. "Come on." She pulled Brooke's coat sleeve. "Let's get to the bus and finish this on the trail."

"Oh, no you don't. Who is Joanna?"

"Gym Woman. Come on." Charley looped her arm with Brooke's and pulled her through the crowd toward the bus.

"Is there anyone else you forgot to mention?" Brooke asked testily as they settled into the front seat of the S57 bus.

"I didn't plan on any of this, okay?"

"But apparently you planned on not sharing any of it with me."

Charley looked out the window.

"Am I really that bad?"

Charley rolled her eyes. "You have no idea. Do you?"

Neither of them spoke for the rest of the short trip to the gates of the Greenbelt Conservancy. Once they were on the trail, Charley felt herself relax, just the slightest bit. She inhaled the warm air, everything around them smelling so pungent, deep scents of autumn rising from the wooded land around them.

After a few minutes, Brooke broke the silence. "Okay, maybe I'm overbearing sometimes, I get that. But I feel like all we've done for the past two weeks is piss each other off and then apologize. I was going to have a nice day shopping today and maybe go to a movie or sit in that champagne bar on Fifty-Fourth Street. Why are we here?"

"Because Annie made us do this. And because it's our pattern. One of us does something stupid, the other one has to step in, we kiss and make up."

Brooke adjusted her backpack. "We might as well be married to each other."

"We never would've made it as a married couple. That's why I broke up with you when we went home after freshman year. Do you want to hear about Joanna or not?"

They walked on toward Lake Ohrbach. As painful as it was, Charley admitted to Brooke that the encounter with Karen had made it abundantly clear that when she'd shut the door of her life after Tricia, it was so airtight that she couldn't breathe, and the ease with which Neely kicked it open and walked through it stole what little breath she had left.

"So why did you walk out on Karen, then?"

"She's still too raw after her breakup. I'm not a hand-holder and I won't be a rebound."

Brooke nodded. "Okay. She did talk all about her ex after you left."

I knew it. My assessment of her was spot-on.

"So, Neely's gonna be the one you eat cheese and crackers in bed with?" Brooke smirked.

Charley laughed. "Probably not. I just know I like her. And we're going out again Friday night."

"Hmmm…And you *will* call me Saturday morning?"

"Yes."

"That leaves Joanna? And you're workin' real hard to avoid telling me how you really feel about her."

Charley picked up several pine cones and flung them at Brooke.

Brooke put her arms up in defense. "Hey, not judging, so you have to tell me."

"I have no idea."

Brooke emitted the sound of a buzzer. "Wrong answer, Cassandra. You know exactly how you feel. You haven't talked about anyone in years, and you brought her up at dinner, so that means she cut through your fortress and made an impression on you. She's on your radar."

Charley sighed. "She's…" She painted a full picture of Joanna, from the aloofness with which she'd first treated Charley right down to the blue Speedo that hugged every curve and every plane of her body like a second skin.

"Not that you noticed. And?"

"Well, aside from being drop-dead handsome? I could get lost in her eyes."

"Ask her out."

"I did. She said no."

Brooke laughed incredulously. "Wait. You've gone from being Punxsutawney Phil to Carrie Bradshaw? In one week?"

"Okay, so I really took your advice to heart. I got two women, and I've been too busy to talk to you."

"You are a piece of work sometimes, Owens. If Joanna said no, you had one night at home to call me."

"Then she said yes." They'd arrived at the lake and walked the perimeter of its thin strip of beach toward two small boulders that were barely discernible in the fringe of tall dune grass.

"Oh, I'm so confused."

Charley repeated the two short conversations to Brooke, the one in which Joanna turned her down in the hallway, and the one in which she came to the sauna and accepted the invitation for coffee.

"Toxic, huh?"

"And she thinks my mother is funny." Charley sat on one of the boulders and pulled two foil-wrapped packets from her bag, then tossed one to Brooke.

"Well, she's right about that."

"You don't go out with someone because you think her mother is funny."

"No, you go out with someone because you find her irresistibly attractive. So check that box on your scorecard." Brooke brushed the boulder off, sat down, and unwrapped her bagel, licking her thumb when she got cold melted cheese on it. "Why do you suppose she's toxic?"

Charley focused on the lake. "I don't know. This woman is enigmatic. Something about her reminds me of—" Charley caught herself before she said Tricia.

"Please don't say Tricia."

"Fine, I won't."

Brooke narrowed her eyes at Charley. "How much older than you is she?"

Charley realized where Brooke was coming from. Her coterie of friends had never liked that Tricia was thirteen years her senior. "I'm starving," she said, taking a bite of her everything bagel with cheese and bacon on it. "This is such a bad breakfast after such a good hike. Did you bring the hard-boiled eggs?"

"Charley!"

She held out her hand and Brooke took a Ziploc bag out of her backpack and tossed it to her.

"I already peeled them for you. And we need a hearty breakfast after this hike. Plus, we still have to get back to the ferry."

"Thank you. She's about our age."

"Well, well, well, Scarecrow. Playing with a little fire, are we? Our age, which might mean she can see right through you. Is she single? Maybe she's as scared and vulnerable as you are."

Charley snorted, the sip of coffee she'd just taken from her thermos almost coming out her nose. "I'm none of those things!"

"Said the frightened woman who's been hiding in her apartment for three years." Brooke leaned back, her face to the sun. "I do love it here."

"Me, too." Charley set her thermos in the tall grass.

"And we've been coming here, what, twenty years?"

"Easily."

"Sharing all kinds of things with each other."

Charley sighed, defeated. "I really don't know how I feel about her, Brooke."

"Is she single?"

"Don't know."

"Is she even gay?"

Charley looked at Brooke like she was the village idiot.

"You asked her out. We've been trying to get you to do this for two years, and out of nowhere, you take someone on. Two someones. But this woman's obviously having quite an effect on you. Please tell me it's not because she's like Tricia. No one was as difficult as Tricia."

"Thanks. I appreciate your assessment."

Brooke shook her head. "I kept my counsel for years, sweetie. I sure don't want to see you get involved with another demanding woman."

"Can I let you know what she's like Tuesday?"

"Coffee's on Monday?

"After Anita's class." Charley began gathering things into her backpack. "Come on, let's walk around the lake."

Brooke found a long piece of broken tree branch in the grass and decided it would work as a walking stick. "You know everyone's going to want to hear all about Neely and Joanna at the next dinner after all the work we put in trying to find someone for you."

"No. Absolutely not. And don't you say a word to anyone."

"Oh, come on, that's cruel!"

"I'm not ready to share this with anyone else. Not until I know what I'm doing, anyway."

"All right, I can give you three weeks before I let it all out of the bag at our October dinner. Maybe you'll be in love by then."

"Now who's being cruel."

Brooke chuckled. "Or maybe you'll just be in heat. Where's the security guard taking you Friday night?"

"You *could* refer to her as a writer."

"When she publishes something, I will."

"She wants to go dancing again. But I'm not so sure I can handle another night like that with her friends." Charley looked at Brooke. "They're just so... Were we so dramatic and bitchy and life or death about everything?"

"You don't remember? Of course we were. It's what you do until you're forty and you realize you haven't done anything *with* your life, and then you become cranky."

"Hmm." Charley checked her phone's bus app now that they were close enough to civilization that she could get one bar, and it showed that the S57 was nearly at their bus stop. They hustled across the street.

On the ferry back to Manhattan, they sat against each other on the open-air upper deck, basking in the sun like a couple of seals on a rock. Charley's phone dinged. It was Neely, sending the website with her short story. Charley hit the link, looked at it, and showed it to Brooke. "See? Published."

Brooke nodded. "Fine. You're dating an author. A very young author."

Charley texted her back. *Thanks! Will read when I'm home.*

Neely*: Let me know what u think. And when do I get to see yrs? Really?*

Neely: *I showed you mine.*

Charley chuckled. *Okay. Give me your email.*

When they got back to Bowling Green, Brooke headed outside in search of a cab. "I'm going home to shower and then to Bloomingdale's. I already know your answer, but I'll ask anyway. You wanna come?"

Charley wrinkled her nose. "I know you want to be buried there, but if I never set foot in that store again, or any retail store, for that matter, I'd be fine."

"You know what Jamie said when we started looking for women for you," Brooke said as she hugged Charley good-bye. "Too bad L.L. Bean doesn't carry a line of lesbians. We'd have found someone for you right away."

When she got home, Charley emailed Neely, attaching the first original five chapters and the rewrites.

I thought you should see the chapters I wrote twenty years ago before you look at what I'm reconstructing. Be gentle.

Part of her was surprised she was so easily trusting this work to someone she'd only just started talking to, but she felt Neely would treat it respectfully. She made a mental note to tell Brooke she'd begun working on the manuscript again. She didn't want to hide anything else from her now. A few minutes later, the buoy tone sounded.

Neely: *looking forward to reading!*

Charley's leg muscles had tightened on the subway ride home and her knee was beginning to throb after the morning's workout, so she took two Tylenol, went to the bedroom closet, and grabbed the webbed strap she used to stretch every day. It had been a gift from the physical therapist who'd helped her through rehab. Bob heard the strap snapping off the rack and vaulted onto the bed as she lifted her leg and counted to thirty. He hunkered down as close to the strap as he could, waiting for it to move when she lowered her leg. Then he pounced and Charley laughed as she raised her leg again, watching Bob, now an eight-pound weight, go with it, his claws and teeth sunk into the lime green quarry. He chased the strap through the entire set of stretches, much to Charley's amusement.

Twenty minutes later, Bob was flat out against the pillow and Charley, feeling much looser, rested on the quilt, its warmth and softness reminding her of being wrapped up with someone. Joanna flooded her mind. Closing her eyes, she imagined Joanna's arms encircling her, pulling her securely to her. She could see her lithe form, all her curves, her flat belly, and wondered what she might feel like hewed to Charley's back and butt as they lay in bed together, their legs entwined. *Will she be there tomorrow night? And is Brooke right, is she as vulnerable as I've been feeling? Can she see right through me?* Neely was sweet, but sweet had never been a part of Charley's palette. She needed to be challenged in her relationships. Startling herself that she was thinking "relationship," she sat up. Bing peeked around the corner of the bedroom door and meowed irritably. Grateful for the diversion from her disturbing thought, she scooped him up and made her way to the kitchen.

After feeding the cats, her curiosity led her to the computer where she opened the website link that Neely had sent her on the ferry and found herself looking at the cover of the *Virginia Quarterly Magazine* where her latest short story had been published. Twenty minutes later, she sat overwhelmed by the piece, knowing it had come from a deep well within Neely, yet she had made it so universal. The language was stunning, the structure was masterful, the point driven home so unassumingly from the very first word that she realized it slipped the rug right out from under you when you reached the final sentence, leaving you standing on nothing but your own emotions.

She wanted to tell Neely what she thought before the goose bumps settled, and sat down to email her, but found one from her instead. She hesitated to open it in case it was in reply to the chapters she'd sent earlier. She wasn't nearly in Neely's league as a writer. Finally, she clicked on it.

Okay, wow...you should've sent that novel out. I can see what yr trying to do w/rewrites and it'll work. But I will be honest. You've lost some of yr elasticity, but technique and style come back, it's like batting practice. I would be more than happy to edit for you while you work. I've already made some changes in margins. May I send them? Also, noted some ideas. We could work together one night a wk, like Tues? No football on then. I checked.

Charley wasn't sure if she was being rescued or if Neely was merely being kind. Either way, she was going to grab the life preserver, figuring Neely wouldn't waste her time if there wasn't something there.

I would love your help. Yes, send changes! And your story knocked me out. I want to read more. See you Monday.

Charley sat at the computer waiting, and a few minutes later, Neely's edits arrived. She opened the attachment and began reading.

Chapter Eight

The weather channel reported a cool morning with a bracing breeze. Charley's open windows confirmed it. She had to admit fall was really here as she slipped a pair of khakis over her bathing suit and draped a sweater over her shoulders. She and Brooke just might have hit the last perfect day of Indian summer for their impromptu hike yesterday. Heading to the Y, she began a mental to-do list. Emily was at the top, back after her bout with the flu. A call to her mother would be next.

Standing outside the doors for a few minutes, Charley watched Neely at the desk and felt a sense of awe at her creative skills. She liked her, of that she was certain. Neely was funny, kind, and intelligent. And handsome. And so young. But she couldn't lead her on when it was becoming obvious to her that it was the writer in Neely who was captivating her. After all, it wasn't *her* face Charley saw when she closed her eyes at night. She was going to have to address that.

She walked into the building, aware of what had changed between them, but unsure of how to handle it.

"Hey."

"Hey yourself."

"It was probably too late for you to look at my edits last night—"

"No, it wasn't. They were…you're brilliant."

Neely smiled. "Workin' with good material. You okay for getting together Tuesday nights? That is, if you really do want my help. I don't want to intrude on your process if you don't."

"Yes, I do!" Charley jumped at Neely's offer. "I want whatever you can give me."

Neely's grin shifted the landscape.

"About the work. Flirt!" Charley headed for the stairs, Neely's laughter following her.

Forgoing laps, she left right after class, knowing Emily would've come in early loaded down with receipts and notes not only from the trip, but from the days spent at home nursing the flu. She'd managed to send a barrage of emails to Charley concerning meetings she needed moved around and ones to set up for the remainder of the week and had even phoned her Monday and Tuesday. It was clear from her gravelly voice and foggy demeanor, though, that the antibiotics were laying her low, but she'd promised to be in today. Charley knew Emily well enough to know she'd be in fighting form regardless of how she looked or felt, so she wasn't surprised to see her standing in her office door looking crisp and chic in a gray pinstriped suit and gray heels, two fat files in her hand.

"Don't hate me," she said, handing the files off to Charley.

Her bag still on her shoulder, Charley riffled through the first file, which was full of receipts. "Listen, Lady Bountiful, if you didn't take all these trips and pick up the tab everywhere, I might not have a job, so don't apologize. How are you feeling?" Charley set her bag down, put the first file on the desk, and opened the other one to peruse the contents.

"Like shit, but I couldn't watch any more of those annoying morning shows. Plus, if I'm keeping food down, I can't justify staying in bed."

"All right, well, we all thank you for bringing in your germs. What's this other file?"

"I'm not contagious anymore." Emily looked over Charley's shoulder, pushing a piece of her modified pompadour that had fallen down back into place. "These are notes from some of the London meetings that I need you to transcribe pronto. I have to go to Abu Dhabi in two weeks, and everything I need for that trip is in those notes. I'm already way behind the eight ball because of this damn flu."

"Abu Dhabi? Care to share what's going on in the Middle East?"

She glanced around like she wanted to make sure she couldn't be overheard. "I realize I should've told you. It's a huge new start-up, possibly a takeover for us, but a merger for sure. That's what the London trip was really about. Donnie and I secured most of the deal, now we've got to sew it up for Hans. Come into my office, though. There's something I want to go over."

Charley stowed her bag under her desk, wondering if she should be worried, and picked up the log and a pen. Mergers weren't necessarily good news for employees like her. And she had never liked Hans Wolff, their CEO. Brought in by the board several years ago to consolidate things, his first move had been to ax three of the conglomerate's oldest companies and their many employees. The stock had risen, but Charley knew that what had been lost could never be quantified. And it had become patently clear in the ensuing years that he didn't care about his employees.

Sitting in an almost formal manner, Emily thanked Charley for unpacking the last of the boxes that her previous employer had finally sent over right after she'd gone to London. "I can't believe it took them nine months to clear the last of my things, those sons of bitches. Anyway, you left this one."

"It was marked 'personal,'" Charley replied, noticing that it had been opened.

Emily slid out a framed photo and handed it to Charley. It was of a very handsome woman, about Emily's age, with short jet-black hair and intense light blue eyes. Charley hoped her noncommittal expression held, not sure what was coming next, but, her gaydar having pinged on Emily months ago, she suspected her boss might be coming out to her.

"That's Terry, my wife. We've been together ten years."

Charley nodded; she was right.

"I asked her to call on my cell phone until I had my bearings here and with you. My last assistant had a problem taking Terry's calls. Had a problem with us."

"I'm sorry. That should never happen."

"Hmm. In a perfect world." Emily looked down at her hands in her lap, and then back up at Charley. "I told HR that couldn't be the case here. But I've sensed it won't be."

"No, it won't."

She nodded. "Then Terry will be calling on my direct line now."

"As she should."

"Good. I thought you'd be okay with it. Nothing seems to ruffle you."

"'Impossible to ruffle' is, I believe, at the top of my job description."

"I think the building could be burning around you and you'd go right to the fire extinguisher without a second thought for yourself, wouldn't you?"

Charley laughed.

"That's why…" Emily picked up an envelope on her desk and bounced the corner of it on the blotter. "I have something else here for you." She handed it to Charley.

Charley slit the envelope, took out a piece of paper, and unfolded it. Reading it, she blinked several times, speechless.

"When I first signed on, I told HR that I needed a crackerjack assistant, the deal being that I would cycle through assistants until I found the right one, but that when I did, he or she should be fairly compensated for what I'd be asking in the way of time, temperament, and loyalty. Someone clearly did their homework to match us up."

Charley was still stunned at the amount of the raise. "Thank you."

"Well, you may not want to thank me down the road. This is my way of putting a pair of golden handcuffs on you. It comes with a fifth week of vacation. You'll be earning all of it. But this stays right here. No one else on our team is receiving further compensation until well into next year."

Charley nodded.

"Now, let's talk about the Middle East."

An hour later, Charley was making calls to the new venture in Abu Dhabi, connecting with the assistants she'd be working with, most of whom were British or German; she appreciated how organized they were. No matter what the outcome of the merger, she already knew some of these men and women would become part of her extensive worldwide network of assistants she could call on for almost anything at almost any time.

That evening, on her walk to the pool, her mind was on tomorrow night's date with Neely. Until she wondered if Joanna would be here, and all thoughts of Neely disappeared. The internal excitement hit her. In the locker room, her favorite row was empty. She went right to the last row, though, closed her eyes for a second, and turned the corner. Joanna wasn't there. Then Charley remembered that she was working tonight and would be tomorrow night as well.

At the Amish market after class, she picked up dinner and went right to the computer to edit Sunday's work. Bob was curled up on the desk, one paw draped across the keyboard as if claiming it his territory. He looked her up and down unblinkingly and Charley laughed at his show of ego, shooing him off the desk. Just as she was getting to work, her phone dinged. She checked it and found it was a text from Neely.

Neely: *pick you up fri night again?*

She hesitated. But she knew what she wanted. *Can we go out to dinner instead?*

Neely: *??*

Would be nice to talk, just the two of us.

Neely: *k, gd idea.*

Charley breathed a sigh of relief. She couldn't have faced another night in a noisy club, or another second of Stacey. Her phone dinged again. Neely had sent the name and address of a restaurant in Hell's Kitchen, and a clock face that read seven o'clock.

Terrific. See you there.

Neely: *no, c u there.*

Charley was confused. Had she missed something? She sent Neely a question mark.

Neely: *abbrevs r faster.*

Charley was a little astonished. She wasn't used to being corrected, and most definitely not used to how Neely's generation handled social media. But she sent back a thumbs-up emoji. A moment later, Neely replied with a smiley face and the kiss lips.

A half hour after kickoff of the Raiders-Broncos game, Charley took a break, turned on the TV, checked the score, and brought her swim bag to the bathroom to hang up her suit. She noticed the message light blinking on her phone. Pressing play, she expected to hear her mother.

"Charley," the familiar voice spoke quietly, "please don't hit erase before you hear all of this message. I need your help. Otherwise, I wouldn't be calling. Please call me back." Hearing the note of fear in her voice, Charley reached for the pad and pen by the phone as Tricia left her number. After a moment's hesitation, she erased the message, ripped the sheet off the pad, balled it up, and hurled it into the trash can. She was still staring at the phone when it rang again. Brooke's name came up on caller ID, but Charley was frozen on the bed.

"Hey, pick up, I know you're there. I want to watch the game with you."

Charley picked up.

"You up for the game?"

"Yeah, sure."

"Uh-oh. What's wrong?"

Agitation bubbled below the surface of Charley's skin. "Tricia called." The anger she hadn't allowed herself to feel when she'd heard Tricia's voice came through her like a backdraft, and it blew a hole in the wall she'd spent the last three years carefully constructing around her emotions. "One fucking phone call! That's all it took, Brooke!" Charley could hardly breathe she was so angry. "Why does she think it's okay to call me? Does she know what it would cost me to have to deal with her again?" She wanted to throw something or fling open the window and scream.

"What does she want? What did she say?"

Charley struggled to control her voice. "I don't know. She left a message, something about needing my help."

"Okay, take a deep breath and sit down."

"She left her number. I know she's going to call again."

"Then let's talk about what you're going to do when she does."

Charley began to breathe little by little, knowing Brooke was throwing her a line and would pull her back in. She picked Tricia's number out of the trash.

CHAPTER NINE

The next morning, Charley handed her ID over the counter to Neely. Neither one of them acknowledged that they'd be seeing each other tonight. They simply exchanged glances, and as she headed for the stairs, Charley laughed at the feeling of covert flirtation she hadn't felt in years.

At work, Charley immediately knew something was wrong. Eavesdropping on Emily's phone conversations, she gathered that there had been a fight between her and Donnie in Hans's office early this morning. Emily hadn't come out on the winning end. She decided to hold her counsel and let Emily come to her if it warranted bringing her in on the problem. It occurred to her that office politics were just as bad as lesbian drama, and there could be just as much on the line.

Charley dashed home from work to get ready for the date with Neely. She wanted to make sure tonight was simply a laid-back evening and that her attire said nothing more than "friends," so she opted for jeans, sneakers, and a button-down. Shortly before the appointed meeting time, she stepped off the crosstown bus into the Hell's Kitchen neighborhood that had been her home away from home thirty years ago.

Looking around at the stores and buildings, it seemed like everything had changed. Her first job out of college had been at a hardware store nearby, a placeholder until she could break into the corporate world. It was now a vegan restaurant. And she had spent many nights in bars and clubs up and down these streets with her friends who had lived here before it became the gentrified Clinton, before the AIDS epidemic. The clubs were all gone now, those friends long dead, part of the reason she never came to this neighborhood anymore. She didn't want those memories.

Down the street, she noticed the Westway Diner. It seemed to be the only holdover from that time.

She spotted Neely a block away, the black leather biker jacket unmistakable, especially with Neely's cherry-striped curls spread over the shoulders. She had on a sheer white shirt beneath the jacket, tucked into a pair of black jeans, a black bra visible underneath the shirt. Neely's kiss was tender, the desire clear in her eyes. Charley began to worry about how best to distance the possibility of anything physical between them without losing the friendship that was fast becoming important to her.

"Wait, don't move," Neely said, her arms still around Charley's waist. She kissed her neck, inhaling. "I can't get enough of that perfume. Are you ever going to tell me what it is?"

"Maybe. But not tonight." Charley disengaged herself from Neely's arms and held open the door of the restaurant. "Tonight, I want to talk about your writing process. That short story you got published was exquisite."

Neely smiled ruefully. "I was pretty sure when I was writing it that it was good. Yeah, sure, we can talk process."

"And tonight, I pick up the tab because I asked for the change of venue."

Neely nodded. "I won't fight you tonight."

"Good, because I wouldn't let you." A waiter led them to a table in the window. "I remember how tight things were when I was in school."

"But you had Tricia."

"Doesn't mean I let her help me. Or that she would have." Charley looked over the small menu.

"But you were a couple."

"With separate financial lives."

"No, come on. Really?"

"She was particular about her money. And I would never have let her pay my way. It was too important to me to prove that I was independent."

"This blows my mind. And scares me. I didn't think couples did that."

"Well, I did, we did. I never wanted to be beholden to her. She was always going to outstrip me financially. I will admit, the times I got laid off in the eighties and nineties, she ended up supporting me, but she got something in return." Charley arched an eyebrow.

"Oh, I'm not going to touch that..."

She smiled and shook her head. "Whenever I landed a new job, she got a very expensive piece of jewelry with my first paycheck. Diamonds were her drug of choice, so I supplied whenever I could."

"Wow. I can't imagine not sharing my money with my wife."

Charley was floored by what she perceived as Neely's naiveté, but recovered as quickly as she could.

"So...what is *your* drug of choice?" Neely asked.

"The beach. Any time of year."

"You did tell me you're a beach junkie. And you've used the setting to maximum effect in your novel. Good, evocative."

"That means a lot...thanks."

"Let me look this over," Neely said, waving the menu, "and then I can talk about another idea I had for your last chapter."

Charley studied her, trying to fathom where the writer in her came from, and where she was going. When Neely looked up, Charley fiddled with her silverware for a moment, the question on her mind a difficult one. "Why did you take a break from your novel? I know you're sending short stories out to websites and contests, but they don't pay, do they?"

"Some do. Ultimately it doesn't amount to anything more than good PR and a fishing lure for an agent."

"But are you jeopardizing the bigger picture? I'd hate to think you're making a mistake by putting that novel down."

"I'm not. It's not writer's block like you, if that's what you're worried about."

For a moment, Charley felt like she'd been slapped in the face, although she knew Neely hadn't meant it that way.

Neely reached into her pocket and handed Charley a flash drive. "This is the first half. No one but my professor has seen it. So, as someone said to me recently, be gentle." Neely smiled sheepishly.

"You're really trusting me with this?" Charley slipped the drive into her jacket pocket and zipped it up. "I'm honored."

"Don't stop your work too long to read mine."

Once they'd ordered, the conversation turned to the art of writing and Charley questioned Neely about her work habits, her trade secrets, and many other things born of her own frustrations with her manuscript of late. Before she realized it, the check arrived at the table and the waiter hinted that with a line out the door, he needed their table.

Heading up Ninth Avenue, they moved from one topic to another, agreeing, disagreeing, finding common ground and the occasional chasm that Charley realized their age difference couldn't bridge. When they threaded their way up Tenth Avenue looking in store windows and car showrooms, it was clear to Charley that neither of them wanted to leave the other's company. She sensed she'd have to make the first move to call it an evening. Soon, however, Neely guided them toward Twelfth Avenue.

"I get the feeling you know where we're going," Charley said.

"I thought we could sit on the bleachers at the baseball field. It's such a beautiful night, you wouldn't know it was late September."

Neely was right. After the cool days earlier in the week, it was almost like a summer night again. A game was in progress when they got there, so they settled in to watch among a handful of spectators in the stands. Half an hour later, the game ended, and everyone drifted out of the park, leaving Neely and Charley alone in the middle of the bleachers. They sat in contemplative silence for a couple of minutes until a few of the lights around the perimeter of the park buzzed statically and blinked out.

"I think that's the universe telling me I need to say good night. I've had a wonderful evening, but I need to get home." Charley stood up.

"Do you, though? Need to go?"

For a minute, her resolve wavered.

"We could still go downtown and join everyone in the club. It's only eleven."

Charley laughed and touched Neely's face. "I have an admission to make. My clubbing days are limited." She took Neely's hand. "Come on. Help me down."

Neely walked down a step ahead of her, holding her hand up, steadying her.

"Look, we could do something else," she said when they reached the lawn and Charley started walking toward the path leading to the gate.

"Such as?"

Neely pulled her into the shadows under the bleachers and kissed her. It was one of those long, slow kisses that made her stomach drop like an elevator. When Neely pulled back to look at her, she couldn't even speak, unable to remember the last time she'd been kissed like that. Intoxicated, she grabbed the lapels of Neely's jacket, so Neely kissed her again, her lips lingering until Charley could hardly breathe. As she skimmed across Charley's jaw, kissing slowly down her neck and throat, Charley pulled Neely's shirt out of her pants and ran her hands up Neely's back, feeling the strong muscles move beneath her touch. Neely unbuttoned Charley's shirt and tugged at it, and all she could do was moan in response. Taking that as a green light, Neely wrenched her shirt open and continued kissing her across her collarbone and down the rise of her breasts, putting both hands on them, her thumbs pressing into her nipples through the lace of her bra. Charley involuntarily arched into her, slipping her hands down the back of Neely's jeans to her buttocks. Neely's hand responded in kind down the back of Charley's jeans, pulling her to her at the same time as she slid her tongue into Charley's mouth and her other hand into Charley's bra, her fingers hunting a nipple. Charley didn't recognize the sound that broke its way out of her throat, but she thrust her hands farther into Neely's jeans chasing the twin globes of the taut ass she'd admired a number of times on the dance floor last weekend. Neely's tongue moved deeper and faster, and her hand made an inroad right between Charley's legs.

A police siren shrieked two short blips. Charley jumped, the two of them broke apart, and she searched the street for the source of the interruption. A squad car rolled slowly outside the park, its lights revolving.

Neely hurriedly buttoned Charley up. "I *am* so sorry. I didn't know they patrolled like this."

"The park is closing," came a female voice through the car's bullhorn system. "You'll have to exit now."

"Oh, thank God," Neely said shakily. "I thought they saw what we were doing and were going to ticket us."

Charley giggled. "Lewd and indecent behavior?"

"Something like that," Neely replied. "My God, I'd be mortified."

"I think we're fine. Considering what goes on in this city, I'm sure we're a nice break from the murder and mayhem these cops deal with on a daily basis."

Neely laughed. "Probably. I didn't think of it that way."

They walked toward the front gate, a cop waiting to lock it behind them.

"Thank you, Officer," Neely said to the woman, moving past her.

"We hated to interrupt you ladies. It looked as if you were having fun, but we have to close the park." The cop winked at her and Charley smiled back, wondering if she was a sister.

"Where to now?" Neely asked after the cops drove off. "Your place or mine?"

"Ohhh…" Charley wasn't sure how to handle Neely's assumption. The conflagration she'd started against the bleachers still resonated and had made Charley yearn for a night in bed beneath a strong woman who could take charge. But that careful core that had become her guide over the years poked its head up, effectively silencing Brooke's advice to walk on the wild side. At least for tonight. She needed to sort out her feelings, needed to make sure that when she went to bed with Neely…if…it was the right thing to do in that moment. For both of them.

"You're bailing, aren't you?" Neely asked.

Charley nodded.

"Did I jump the gun? Did I push you?"

"No. I…" Charley ran her hands over Neely's leather jacket lapels.

"You need time. I get that," Neely said softly.

"I don't know if you do. Maybe sex means different things to us."

Neely cocked her head, a questioning look in her eyes.

"I don't think I'm as casual about it as I was when I was younger." She felt safe confiding in Neely after all the ground they'd covered getting to know each other.

"Okay." Neely nodded. "Well, why don't we work together Tuesday night in the library, like I promised you, and have dinner next Friday and talk about what sex means to us."

She had no idea what that conversation would look like, but she'd have a whole week to think about it. And she wanted to work with Neely in person on Tuesday after everything they'd talked about over dinner.

At the M50 crosstown bus stop, Neely protectively put her arm around Charley. On the ride to Second Avenue, she picked up the thread of a conversation they hadn't finished earlier, and Charley was grateful for how easily they fell back into it.

Chapter Ten

In the elevator, Charley pulled her phone out of her pocket and texted Brooke. *Just got home. We didn't go dancing. I took her out to dinner. We talked and walked.* Brooke sent her a scowling emoji. Charley walked down the hall to her apartment and leaned against the wall by her door. *And then we made out like randy teenagers under the bleachers of that baseball field on Twelfth Ave. But the neighborhood police patrol broke up our session, and I sent her home. I am officially an old fart.* Her phone rang an instant later and Charley laughed out loud as she unlocked her door.

"You're joking, right? Please tell me you're joking," Brooke said.

"Nope. I got possessed by the devil for an instant, but I'm not ready yet for a night in bed with her. If I even cross that line."

"Please cross it. Just for one night. I can't believe I'm rooting for the security guard here."

"Brooke." Charley had entered the bedroom, and the blinking message light on the phone caught her attention.

"Okay, okay, the writer."

"No. My message light is blinking."

There was a moment of silence between them.

"If my mother really needed me, she'd have called my cell phone."

"Okay, so find out who it is. If you need me, call me. Otherwise, you have to call us in the morning and tell us every dirty detail of this date tonight."

Tossing her cell phone on the bed, she hit the message button.

"Hey, babe, it's me."

Charley couldn't possibly miss the sadness in Tricia's voice this time. "I left you a message yesterday. I guess I didn't expect you to call me back, but I do need you to. I can't discuss this over the phone, but...I need your help. Please call me."

Charley smoothed out the crumpled paper with Tricia's number on it and reluctantly picked up the receiver, but then looked at the time on the clock and put it back down again. *Where is Reagan? Why is she calling me?* And then it dawned on her: Reagan must have left Tricia. Or vice versa. *I hope that's not what this is about...*

As she brushed her teeth, she couldn't help picturing Reagan and Tricia the night she'd stumbled upon them sitting at a table in the window of that Chelsea restaurant. She'd known immediately that they were lovers. Unnoticed, she had turned the corner and thrown up in a trash can. Hours later, she'd confronted Tricia, gotten the confession that she was fucking her new young associate, slammed out of the apartment, and taken a cab to Brooke's.

Why do I do this to myself? Needing to staunch the rising stress level, she headed for the cats, who were curled up on the bed, tail to tail, two mismatched bookends. She pulled the covers back slowly so as not to dislodge them, slid into bed and kissed them each on a furry shoulder. Bing sighed. Bob shifted and opened one eye. Finally on the verge of falling asleep, Charley pushed aside the past and felt Neely pinning her against the bleachers, her lips setting her on fire, her hands adding fuel to that fire, her own hands full of Neely's luscious ass, and she reached beneath the covers to quell the insistent pulsing that arose between her legs

In the morning, with the college football countdown show providing background "music," Charley called Brooke and put the phone on speaker mode so that Annie could hear about the date, too.

"Are you listening to those stupid talking football heads?" Brooke asked. "They're so full of hot air."

"I have to listen to something while I clean the lab experiment in my refrigerator. I have no idea how this happened, but even the cats left the room when I discovered it this morning."

"Oh, thanks so much for sharing that."

Annie laughed. "Never mind that, Mrs. Clean. How was the date?"

An hour later, feeling like she had shared almost every minute of the date, her pantry shelves cleaned in addition to the refrigerator, Charley finally hung up, made lunch, and sat down at her computer to work on the next set of chapters. She lost track of time until the cats reminded her they needed sustenance. Charley made dinner for all three of them, watching some of the Boise State game as she ate hers, and then went back to work again.

Sunday morning, she felt the effects of sitting too long the day before and did something completely out of character: she left everything where it was, picked up her coat and canvas bag, slipped her last several chapters into it, and got on the subway to Woodside for the train to Long Beach. It was a perfect fall day, a cool seventy degrees, blue sky as far as you could see, and hardly anyone else on the train with her. She walked the beach from one end of the small town to the other, allowing her thoughts to run rampant without making any tidy conclusions, which was anathema to her very nature.

She sifted through problems like her mother's increasing needs and her brother Robert's recent request for more help from her. *I'm going to have to give him more of my time, but when?* She worried about the possible merger Emily was working on. That generous pay raise suggested everything would be fine, but what if it wasn't? Parts of her world that had been safe for so long suddenly seemed to be in flux. And now her previously nonexistent love life had become a thing. She climbed the ramp to the boardwalk and sat on a bench, turning so that the sun's late afternoon rays hit her shoulders and back. *Neely doesn't fit into a neat box I can tie up with a pretty ribbon.* As confused as she was about dating her, she was reluctant to lose the sense of life at full throttle that it was giving her. And she didn't know enough about Joanna to know what might happen tomorrow when they met for coffee. What if her hunch proved wrong? At least she'd have a new friend. Two new friends. She was going to have to do something she rarely did. Let go, and let things happen.

She took the chapters she'd brought with her out of her bag. *This is one thing I can control.*

CHAPTER ELEVEN

A nyone walking down the main hall of the Legal Department could see Emily Dunn's big glass office at the far end, and as Charley made her way to her desk, Emily was sitting there staring into space, a piece of paper in her hand. Charley sensed trouble, dropped her canvas bag on her chair, and went in. "What's up?"

Emily looked at her absently. "Hans contacted another company to help with the Middle East deal, but Donnie went and screwed things up with their CEO." Emily rubbed her eyes. "God, Donnie is such a stupid prick, and I had no idea this was going on. If it's what I think it is, Hans didn't even clear it with the board. And now he's tasked me with fixing everything. Trouble is, I don't know anyone over there."

"Where?"

Emily handed the piece of paper to Charley.

She looked at the information in front of her. It was a financial breakdown of their biggest competitor. "Okay."

"Something doesn't feel right. But beyond that, I'm not sure how to get in the door."

"Emily, you know everyone in this business."

She hung her head. "What I should've said is I've burned so many bridges getting *here* that I'm sure no one will answer my calls."

"Who do you need to see there?"

"Paul Whitney, the CEO."

Charley went out to her desk, opened her digital Rolodex, and dialed the number that popped up on the screen. A moment later, Emily was leaning over her shoulder reading the screen, and Charley felt her freeze. She was amused by the surprised look on her boss's face as she secured her an appointment with the CEO and a date for drinks with his assistant for herself. "You're in," she said, hanging up. "Nine thirty Wednesday morning."

"Shit. How do you know Paul Whitney's assistant?"

"Worked with Payton years ago in advertising. My Rolodex is full of assistants I never lose touch with or track of. Never know when you're going to need to pull a rabbit out of a hat. Consider Payton said rabbit."

"You've never burned a bridge in your life, have you?"

"I wouldn't go that far."

"Wow. Okay, well, I need to think about what I'm putting together for this guy." Emily went back into her office, then came out again. "How does Payton know he'll see me? Considering Donnie's utter incompetence, I'd think he'd cancel me in a heartbeat when he spots the appointment in his calendar."

Charley snorted. "Payton's been working with him for fifteen years. If she put the meeting in his calendar, he's going to trust that there was a damn good reason. Besides, she knew I was begging. I owe her now."

Emily sat down at her desk, got up again, and walked to the doorway. "Bring me the receipt for your drinks when you meet with her. I'll expense them."

"You know that's not kosher, don't you?"

"I have an assistant who's good at burying that sort of stuff deep in the expense reports," Emily said as she returned to her desk.

Charley laughed.

An hour later, she had the notes for Emily's presentation to Paul Whitney. Looking them over, she realized Emily was angling for a joint rollout with this new digital company they needed help with, positioning it as a win over the possible takeover Hans had obviously sent Donnie in to sell to Paul. *She's trying to save us. Hans was going to give us away, and she knew that.*

Emily's accompanying instructions made her smile. *Work your magic, make this sing.*

It took her all day to fashion the ten-minute PowerPoint, going back and forth with Emily as they tried to get it right, adding and deleting fade-ins and experimenting with an animated pie chart, finally settling on revolving financial charts, all the while trying to hide her surprise and fear at the information indicating how much trouble the company was experiencing, knowing that that was why Hans might've been trying to unload it. By the time she left for the pool, she had a headache and was exhausted on many levels.

Charley didn't see the telltale blue Yale lock anywhere when she arrived in the locker room, and the sensation she experienced in the pit of her stomach wasn't good. Joanna hadn't seemed like the kind of woman who would leave someone high and dry over a simple cup of coffee. But then, it wasn't like Charley knew her at all. What if the whole date thing had, in the end, scared her off?

Hoping she was just going to show up later than usual, Charley headed down to the pool and the comfort of Anita's regimentation, opting for the heavier blue Styrofoam water weights so she'd have to keep focused on the class. She knew she'd pay for that choice tomorrow.

Back upstairs an hour later, there was still no blue lock in sight. On any locker. Charley checked the whole room. Should she wait? Get dressed and sit in the little TV area for a few minutes? And how long should she wait before feeling foolish? Charley didn't want to get angry because maybe there was a really good reason Joanna didn't show up. And making plans for coffee wasn't exactly ironclad. She got dressed and went home.

In the kitchen, Charley dropped the salad she'd bought at the Amish Market on the counter and headed for the bathroom to toss her suit into the sink. The blinking red message light caught her attention as she passed the phone on her night table. She wasn't sure she wanted to find out who it was.

"Hey, Charley. I'm sorry I'm stalking you, but I need you. It's something serious. Please call."

She sat on the bed and tried to measure her feeling of inadequacy at not calling against her anger that Tricia was trying to contact her, and then got mad that she even considered herself inadequate. Whatever Tricia wanted, the call was going to be hard. She sat on the bed for a few minutes, rehearsing in her head what she and Brooke had talked about, and picked up the phone to dial, but before she hit the last number, she hung up.

Instead, she rinsed out her suit and walked out to the kitchen, fed the cats, picked up a fork and the salad, and went to her computer to bury herself in editing and reshaping the next batch of chapters.

❖

"Are you ready for tonight?" Neely asked when Charley handed her ID over the desk Tuesday morning.

"Yes."

"There's a room I work in at Hunter Library. No one seems to know about it, so I have it to myself. I'll meet you downstairs with a guest pass at eight. Is that okay? I've read the next five chapters, so we can take a look at my notes and decide if they work for your overall vision."

Neely looked so serious as she handed the ID back. Charley would have to reconcile this mentor with the woman who had flirted relentlessly with her all year and then set her on fire under the bleachers Friday night. Neely was more complicated than Charley had realized, and she wondered, again, what she was doing dating her.

The morning slipped by with Charley working through everything Emily thought she would need for tomorrow's meeting with Paul Whitney. When she finally looked up, Emily was coming down the hall with two bags from Chop't, the salad place around the corner.

"You've done yeoman's work lately so I'm treating you to lunch. You go to this place all the time, don't you? Come on in and we can go over what we've got before my two o'clock."

Toward the end of lunch, Emily kicked off her heels, tucked her feet up on the couch, and began dishing about many of the company men. Charley had never seen this side of her boss. It was amusing, and it also made her feel a little more secure. A good relationship with your boss wasn't something that came easily.

"Of course, all this stays right here," she said when she finally uncurled herself and stepped back into her heels.

"I should be horrified that you even asked," Charley said.

❖

Neely was in the lobby of the library, pass in hand, when Charley walked through the doors.

"They all smell the same, don't they?" Charley said as they stepped into the elevator. "Academia. Books. Leather bindings. Even the dust."

"And now it'll smell a little bit like you..." Neely hooked her finger into the front of Charley's shirt and kissed her, but when the doors opened, she became all business again. Sitting in the small space that contained a table, a chair, and the old overstuffed leather chair Neely admitted she'd dragged up from the second floor reading room, they discussed her notes, the edits, and the cuts she'd made that tightened the chapters and telescoped Charley's story line. They also looked at Charley's technique and style. She hadn't had anyone to discuss those things with in a long time and reveled in it.

"What you've done is amazing," Charley said.

"I keep telling you, I'm working with good material. And you're getting that muscle back."

Hours later, when Charley collected everything together to leave, Neely caught her up in her arms and kissed her, and like she had on Friday night, Charley surrendered to her soft lips, this time kissing Neely back, wrapped in the intimacy of the moment.

"Am I seeing you Friday night?" Neely asked, Charley still in her arms.

Charley hesitated. Closing the door on Karen had opened a window she hadn't known was there. So much in her world had shifted, the biggest surprise being Neely and what was happening between them. There hadn't been any contemplative time to iron it out, to figure out what she really wanted. Or what would be right for both of them. Friendship, yes; sleeping with her, a very possible yes, although the prospect of that hard young body against hers was daunting every time she thought about it despite knowing she wanted it. And what would the repercussions be? At this point in her life, the responsibility to consider that was paramount; she knew the outcome, emotional and practical, would never be on Neely's mind. For this moment, though, the plausibility of another Friday out was off-putting.

"Or do you want to punt to next weekend?"

She closed her eyes for a moment and nodded. She didn't know if Neely instinctively understood she needed time, or if she just thought she was tired, but either way, Charley wanted the time to herself again.

Once she was back in her apartment, she sat down at the computer to begin working on the new edits, stopping only long enough to get a bottle of seltzer and a pint of raspberries from the refrigerator. Bob picked his way over the keyboard when he saw her coming back, attempting to insert himself front and center, but she put him on the floor and popped some of the fruit into the seltzer bottle. Charley loved the way the berries bubbled and exploded when she flattened them with her tongue after they'd been sitting in the effervescence for a while. It was a sweet release. The first two berries rolled up the neck of the bottle, and Charley closed her eyes, the eruption filling her mouth, dripping down her chin and fizzing up her nose.

And suddenly she was under the covers, way down under the covers with Joanna. She froze, a tangy raspberry crushed on her tongue. *Why is it with her and not Neely?* She sat back, confused by her own mental confluence. How had this woman she didn't even know yet become the face of her sensual meanderings? Swallowing slowly, Charley eased the berries down her throat. She wiped her chin and reluctantly scrolled to the beginning of the next chapter.

On the way to work Wednesday morning, Charley texted Emily. *Good luck. Knock him dead.*

A moment later, she had a short *Thx* in reply.

Midmorning, Emily came down the hall with a small bag in her hand and set it on Charley's desk before continuing into her office and tossing her briefcase on the couch. Her coat and suit jacket followed.

Charley, right behind her, held up the bag. "La Maison du Chocolate? That can be good or bad."

Emily opened her arms wide. "I'm presenting to their board next week."

"That's huge."

"Well, I'm not out of the woods yet."

Charley hung Emily's coat and jacket on the back of her office door. "You're not selling this as the 'merger' Hans wants, are you?" She used air quotes, wanting to make sure Emily knew what she meant.

In the long moment of silence that hung there, Charley thought she might've made a mistake. Until Emily folded her hands, prayer-like, under her chin. "You understood my presentation, then...I didn't come here to be part of the dissolution of this company. I was brought in to save it. Hans has been a less than stellar captain of industry. We're actually in financial trouble here." She put her finger to her lips, and Charley understood. "And he can tuck his balls away if he wants to and arrange to palm us off on our competition right under the board's nose for a big payoff to *his* wallet, but..." Emily inhaled and let her breath out very slowly. "And I know I'm playing a risky game of chicken here, but if I win, which I'm pretty sure I will, the board will know what he's been up to, and what I had to do to stop him."

Oh my God...I was right. We were being offered up to the competition. "And the company will be yours?"

"Or the board could dismiss me for fiduciary negligence. Either way, before this all pans out, I'm taking you to dinner at the most expensive place you can think of because without your help, I couldn't have pulled this off so far. I have a feeling whether I succeed or not, Hans will try to fire me for insubordination and bury it before the board finds out, so we might as well make hay while the sun shines."

"Expensive I like." Charley grinned, although she was unsettled by Emily's forecast.

There was a cool edge to the evening air when Charley left the office for the Y Wednesday night. Zipping her fleece, she sighed. Winter was reaching for the calendar with tentative fingers.

Trying not to, she hoped to see Joanna's blue Yale lock on her usual locker. There hadn't really been a moment during the day to think about what she'd say to her, but now her mind went back to her walk on Long Beach on Sunday, and the realization that she just had to let go in certain cases, not something she did easily. Or at all. She made her way to the back bay of lockers and found Joanna sitting on the bench in her suit, her towel next to her, her eyes on the floor. Charley stood looking at her for a moment, still caught by her striking beauty. Then Joanna glanced up, saw Charley, and a mix of relief and anguish raced across her face, along with something Charley couldn't identify but that was followed by a blush.

"There you are. I'm so sorry!" Joanna stood up.

"Are you okay?" It was all she could think of to say in this moment. And she really did want to know if everything was all right.

Joanna's hands twitched awkwardly at her sides. Charley could tell she wanted to do something with them. "Irene lapsed into heart failure Sunday night and I had to rush her to the hospital. I stayed with her until she was stabilized yesterday morning. And then I realized I left you hanging Monday, but I had no way to contact you."

Charley closed her eyes. She'd foolishly made it all about her, barely considering that something could've gone wrong in Joanna's life. And of course, they didn't have each other's phone numbers. "Is she all right? Are you all right?"

"Yes, they stabilized her. They're keeping her until Friday."

"And you? Are you okay?"

"I'm fine. I just felt so bad. Do you know how many C, or Charley or anything resembling a Charley Owens there are in the online white pages? I even called information. I didn't think they existed anymore, but you can still call four-one-one. And the operator can still tell you that without an address or a proper name, she can't help you."

"You didn't have to—"

"I even went back to Irene's apartment when I left the hospital to see if she had your mother's phone number in her address book, and she had two of them, both crossed out, so I called the last one just in case and woke up some poor woman at eight fifteen in the morning. Not your mother, by the way."

Charley smiled at the thought of the poor woman being woken up, and at the persistence with which Joanna had tried to find her. "I'm sorry. I didn't mean to put you through such a wringer. I don't know why we didn't exchange numbers."

"Because we're idiots."

Charley got out her phone and handed it to Joanna, the back of it facing her. Joanna looked down at it and saw the tiny label with Charley's phone number on it. She laughed.

"You have your phone number on the back of your phone?"

"Yes, because I'm an idiot."

A look of surprise flashed across Joanna's face.

"When the ambulance crew who came for my mother last winter asked for my cell phone number, I went blank. I knew that could never happen again, so…" Charley shrugged.

Joanna shook her head sympathetically. "Been there, done that. Hold on." She tucked the phone under her arm and opened her locker, pulled her own phone out of her pants pocket, and sat down to add Charley to her contacts.

"You know, we could've done this when we actually *do* get together for that coffee," Charley suggested.

"Oh, no, because if one of us nearly drowns in the pool tonight and gets hauled out by ambulance, we'll still have no way of getting in touch with each other. Not hazarding that again."

Charley snorted. "I have no intention of drowning in the shallow end of the pool tonight."

"Yeah, well, Irene didn't have any intention of almost meeting her maker Sunday night, either."

Charley sobered up quickly. "Touché."

"I can get that coffee tonight if you still want to," Joanna said, glancing up at Charley. "Obviously, I'm not on duty."

"I'd love to," Charley said.

"You've had a tough week." The waiter set cups of coffee down in front of them, and Charley thanked him. "Maybe we should've gone out for a drink."

"Oh, I'm too tired for that. I'd fall flat on my face if I had a drink right now."

"Why didn't you say something? We could've done this next week. I should've realized."

"No, I proposed it. I wouldn't have done if I was that tired. Besides," Joanna said, studying Charley, "I really did feel bad. I never leave people hanging like that. You have to understand that about me."

The earnestness reflected on Joanna's face touched Charley. "You're as dependable as the sun coming up, aren't you?"

"Well...I have to be. I'm responsible for someone's life."

Charley smiled. "I'll bet you were like this long before you became a nurse." Pieces of the puzzle began to fall into place. She took in the light freckles sprinkled across Joanna's nose and cheeks and knew they were echoed on her neck, shoulders, and chest. She loved the crinkled lines at the corners of her eyes, the fading summer tan.

"Okay, yes. I come from a military background, so I learned growing up that when the watch bells chimed, you'd better be where you were supposed to be because someone's life just might depend on it."

"Wow. That's a lot for a kid, isn't it?"

"It was good training, a solid foundation for whatever I was going to do in life. And that reminds me." Joanna pointed her spoon at Charley. "You know, I have no idea what you do for a living. You come in with your suit already on under your clothes, and half the time you're in shorts. Didn't anyone tell you summer is over? Are you some kind of tech guru who makes her own hours?"

Charley laughed. "Very much the opposite." She told Joanna about her nine-to-five life, which, she pointed out, meant "nine to five" wherever Emily happened to be in her international travels.

Joanna sat back. "So, you're as dependable as the sun coming up, too, aren't you?"

Charley had never thought of it that way. "I'm what's called a gatekeeper. So I have to be right with her at every step."

"Well, I'll bet *you* were like this long before you went to work for *her*." Joanna stifled a yawn.

"Okay, that's it," Charley said. "You need to get home and get some rest."

"I know, but I'm having a good time," she protested.

"You say that like you didn't expect to."

"I'm not sure what I expected."

"On this 'not a date.'"

Joanna chuckled.

The waiter had dropped the tab on the table. Charley picked it up, a ten-dollar bill already in her hand and waved him back over.

"Hey, come on, let me put in for my coffee."

"It's the least I can do considering what you've just been through," Charley said.

Out on the sidewalk, Charley put on her coat. "Do you have far to walk?" she asked, hoping Joanna didn't notice the fishing expedition.

"I'm right down the street, Ninth Avenue. But it's a nice walk most nights. You?"

"I'm around the corner at First Avenue. And Ninth is not right down the street."

"Takes me less than half an hour. Unless it rains, it gives me time to unwind."

They looked at each other for a moment. The soft light from the streetlamp spilled around Joanna, and Charley was again taken by her arresting handsomeness, almost forgetting that she needed to say good night.

"Thanks for the coffee. I'll see you...next week, I guess?" Joanna asked.

"Yes. Monday night. Get some rest. And maybe text me, let me know how Irene is doing? And how you're doing?"

"I will. Thanks."

Joanna turned and disappeared down the street, and Charley watched her go until she couldn't see her anymore.

CHAPTER TWELVE

The end of the week was quiet enough in the office, with Emily spending hours preparing for her presentation to their competitor's board next week and giving Charley time to catch up on the kind of housekeeping she hated: filing, archiving, purging paperwork and e-files, and ordering supplies. It was the dreary but necessary cog-turning that could gum up the works if not done on a somewhat timely basis.

Friday night, she thought about plugging in the flash drive Neely had given her last weekend and beginning to read her novel, but she didn't have the concentration level she wanted to give it. Instead, she crawled into bed to watch the end of a college football game and the news. It felt good to do something so mundane. She read for a while afterward, and just as she was about to turn off the light, the buoy tone sounded on her phone. She picked it up expecting to see a snarky message from Brooke.

Joanna: *Patient home and doing well. Nurse not so bad, either.*

Charley smiled. *Terrific!*

Joanna: *Just realized you might've been asleep. Sorry!*

Charley sent back a wide-eyed, wide-awake emoji, and Joanna sent back one of a devilish nurse with a squirting needle in her hand.

Joanna: *I can give you something to take care of that.*

I'm good, thanks! Special relationship with the Sandman.

Joanna: *Really? We'll have to talk about that. I had a good time Weds. Drinks Mon.?*

Charley's stomach fluttered. *Yes.*

Joanna: *Good. Go find your Sandman.*

Charley pulled up the covers, savoring the unexpected moment. Then, not setting the alarm, she turned off the light.

When the phone rang, levitating her out of bed, she didn't know how long she'd been asleep. It took her a moment to focus on the hands of the clock on her nightstand. Six a.m. A call at this hour was never good. She thought it would be her mother, but then she saw the number. *Dammit.* "Hello."

"Charley, I'm so sorry to call you at this hour, but it was the only way I knew to get you to answer."

Short and determined, that was Brooke's advice. "I've answered, Tricia. What is it?"

"I...I need your help. During my physical three weeks ago, my doctor discovered something she didn't like and sent me for tests."

"Okay," Charley said as evenly as she could, although a wisp of fear snaked through her.

"Still unflappable, aren't you?"

Charley didn't respond.

"I always knew whatever was wrong would be all right when I heard you say 'okay' like that, that the news wouldn't bowl you over, that you'd handle it with me..."

"What happened with the tests, Tricia?" She kept her voice determinedly cool even as apprehension stole over her and long fingers of fear closed on her throat.

In the moment of silence between them, Charley heard Tricia struggling with her words. "They found stage four lung cancer, Charley. And I don't know what I'm going to do."

The air went right out of her, her pulse pounded, and her head buzzed. When the effects subsided a moment later, she tried to control the tears she felt welling up before she could say anything. She grabbed a tissue and sat up in the bed.

"Where is Reagan?"

"She left me. A year ago."

The confession exploded in Charley's head like cheap fireworks.

"Go ahead. You can laugh, say I told you so. You were right. I threw away twenty-five years for a couple of quick fucks. I'm surprised she stayed the two years. Probably only because I gave her everything she asked for, like a fool, until I didn't."

Under different circumstances, Charley *would* have laughed. She wondered what "everything" meant, even as she supposed Tricia had left herself open to it. "I'm sorry it turned out the way it did."

"You don't need to be kind, Charley, I'm not a charity case. I hurt you very badly. I'm sure you never want to see me again, and I wouldn't be surprised if you told me you hate me."

"I don't hate you, Trish." It was the first time she'd admitted to herself that she probably still loved Tricia on some level, and it hit her, in this moment, that that was what was behind the anger that she'd held on to for so long. Tricia had been her world. She had, indeed, grown up with her. But that was then. And now? Brooke had been right. The baggage was holding her back. Although it seemed she'd put at least one piece down after meeting Joanna, and another right after her first date with Neely. And kicked the rest to the curb when Neely had nearly made love to her under the bleachers. "I'm still angry, but I certainly don't hate you."

She could hear Tricia exhale in relief. "That's what I was hoping to hear. I wanted to know I could turn to you, and you wouldn't shut me out."

Charley sighed. "Tell me what you know. And what you need me to do."

Tricia walked her through the diagnosis, the follow-ups with her doctor, the team that had been assembled at Memorial Sloan Kettering, and the plan of attack they had laid out for her, so Charley took notes, trying not to be frightened by what she was hearing.

"Can you come with me on Wednesday to meet my medical team?"

"What time is the appointment?"

"Eight fifteen. I figured it was early enough that you could still get to the office on time."

Charley was already formulating how she would handle this with Emily.

"I know I'm asking a lot of you…"

"Let's just take it one step at a time, okay?"

"That's what I'm trying to tell you. I don't think we can. It's a big picture kind of thing. It's already engulfing me. And I know I'm going to suck you right in with me. I'm trying to apologize now for what I know isn't going to be easy."

"Okay. But we should still take it one step at a time."

"Charley, I'm not going to beat this," Tricia said quietly.

The tears rose again, and this time it was Charley struggling with her words. "Can you let me hear what the doctors have to say first?"

"Of course. I'm sorry. I shouldn't hit you with all of this at once."

"Do you...do you need me to come over this weekend?"

"No, but could we talk maybe Monday night? Watch the game together on the phone?"

"Yes. Give me your number so I have it now. And your email. Are you still working?"

"So far. You have my number. I called several times."

Charley didn't say anything. Tricia laughed. "You deleted me. You didn't keep the number, did you?"

"Well, you're the one who suggested I hated you." Charley picked up the crumpled paper with Tricia's number on it that she'd tossed onto her nightstand and smoothed it out.

"I got worried when you didn't call me back. I told you it was serious."

"That was wide open to interpretation. You didn't say what *serious* meant."

"I couldn't tell you what it was over the phone. Who leaves that kind of message, 'Hi, this is your ex, I'm dying of lung cancer, please call me.'"

"I can see that now. And please stop saying that. You can't tell me your doctors have said you're going to die."

"Doctors never say that. They fight even when you're on life support."

"If they're going to fight, you're going to fight. Do you understand me? I'm not signing up for anything else."

Tricia was silent.

"Oh, fuck, I'm signing up for everything, aren't I?"

Tricia sobbed, catching Charley off-guard. She wanted to reach through the phone to hold her.

"Tricia, I'm here now. I will get you through this." It hit Charley what finality those words might hold. Charley heard Tricia clear her throat and knew she was pulling herself back together.

"I'll call you Monday. You'll pick up?"

"Yes, smartass, I'll answer."

"I do love hearing you call me that again." Tricia gave Charley her address, too.

"Nice 'hood. Wow."

"It's where..." Tricia hesitated.

"Where Reagan wanted to live."

"I'm sorry..."

"Look, I think we have to stop apologizing for what's in the past now. There's too much we'll be dealing with going forward to let that get in the way."

"I will apologize til the day I—"

"No. No more apologies. Let's be done. You want me on board? We're done with that."

"Okay. Truce."

"Thank you. Monday night, then. Oh, wait." Charley couldn't believe she'd nearly forgotten Joanna's text asking to go out for drinks Monday. "Look, I may not be home until close to nine."

"Oh. Something going on?"

"Big presentation at work. Emily needs me on tap." So much easier than lying to Brooke.

"Wow. Your boss kind of owns you, doesn't she?"

"Not really. I like what I do."

"Okay, nine. And, Charley?"

"What?"

"I love you."

Charley closed her eyes to ward off the pain and found it surprisingly diminished. "I know."

Tricia hung up. Charley sat back against the pillows and reached for Bing as the tears came. Because she didn't expect them, because she thought she had better control, because she knew Tricia was now in her past in more ways than one, they swept her away. She cried into Bing's fur until he became alarmed and evacuated the bed with Bob in tow.

When the tears abated, she lay back and went over the conversation with Tricia. She knew she had, indeed, signed up for everything. She was suddenly overwhelmed, feeling at a loss and adrift again, but it wasn't from the same place she'd been when she'd left Tricia. That had felt akin to being alone on an ice floe in the Bering Sea, even with all the support from her friends. As she picked up the phone to call Brooke, the time on the alarm clock came into focus. Seven fifteen a.m. She couldn't call her at this hour.

Needing to get out of her head, Charley fed the cats and got to work cleaning the bedroom. It was way too early to move any furniture to chase dust bunnies, so Charley worked some of her tension off cleaning the moldings instead. *Then, I'll sit down at the computer and research "lung cancer." Then I'll call Brooke. After that, maybe I can jump out the window.*

A half hour into the research, Charley found herself fighting a stress headache and took some Advil. Staring out the window while waiting for it to work, she wondered how old the child would be now that Tricia had wanted to have. Or rather, that she'd wanted Charley to bear for them. But children had never been in her life plan. She'd fought her on the issue even as she put in applications for graduate school from Iowa to NYU, and she had lost the battle around the time she worried over the essay to Columbia University. Tricia's arguments wore her down so she struck the bargain: *If I don't get into school, we can get pregnant. But if I get in, no more talk about children.* Tricia had agreed. And Charley went to church to pray for a master's degree.

One of the many saints she entreated must've taken pity on her; she received the letter of acceptance from Columbia University on April Fool's Day. But Tricia had brought up the children question again right after Charley graduated, and she answered by taking her degree off the wall, handing it to Tricia, and walking out of the room. If she'd let the bargain go then, that child might be twelve or fourteen, would have weathered a nasty divorce, and would now possibly be facing young adulthood without one of her mothers. Charley wasn't sure she could've handled that.

At one minute past nine, Annie answered the phone. "You may get up early on a Saturday, but the rest of the world doesn't."

"I am so sorry, Annie. You know I wouldn't call at this hour unless it was important. Is she there?"

"I'm doin' pretty good, thanks. And you?"

"Ouch. Okay, I didn't think you wanted small talk."

"I'm busting you, sweetie. Hold on. She's actually in the shower. We've been up for a while."

A moment later, Brooke picked up. "Hey, what's up?"

"Hi. I'm sorry to interrupt your morning."

"Not interrupting. I finished putting a smile on Annie's face about an hour ago. You're cleaning, I'm sure. Unearth King Tut yet?"

"Tricia called me at six."

"Whoa. You really did unearth King Tut. And six a.m.? That's nasty. What is wrong with her? Did you carry out our plan?"

"I couldn't. It's far more serious than I thought. She has lung cancer, Brooke."

"Oh my God."

"Reagan left her a year ago. She's asking for my help."

Charley heard Brooke exhale. "This is bad. And I know the answer, but I'll ask anyway. What did you tell her?"

"Of course, I'll help her. I would hate myself if I didn't." Charley told her what she'd learned online and how overwhelmed she felt already.

"Look, we all despised her for what she did to you, but we will all be here for her. But really for you. And don't believe everything you read online. What hospital is she using?"

"Memorial Sloan Kettering." Charley related the entire conversation.

"What a nightmare."

There was a long moment of silence Charley didn't have the strength to try to fill.

"Are you going to tell Neely? And you had a date with her last night, yes?

"I canceled it. And no, I'm not going to say anything to her yet." Charley wasn't sure if she'd say anything to her at all.

"You canceled? Are you okay?"

"Still not ready yet."

Brooke sighed. "Hey, do you want to bring her to the dinner next Saturday?"

"Brooke, next weekend is kind of far from my mind right now."

"I'm sorry, I'm not doing a very good job being your shoulder, am I?"

"I know you'll be there when I need you."

"Well, I think I should be there for you tomorrow night. I know you're already thinking of bagging the NFL dinner. Don't. Let me come get you and we'll go together. Might do you good to get your mind off this."

When they hung up, Charley put on ESPN's *College GameDay* and sat down to listen to the commentators fight over the day's games. It was easier to float away on football than to try to make sense right now of what lay ahead.

Chapter Thirteen

Monday morning, Charley already had a game plan for talking to Emily about Tricia and went right into her office without even knocking, shutting the door behind her. She didn't want any staff member walking in on this conversation. Emily looked up in surprise.

"Good morning. I hope you had a better weekend than I did." Charley laid the whole scenario out. Of course, it meant coming out to Emily, which she'd chosen not to do when the perfect time had presented itself several weeks ago. She supposed she was still conditioned by the years when one didn't in Corporate America. Emily listened first with surprise, then with growing concern, asking questions. Charley had anticipated the kind of time she'd now be spending with Tricia, between medical appointments and help she might need at home, and she let Emily know how she intended to dovetail that in such a way that it wouldn't affect her presence in the office.

Emily nodded. "Whatever you need in the way of time, take it. Let's talk every morning, though, so I know how you're both doing and so we can keep on top of things here without them overwhelming you."

Charley nodded and turned to leave.

"And, Charley, thank you for letting me know. I realize you could've kept this as hidden from me as I kept Terry from you."

"No, I couldn't. You're right, I'll probably be needing things down the line...time off, maybe even a short-term leave. And you deserve to know what's going on. We can't be a good team if we can't trust each other."

Charley pushed the envelope to get everything on Emily's list done before walking out the door for Anita's class. Burying her emotions in the job at hand had always been her way of getting through. Today was no different.

The stress of the day fell away as Charley walked to the Y. She wound her way through a route she'd never used before, a hiker's way of forging a new path, called a desire line, through unknown territory to discover what was there. Only in this case, it wasn't unknown territory, but the concrete canyons of the city she knew so well. With stores and restaurants always closing, though, new places opening in their spaces, and old buildings being pulled down all the time, replaced by new modern glass slivers, it was like discovering new territory. With every step, she thought of meeting Joanna for that drink tonight after class, and that Joanna had asked *her* this time. Before she could examine it too closely, she was at the door of the Y.

There was a Post-it note on Joanna's locker. Charley pulled it off. *In the weight room. See you after class.* Charley got the pen out of her jacket pocket and drew a small picture of a thumbs-up on the bottom of the note and put it back on the locker higher than she'd found it so Joanna would know she'd seen it.

After class, she found Joanna sitting on the bench in front of her locker, a towel around her neck, defeat seeming to rest on her shoulders beneath it.

"So," Charley said, "the weight room win this round?"

Joanna looked up and shook her head. "I ramped each machine up forty pounds. I think that might've been a mistake."

"Ouch. How long have you been lifting whatever you've been lifting?"

"Not long enough, apparently." She rubbed her right bicep.

"Think you can still lift a drink?"

"Very funny."

"We can always postpone our second 'not a date' if you need to."

Joanna shot her a look of warning.

Charley ignored it, smirking. "Well, you *did* say you had a good time the other night when you asked me out for this drink tonight."

"Do you get a hernia carrying that ego around?"

Charley was a little surprised despite hearing the dry humor in Joanna's voice "I don't have...I have an ego, don't I?"

Joanna pulled her shower gear out of the locker, the trace of a smile on her face.

"Fine, I was just poking fun at your facade, anyway."

"I don't have a—" Joanna put a hand on one hip and cocked her head at Charley.

Charley heaved a false sigh and laughed. "I'll be ready in five minutes so why don't I meet you upstairs?"

In the lobby she settled on one of the upholstered benches and watched the members, a fascinating crossroads of many nationalities, come and go. Appreciative of well-dressed women, Joanna being one, Charley wondered what ensemble she'd have on tonight, and she wasn't disappointed when Joanna finally came up the stairs and scanned the lobby for her. She wore the sharply pressed navy slacks Charley had seen before, with a thin red belt at her waist, a white sweater over a white shirt, both smoothly tucked into those pants, and a plaid down vest tying it all together. Red tasseled loafers and the red scarf around the jacket's collar completed the outfit; she looked like she'd stepped out of the window display at Brooks Brothers.

Being the object of Joanna's search gave Charley a sense of power that resonated in her core. She relished it right up until the moment Joanna was standing next to her and she saw the tiny pair of handcuffs on the silver chain at her throat. The sight froze her. A second later, she felt the reverberation between her legs. A gold cross, a seagull on a delicate diamond-laced chain, Charley had even seen a necklace with an emerald caduceus on Joanna once, but never anything like this. She was forced to refocus when Joanna touched her arm to get her attention, and by the ghost of a smile that passed across her face, Charley knew she'd been caught staring at the jewelry. And then Joanna's light lemon scent washed over her, rendering her immobile again.

"I thought we could go to Bar and Books over on First Avenue and Fiftieth," Joanna suggested. "Have you ever been?"

Charley smiled.

"I thought you'd like that."

As Charley opened the Y's front door, it was evident that the temperature had dropped, but not significantly enough to affect her.

"You're not cold?" Joanna snuggled the scarf into the vest, zipping it to the very top as a cool breeze from the East River swept down the street.

"I grew up near the Canadian border. This is still Indian summer in my book. Where are you originally from?" Charley asked.

"California."

"Ah. Whereabouts?"

"Southern part."

Charley hoped she would mention a town. "Nice and warm, not like here. A beach town?"

"Mm-hmm."

Charley asked several more questions of Joanna about her past, getting successively succinct answers, which caused her to wonder if she'd somehow gotten off on the wrong foot tonight. Joanna had definitely not been this cagey last week. She began to wonder if ivy found it as difficult trying to gain a foothold on a brick wall. The silences that Charley decided to fill with odds and ends about herself were one thing, but there was so much she wanted to know about this woman. The thought crept in that Joanna might be a different kind of difficult than Tricia, but she dismissed it. Hardly enough evidence. She sought the *balance* stone in her pocket and reminded herself of her beach walk advice to just let go. But she couldn't. The necklace kept coming back, too. Was it merely a fashion statement skating the edge of that "bad girl" persona that some women liked to try on? Charley was inclined to think otherwise. Joanna seemed too comfortable in who she was to try anything on. There had to be a reason for that particular necklace. Or was there another woman behind it? That would be difficult…

Charley thought about what she could ask to discover answers to those questions as they entered the intimate space that was Bar and Books, but she drew a blank. In truth, she wasn't sure she wanted to know the meaning behind the necklace or who else might be attached to it.

Joanna picked out a small table in the back of the room, near the fireplace, not waiting for the maître d' to seat them. Charley stood by the wingback chair and perused the titles of the books that lined the shelves near her, sighed, and eyed the rest of the shelves full of books that stretched in either direction all around the bar.

"D'you know, I think I could live here." Charley sat down, giving the shelves a backward glance.

"Mmmm. No, I'd choose the beach."

"Oh, now wait. Now I have a problem."

"You don't like the beach?"

"I could also live there," Charley said, seeing Long Beach in her mind.

"I don't know. You can only live in one place."

The firelight caught Joanna's necklace, and Charley was drawn to it again. "I beg to differ. Lots of people have second homes."

The young woman working the room arrived at their table, and Joanna ordered a Johnnie Walker Red and asked her to bring the check with it.

"Make mine Black," Charley told her.

"You don't strike me as a second home kind of woman."

"No?" Charley was intrigued. Did that mean Joanna had been giving some thought to what kind of woman she was? And did that mean there wasn't another woman in her life?

"I'd say you're a minimalist."

Charley nodded slowly, thinking of everything she'd left behind when she'd walked out on Tricia. "You could be right. But it didn't happen by choice."

"Hmmm." Joanna studied her. "Hurricane?"

Charley studied her for a moment. "You might say so. Divorce."

"Oh…"

The young woman brought their drinks, along with a bowl of nuts and another of pretzels. She handed Joanna the check.

"I hope you're not thinking of picking this up," Charley said, nodding at the check.

Joanna shrugged. "Do you want to tell me what happened?"

Did she want to tell her? Charley shifted in her chair. "We were together twenty-five years and she had an affair with a younger woman. I walked out and left everything but my clothes. That was three years ago." Charley was surprised by the stunned look on Joanna's face.

"That's a lifetime, twenty-five years. How could she do that?"

Charley picked up her scotch, breathed in the essence, and took a long sip. "In her defense, she was seduced and stolen. And I should've known better since I originally stole her from someone else."

"How can you defend her?"

"Because I loved her." Charley looked directly into those iridescent green eyes.

Joanna blinked. "You still do, don't you?"

"I always will. But not the same way I did when we were together." Clarifying that difference out loud felt like a key turning somewhere inside her, a door long shut springing open.

"Are you still in touch with her?"

Charley couldn't read the expression on Joanna's face, but she was aware that it had changed. "She…recently came back into my life. Because she needs a friend." Her emotions surrounding Tricia were still too raw after their phone conversation Saturday morning. She didn't think she could, or should, share the reason with Joanna. "And I found I couldn't say no."

"Hmmm. That's beyond nice of you. Because I'm sure the current Mrs. Owens couldn't have been happy about that?"

Startled, Charley almost laughed out loud. Joanna easily vaulted all the questions Charley had asked and was clearly fishing for an answer of her own. "The current Mrs. Owens would be my mother. No one in my life since the divorce."

"At all? No dates, no dalliances…"

This time, Charley laughed. "Dalliances. I love words that wear gloves."

Joanna chuckled, and Charley swore that even in the low lighting, she saw a blush.

"Well, not for lack of my friends trying, that's for sure. They've spent a lot of time setting me up the last couple of years because they think I'm, well, in need of company." Charley made air quotes around the word "company" with her fingers.

Joanna nodded. "Are you?"

Charley looked down at her drink and swirled the cubes around in the glass. She sensed this already might be a crossroads, and in this moment, she wanted to choose her path carefully. "I didn't think I was until someone I've known for a year asked me out recently and shed a little light on that for me."

"Ah."

"Mmm, perhaps not what you think. She's…well, kind of young and it's really her skills as a writer that I appreciate at this point, so, if anything, it'll be a friendship."

"Kind of young? And a writer?"

"And what about you? No Mrs. Caden waiting at home for you tonight?"

Joanna nodded slightly. "All right. Turning the tables. I suppose I deserve it. I'll go along with your ruse. No, no one in my life. And I doubt there will be again."

The admission startled Charley. "That's a lengthy self-imposed hair shirt, isn't it?"

"I wasn't built for long-term relationships. Too much of me goes into my work."

"It shouldn't be a problem if she understands that about you, and if you're there for her when you're home."

"I'm guessing she didn't, and I wasn't."

The waitress asked if they wanted another drink and Joanna responded by handing her a credit card and the tab.

"So there *was* someone recently."

Charley pulled some bills out of her pocket as she watched Joanna, lost in the eddy she created in the glass in front of her. Her fingers circling the rim were slender, delicate, the perfectly manicured nails polished a deep mauve, and Charley imagined those hands somewhere other than that glass.

"A while ago. And when it was over, I vowed I would never let a woman do that to me again." Joanna looked at Charley. Was it a warning shot over the bow?

"You can't condemn yourself to a life alone."

"Yes, I can. I don't want that kind of pain again."

Charley thought about her own vow to Brooke recently that there wouldn't be another relationship. "Pain lets you know you're alive."

"So does heartburn, but I don't recommend either one."

Charley snorted.

"On that note, it's getting late and I have to get home."

"Mmm...so do I." Thinking of the cats and her promised call with Tricia, Charley handed a twenty across the table to Joanna.

"Nope," she said as the woman came back to the table with the credit card and receipt for her signature.

"Well, that's not very fair."

Joanna shrugged.

"All right, then, since we both left so many things unanswered, why don't we do this next Monday? Not a date, of course." Charley saw the reflected firelight dancing in Joanna's eyes and her breath caught in her throat.

Joanna's laugh was soft, gentle, and it made Charley shiver. "And who will be answering what, I wonder."

The breeze was markedly warmer than it had been earlier, and as they walked down First Avenue, Charley couldn't help the feeling of belonging, of ease, which swept through her in Joanna's company.

"What a lovely night," Joanna remarked.

"I told you it was still Indian summer."

When they reached the Isaiah Wall across from the U.N., Charley pointed at the stairs leading up to the little neighborhood tucked above First Avenue. "This is me. You don't have to walk me up, though."

Joanna leaned in to hug her good night, the lemon scent washing over Charley like a balm. "See you Monday."

Upstairs in her apartment, Charley turned on the NFL game. "Hey," she said when Tricia picked up on the second ring. "Sorry I'm late."

"I almost thought you were ditching me. Then I couldn't remember if I was supposed to call you at work, but no one answered the main number and you guys don't have a phone tree."

"The company's too big to have one of those."

"Well, then I realized I never got your phone number. So you ended up working really late."

"I should've given it to you. No, actually, I ended up over at the Y." Charley turned down the sound on the game since she could hear it clearly on Tricia's end.

"The Y?"

"I use the pool there."

"Wow. I'm impressed. You must look terrific."

"Hardly. Still working on losing all that weight I gained when I quit smoking." The realization of what she'd said hit her like a two-by-four. *My God, I smoked in that apartment for fifteen years. Is her cancer my fault?*

"So, what's your cell number?" Tricia didn't seem to notice the correlation.

She had to have considered my smoking when she got the news. Charley recited the ten digits, feeling ill at the possibility. "Do you want me to come downtown and get you Wednesday?"

"No. Meet me at the York Avenue entrance of the hospital at eight. I've been watching this game for over an hour. Who's winning tonight?"

"I'm not really invested in this one."

"That's not like you. How are my sweet Bing and Bob? Do they still watch football with you?"

Charley hesitated. She'd taken the cats with her when she left Tricia. Having been their primary caretaker, she felt they were rightfully hers. Those first few weeks in her new apartment, when Tricia called almost daily leaving messages begging her to come back, she also left messages for them, cooing to them, and telling them she missed them. Charley would never let Tricia know that they'd quietly sat at the front door for months, little sentinels waiting for her to come home. "Bob was never sweet, you know that. And they're fine. Older, but fine."

After Tricia hung up, Charley gave the game another half hour, but her thoughts were really on Joanna. Why had some things been up for discussion, like the fact that there was no one in her life, but others were not, like where she'd grown up? And that Joanna had struck the first blow when it came to finding out if she was single had surprised her.

Since she could chase her own tail to no avail with questions like this, she decided there was only one way to quell her thoughts, and she got Neely's flash drive out of her coat pocket. Bob, wrapped around the bottom of the computer screen, complained mildly as Charley plugged the drive in, swatting once at the mouse. Charley gently rubbed his head and began to read. Within minutes, his purring ebbed, he was asleep, and Charley was lost in 1945 post-war Chicago with Rose and Pearl, two young black girls, one of whom Charley was pretty sure would grow up to be Neely's grandmother. Two chapters in, she began making notes to take to Neely tomorrow night.

❖

Wednesday morning, Charley was standing under the massive metal overhang in front of the doors of Memorial Sloan Kettering, feeling almost hung over. She'd worked on her novel well into the night, finding solace in the hours of creativity.

Each cab that pulled up to the curb had Charley's undivided attention. She was afraid of seeing Tricia after all this time and wondered if old feelings would come flooding back. Would she look different? Treat Charley differently? Would she push all those old buttons again? Or, perhaps worse, would Charley be able to see in her former lover's eyes that even the most intimate of things between them was now in the past, irrelevant? So she studied every cab as, one after the other, doors opened, disgorged passengers, took on others, and closed. Shortly after eight, the cab she'd been dreading stopped half a block away and Tricia emerged from the back, her tall figure unmistakable in the tightly-belted white trench coat, the highlighted brown hair swirling around her shoulders over the fashionably turned-up collar. *Some things never change.*

Charley smiled to herself as she took in the navy and white scarf at Tricia's throat, the navy leather gloves, and the small navy purse tucked under her arm. The memory of her Shalini perfume got to her senses well before Tricia was close enough for it to actually hit her, and when Tricia kissed her cheek, Charley breathed in the indelible scent. She studied Tricia's face. Even at sixty-four, she was still a beauty, her high cheekbones more prominent, the aquiline nose still seeming to point to those perfect bow-shaped lips. Charley was more familiar with the landscape of Tricia's dark eyes than she was with the backs of her own hands. In a fleeting instant, she saw gratitude, love, fear, and pride. But nothing sparked inside her. The only thing she felt was the sense that she would be helping where no one else could, harnessing a bond no one else had with Tricia in service of what was to come.

"Thank you for doing this with me," Tricia said.

"You would do the same for me."

"I would, but you would never have called me in the same situation." Tricia headed for the front door of the hospital.

"You don't know that."

"I do know that. You would never have asked for my help, and Brooke would've mustered every living being to stand between the two of us if you had. You were always so lucky with friends."

Charley had no rebuttal.

Tricia walked toward a set of elevators behind the front desk. "And I'm sure Brooke wanted to spit nails when you told her about this."

"No, actually. She was quite concerned for you."

"The concern was for you, not me." The elevator doors opened, and Tricia punched the button for the eighth floor.

"Yes, she is concerned for me. But she promised me she'll be there for you, too."

"Only because *you're* here for me."

"Still pig-headed, aren't you?"

"No, a realist. I know what your friends think of me, and they're right to be so protective of you."

"I won't argue with you."

Tricia held the elevator door for Charley when it opened on the eighth floor. "Straight ahead. I bet Brooke never told you I contacted her when Reagan left me."

Charley stopped and grabbed Tricia's wrist. "You what?"

"I didn't have the guts to call you myself. So I called Brooke and asked her to call you for me. Do you know what she told me?"

I can only imagine, and I'm gonna kill Brooke.

When Charley didn't reply, Tricia gently disengaged her wrist. "She told me to go to hell and to fuck myself on the ride down."

Charley laughed out loud.

"So, you can see I'm not being pig-headed here, although I *am* well known for that trait. Your friends hate me." Tricia opened the door to suite 803. "I know why *you* don't hate me. But I still went to church Saturday morning after I hung up with you to thank God that you said yes." She walked over to the receptionist's desk. "Tricia

Sullivan. I have an eight fifteen appointment with Dr. Gerard." She turned to Charley. "That's the second time in thirty years I thanked God that you said yes to me."

Tricia took off her coat and sat in one of the waiting room chairs. Charley stood at the desk, dumbfounded, unable to breathe or move for a moment. When she sat down next to Tricia, she took her hand.

"I don't deserve you," Tricia said. They sat in silence until the receptionist called Tricia's name, opened the door to the examination offices, and led them to a sunny conference room at the end of the hall. Charley was intimidated by the sight of six men and one woman, all of them in white lab coats, sitting around the table.

"I don't even remember all their names yet," Tricia said. "But I have some decisions to make with them about what route to take to treat this. Or not."

Dr. Gerard, an imposing man with a patch of silver making inroads through the black hair at his right temple, stood to greet Tricia and introduced the group to Charley. For the next half hour, the oncologists reviewed the various treatment options, from targeted therapy to anti-angiogenesis therapy that would starve the blood vessels that the tumor needed to continue growing, and from radiation to chemotherapy to combinations of all of them. The X-rays and scans were on a laptop on the table, and from time to time, a doctor would turn it toward Tricia and Charley to illustrate what he or she was talking about. Tricia had several questions for the team. Charley took notes as the doctors spoke.

"Why don't you two take a couple of days to think about all of this. Come in on Friday morning and let's make a decision as to which direction to take."

"I could also choose to do nothing, correct?" Tricia asked.

Dr. Gerard's face didn't register a single flicker of emotion or that he'd even heard the question. Charley could feel the stunned silence emanating from the rest of the team.

"Yes. You could." He nodded thoughtfully.

"Because I'm not sure I want to put myself through any of this if the outcome is going to be the same. Or if it buys me six more months. At what cost? I might just want to make the best of whatever time I have left."

"Then let's talk about that Friday when you and Charley have had a chance to talk." He gave Tricia another hug. "Please think about it, though. Stage four doesn't mean we can't turn it around."

In the most uncommon move Charley had ever seen Tricia make, she touched Dr. Gerard's cheek and walked out the door.

"Thank you, Dr. Gerard." Charley extended her hand.

"I'm glad you came this morning, Charley. Tricia needs you. I think we'll be seeing a lot of each other over the next several months."

Watching Tricia walk down the hall, she responded, "I'm not so sure about that." She caught up to her at the elevator.

"Don't say it."

"I wasn't going to say anything," Charley said, stifling the rebuke that she'd been about to make.

They rode to the ground floor in silence. Outside, Tricia turned to her. "Have dinner with me tonight. I can't make this decision without talking about it."

It hadn't occurred to Charley that there would be such choices to make. She'd only thought about treatments, handholding, being there for Tricia at odd hours.

Stepping off the curb, Tricia whistled for the taxi half a block away at the red light and turned back to Charley. "What about seven?"

"I still marvel at this dichotomy, the chicly-dressed woman whistling for a cab," Charley said.

"I may have buried the farm girl in haute couture, but I never forgot how to get a job done." She opened the door and held it for Charley. "You take this one."

"I have an aquatics class at six. I can be at your place about eight."

Charley was typing up the notes from the doctors' meeting when Emily swept by her desk. "Come on in. Talk to me."

Charley went in, shut the door, and gave Emily an abbreviated version of Tricia's appointment.

Emily nodded. "Will she do nothing?"

Charley shrugged. "She might actually be considering that."

Emily ran a finger along the edge of her desk. "That would certainly simplify things. Are you okay with that?"

Charley was stupefied for a moment. "I can't...it's really her decision, not mine. I can be there for her, but I can't ask her to fight this if she thinks she won't win. Tricia was always about winning."

Emily nodded. "I'm sorry. This must be hard for you."

Charley looked down at the floor, fighting tears.

Emily sighed. "Okay, well, I had a message from Paul Whitney early this morning. He wants to see me Friday afternoon, before the board meeting. I don't know if this is a kiss-off or a handshake, so I need something I can hide up my sleeve in case it sounds like they're going to say no. We literally can't afford to lose this deal. Move my meetings and buy me two hours to noodle around. I have to see what I can get on paper that will have him saying yes even if he thought he was about to say no."

Charley had the sensation of being underwater as she left Emily's office.

Chapter Fourteen

The conversation with Emily continued to reverberate in Charley's thoughts as she left the Y after her aquatics class. Instead of grabbing a cab down to Tricia's, she walked over to Fifth Avenue and took the bus. The long ride gave her time to think about how she fit into the equation of Tricia's care. All that came to her was that she was probably going to have to level with Tricia and ask her what her expectations were, because she was clueless. She wasn't used to that. She'd made a career out of anticipating everyone's needs. It was part of what made her an exceptional executive assistant. She pulled the cord at Tenth Street. The bus left her right in front of Tricia's building, and as she approached the massive glass door, the doorman swung it open. "You can go right up to twenty-one, Miss Owens. Miss Sullivan is expecting you."

Charley almost glanced behind her to see if the doorman was talking to someone else. He had obviously been told to expect her.

"Thank you. Twenty-one what?"

"Twenty-first floor is the penthouse. She'll be there at the elevator door."

Charley didn't know whether to thank him or throw up. She settled for a nod and walked through the marbled lobby. She thought of the small apartment she and Tricia had first lived in on the Upper West Side, of all their conversations about where they might move when Tricia made partner. But it was a simple two-bedroom apartment they'd settled for a few blocks away because Charley couldn't bear leaving the neighborhood. Now her own stupidity stared back at her in her reflection in the gold elevator doors. Then the pain of what she'd gone through three years ago as she'd watched twenty-five years of her life go up in smoke between some other woman's legs hit her again.

The elevator glided up twenty-one floors, and Charley put the lid on the past as best she could.

Tricia was there when the elevator door opened, and Charley was stunned to see her in a pair of sweatpants and a T-shirt. Well, at least Reagan was good for one thing if she got Tricia to loosen her regimental dress code. Charley stepped into the tiny hallway and across the threshold into a large foyer. The size of the place overwhelmed her. Beyond the foyer was a spacious living room with wide floor-to-ceiling windows. Hallways disappeared in either direction. Even from where she stood, she could see the lights of lower Manhattan glinting everywhere, Lady Liberty watching over the harbor in the distance. Charley wanted to walk into the room, but she stepped aside and waited for Tricia to throw the deadbolts.

"Come on, I have something set up for us in the kitchen."

Charley followed her down an Oriental-carpeted hall past a large dining room. In the low lighting of a recess behind the head of the table, she recognized a large Modigliani painting on the wall and stopped to stare. When had she acquired that?

In the kitchen that a professional chef would've appreciated, Tricia took a platter of fruit and cheese out of the refrigerator. Charley perched on a chair on the other side of the marbled work island.

"Wouldn't you rather sit at the table by the window?" she asked. "I have a nice view of the tip of Manhattan from here. Beats the one we had of New Jersey on West End Avenue."

The irony didn't escape Charley. Taking her typed notes from her canvas bag, she moved to the table.

"Why do I smell chlorine?"

"Because you do," Charley replied. "My bathing suit is in my bag."

"Right, you said you were going to the pool tonight. You swim now? I wanted to tell you this morning that you look really good, but I didn't want you to get mad. How often do you go?"

"Every day. What do you mean, get mad?"

"I know I picked on you about your weight after you quit smoking. It wasn't good for our relationship. And then, anything I said after that seemed to piss you off."

Charley cocked her head and stared at Tricia, angered by the remark and at the same time amused by her stupidity in putting it right out there. A second later, Tricia realized her gaffe in bringing up an old issue that had driven a stake between them years ago.

"That was…I'm sorry. I didn't mean it the way it sounded. And I shouldn't have said it."

"You think?" Charley stared at Tricia until she folded.

"So…" Tricia hesitated. "Where do you live? Where do you swim?"

"I'm in midtown. East Side."

"You left the West Side? You were such a West Side girl. Whereabouts on the East Side?"

"You left, too."

"Yes, well…"

Charley raised an eyebrow. "Suffice it to say I had to go where the apartments were affordable."

Tricia took a bottle of wine and a can of Coke out of the refrigerator and set the soda in front of Charley.

"I don't drink that anymore."

Tricia got her a bottle of water. "I have Johnnie Walker."

"Water's good."

"Okay, let's talk about something safe, then," Tricia said, settling at the table and picking up a handful of grapes. "I looked up Emily after you mentioned her name. She's quite the grand poobah over there. How did you come to be her assistant? I thought you were in A&R?"

"They moved me when she came in. Someone thought we'd be good together."

"And are you?"

"Mmm-hmm." The arthritis in Charley's index finger made it impossible to open twist caps, so she picked up the napkin Tricia had dropped on the table, wrapped it around the cap of the water bottle, and wedged it into the soft pad between her thumb and forefinger, turning it. When it didn't open, Tricia took it from her.

"How good? Because I know she's gay."

"Oh, Tricia, please. I'd sooner get involved with Satan than with a boss. You know that." The minute it was out of her mouth she regretted it, although she wasn't the one who'd been caught out involved with her young associate.

"Okay, just asking," Tricia said. "And *are* you involved? Is there anyone in your life?" Tricia poured herself a generous glass of wine.

"Not that it would be any of your business, but no."

Tricia sighed. "Is there anything about your life that I can know?"

Charley took a long swig of water, popped a piece of cheese in her mouth, picked up the notes from the morning session with Dr. Gerard, and began paging through them.

"Okay, I'm treading where I don't belong, but I'd like to belong there, just a little."

The note in Tricia's voice revealed a step back, a supplication Charley had never heard. She nodded at Tricia's outfit. "Sweatpants?"

"Reagan hated suits, wouldn't allow them at home. Turns out, I really like being comfortable."

Charley looked back down at the notes.

"I'll trade any piece of information about my life that you want," Tricia said.

Charley saw the banked ember of interest in her eyes. "I don't want any information about your life."

Tricia looked down at her hands. "Of course you don't."

Charley was possibly the only person on earth who knew that Tricia had vulnerabilities and insecurities that she shielded like they were the White House nuclear codes, and the defeat in Tricia's eyes made her take pity on her. "I recently began seeing two women," Charley said quietly. "But one of them isn't right for me. She's too young. She's a writer, though, and a good one, so I think we'll be friends."

Tricia nodded. "And the other woman?"

"I don't know." Charley concentrated on the pages in front of her again, but she felt the heat of the blush creeping up her neck.

"You do know. It's manifesting itself on you right now."

Charley hated that in opening the door this tiny bit, Tricia could slip in so easily, even as her arrogance beat her through it.

"You think she could be your beach, don't you?"

"We really need to go over these notes."

"I know I was a handful, but I was your beach. You need to find someone whip-smart, Charley, someone who makes you reach, but more importantly, who's your place of peace, your home."

"I know what I need, Tricia, thank you." Charley tapped her pen on the notes. "Now can we go over what we talked about this morning with your doctors?"

"I don't want to. I don't need to."

And just like that, Tricia had crossed back into her reality. The panic that Charley felt blossoming inside her chest was mirrored in Tricia's troubled eyes.

"I know what you're going to say." Tricia tucked her leg under her.

"Maybe you don't."

"You're going to tell me I'm being foolish."

"No, I wasn't." Charley took a deep breath. "I was going to ask you if you'd made up your mind before we left the meeting this morning. And if that was the case, why did you want me here tonight?"

"If we were still together, would you support my decision not to do anything?"

"That's irrelevant. I will support whatever you decide." She wasn't sure if it was true.

Tricia moved her wine glass in a little circle on the table. "I don't see a point in fighting this. I researched it. It's not good." Tricia looked down at her glass, and Charley could see tears welling in her eyes. She quickly moved to the chair next to her and took Tricia into her arms. The tears wet her neck before Tricia went to pieces. Deciding there was nothing she could say, she kept Tricia in her embrace until her body had gone quiet.

"If you're sure," Charley finally ventured, "if this is what you want, then we still have to talk about what to ask the doctors to expect. I need to know what's going to happen to you step by step, what signs I need to be looking for, what you might experience, what kind of drugs are available for what, do you need nurses and if so, when. And anything else they think I should know." Tricia still rested against her shoulder and Charley ran her hand through her hair. "But if you want to trust in Dr. Gerard that stage four can be beaten and you want to fight, then I will be in your corner. Either way," Charley said, wiping the tears from Tricia's cheek with her thumb, "we need to inquire about hospice because you might need it if you fight, and you will need it if you don't."

"I looked into that today," Tricia whispered.

"You did?"

Tricia nodded.

"I should have known. You were always about the end game first."

"And you did the leg work up front. It's why we made such a good team." Tricia sat up and dried her eyes. "I'm scared, Charley. But I'm not stupid. I know where this is going. Let's put the questions together. You can be the warrior for me. It's why I called you."

Charley set the notes from the morning meeting aside and reached into her bag for her spiral notebook. This would be the most difficult logbook she would ever keep. But it might be the most valuable thing she could give Tricia now.

CHAPTER FIFTEEN

Tricia's call Thursday night had brought Charley right downtown to her apartment. They sat on the couch and watched the NFL game. Charley sensed that if she brought up tomorrow's meeting to let the doctor know her decision, Tricia would lose it, so she went to the kitchen during halftime and made a pot of hot chocolate. She searched the cabinets for the tiny marshmallows they used to keep on West End Avenue for evenings like this, cold rainy evenings or sad evenings that called for the comfort of a steaming mug of hot chocolate, but found none. Reagan must've banned them, too, like Tricia's suits. She'd hardly seemed the marshmallow type. In a last-ditch effort, Charley checked the refrigerator. Cold, hard marshmallows would be disgusting but they'd warm up and melt. No marshmallows there, either. Instead, she found a can of Reddi-wip, shook it, and blasted each mug with a mountain of white cream. *Just what the doctor ordered...*

Tricia smirked and shook her head when Charley came in carrying the tray. "That whipped cream might be left over from last Thanksgiving."

"There's enough sugar in this crap for a nuclear half-life of fifty years. I think we're safe."

After she'd drained her cup, Tricia settled against Charley and yawned. "Not a great game."

"It's the Giants. We're only watching for the eye-rolling comic moments." That, she knew, would be the extent of the discussion they'd have pertaining to tomorrow morning's appointment.

❖

Charley opened the window before she got into the shower and saw a dark, unruly sky that matched the feeling inside the apartment. She hadn't thought to grab her umbrella. Maybe Reagan had left one behind in a closet. She dressed quickly and found Tricia pacing in the living room, waiting to head down to the street. They'd hardly said anything to each other all morning, and the tension could be cut with a knife.

At five past eight, after peering intently down the street for five minutes, Tricia swore under her breath and deemed the town car late. Angrily, she pulled out her phone to call her assistant. Charley put her hand on Tricia's arm to intercept that call, knowing it was less about the car than where they were headed, and her assistant shouldn't bear the brunt of that. "She's not going to know where the car is."

"No, but she can find out!"

"So can we. What company does your firm use?" Charley knew all the limo companies in the city; every boss she'd ever had used a different one, making it imperative that she have a tab in her contacts listing them all.

"Executive."

Charley pulled out her phone, scrolled to the contact, and hit the number. Several fat blobs of rain fell on her head as the call connected. She looked up at the threatening sky, and a second later, it was obliterated by the doorman's umbrella. Thankfully, the car pulled up and Charley slid into the seat, the doorman opening the door for her. Grumbling, Tricia got in beside her. Nothing was said as the car rolled uptown through rush hour traffic. At one point, she looked at Tricia, who was looking out the window at something so far away Charley knew it wasn't actually there. For her sake, she began to get herself mentally ready for the meeting with Dr. Gerard.

An hour later, Charley walked into the solarium on the ground floor of her office building seconds before the downpour finally hit. After getting a cup of tea from the Beanery kiosk, she sat at a table and watched the rain pelt the window, trying to collect herself before she went up to her desk. Still in shock over Tricia's decision to refuse much help from the hospital team, Charley shifted her attention to the tea that swirled hypnotically as she stirred it. Dr. Gerard had looked at Charley after Tricia laid out her case, and she had looked at the floor. He had to understand that it was out of her hands. Since she wouldn't be the one enduring treatment, or sacrificing her quality of life, she couldn't judge Tricia.

A clap of thunder brought Charley back to her surroundings. The rain was coming down so hard now that the street was nearly invisible. She knew she should go up to her desk and make sure Emily had everything necessary for her meeting this afternoon with Paul Whitney, but she couldn't bring herself to move. Maybe the weather was a sign. "Emily Dunn, Rainmaker," the *New York Times* had called her when she joined this firm, "the most ambitious and creative young executive in the field." *If ever she makes it rain, it has to be today.* Why Wall Street hadn't sniffed out their financial problems yet was beyond her; someone in the executive offices was hiding it well. If Emily didn't succeed in bringing Paul's company into this deal, though, and as a partner instead of a buyer, they'd be in the kind of trouble they couldn't hide any longer. It would be all over the news, their stock would tank, Hans would throw Emily under the bus to avoid his own disgrace, and Charley could be facing the prospect of a job hunt, something she didn't relish at her age. Not a pretty picture.

The storm was full force when she finally made her way to the lobby, matching her mood. Passing through security and heading for the elevator bank, Charley brought her emotions back under control so that by the time she closed Emily's office door and filled her in on the meeting with Tricia's doctors, she was all business. And it was a short task. "Anything I need to know before I get to work?" Charley asked.

"I have a car at two o'clock?"

"Yes. And it will wait there for you indefinitely. It didn't make sense to schedule a pickup since we don't really know what time you'll be finished."

"Okay." Emily toyed with a paper clip. "And I'm going to assume that you are doing okay for the moment?"

"Yes. Are you mentally ready to face their board?"

"Think so, yes."

They were both lying.

When Emily left for the meeting, Charley sat back in her chair and stared out the window; it was still pouring. Her phone rang. She didn't recognize the number, but she picked up in case it was the driver looking for Emily, who had a habit of wandering from in front of the building to look for her car if she didn't see it right away, causing all sorts of communications problems with the limo company.

"Charley Owens. How can I help you?"

"Hey, Charley, I'm at a pay phone 'cause my battery died," Neely shouted over the thunder that was now hitting the city. "I sold a story to *The New Yorker*!"

"You're kidding?" She could hardly believe what she was hearing. And then all that came over the line was Neely's breathless laughter.

"*Are* you kidding?"

"No!" Neely said. "I'm in shock!"

Charley started laughing, Neely's infectious giggles touching her like champagne bubbles.

"They never publish people like me. I'm a nobody!"

"Not true," Charley said. "And we have to celebrate. Let me take you out to dinner tonight."

"No. I wanted you to come over tonight. That's why I'm calling. I'm just walking home from the market. I want to make dinner for you. It was your notes that helped so much."

"But I've been giving you notes on the novel," Charley said, confused.

"I extracted two chapters and molded them into a short story. Please, come over tonight."

Charley gladly acquiesced. When they hung up, she was able to face the shorthand she'd taken at this morning's meeting with Dr. Gerard, transcribing it and typing it up to email to Tricia. A few minutes later, her phone rang.

"Can you talk now?"

"Yes. Are you okay?"

"I looked over the notes. Can you come over for dinner tonight?"

Charley hesitated. She knew Tricia needed her now emotionally, but she couldn't turn the clock back to the time when she would've dropped everything for her.

"Actually, no."

"Oh?"

"I'm having dinner with my young writer tonight."

"Oh. Okay, well, what about lunch tomorrow?"

Charley heard Tricia's other line ringing.

"I'll call you right back."

Charley checked the time on her computer. Emily would be deep into the meeting with Paul and his board. She sent up a little prayer. Needing to keep both her lines clear if Emily called, she opened another email to Tricia.

"I'll come by at 1:00 tomorrow. Salad for lunch, okay? Balsamic vinaigrette. I don't use French dressing anymore. And get some lemons for the water, for God's sake. Didn't I teach you anything?" She hit Send.

Several minutes later, she had a response from Tricia. *I had lemons the other night. You didn't ask.*

Charley fired off a reply, finding comfort in the normalcy of their old-style banter. *I need to ask?*

Mea culpa, came Tricia's response. *From now on, my refrigerator is your refrigerator. Oh, and by the way, my doorman on the weekends is a woman, quite a stunning Black Irish beauty. Try not to add her to your dating roster on the way in tomorrow. Have fun tonight.*

Charley sent back an emoticon sticking its tongue out. Then, wanting to ward off the tension that had her in its grip as she waited to hear from Emily, she pulled her Lysol wipes from the cupboard. Her cubicle looked like Miss Havisham's study. No use trying to concentrate on anything real. Before she'd gotten to the last bit of cleaning, the tops of the filing cabinets, the Instant Message blinked open on her computer. *Book flight to the Middle East. And the most expensive restaurant you've always wanted to try.*

Charley walked into Emily's office, relief washing over her, and plopped into Emily's chair. She looked out at her city. From the thirty-fifth floor, Central Park shimmered in the aftermath of the storm, and all the day's stress began leaving her body. Emily had made it rain. *Maybe now I can allow myself to think that life will be good for a while.*

CHAPTER SIXTEEN

Charley had no idea Emily had put a split of champagne in the little refrigerator in her office earlier in the day. They opened it in her conference room, just the two of them. Charley went over the travel plans she'd made days ago, hoping that locking the flights down ahead of time would serve as a good luck charm and knowing they were easier to cancel than to make this close to the date Emily wanted to depart.

"And the restaurant?"

"Made reservations for three at Per Se for two weeks from Saturday."

"You can't get in there before next April," Emily said dismissively. "I know, I tried, for Terry's birthday next month. Even *my* name didn't open the door."

"Oh, you should've come to me. I have connections there."

"Seriously?"

"I told you my Rolodex is full of rabbits I pull out of hats."

Emily laughed. "Yes, you did. I'm beginning to think you're a member of the Mafia."

Charley smiled. "The executive assistant Mafia. There's a difference."

"Hmmm. I don't think I want to know."

Emily left early, and for once, Charley was right out the door behind her. She stopped at her apartment to feed the cats and change, deciding quickly on the old standby of a pair of jeans and a white button-down. She left the pearls on. That damn lobster clasp was such a pain in the ass. Moments later, she was on the Third Avenue bus heading up to Neely's apartment. In the corner bodega, she bought a single red rose to bring to her.

The listing on the buzzer told her Neely lived on the fifth floor of the walk-up. She took a deep breath and began the hike up. As she rounded the last landing, Neely opened the door, a frosted glass of white wine in her hand.

"Oh, thank God," Charley said.

"I was going to send a Saint Bernard down with it, but then I figured you'd just sit down on the step and drink it there."

"Very funny."

She took the glass from Neely and peeked inside the door. "This is cute." Stepping into the apartment, she was immediately in the kitchen, a compact affair, with the sparsely furnished living room on the other side of a pine breakfast bar. Charley assessed the space, turning in a 360-degree circle. She went over to the French windows that overlooked a series of backyards below. "Nice."

"Would you like the official tour?" Neely asked.

"Of course."

"Kitchen, living room," Neely said with a sweep of her hand. "Bathroom down the hall." Neely led her to the hallway. "And beyond, the bedroom."

Charley flicked on the bathroom light, took stock of the walls stenciled in lilacs and green leaves, and wondered if Neely had done the work herself. It was a beautiful but tedious art that she'd decorated a long-ago apartment with, and then had vowed to hire an artisan the next time she wanted it. She followed Neely into the bedroom. There was a comfortable feel to it, the room done in a light lilac, unpainted pine furniture softly lit by one floor lamp. On the wall above the king-sized bed hung an enormous photograph of violet-colored hydrangeas spilling over a picket fence.

"Neely, this is lovely. Where do you write?"

"Mostly on the couch." Neely turned off the lamp and headed to the kitchen where she put a deep sauté pan on the tiny stove, turning up the flame under it. She retrieved a block of lard from her refrigerator and a thermometer from a small jar of utensils on the counter and set them next to the stove. She went back to the refrigerator for the bottle of wine and a small dish of crudités and dip, setting them both on the breakfast bar.

"You're going to have to stay over there when I begin to work," she warned Charley as she cut the lard into the pan. "And I hope you don't mind, but I still do this recipe like my grandma did." She held up the lard. "It wouldn't taste the same otherwise."

She brought a large bowl containing chicken pieces in an egg wash out of the refrigerator and threw a large pinch of salt, pepper, and Cajun seasoning into the pan, dipping the thermometer into the sizzling lard and holding it there. Satisfied with the reading, she coated each piece of chicken with flour in a large baggie that had been sitting next to the utensil jar. There were red specks of some kind of seasoning in it. "Okay, I'm putting this in the pan. Stay where you are. I don't want your clothes to get splattered."

The crackle of the chicken hitting the pan caused Charley to jump as a shower of spattering fat burst over the stove. The sweet smell of the lard was eclipsed by the stronger spices and the gamey pungency of the chicken itself, making her hungry. While Neely worked, they talked about how her grandmother had taught her all her cooking secrets as a way of healing her after her mother had disappeared into drug addiction when Neely was ten. Charley wanted to hug that child but knew she was long gone, grown into the interesting, contemplative, kind woman full of light and laughter who stood at the stove cooking for her. A woman who was now about to be published by one of the most prestigious magazines in the country. If she wasn't so happy at the turn of events for her, Charley would've been jealous.

"I've been meaning to tell you," Charley said, dipping a carrot into the hummus. "I know I've been giving you advice in pieces and parts over the last couple of weeks, but I read the entire first half from start to finish two nights ago."

Neely carefully turned the chicken. "What did you think? Does it work?"

"It's a complicated and beautiful story, which I don't think I really told you before. I've been sucked right in."

"Okay." Neely nodded.

"I know Pearl is your grandmother, and I've really grown to love her. But I hate that she's wrecking her life."

"Rose is wrecking Pearl's life."

"No, Pearl is letting it happen. She could stop it, but she doesn't."

"No, she's defenseless against her sister."

"No one's defenseless, Neely. No one can use you unless you give them permission to, and that's what Pearl is doing."

Neely turned to look at Charley and then sat down on the stool next to her. "My God, that's it. Pearl *is* making a choice…I didn't see that."

"But she's your character. Everything she does is in your hands."

"No, I don't always have control. Things come out my pencil, I don't even know where they come from sometimes. It's like I know this story, but I don't." Neely kissed Charley on the forehead. "And you just gave me an invaluable note."

"Well, finally. Something I can do for you."

Neely checked on the chicken. "You do more for me than you know." Wiping her hands on a towel, Neely went to plug her iPod into a speaker on the coffee table. Charley kicked off her shoes and joined her, curious about what artists she had in her library.

"It's my version of the American Songbook," Neely said. "All the artists are black. And you can look at the list later. Right now, let's eat, you listen." She went back to the refrigerator for a bowl of potato salad and then put two green salads on the table.

Oh, thank God, Charley thought, seeing the greens. She'd been a little worried about how the chicken fried in lard might affect her, but the minute she bit into a thigh, cracking right through thin, perfectly seasoned skin, and the hot juices spurted out, all thoughts of healthy eating sailed right out the window. This chicken was heaven.

For the next three hours, they ate and talked, and Charley listened to a host of artists she knew: Ella, Lena, Sarah, Nat King Cole, and many lush voices she didn't recognize. Neely pushed their second bottle of wine toward Charley's glass.

"Oh, no you don't. I can't drink like that."

"Why don't we move to the couch," Neely suggested. "My bones hurt from sitting on this stool so long."

Charley began to clear the dishes, transferring them to the sink and running water on them. Neely came up behind her and swept her hands through Charley's hair, surprising her. "I love these curls."

She buried her nose in them and inhaled. Then she kissed her neck. "Leave the dishes. I'll do them later."

Charley turned around to face her. She had a nanosecond to decide what to do before Neely was kissing her, softly at first, her hands gliding up the front of Charley's shirt. Neely pressed her against the counter and Charley pushed back, desire kicking in as Neely kneaded her breasts. She moved her hands to Neely's butt, pulling her apart beneath the soft fabric of her jeans. Charley could feel her heat, and within seconds, she went up in smoke when Neely reached between her legs. Breaking the kiss, breathing unsteadily, Charley wondered if Neely could feel how wet she'd made her at a time in her life when that didn't physically happen anymore.

Neely tilted Charley's chin up. "I don't want to sit on the couch."

"I know you don't."

She took Charley's hand and led her toward the bedroom, turned the lamp to the lowest setting, and unbuttoned Charley's shirt. Trying to control the trembling as Neely draped the shirt over the chair, Charley thought of all the times she'd imagined a moment like this since leaving Tricia. None of them measured up. She was afraid to let Neely know how like her very first time this felt, or how surprised she was at how much she wanted this. She was also afraid that once Neely saw her completely naked, she might not find her attractive, might draw back. Despite all the classes she'd taken in that pool over the last couple of years, there were some things that time couldn't hide. She let the thought go and unbuttoned Neely's shirt, trying to take her time but unable to keep her fingers from flying through the task. She quickly unclasped Neely's bra and tossed it onto the chair. Neely reciprocated. But before she could get to Charley's pants button, Charley had her hands on the buttons of Neely's pants. She slid them down Neely's legs, pulling her boy shorts down with them, then dropping them on the chair with the other clothes.

She caressed Neely's stomach, admiring the muscles. Neely's sigh deepened into a groan as Charley dipped her hand between her legs, relishing the tight curls now drenched with her arousal. She inhaled her essence and laid her head on Neely's shoulder, her hand on her breast, as she stopped long enough to realize that this was happening. Neely unbuttoned Charley's pants, slipped them over her hips, and traced her fingers down the sheer fabric of Charley's panties. She shivered when Neely outlined the small fan of hair that rose from the top of her sex, then cupped her hand between her legs, moving in and out slowly. Charley put a hand on Neely to steady herself. Neely stood, lowered her to the bed, and gazed at her. Charley stretched her arms over her head and arched her back, as much out of need as to tease Neely as she took her in, the powerful shoulders and toned arms she'd felt under her hands when they were dancing, what Charley could only define as a six-pack, tautly muscled hips and legs. *Oh my God, she's Adonis and Aphrodite rolled into one.* Charley reached to unfasten the pearl necklace.

"No." Neely stopped her. "Leave it. That's a beautiful sight. You nearly naked, and the pearls against your skin."

Before Charley could slide up onto the bed, Neely stripped her panties, went to her knees, and opened Charley's legs, her tongue stroking the length of her sex and toying with the hood that protected her clitoris. She braced herself with one foot on the floor and held on as Neely drove her tongue as far inside her as she could. Charley had forgotten how moments like this could rob her of all her senses as she struggled for a breath of air. Neely teased her, sank her tongue in again, and Charley cried out. Grabbing fistfuls of the bedspread, she arched into Neely's mouth, her stomach muscles tightening, Neely's tongue again tracing her sex, thrusting inside her, drawing out, seeking Charley's clit, flicking it over and over. Charley moaned and rose against Neely, who slid her hands under her, lifting her higher, her tongue plunging in and out until the anticipatory flame of an orgasm gathered from her toes to her neck. She went rigid, and the single touch of Neely's lips at her clitoris sent her cascading over the edge. Neely held her hips, her mouth riding Charley until she peaked for the third time and slowed, finally lying still, her legs draped over Neely's shoulders.

"I can feel your heart beating all the way down here," Neely whispered, her cheek against Charley's thigh.

"Can you send it back up to my chest, please? I'm about to fall off the bed."

Neely helped her onto the bed and lay down next to her. She wedged her hand against Charley's pussy as she entwined their legs. "Hmm. Terrible…you've been rode hard and put away wet."

Charley punched her playfully. "All this bed and you made love to me on the razor's edge."

"I couldn't wait another second," she said, playing with Charley's curls. "I've wanted this…you…for so long. Besides, we have all night to use every inch of this playing field."

Charley lifted her head to regard Neely.

"You are staying the night, aren't you?" Neely asked.

"I like playing fields," Charley said, rolling up to a sitting position. She tucked one leg around Neely's hip and scissored her other leg under her, repositioning her smooth pussy against Neely's wiry curls, beginning a slow grind against her. She watched Neely slowly lose control as her need to climax grew, driving her to move against Charley. It was a powerful feeling, riding a woman this way, bringing her to the brink, and Charley loved that sense of command.

"Oh, dear God." Neely moaned.

Charley reveled in the look of ecstasy on Neely's face as she shifted against her like a belly dancer.

"Not in my wildest dreams…" Neely whispered.

Charley felt Neely getting slick again, swung her leg out from under her, and lowered herself on top, pushing her thigh between Neely's legs, running her tongue from her earlobe down the side of her throat to the hollow of her neck, pausing for a series of unhurried kisses as she provoked Neely's nipples to stiff buttons with her fingers. Neely undulated beneath her and Charley felt the rhythm and matched it, pushing her thigh hard against Neely's slippery wetness as Neely ground into her. Then, one hand on the bed to steady herself, she began stroking between Neely's legs, keeping up the tempo she had set. Neely put her own hand on Charley's, moving with her and guiding Charley to where she wanted her. Capturing her breast in her mouth, she elicited low moans as she tongued her nipple. Neely's clit receded into its protective hood and she eased down to chase it, drawing the tip of her finger through Neely's sex, teasing it open to reveal the silky pink inside, feeling a tremor of pleasure rip through her at the touch. Kissing and nipping her way up first one, then the other inner thigh as she pressed a finger lightly against Neely's anus, she continued playing in her wet heat, found her clitoris, and tenderly pressed its fullness from beneath.

Neely's reaction would've been audible to the neighbors. Charley moved in with the tip of her tongue and swirled circles to the rhythm of Neely's rocking hips, reaching up to caress her breasts. Neely's clit grew rigid; Charley closed her mouth over it and ran her tongue up and down the little shaft. Neely gasped, her body stiffened and arched. Charley slipped her fingers inside as the orgasm burst and overtook Neely, and she rode it out until they both settled onto the bed. Neely, her breath coming in ragged gasps, rolled over onto her side and brought her legs up tightly together.

"I didn't hurt you, did I?" Charley was alarmed.

Neely spoke haltingly, but she didn't roll back toward Charley. "No. I'm trying to hold onto this orgasm the best way I know how."

"I can give you another one, you know."

Neely giggled as Charley rolled against her back and held her, breathing in the familiar sweetness of cocoa butter mingled with the redolence of sex. "Oh my God, I love the sensation of a woman against my back. Stay right there."

Charley combed her fingers through Neely's hair. "Can I ask you something?"

"Oh, that feels good. Of course. Anything."

"You said you've wanted me for a long time?"

"Since you walked through the door of the Y the first morning I was on duty."

"What was it? That made you want me?"

"Really?" Neely rolled over and kissed Charley. "I can't even begin to tell you what you do to me." Neely ran her hand through Charley's curls. "Everything about you makes me a little crazy." Neely eased on top of Charley and kissed her again. "And a little nervous." She kissed Charley's nose. "And a lot hot." Neely stroked a finger across Charley's eyebrow.

"And…" Charley saw the sheepish look on Neely's face as she wrestled with what she wanted to say. "Something told me you were way experienced in bed."

Charley laughed. "I think you've got some solid cred yourself there."

Neely kissed a path down Charley's neck, taking the pearl necklace gently in her lips. A moment later, her palm was on Charley's sex and she entered her. Charley groaned, grabbed Neely's butt, and found her damp slit, opening her. Neely dropped the necklace, her head falling back when Charley penetrated her. They moved in tandem, Neely's eyes locked on Charley's, Charley's legs wrapped around Neely. She moved faster when she found Charley's hard clit.

"Come with me," Neely begged.

"Higher, up higher," Charley ordered. "That's it. Now match my stroke."

Neely slowed down. "Do I have you?"

Charley answered by digging her heels into Neely's thighs. It had been a long time since anyone had played in bed with her like this. She didn't want it to end. She felt Neely growing against her finger, slipped under her clit and stroked the shaft. Neely's body stiffened against Charley and she came. Charley kissed her, felt the muscles working in her shoulders, skimmed her hands over them, and as her own orgasm triggered, she raked her nails back across the same path.

"Oh, my God," Neely breathed.

Charley could barely get enough air. Her head dropped into the pillow; tingling rose from her toes to her fingers. She closed her legs around Neely's thigh, her sex tight against it as she hugged Neely to her chest, her nails digging into Neely's back.

"Oh my God, I can feel you throbbing against my thigh." Neely's eyes widened.

"Don't let me go until it stops."

Neely buried her face in Charley's breasts, put her hand under Charley's thigh, and held it firmly against her.

"How often do you work out?" Charley asked, running her hands up and down Neely's back. "Your muscles drive me a little crazy."

"I'm at the Y every day, remember?"

"Of course. What was I thinking? Can I ask you something else? And you'll answer me truthfully this time?"

Neely looked up at Charley from between her breasts. "Anything," she said, her voice muffled.

"How old are you?"

"Thirty."

"Oh God..."

"Why?" Neely lifted her head. "How old are you?"

"I'm fifty, Neely."

"You are not."

"How old did you think I was?"

"Forty-two, maybe."

Charley trailed her fingers around Neely's lips and down the center of her nose. Neely hadn't seemed to notice or care that she was a little pudgy, and that there were age lines on her face Charley hadn't seen a year ago. Would her admission of her age change that?

"Does it matter?" Neely asked. "We just blew up the sheets. And we weren't even in them."

"Speaking of which, can we get under the covers?"

"You're still throbbing. A little."

"And I'm getting a chill."

Neely pulled the covers back and Charley got under them.

"Let me hold you," Neely said.

"Okay, but only for a little bit."

"You don't like to be held? What woman doesn't like to cuddle after sex?"

"I love to be held. But you said you love the sensation of a woman against your back, and I'd like to fall asleep with you in my arms."

"You'll stay the night?"

"Mmmm. Let's just enjoy this moment and fall asleep with each other." Charley caressed Neely's arms as she sighed and pulled Charley closer.

"This is so nice," Neely whispered. "When is the last time this happened to you?"

Charley hesitated, thinking about the last night she and Tricia made love. "Four years ago."

"Four years and no sex? Ouch." Neely played with the pearl necklace.

"I'm a big girl. I can take care of myself."

"Oh, don't do that to me…"

"What?"

"I just got a mental picture of you 'taking care of yourself.'"

Charley laughed out loud. "Turned yourself on, did you, imagining me lying in my bed with my hand between my legs?"

Neely's moan came from deep within her chest. "Just your hand? No toys? You live on the edge. Or is that another generational thing we can discuss later?"

Charley drew away. "We have run across a few of those, haven't we?"

"Yeah, but I don't care about 'em right now." Neely rolled over and settled on her hip and stomach, her arm under the pillow. Charley snuggled in behind her and gathered her close, pressing her breasts into Neely's back.

"Oh, my God. I've died and gone to heaven."

Charley shifted around slightly, teasing Neely.

"You keep that up and I'm gonna have to blow you again."

"Promises, promises. The necklace isn't going to hurt? I can take it off."

"No, it feels as good as your breasts."

"You're so funny, asking me to keep the jewelry on."

"I think there's nothing sexier than a naked woman adorned in jewelry," Neely said softly, "especially when she's lying on her back beneath me."

A few minutes later, Neely's breath became slow and even with sleep. Charley ran her hand up and down Neely's thigh and hip and kissed her shoulder, amazed by the strong young body next to hers. But she was acutely aware this would be the only time that wall should come down. She didn't belong here. And she couldn't ask Neely to continue with a liaison whose outcome wouldn't end in happily ever after.

She very slowly extricated her arms from around Neely, slipped out of the bed, and gathered her clothes. In the living room, she dressed, found a piece of paper and a pen, and sat down.

My sweet Neely,

I think our coming together is kismet. What you gave me tonight can't be measured, and you have no idea how grateful I am for it. But it's what you give me Tuesday nights that is having the greatest impact, and it's what I need most from you. You are gifted, probably more than you realize, you are a natural teacher, and I'd like to be your student. Until I can catch up. If that will ever be possible.

"Kismet" comes from the Turkish and Arabic for "portion" or "division," to working our way through the chapters or sections of our lives to reach our destinies. I'm hoping that when I show up at the library Tuesday night, you'll be there, wanting the next chapter, too. I think that's the future we can ask of each other. And if you're not there, I'll understand.

Charley

She took the rose she'd brought from the vase Neely had put it in, tiptoed into the bedroom, laid it on the pillow with the note, and quietly let herself out of the apartment.

CHAPTER SEVENTEEN

Minutes later, in a cab heading downtown, the driver chattering about the loneliness of the city's streets at this hour, Charley pulled out her phone, clicked on Joanna's contact, and looked at the blank space where a photo should've been. But she didn't need a photo. Over the prattle of the cabbie, the soaring orchestrations of "Johanna" from the musical *Sweeney Todd* began playing in Charley's mind, and she heard the young suitor swearing that he thought he'd been dreaming but woke to find she was real... Neely hadn't been a dream, and although Charley and Joanna had only been out together twice, she knew, like she'd never known anything before, that there could be something real there. But would she get the chance to find out?

Bing popped up from the couch when she opened the apartment door, blinking against the too-bright hall light behind her, his fur sticking out at peculiar angles in his newly wakened state. She asked him if he wanted breakfast; he answered by stretching the length of the pillows and was asleep again before she hung up her coat. Making her way to her bed, she dropped everything on the floor and crawled under the covers. But she was wide-awake. Everything about the last few hours with Neely played through her mind. She hadn't had sex like that in years. Moving into a more comfortable position, she realized when her sciatic nerve complained that she'd be paying for it over the next couple of days. She didn't care. In fact, for a moment she thought about going back to Neely's apartment and...what? Tell her she'd made a mistake leaving like that? No. It hadn't been a mistake.

It was the right decision for both of them. And for what she hoped might happen with Joanna. A conversation she'd had in the library with Neely the other night came back to her, and she realized she was still smarting from it. She'd asked Neely what path she planned on following when she finally got her master's in May. Neely had looked at her blankly until she prompted her to think about what kind of employment she'd seek.

"I'm going to write," she had answered.

"And pay the rent with what?" Charley had asked.

"I'll figure it out. But I won't be you. I won't take something nine to five to pay that rent and sacrifice my craft."

Not for the first time, the fact that Charley was old enough to be her mother had resonated with her.

Bob jumped up on the bed and poked his cold nose against her cheek like a brief kiss. Then he settled his fluffy little body alongside hers, facing her, stretched one paw out to protectively touch her wrist, sighed, and closed his eyes. *I have a special relationship with the Sandman,* she'd told Joanna. Where was he now? She thought about popping a couple of ibuprofen but didn't want to wake Bob. Staring out the window at the inky darkness giving way to dawn, Charley realized she was on a desire line in her life right now. She'd departed from the tried-and-true path the night she'd met Joanna and had forged further off it with Neely. For all intents and purposes, she was in the middle of nowhere now. Of one thing she was certain: she didn't want to go back to the worn path. She closed her eyes and saw the two glittering green eyes that seemed to haunt her sleep almost every night now...

Late Saturday morning, Charley carried the pail of sudsy water from the kitchen to the bedroom and began moving furniture to clean, finding pockets of dirt that made her crazy. *How does this stuff get in here? I have screens on every window.* The armoire door was still ajar from having moved it to clean behind it, and when she slipped her hand inside and braced her shoulder against it to move it back into place, something squeaked, the door banged open, and a panicked Bob flew out. Charley screamed and then fell on the bed laughing.

When she recovered, she headed to the bathroom to take care of last night's clothes still in a heap where they'd been tossed. The scent of sex was on everything. She put the lingerie into cold soapy water in the sink. Sitting on the side of the tub for a moment, she thought about last night. Her phone hadn't rung, there were no texts or emails. Was Neely okay? Or was she licking her wounds? Charley would know for certain Tuesday night. It had been difficult asking Neely, in the note, to meet her this coming Tuesday at the library, as usual, but it was the only way she knew to preserve the relationship she wanted with her, and to give her the same avenue.

Rinsing the lingerie, Charley then gently wrung out the pieces in the sink, hung them up, and tossed everything else into the laundry hamper.

The armoire needed tidying, but she found a rugby shirt and a pair of capri pants, and pulled them out. It was a balmy autumn day and she wanted to take advantage of the sunshine on the walk downtown. Half an hour later, she was standing at Tricia's front desk admiring the woman behind it who was calling upstairs. Tricia's warning that her weekend concierge was stunning had been an understatement.

Tricia was waiting when she stepped off the elevator. Charley could tell that something had shifted in the night. It didn't take her long to draw it out. Tricia had had second thoughts about the levels of pain she might be facing after going over Charley's notes, and she wondered if she shouldn't consider radiation to manage the tumor. Before Tricia could rethink it, Charley texted Dr. Gerard asking how soon the first treatment could be arranged. His responding text arrived soon after and they read it together. He had set up the appointment for early Monday morning, explaining that this would be the simulation. The radiation oncologist would fit molds and blocks on Tricia's prone body to pinpoint the precise area to hit with the measured radiation. With that map, Tricia would be in and out five mornings a week, and each session would only be a matter of minutes. Charley blanched, realizing the possibility of spending every morning with Tricia could become reality.

"You know," Tricia said, "I can probably get through the treatments myself. A few minutes is not a big deal. So you're off the hook, Sancho Panza."

Charley's relief was quickly replaced by guilt, neither of which she wanted Tricia to know she was experiencing. She left Tricia's after lunch. Ensconced on the couch watching the Clemson game, she realized she'd lost track of time thinking about Tricia when Bob jumped up onto her chest and gently poked at her nose with his curled paw. She hoisted the cat under her arm like a football and did the Heisman Trophy run to the kitchen, Bob complaining loudly until she put his dinner plate down. Bing sauntered in and hunkered down in front of his plate. Charley left them happily eating and headed out to Brooke's.

Following nearly the same route to Brooke's as she had to Tricia's, Charley marveled at the irony that Brooke and Tricia only lived a few blocks apart and hadn't known it. They had never liked each other. Brooke thought Tricia was high-handed and arrogant, and Tricia thought Brooke was flip and judgmental. They'd both been right.

The one silver lining of tonight's get-together: her friends hadn't invited a woman for her to meet. For the first time in a long time, though, she wasn't looking forward to the evening. And that bothered her. She loved these dinners, which had started out so many years ago as Brooke's way of keeping their circle of college friends together. They'd become an anchor for her, a place to be completely herself with the women she knew best. Girlfriends had come and gone, or, like Annie, become wives and stayed. That Jamie and Lindsay finally realized they'd had a thing for each other since sophomore year, had acted on it, and become a couple several years ago, amused them all no end. But tonight, she'd actually considered telling Brooke she wasn't feeling well and staying home.

She bought a bottle of white wine on the walk down, not wanting to be the empty-handed guest she'd been last month. Lindsay answered the door, drew Charley inside, and hugged her, offering an apology.

"Let's let that go, Linds. I'm fine, I'm sure Karen is fine. So don't take on any guilt for either one of us." Charley poured a short Johnnie Walker Black and asked who'd seen the most recent plot twist on *The Blacklist,* and like that, Karen was quickly forgotten, traded for the intrigue of Red Reddington, and then for all the current troubles in their lives. Charley was content to sit back and listen to each of them sort out the other's problems, forgetting everything about her own. Toward the end of dinner, her phone vibrated, and she slid it out of her pocket, figuring it was her mother. After a recent series of emails with her brother Robert, she'd taken on her mother's grocery duties and now received all manner of texts from her asking for one item at a time, giving her insight into why Robert needed help. Instead, it was Joanna.

Joanna: *Just a quick drop-in to say hi, how are you, and where are we going Monday night?*

Charley was surprised. And thrilled. She got up from her chair and moved to a window in the living room. *Hey! Nice to hear from you, I'm fine and I was thinking about Pietro's because it's a block from the Y. Is that okay, and how are you?*

Joanna: *Irene having an off night so I'm hovering. Just thinking about what to wear this week if I don't do laundry Mon.*

Charley quietly laughed. *And here I was thinking you were thinking about me. Hold on while I put this ego down. There, much better.*

Joanna sent back an eyeball-rolling emoticon.

A local Italian place, wear jeans if you want.

A thumbs-up emoji came back. When nothing else followed, Charley returned to the table and was met with several inquisitive looks.

"Was that your mom? Everything okay?" Brooke asked.

"It was a...friend."

"Really?" Jamie asked. "Because you're all pink."

Charley scrambled. "Must be the heat register. I was standing right near it."

Annie came out of the kitchen with a pot of coffee and put a raspberry cobbler in front of Brooke. She leaned over Charley's shoulder and quietly asked her if she wanted to talk to them about Tricia over dessert. Charley shook her head.

"Who wants cobbler?" Brooke asked, the knife poised above the dessert. Everyone raised their hand.

"Charley, you've been awfully quiet tonight," Lindsay said.

"Except for that text message from your friend," Jamie noted, putting air quotes around the word.

"I do have friends other than you guys, you know."

Brooke coughed and Charley shot her a warning look.

"Okay, you two," Jamie said. "We know your Laurel and Hardy routine."

"Charley's seeing someone," Brooke said. "Two someones."

Charley shook her head at Brooke and looked out the window at the traffic pouring up Sixth Avenue, a little ticked off.

"What the heck?" Jamie asked.

Annie poked Brooke's shoulder. "You could've let her tell us in her own time."

"She wouldn't have, then," Brooke replied.

"Are you?" Lindsay asked.

"That's why you left the table with your phone," Jamie said.

Charley cleared her throat. "I suppose I owe you an explanation after all the work you did so *ceaselessly* on my behalf in the last year, hoping to find someone for me," Charley said sarcastically, "although I never asked you to."

"You'd have done the same for us."

"Would I, Jamie? Or might I have respected your process and let you come to your own conclusion about the timeline you needed to get over breaking up with Lindsay and finding someone else to warm your bed?"

"Okay, you guys," Lindsay interrupted. "We feel bad enough about our culpability all around, and maybe, Charley, we should've asked you first before trying to fix you up, but you would've said no, and we did it because we love you and you were stagnating." Lindsay held up her hand when Charley moved to interrupt. "You were. You shut yourself off. And it was hard for us to watch your world getting smaller each year."

Charley looked down at her hands in her lap. Maybe it was hard for her to admit that they were right, as hard as it had been to tell Brooke she'd realized how lonely she'd become.

"And now, look," Lindsay noted. "Maybe we jarred something in you. Who is she?"

"You mean who are they?" Jamie said. "Brooke said there are two someones."

"Well, she's wrong. As of last night."

"What happened last night?" Brooke asked.

"I'm sorry I didn't call you, but I'm still processing. I slept with Neely and then I...I don't know, I broke that part of it off with her."

"Wait a friggin' minute," Jamie interrupted. "I need to throw out the penalty flag here. I didn't see any of that play and I feel like that's a hit on a defenseless player. On all of us."

"Why don't you start at the beginning," Annie said, a protective hand on Charley's shoulder.

Charley quickly wove together the facts of the last few weeks, frankly told them about the note and the rose she'd left on Neely's pillow, and about seeing Joanna again on Monday evening.

"Holy shit," Jamie said. "Where did this all come from?"

"Somehow Karen jarred something loose," Brooke said.

"Something like that," Charley said, leaning her elbows on the table.

"Okay, so we succeeded," Lindsay said. "Even if it wasn't with any of the women we introduced you to."

"Something like that," Brooke reiterated. "So, was Neely amazing in bed?"

"Brooke!" Annie admonished her.

"What? Inquiring minds want to know," Brooke said shamelessly.

Jamie laughed. "You can be so inappropriate, you know that?"

Charley cleared her throat. "She was...yeah. It was smokin' hot. I'm still sore."

There was total silence for a moment.

"And you're all jealous," Charley added.

She was met with a chorus of "No," "Oh, hey, we're good," and one "I love my wife," none of them convincing to Charley's ear, and all of them tinged with embarrassment.

"Glad you did it?" Brooke asked.

Charley looked at her entwined fingers. "Not sure. Think so. There's just so much going on right now, I don't need any complications in my life."

"What's going on?" Lindsay asked.

Charley fiddled with a spoon, wanting the question to go away, but of course it wouldn't, and she was going to have to deal with it sooner or later. The silence hung there. "Tricia called."

"Well, I'll be damned," Jamie said. "Destry rides again."

"Hush!" Brooke said.

Charley paid no attention to Jamie's remark. "She's been calling me for weeks. And it was too hard for me to call her back. But she finally caught me last Saturday." Putting her hand into her pocket for the *balance* stone, Charley looked at each one of these friends that she'd known for so many years, certain she could count on them to help her get through what she was about to tell them. They'd been there for her every time she'd needed them, and they would be now. She poured herself another scotch and gave them the news.

CHAPTER EIGHTEEN

Charley had called Tricia Sunday night to invite herself to the radiology appointment Monday morning, and when she hadn't protested, Charley confirmed her suspicion that Tricia was frightened and actually wanted someone around. Now, as she leaned against the building waiting for her, she hitched her canvas bag up behind her shoulder blades and moved a little to the left to get out of the morning glare. Glancing up Sixty-Sixth Street, she spotted Tricia in the mix of people heading toward the front door.

"Whoa. Did you take a bus? I didn't see you getting out of a cab."

"Don't be ridiculous. I left it at Third Avenue and walked over. I figured I could use a little exercise."

Charley snorted. "I always hated your metabolism. Whip-thin, ate anything you wanted, didn't even glance at a gym as you walked by."

"Some of us are genetically lucky and some of us aren't. I guess I'm both now. So," Tricia said, hitting the revolving door, "how was the rest of your weekend?"

"Fine."

Tricia eyed her in the elevator. "*Fine* was always your smoke and mirrors."

Charley faced her, one eyebrow raised.

"I know something is up. I knew it on Saturday."

The elevator doors opened, and Charley looked around. "Which way is Radiology?" Tricia found a map on the wall and they studied it together.

"Oh, here." Charley pointed to a line on the map. "Green hallway over here." She headed down the hall.

Tricia followed. "Come over to dinner tonight. We can talk about this radiology and you can tell me what's going on. Because something *is* going on."

"I'm not doing this with you, Tricia." Charley opened the door to the Radiology Department, almost let it slam on Tricia, and went to the desk. "Tricia Sullivan, a seven thirty appointment with Dr. Chadha."

The receptionist checked a list and picked a file off the top of the stack on her desk. "Right this way, Miss Sullivan, Dr. Chadha is ready."

"No, she's Miss Sullivan, I'm here to observe," Charley said, pointing at Tricia.

"Only if you agree to come to dinner tonight. Otherwise you can sit out here," Tricia said as she took her file and walked through the door ahead of Charley.

"Radiology One is on the right," the receptionist advised her.

Charley grabbed the door handle before it shut.

"I hear footsteps," Tricia said. "You must be coming to dinner."

"You are completely insensitive, you know that?" Charley hated when Tricia did this sort of thing to her. She'd always hated when Tricia won, too. "I can't come to dinner. I…have to work. Emily's going to the Middle East. I have a lot to do to get her ready." She wasn't about to share Joanna with Tricia.

"Again? You may not think so, but from where I stand, Emily sure as hell owns you. All I want is for you to open the door for me." She held the door open for Charley, who went through it, glowering at her as she did. "I need you and you just might need me. It's that simple." Tricia went into the changing room and picked up the paper gown sitting on the table. There was no vulnerability to her argument. Simply her truth. "So, come down after you finish, and we'll have a light supper. We'll order out."

"Do you want me to come down because you're afraid of the radiology?"

"Wouldn't you be?"

Charley took notes as the simulation unfolded in front of her, the technicians making small marks on Tricia's chest, further delineating the area to be radiated with blocks and plastic cutouts until they had several tiny precise circles mapped out. While they worked, Dr. Chadha, the radiology doctor, came in and explained how this would play out for the next two weeks, how the maps created today could change as the radiation had the desired effect, if it did, of shrinking the tumors and what the possible next steps could be. When the technicians finished, she and Charley stepped out into the hallway to wait for Tricia. It was the opportunity she'd been seeking.

"What kind of fatigue will she be facing from all this? I know we talked about it in that first meeting, and about a lot of other effects she'll be feeling, but I'm not sure I understood as much then as I do now."

"I think the cumulative effect will get to her by the end of the first week. The sessions will be less than fifteen minutes, and she could be fine until the end of the day. She may need someone then. She'll certainly need support by the end of the week. She could experience some epidermal burning, and some soreness deep in her body that might manifest itself outwardly."

"She thinks she'll be okay, that nothing will really affect her."

"These are pretty sizeable tumors and I'll be going after them with all I've got. We don't want this to metastasize. She *will* be affected."

Tricia came out of the changing room and eyed Charley with Dr. Chadha. "Same time the rest of the week?" she asked the doctor.

"Yes. The technician can take care of you. I'll be back on Friday," Dr. Chadha said.

Tricia turned and walked away. "Coming, Sancho?"

Charley caught up to her.

"I know you're about to protest or be noble about this, but really," Tricia said as she pressed the elevator button, "I don't need your help with this part. Go to the pool."

"Tricia, it's a lot of radiation they're throwing at you. Wasn't this sort of thing the whole reason you called?"

"I spoke with Dr. Gerard this morning. We went over everything radiology. I'll be fine to do this on my own. I don't want help yet. I don't want it until I absolutely need it. And I wish you hadn't questioned Dr. Chadha."

"Well, if you're not going to share information, where else do I get it? You know what?" Charley stepped into the elevator that had just opened and held the door for Tricia. "I'm happy to go back to my life." Sure enough, Tricia had pushed a button. And Charley was instantly furious. "But you are aware you have a track record of waiting too long to ask for help. And then, you're halfway over the cliff's edge and I have to chase you and clean up the mess."

"That elevator is going up," Tricia said quietly. "We want to go down."

Charley looked at the green "up" arrow on the panel, apologized to the people standing behind her, and got off.

"I'll strike a bargain with you," Tricia said as the arriving down elevator pinged.

Charley regarded her warily as they descended, working to check that familiar anger.

"I will ask the nanosecond I feel the need, and I won't bury it and try to be strong if you open the door. Just as a friend. You can put up the stop sign any time you want. And you can help me all you want, then. Come down every night if you feel like it."

Charley felt the sigh coming all the way from her toes. "Oh, Tricia. You never stop, that's the problem."

"I'll take your secrets to the grave, I promise."

"Not funny!"

"I kind of thought it was." Tricia walked through the revolving door. "Look, I promise you, everything will be on your terms with us now."

Charley concentrated on the cabs coming down the street as Tricia put her arm out to hail one and wondered how anything between them now would ever be on her terms when everything for the foreseeable future would be about Tricia's needs. She sighed again, knowing the answer. "You *will* ask, and not make me guess and chase you or pull you back from the precipice?"

"Absolutely."

"And when I tell you 'enough' you will back off from my private life." Tricia crossed her heart and then opened the door of the cab that had pulled up. Charley got in and Tricia followed.

"What time can I expect you, then?" Tricia asked.

"Probably close to nine o'clock."

Pietro's wasn't busy when Charley and Joanna got there. It was what she'd been counting on, wanting the kind of quiet she liked for talking. They were both rather taken by the beautiful young bartender, watching her as she worked until finally Joanna said, "I know I'm an inveterate girl-watcher but somehow, I didn't expect it from you."

"You didn't think I was a second home kind of person either, so I guess I'm as full of surprises as you are."

"I'm not full of surprises, Charley. I'm exactly what you see."

Charley thought of the handcuff necklace. "Well, I was a child bride and moved in with Tricia almost right out of college. All I could do for years was look."

"Seems like you're making up for lost time now, and since tonight is supposed to be about unanswered questions from last week, 'young and a writer'?"

Charley told her about Neely, leaving out the events of Friday night. And then she told her about the novel, its birth in graduate school, the long drought, and how invaluable Neely had become as she worked anew.

"You never let your dream go, did you? Even when it walked away from you. That takes deep reserves. I like that about you."

Charley was a little surprised by Joanna's reaction, and her insight, and studied her drink. "It's all I ever wanted. But I had nowhere else to go but into the nine-to-five workforce when the writer's block became an immoveable force."

"Well, now it sounds like you have two jobs. You must do all your writing after work? That must be exhausting."

Charley thought about it for a moment. "No. It's actually what I always imagined the gods must feel when they returned to Mount Olympus after they'd been gone for a while."

"Wow." Joanna smiled.

Charley's phone rang. She glanced at it, saw it was Tricia, and excused herself.

"You need to go, don't you?" Joanna asked when Charley sat back down.

She sighed. "I told you my ex recently came back into my life because she needed a friend."

Joanna nodded.

"It's really because she's ill and she needs my help."

"Oh, Charley, I'm sorry."

Charley shook her head. "I told her I'd go down and see her tonight, so I should get going. But you realize one of us here didn't take care of some unanswered questions, so we may need to do this again next week."

"I didn't hear you ask any questions," Joanna said as she put on her down jacket.

Charley's laugh was barely audible. "You wouldn't tell me where in California you grew up when you reacted to the cold the other night."

"Oh, that… Kind of drove you a little nuts, didn't it?"

"Yes, it did." In a quickly calculated move, she stepped in and zipped up Joanna's jacket. "Something tells me you like driving women nuts, though."

"It does? So you've given that some thought."

"I've given a lot of things some thought, Miss Hair Shirt." Only a few inches away from her, she could've kissed Joanna in this moment, wanted to, but the serious look that passed over Joanna's face made her step back.

"Oh, you don't want to hear about that part of my life, trust me."

"Well, you have a week to think about it," Charley said softly. She gave the bartender several bills after she told her what the damage was. "Keep the change."

Outside, Joanna hailed a cab for Charley.

"Text me Saturday night again?" Charley asked. "I liked that you did that last weekend."

"I'll think about that, too."

"Mmm-hmm." Charley got into the cab and waved as it pulled away. She couldn't help but wish Tricia had been okay on her own tonight. These snatched moments with Joanna just weren't long enough.

The doorman picked up the house phone the moment he saw Charley and nodded toward the bank of elevators. When the doors opened on the twenty-first floor, Tricia was waiting, a set of keys dangling from her finger.

"Here. These are for you. The staff knows you have them."

Charley slipped them into her pocket, feeling odd about the transaction that was so reminiscent of the first time Tricia had handed her a set of keys to her apartment twenty-eight years earlier.

In the kitchen, they plated the Indian take-out dinner. Charley was getting to know the layout of where everything was, and they worked in tandem almost as smoothly as they had on West End Avenue. She called her mother to check on her while Tricia whisked dressing for a salad she'd made.

"She doesn't know about this, does she?" Tricia asked when Charley hung up.

"No, and she never will." Charley caught the sorrow passing over Tricia's face as she turned to open the refrigerator.

Tricia took the salads and drinks out to the living room and turned on the game. Charley brought the plates of chicken vindaloo to the coffee table and they settled down on the floor.

"That remote could fly a plane, but then your TV is the size of most movie theater screens."

"Reagan liked things big."

Charley glanced at Tricia and almost laughed, seeing the pleased look on her face.

"What? Can I help it if I'm larger than life?"

Charley laughed out loud. "I never thought I'd say this, Tricia Sullivan, but don't ever change."

"As if. Listen, I've been reading the sports pages again. The Colts are going to lose tonight. Their offensive line has huge holes in it," Tricia offered. "And normally I'd wait for your analysis, but I think this game will be over in the first four minutes and I want to know what you've been holding out on me. It's much more than your young writer, isn't it? Is it the other woman?"

Charley picked at her salad for a moment. "Not the radiation, huh? We have to begin with this?"

Tricia looked at her expectantly.

"I want no advice from the peanut gallery, got it?"

"Not offering advice. Just listening."

Charley gave Tricia an abbreviated accounting of what Brooke and company had been doing, fixing her up with women for the last two years.

"I'd say you needed that kick in the pants."

"Peanut gallery, did you not hear my warning?"

Tricia tilted her head in apology, and Charley decided to let her know about how Karen had affected her, and how that had led to Neely.

"A third woman first? Interesting. Why did you let Karen get away without at least one night of fun in bed? You were the queen of short affairs when I met you. Have you lost your touch? Maybe you need to pick someone up in a bar this weekend, make sure everything still works."

"No advice and NO judging!"

"I mean, when was the last time you slept with a woman, Charley?"

"Friday night."

Tricia missed the coaster she was putting her glass on, sending lemon slices, ice, and water cascading across the coffee table, spilling over the edge in a miniature waterfall.

"Oops. Weren't ready for that, were you?" Charley said smugly as she got up and headed toward the kitchen.

"With who?"

"Whom," Charley corrected her as she disappeared down the hall. "If I was out with the writer Friday night, who do you think it was?"

"Neely," Tricia said quietly.

When Charley came back into the living room with the roll of paper towels and set about cleaning up the spill, Tricia was staring out the window.

"You told me she wasn't right for you."

Charley stopped wiping the table, aware that Tricia's concentration on the city below was a ruse for the emotional pain she was likely feeling. "I'm not sure we should discuss this anymore," Charley said. "In fact, I should put up the stop sign."

"Not yet. Why did you sleep with her when there's someone else on your horizon? And you haven't told me anything about the other woman, not even her name."

"Stop sign."

Tricia picked up a forkful of salad. "I already know she's gotten under your skin. We both know how far down that blush came from the other night when you mentioned her."

Charley sighed. "I don't know if I mean anything to her yet. Or if I will. And Neely was my George Mallory moment. Like Everest, she was there. But it's the writer in her that I want, so I left a note of apology on her pillow in the middle of the night." Charley realized she'd said more than she'd meant to when she saw a light dawn in Tricia's eyes.

"You're writing again."

"And what if I am?"

"Well, it's about time, that's all. You were good, Charley, and I was always so sad that you stopped." Tricia took a spoonful of her vindaloo. "It's getting cold. We'd better eat."

Charley gratefully dug in.

"Maybe that's the difference I'm sensing." Tricia glanced at her. "You were always so much lighter when you were writing. But I bet the other woman has something to do with this lightness in you. Who is she? Where did you meet her?"

"Stop sign."

Tricia played with her food. Charley watched out of the corner of her eye, unsure if it had something to do with the conversation or Tricia's appetite after the radiation.

"A note on her pillow, huh? Isn't that like kids today breaking up by text?"

"I wasn't breaking up with her. It was a one-night stand. And you need to eat. You can't afford to lose any weight."

"Not really hungry. Heard from her yet?"

Charley put her bowl down.

"Do you think you broke her heart?"

"Please don't say that."

"Then who's the mystery woman?"

"You promised you wouldn't push."

Tricia put her hand on Charley's. "I don't want to see you get *your* heart broken in this equation. I can't watch that happen to you. I need to know it won't happen."

Charley leaned back against the couch. "I love that you're concerned, but it's my life and my heart. And you are the last person in the world who can protect me or who should step in the way of anything I'm doing with anyone. Understood?"

Tricia sighed and nodded contritely.

The truth was, Charley wasn't sure whose heart would get broken in this situation. Or if Neely's already had.

CHAPTER NINETEEN

There was something wonderful about the way the city smelled on autumn afternoons: brownstone fireplaces burning fragrant pine and oak, restaurant exhaust systems emitting the tantalizing aromas of winter comfort dishes, and the sharp smokiness emanating from the hot chestnut carts that began popping up on street corners. But mostly what Charley loved was the almost bitter pungency of the earth winding down for winter. Decaying leaves mulched, giving off a dense woodsy odor. It mingled with the peculiar perfume of the various hibernating florae planted around all the trees on the streets. Other greenery standing sentinel in decorative pots on either side of apartment door buildings was replaced with small pine and fir trees releasing that clean sap scent, and they'd be decked in lights and Christmas decorations soon enough. She breathed it all in on the walk downtown, jingling Tricia's keys in her coat pocket as she worked on a plan to move her toward hiring in-house help for evenings or overnight stays. She would need them sooner or later, and Charley needed them now for sanity's sake. She'd spent almost every night with Tricia this week and she was tired. Besides, she needed to keep a step ahead of things. Tricia's own fatigue as the week's radiation wore on seemed to compound on itself. Time was of the essence in everything she would be doing for Tricia.

Charley heard the football game on the TV when she let herself into the apartment. Tricia was curled up on the couch sound asleep, so she covered her with a white afghan that was folded up in a basket next to the couch, lowered the volume on the TV, and went to the kitchen to see what the refrigerator held that could be put together for dinner. On the counter was a receipt from the supermarket's delivery service. She read over the list of items Tricia had ordered, opened the refrigerator, and pulled out the rib eye roast. It was the perfect afternoon for a roast with potatoes and vegetables. As tempted as she was to quietly walk through the rest of the rooms that Tricia hadn't shown her, Charley prepped the ingredients for the roasting pan, seared the meat in some herbes de Provence, got it into the oven, and then opened her laptop to work on the novel.

A while later, she went to the living room to look in on Tricia and found her awake, the afghan pulled up to her chin.

"God, there is nothing like a fall Sunday, football, and the smell of a good roast in the apartment. When did you get here?"

"Around three."

"Where have you been? I thought for sure you'd be sitting right here glued to the games. Or were you poking through the other rooms? I realized after you left the other night that I never showed you the whole place."

"Been in the kitchen working."

"Really? What time did the roast go in?"

"Three thirty."

"That's a long time in the kitchen. Don't tell me you're saddled with stuff from work?"

"No, the novel."

Tricia regarded Charley thoughtfully. "Good."

She pushed the afghan aside and sat up. "Oh my God, I'm tired. And I have to pee. Do you want the nickel tour?"

"Sure, and then I'll jump out the window of the last room."

"Don't say that. I was afraid you'd have that reaction. What I did to you depresses me."

"What you did to us."

Charley thought she caught a glimpse of regret in Tricia's steady gaze. "Mea culpa, my sweet. I've paid for it."

She did, indeed, want to jump out the window of the last room because it was a fully loaded laundry room with a view of New York Harbor. *And I do my laundry in a cramped basement space that holds twenty washers and dryers and two five-foot folding tables for three hundred and fifty apartments. I bet Reagan never did laundry in here, but I still hate her for this.*

"Come to the kitchen. I need to talk to you," Tricia said. She opened a bottle of wine and poured them each a glass. "How's Neely? Anything?"

Charley busied herself putting away the dishes in Tricia's drain board. "She took the week off from her job, emailed me to tell me. Said she needed a little time."

"So you did break her heart."

"You said you needed to talk?"

"Is that my stop sign?" Tricia asked.

Charley cocked her head, knowing her stare was the blank one she'd perfected years ago for department store salespeople and other idiots.

Tricia pursed her lips and Charley knew whatever the news was, it wouldn't be good.

"The firm doesn't want to buy me out. They suspect something is wrong. They didn't believe that at my age I want to bow out of the hustle of the Big Leagues to open my own little shop where I can work a couple of hours a day."

"How could they actually know that? What did you say to them?"

"Not 'them.' Schuyler. The board flagged him to my request, which I knew would happen, and he said that whatever I might be thinking, the firm isn't willing to lose my name from the door. So I can retire, but I have to leave them my name."

"Well, then."

"I'm going to hire a lawyer. I want a buyout."

"Why? Just retire. You're gonna be a little busy soon, ya know?"

"I have plans for that money. I want it."

Charley checked herself. "Do whatever you feel you need to do. But understand that this could add unneeded stress to your life, and stress will not be good for you."

"You know I always liked a good fight."

"You forget who you're talking to."

"I'm going to need your help. I can't use my assistant at work."

"Oh." Charley looked at the ceiling. "Well, I signed up for everything, but not that. Hire some kid to temp for you."

"I need your expertise. It would only be for, like, ten hours a week. I'll pay you whatever price you name."

"No." Charley drew a line in the sand, surprised at how easy it was now. "I have precious little time to write as it is. And how long do you plan on continuing to go into the office?"

"Until I can't put one foot in front of the other."

Tricia's medical team had addressed a timeline with her. It had been the hardest part of the meetings for Charley, especially when Dr. Gerard had told her to consider knocking off anything on the top of her bucket list right away. "Why would you do that?"

"Because it's who I am. You know that."

"Maybe you could consider being someone else for once."

Tricia's expression didn't change as she took a sip of wine.

Charley sighed. "I'll get you a top-notch temp. And I think we need to discuss when we should bring in a night nurse. If you're going through with a lawsuit, you're going to be drained at the end of each day. And I can't spend every night here."

"Not ready to discuss a nurse."

"Tricia!"

"I'm putting up *my* stop sign."

Charley studied her for a moment. "Fine. Do you want to eat in the living room, the dining room, or in here? I'm not sure I even know who's playing tonight."

"Seriously? That's not like you. Denver at Indianapolis. It'll be fun watching the Broncos steamroll that Colts front line. Let's eat in the living room with the game."

Fifteen minutes later, they were set up and waiting for the talking heads to come on the air.

"Charley, this is terrific. You have no idea how much I've missed your cooking."

"Let me guess. Reagan complained if she broke a nail calling out for delivery."

"You seem to have figured her out in a hurry."

After dinner, Charley grabbed her laptop from the kitchen and sat back down next to Tricia, who leaned over to look at the screen.

"Don't even try," Charley said.

Tricia turned the sound down on the game.

"I can concentrate with the game on. Sports has become soothing white noise while I work. If the game is actually any good, I'll tune back in, so you can leave the sound up."

An hour later, Charley heard light snores from Tricia, who had stretched out on the couch.

She worked a while longer and then woke Tricia to take her into her bedroom. After settling her in, Charley walked slowly through the apartment, turning on the lights in each room, marveling at what she saw, and ended up in a recessed window well in the formal dining room looking at the Modigliani she had seen the first night. The dark, she decided, was infinitely better, and she turned the light off, sitting in the recessed window again. *This was supposed to be my life. I put in the years getting Tricia from associate to partner. This should've been mine.*

As much as she wanted to, she no longer felt sorry for herself. The travails of the last three years had been her crucible, and she knew now that she'd come through them. Tricia's affair had actually set her free.

Charley went back to the living room and sat down to finish the chapter she'd been working on. But first she pulled out her phone and scrolled to Joanna's contact.

Still thinking about texting me?

Joanna: *Sorry, can't hear you. Do you have your ego on over there? Kinda loud.*

Charley laughed and hit the phone icon. Joanna answered right away.

"Can you talk? I realize I probably should've asked you first."

"For just a minute, yes," Joanna said.

"I really only wanted to find out if you're still up for going out tomorrow night."

"I am, but I realize it's my turn to find a place and I don't really know any good bars or restaurants in that part of town, and I haven't had time to research."

"Do you want me to make any suggestions?"

"I'm not a slacker. I'll find something."

"All right, then, see you tomorrow." She hung up, feeling like a teenager getting ready for a first date. But it wasn't one, right? Not yet.

CHAPTER TWENTY

C harley poured the coffee she'd just brewed into her thermos. "Wow. What are you doing up at this hour?"

Charley was surprised to see Tricia standing in the doorway of the kitchen. She looked pale and worn out. "Going to the pool. My class begins in half an hour. Decided your coffee looked good, so I made a pot. Want a cup? I didn't wake you, did I?"

"No. I've been up a while. I wanted to ask you something last night. Yes, I'll take a cup."

Charley found a mug, retrieved the milk from the refrigerator, and put them both in front of Tricia, who'd sat on a stool at the granite work island.

"I decided your temp idea last night was good. You're right, you shouldn't give up any more time than I'm already asking."

"Great. I'm sure your assistant can find a temp for you."

"I can't ask her to do that! I need you to find this person for me."

Charley sighed. "Of course you do. Send me an email."

"And listen, I can take care of myself tonight. You stay home."

Charley wasn't sure Tricia could take care of herself, despite the fact that all Tricia would have to do was warm up the roast leftovers, but she sent up a silent thanks to whichever saint fielded prayers for caretakers.

❖

Charley saw Neely at the front desk of the Y when she reached for the door. Hoping she'd found some peace, and feeling a little anxiety settle in her own chest, she went in. Neely looked up immediately.

"Hi," Charley said, handing her ID over the counter.

"Hi," Neely said, her tone neutral. "I'm sorry about last week. I just needed a little space."

"You don't owe me an apology. If anything, it's me who owes you one."

Neely studied the desk for a minute. Charley listened for anyone else coming in the door. It would be awkward if they got interrupted in this moment.

Neely swiped her ID and handed it back to her. "No. I think it was something we both needed. Or it wouldn't have happened. I wish it didn't have to end, though. And I'm still working on what you said in your note. But I like being your teacher. So, tomorrow night?"

Charley smiled and headed for the stairs but turned back. Handing the *balance* stone to Neely, she said, "My best friend gave this to me when…well, at a time of turmoil in my life, and she promised me that what's inscribed there would come back to me. It did. I think you need this now."

Neely turned it over and over and ran her thumb across its smooth surfaces. Her eyes watered, and Charley headed for the stairs before she lost her composure, too.

In the afternoon, when Emily left for several back-to-back meetings, Charley was able to concentrate on the search for Tricia's assistant. *I can't believe I'm doing this, but if it takes things off my plate, it's worth it.* Her first call was to a friend who temped full-time to find out what agencies she worked with, and then she contacted the one that most intrigued her, an agency that represented actors between gigs. The consultant she spoke with understood Charley's parameters for the job, and by the end of the day, she had five résumés to peruse. She studied each one carefully, scrutinizing them for bullshit or buzzwords, and settled on two candidates to interview, one male and one female. Tricia hadn't specified, and while Charley knew she'd rather work with a woman, a man might be exactly what she needed now. She called the consultant back and set up the interviews for late Tuesday afternoon, and then headed out for the pool.

By the time she got to the Y, she knew she wasn't going to push Joanna to talk about anything she didn't want to tonight. With the *balance* stone now in Neely's pocket, she decided all she needed at this point in her life was the realization that had come to her during her walk on Long Beach. The idea that she couldn't necessarily control things was still foreign, but she sensed it was the best way to be, especially with Joanna, who definitely didn't seem like the kind of woman who could be controlled or handled.

She spotted the Post-it note on Joanna's usual locker. *Got here early, already in the pool.* She quickly drew a smiley face on the bottom, changed, and headed downstairs to her class. When she got back upstairs afterward, Joanna was nearly dressed.

"You're Speedy Gonzalez tonight," Charley said.

"No, just got here early so I could do the weight room circuit and the pool."

"Wow. Everything okay, or are you just a glutton for punishment?" Charley stood looking at her, her towel around her neck. Something about her seemed subdued.

"Maybe a little of both."

"Many years of therapy have taught me how to listen, if you want to talk."

Joanna pulled a necklace out of her jacket pocket. "I'll think about it." She bent her head to the side in that graceful movement to sweep her hair out of the way, and Charley held her breath, a servant to her emotions. Joanna's fingers met at the nape of her neck to hook the clasp, but she faltered, and a silver heart fell to the floor, the chain dangling in her hand. Charley picked up the heart and took the chain from her, noticing the look of surprise in her eyes. She threaded the heart onto the chain and stepped behind Joanna to secure it.

"You had a very different pendant on the night we had coffee."

"I did."

"I've never seen anything like it."

"No?"

Charley didn't respond. The tiny clasp locked in her fingers.

Joanna turned to face her. "For all the ways that we're alike, there are ways we're not."

There was no mistaking her meaning, and a slick of fear snaked its way up Charley's gut, a vein of excitement she'd only experienced looking at certain types of photos opening up right behind it.

"A gift? From a friend?"

"A very close friend."

Charley immediately felt like an outsider. There *was* someone else in this equation, wasn't there? Then, Joanna used Charley's towel to wipe water from her face that had dripped down from her hair, and the intimate act brought her back into Joanna's realm. Still, it didn't quell the disquiet that had arisen from this new admission.

"Seems it's my turn to wait upstairs for you," Joanna said, picking up her coat and bag. "Take your time."

Joanna opened the front door when Charley came upstairs, and they headed east. She decided not to say anything at all, but to let Joanna set the evening's tone. She wondered with surprise what that tone might be when they were standing outside the Palm Too restaurant around the corner.

"This is rather high-end," she said.

"I called this afternoon. Apparently, dress codes have gone the way of the horse and buggy. Besides, we're only sitting at the bar."

They'd been there a few minutes with their drinks in front of them when Joanna finally said, "You're not going to rescue me, are you?"

Charley looked at her questioningly.

"You always manage the conversation. Fill in the gaps."

Charley was amused. By her own admission, she'd caught Joanna out. "Silences. I fill in the silences. You leave yawning chasms of them sometimes."

Joanna shrugged. "Well…I'm a minimalist, too, I guess. When it comes to talking about things." She cleared her throat. "Emotional things. I'm not really good at that."

"Well, lucky for you, I *am* good at those. Provided they're not *my* emotional things."

Joanna regarded her, then took a swig of scotch. "We were together for eight years. It ended just over a year ago and she went to San Francisco when we broke up, opened a satellite to her business here, but when the New York shop began to falter recently, she came back. And she called me. Because she needed a friend."

It was another precious piece of the puzzle dropping into place, and Charley waited patiently for whatever was coming next, a sense of dread working its way in and curling around the anxiety she already harbored.

"Her call was like a landmine explosion." Joanna glanced at her. "Sort of like what I imagine must've happened to you when your ex called?"

Charley acknowledged the question with a single nod.

"Our relationship was rocky from the day we met, but Georgia owned me in so many ways. I can't explain it. But I found I couldn't say no when she called. I needed to find out if she still..." Joanna's unfinished sentence hung in the air.

"If she still owns you." And then it dawned on Charley. "That's what the handcuff necklace is about."

"Partly, yes."

"And that's why you told me you were toxic, isn't it?" Charley asked quietly. "Have I complicated things for you?"

"More like you complicated things for her. I was finally back on my feet again. In fact, I was looking to find someone to have some fun with again."

"Oh?" Charley was crestfallen. Was that what she was, a bit of fun?

"And then I met you." Joanna sighed. "And now quite frankly, I don't have any idea what I'm doing anymore."

"Well." Charley picked up her drink and drained it, relieved, realizing the door *was* open to her, and that what she wanted to do was unobtrusively walk through it and close it against Georgia. "It's a good thing you asked me if I needed a pool buddy because I'd say we're both in the deep end here."

"I've complicated things for you?" Joanna asked.

"I never thought my ex would make an appearance again. I'm not the kind who looks for someone to have fun with, and I definitely wasn't looking for another relationship." Charley sucked a partially melted ice cube into her mouth. "And then you showed up out of nowhere."

Joanna had finished her drink and signaled the bartender for the bill. "This could be bad, couldn't it? What do you suppose we should do?"

"Tread water?" Charley asked. "Keep each other from drowning?"

Joanna considered the suggestion as she riffled through the bills in her pocket, pulled a couple out, and set them on the bar under her empty glass.

"Then again," Charley said, "like that blinking orange sign you sometimes see along the highway, we could proceed with caution."

Joanna snorted. "Why do I get the sense that's going to land one of us in trouble?"

"Why *did* you show up out of the blue?"

Joanna looked at her questioningly.

"I'd never seen you before September," Charley said.

"Oh." Joanna was clearly relieved. "I didn't like the pool at the Y downtown. Someone told me your pools were better. They were right."

Out on the sidewalk, Joanna tucked her scarf into her coat and eyed Charley's open jacket. "You're amazing. Not cold?"

"Upstate winters inured me. The cold doesn't bother me until it hits twenty degrees."

"Not going downtown tonight?"

"No. She doesn't need me." Charley reached to free Joanna's hair which had gotten caught inside the scarf, and then she kissed her. She tasted the scotch on her lips, put her hand on the back of Joanna's neck, felt the almost imperceptible pressure of Joanna leaning into her.

"You're not treading water," Joanna said, her lips skimming Charley's.

"No. I thought I saw the orange blinking light." She kissed Joanna again, caressing her cheek.

"You're not proceeding with caution, either. And how is your hand so warm?" Joanna took Charley's hand; hers was cold so Charley clasped it between her hands to warm it.

"How are your lips so soft?" Charley asked. She looked at Joanna's mouth, the lines on either side of it framing it like parentheses, the slight cleft in her chin highlighting it. Asking the question made her feel like a teenager, but she couldn't help it. She'd wanted to kiss her since the first day she'd met her.

Joanna's forehead was touching hers as she looked at their hands. "Anatomically speaking, all lips are soft, Charley."

"Hmmm...I see what you're doing there. The practical nurse in you is weighing in."

Joanna looked at her.

"And she's going to stop us, isn't she?"

"I'm not sure I'm free to do this yet."

Charley ran her thumb over Joanna's lips, inhaled the cold air, and let her breath out slowly. "Georgia. All right. The practical nurse doesn't want to be bandaging anyone."

"But we could certainly continue this conversation next Monday."

"I'd like that."

They walked over to Forty-Second Street in silence, Charley realizing it was the same comfortable sense she'd felt last week as they'd walked down First Avenue from Bar and Books. Except that now Georgia seemed to be with them.

"Text me over the weekend?" Charley asked.

"I'll think about it." Joanna kicked at a bottle cap on the sidewalk. "And...thank you for understanding. It's nice to have a pool buddy."

Charley summoned her Bogart impersonation. "Louis, I think this is the beginning of a beautiful friendship."

"*Casablanca.* I love that movie."

"Then we'll have to watch it together some night."

Joanna headed down Forty-Second Street, Charley again watching her go.

CHAPTER TWENTY-ONE

Tuesday morning, Charley set up a Skype call for Emily with Jenny, the assistant she'd be working with in the Middle East, so they could all go over finalized plans for the trip. She'd sent Jenny a number of delicate questions about the country's customs that she felt Emily should be aware of, and that she couldn't answer even after doing online research and talking to some of the British assistants she'd befriended, asking Jenny to weave the answers in as though they were part of the conversation. She didn't want to embarrass Emily or put Jenny on the spot by asking them herself during the call. The one piece of information she made no bones about imparting to Emily before they dialed up Jenny: that homosexuality in the United Arab Emirates was a crime, so if Emily was the type to wander from her marriage when she traveled, this was not the place to do it.

"I should be scandalized by your thinking you had to tell me that," Emily said, "but I realize you're only doing your job. And probably saving my life if I *was* the type to step out on my wife," Emily remarked as the Skype dial tone sounded.

"I learned a long time ago never to judge a book by its cover or assume that you know everything about someone."

"Hey," Emily said when she closed Skype half an hour later, "you haven't talked to me about our dinner. It's this Saturday, right? At Per Se?"

"Yes."

"Who are you bringing? Is there anything I need to know about her?"

Charley was caught completely by surprise. She was sure she'd told Emily the reservation was for three. "I wasn't going to bring anyone."

"Oh, you have to. To a three-star restaurant of this magnitude? There must be someone in your life who'd jump at this chance. And who'd want to spend an evening with you. By the way, Terry's looking forward to it. She told me to tell you you're a genius for managing to swing this reservation."

Charley felt like she was in some bizarre time warp, caught in one of those moments that used to be at the heart of the Doris Day-Rock Hudson movies of the 1960s where they played a mismatched couple who had to conform to some societal norm for everybody else's convenience and then found they were, of course, perfectly matched. Because she immediately thought of Joanna. But she would be working Saturday night, so that settled it. Charley took out her phone and looked at it. A moment later, she was walking down the hall hitting Joanna's contact, hoping she wasn't waking her. She realized she had no idea what her schedule was on her days off.

"Hey, Charley, this is nice. What's up?"

"I didn't wake you, did I?"

"It's three in the afternoon. I should hope not."

"I have no idea what your schedule is. I've never actually known anyone who works nights."

"Well, this is the beginning of my day. So. Are you drowning in the shallow end, is that why you called?" Joanna chuckled at her own joke.

"In a manner of speaking, yes."

"Oh?"

"Can you by any chance get Saturday night off?"

"I could, yes. But what am I getting myself in for?"

Charley explained the situation. "If you can, I would so appreciate it. No, I'd be in your debt. Whatever you want, you could have."

"Hmmm. Tempting. I'll put that marker in my back pocket. Let me call Alexandra and see if we can trade shifts. I'll text you, but I think it's safe to say you've got yourself a plus-one."

Charley breathed a sigh of relief when she hung up.

Late in the afternoon, Emily had a meeting that took her out of the building for the rest of the day, and Charley had set that time to interview the candidates for Tricia, using the department's small conference room. Anyone seeing her name on the door would figure she was preparing for Emily's trip. She spent almost forty-five minutes with each candidate. Having had enough interviews in her day, she knew exactly what she was looking for with every question she asked. Blaire smacked of Lauren Bacall, just the kind of sultry efficiency Tricia usually hired. But it was Ted who won her with his outgoing demeanor, and the style that extended from his handshake to the pocket square that matched his tie, to the way he artfully painted a picture of who he was with every answer he gave her. She set up follow-up interviews for both of them with Tricia for Thursday evening at her apartment.

Walking home, she talked herself through her sense of trepidation at working with Neely tonight at the library. Of course she knew plenty of women who'd remained on good terms with their exes, although she really couldn't categorize Neely as an ex. Except in the case of Brooke, and by happenstance, Charley had never been of that camp, finding it incongruous to make small talk with a woman she'd been intimate with in bed for several weeks and then dropped. But this was different, with Neely. There was something deeper here, above and beyond that physical moment. At least there was for her. And she guessed there would be for Neely once she could get past it and see Charley in a new light.

Bing was waiting by the door when she came into the apartment, but Bob was nowhere in sight, baffling her. He was usually the one pacing by the dinner bowl. She got out the can of cat food, sure he'd come running when he heard the lid pop. Nothing. Worried, she put the bowls down on the floor and walked toward the bedroom. And that's when she saw the masses of toilet paper spilling out of the bathroom like a big white snowdrift. *Why, you little devil!* He hadn't run amok with the toilet paper in a while, and she knew exactly where he hid when he did. She bent down, lifted the dust ruffle of her bed, and saw him cowering in the far corner. "Don't bother to come out for dinner, you little dust bunny. Not until I'm gone, anyway." She couldn't really yell at him...he only acted out like this when she wasn't home enough, so now he had her feeling guilty as she changed into jeans and a long-sleeved polo shirt and left to meet Neely.

❖

Tricia called her in the middle of the night and Charley went right down, hearing the note of panic in her voice. Tricia had spiked a fever but couldn't stop shivering. Charley had held her in bed to warm her up.

"Listen, it's not that I mind coming down when you call—"

"But you do. I know."

They were sitting on the couch watching the sun rise, Charley holding Tricia and gently running her fingers through her hair like her own mother had done when she needed comforting as a child. "These nights at your place are beginning to chip away at me. We need to talk about a night nurse, don't you think?"

"No, not yet. I'll go it alone until Friday."

"You're aware you're fraying a bit around the edges. I'm not sure I want to leave you alone."

"Double-edged sword for you."

Charley was slightly alarmed at the recent change in Tricia's pallor, the beautiful rose of her skin slowly taking on a chalky color over the last couple of weeks. And she could feel the utter fatigue in her body as she lay against Charley. "I have a friend who's a private duty nurse. Let me to talk to her." Charley could still feel Joanna's kiss on her lips two days later, but she wasn't about to share that with Tricia.

"I've already researched. I can go over it with you later. I'm not ready to admit I need it this soon. Give me a couple days. I won't go over the cliff. I promise."

"Well, at the very least, we should have breakfast before one of us goes over the cliff." Charley disengaged herself from Tricia and headed for the kitchen. While the eggs poached, she put the hollandaise sauce she'd made the other night into a small saucepan with a dash of hot water, whisking it back to life. When she threw a handful of spinach into the microwave, the time on the clock caught her attention: she was going to miss her aquatics class. A moment later, she realized

Neely would wonder if something was wrong after how smoothly last night had gone, the two of them talking over each other's edits before spending a couple of hours working in peaceful silence, so she texted her to let her know where she was, and why. Moments later, she had a short reply with a hug emoji. They'd weathered not only the awkwardness of seeing each other every morning when Charley went into class, but now they'd also begun to forge a deeper friendship.

When the cab dropped her at her apartment a couple of hours later, she was tempted to text Emily that she'd be in late so she could get some sleep, but she didn't want to borrow on that bank of time yet. Something told her to build up a deep reserve because she was going to need it. So she took care of the cats, a contrite Bob hanging back as she dished out breakfast. Then she dressed and went into work.

With Emily's flight to the Middle East set for Sunday night, Charley and Emily spent the rest of the week working on the finalized presentations with the rest of the legal team. Emily had finally brought them in on what was going on after Charley had questioned the wisdom of keeping them out of it.

As Emily put on her coat to leave on Friday, she told Charley that Terry had talked of nothing all week except the dinner tomorrow night. "I live with a food groupie," she admitted. "My kitchen counters are stacked with recipe magazines. Have you ever looked at any of them?" She shook her head. "The photos border on porn, but for food. This restaurant had better live up to its stars. Oh, and we're looking forward to meeting Joanna."

When she hadn't been concentrating on the tasks at her desk, that was what Charley had worried about all week. She and Joanna had exchanged several texts and calls after Joanna had let her know Alexandra was trading shifts with her, Saturday for Monday, which meant their Monday night drinks were canceled. She also wanted Charley to know she'd done her homework, researching both Emily and her wife on Google so she could carry on intelligent conversations with them. She'd even asked her what she planned to wear, and when Charley had posed the question back to her, she'd told her she was undecided.

"But I promise I'll look appropriately 'corporate night out,'" Joanna assured her.

"I'm not worried about that," Charley said.

"But you're worried."

Charley didn't have an answer.

"You worry a lot, don't you?"

"Worry and anticipation are the twin rulers of my life."

"I'll tell you what. You leave it to me, I promise I'll look like I stepped off the cover of *Vogue*, I'll be refreshingly conversational, and all you'll have to do is look pretty."

Charley laughed. "Yawning silences, remember? You called on me to manage the conversation that night, as I recall."

"That was a momentary blip because I had to come clean about Georgia. I'm usually very entertaining in these situations."

"I can hardly wait," Charley said. "And all I'll have to do is look pretty?"

"Hanging up now, have to go root through my closets for something to wear. Talk to you tomorrow."

That night at Tricia's, Charley made a beef stew on the stove top and put a meatloaf in the oven. When Tricia came out to the kitchen to collect the silverware and napkins, she asked Charley if the Fifth Regiment was coming to dinner.

"Very funny. I'm not coming down tomorrow night, so you can reheat the stew, and Sunday, I don't want to cook. This way, it's done."

"What's going on tomorrow night? I thought you and Neely were over."

"We are. Dinner with Emily. A thank you for all my work recently."

"Oh, nice. Where?"

"Per Se."

"Very nice. Just you and Emily?"

"And Terry, her wife. And Joanna."

"Really? Wow. So, does this mean you mean something to her now?"

"She's rescuing me."

"From what? You've never been the damsel in distress type."

"Emily seemed to think I should bring someone, and her request almost felt like a test of some sort. I asked Joanna. It seemed safe."

"And I was just about to tell you that you didn't have to come down on Sunday because I hired Ted and he's beginning Sunday morning."

"Good. I didn't think you'd take my advice."

"Well, quite frankly, you were right. Ted was exceptional. Blaire *was* nice eye candy and I would love to have had that around, but…"

Charley laughed. "You are such a male chauvinist pig sometimes."

"Oh, we can't say things like that anymore, Charley, it's libelous. I believe the term would be 'enthusiastic binary gourmand of the female faction of humanity,' or some such bullshit."

Charley rolled her eyes. "I was planning on coming down for dinner anyway. And you can't make Ted work those kinds of hours."

"We're putting together a schedule that suits us. I don't need him that much during the week. Yet. But I do on the weekends. Anyway, not really your business since you're not his union rep. Are we watching tonight's college game with dinner?"

Charley dished up the stew and followed Tricia to the living room.

CHAPTER TWENTY-TWO

C harley always took time to stand back and look up at the resplendent glass Time Warner Center on Columbus Circle whenever she came over for concerts in Lincoln Center's Appel Room. The cabaret venue, with its floor-to-ceiling windows, had a spectacular view of the corner of Central Park where south meets west at the imposing statue of Simon Bolivar astride his glorious steed. At night, the winking headlights of the cars moving along Central Park South, the warm lighting emanating from the apartments in the turn-of-the-century buildings along the avenue, and the spotlights on Bolivar provided a luminous backdrop for the concert. It was the same view Per Se had, only the restaurant was several floors higher. She didn't even glance around, though, when the cab dropped her off tonight, instead making a beeline for the elevator, hoping to arrive before Emily and make sure everything was flawlessly set for this evening. The maître d' patiently explained that he couldn't seat anyone until everyone in their party had arrived, and Charley assured him she knew that, that she just wanted to see for herself that everything was ready and perfect because she was dining with her boss, Emily Dunn.

"Ah, I see." The maître d' nodded toward the cocktail lounge. "They came in half an hour ago," he said. "They wanted to have a drink and take it all in. But rest assured, we are always perfect here."

Charley thanked him and walked down the short hallway toward the lounge trying to decide if she should join Emily and Terry or wait for Joanna. She peeked in, not wanting to be seen, and spotted Emily seated by one of the enormous windows. Terry stood next to her, motioning at something out there with her glass of wine. Charley decided to wait for Joanna and went to the ladies' room to check herself in the mirror one last time, straightening the fine black mesh that covered her shoulders and met the rest of the cocktail dress at her cleavage. Then she walked back to the big glass front door. A moment later, the elevator across the hall opened and several people got off. Charley didn't recognize Joanna at first, until she registered the graceful athletic way the well-dressed woman walking toward the door moved. Her hair was up, her coat over her arm, and she had on a short white jacket with black thread piping at the collar, down the front and around the bottom, repeated on the cuffs and the pockets. Two buttons mid-torso held it closed, a black silk shawl shirt barely visible beneath it. Black palazzo pants and black heels completed the outfit. The ever-present set of silver bracelets hung on her wrist. For a moment, Charley couldn't move, stunned by Joanna's elegance. And then she reached for the door.

"The cavalry has arrived, ma'am," Joanna said. "Are there any last-minute items I should know about that we haven't already discussed in detail this week before we launch this offensive?"

Charley shook her head and smiled. She wanted to kiss Joanna right here. Right now.

Joanna handed her coat over the counter to the young man in the coat-check room and took her chit from him. Turning, she held out her arms and slowly did a three-sixty. "This was the best Rock Hudson I could come up with. But you've certainly mastered Doris Day, haven't you?" She brushed a piece of nonexistent lint from Charley's shoulder. "Very nice. Are you ready?"

She reached for Joanna's hand and led her to the bar, where Emily and Terry were clearly watching for them.

"Oh, my God, is that a Chanel jacket?" Terry asked.

"It is," Joanna said. "It was my mother's. Luckily, it fits me."

Surprised, Charley registered another piece of the puzzle, and a new admiration for Joanna's wardrobe finesse. The topic of family was a place Joanna seemed reluctant to go despite Charley having told her everything about hers.

"May I touch?"

Joanna held out her arm and Terry ran her hand over the material.

"Do you know what year she bought it? It's so vintage."

Joanna chuckled. "She didn't. She borrowed it from her sister and never gave it back. But my aunt was fifteen years older than her, so I'm guessing it's from the mid nineteen fifties."

"Ho! I'm surprised your aunt ever spoke to her again."

"My mother was the baby of the family." Joanna looked at Charley. "There's something about being the baby, you can wrap everyone around your little finger."

Charley blushed. Joanna *had* been listening when she talked about her older brothers.

"You two look incredibly chic," Joanna said to Terry. "I admire women with style."

Their outfits hadn't registered with Charley, but now she studied Emily and her wife. Although Charley had met Terry only once in person when she'd come to pick up Emily at the office one Friday night, she didn't think of her as tall. Perhaps tonight it was the black suit perfectly fitted to her willowy form, or maybe it was the legs of the slacks ending at a pair of four-inch black heels with quarter-inch red grosgrain ribbons slashed at an angle across the toe, but suddenly, Terry seemed Geena Davis tall. The collar of the suit jacket and a cherry red shirt stood up against her neck, the shirt unbuttoned as far as propriety would allow. Charley had always thought Emily could wear a burlap sack and looked stunning. She was in a long-sleeved cherry red dress with black buttons down the front, black piping at the collar, sleeves, and hem, and black heels. Charley noticed the reds in both outfits matched. Even if they shopped together and were partial to the same designer, the chances of hitting identical reds was one in a million because matching a color outside a dye lot was nearly impossible. And while the two women reminded Charley a little of Barbie and Ken, or Barbie and Barbie, a pairing she'd always dreamed about when she was eight or nine, she had to admit Joanna was right, they were quite a stunning pair.

As they walked to their table, she overheard Joanna and Terry talking fashion designers and wondered how this side of her had never come out in their Monday nights together.

True to her word, Joanna effortlessly kept all the conversational plates in the air as course after course of delicate, delectable, exquisitely arranged food was delivered to the table by a phalanx of waiters. She pulled gossip about the authors she represented from a usually highly professional Terry; got Emily to talk about her first job in high school waving one of those giant arrows outside a car dealership in her hometown of Los Angeles, leaving Charley out of breath with laughter at the visual. And then she told them about growing up all over the world on Marine and army bases until her father landed the coveted position running the Imperial Beach Navy SEALS base in California. Charley was astounded. This was information she'd been trying to glean for weeks, and she tucked it away.

"So, Charley, you're dating the admiral's daughter."

Charley didn't miss the amusement in Emily's expression. "Oh, we're not dating. We're just friends."

Joanna glanced at Charley.

"Ah, I see," Emily said, unconvinced.

Sometime later, with Terry and Joanna still deep in conversation about food, recipes, and the *New York Times* food critic, Emily turned to Charley. "We're going to have to break this up or I'm afraid they could talk food all night."

Charley sighed and rolled her eyes.

"You didn't know she was like this, did you?"

"About food and recipes? No. We usually go out for drinks."

Downstairs after dinner, Charley told Emily she'd hold down the fort as usual while she was in Abu Dhabi, and she and Joanna let Emily and Terry take the first cab.

"Where to now?" Joanna asked.

Charley looked at her, surprised.

"I thought you might want to debrief."

"You really *are* the admiral's daughter, aren't you?"

"Actually, I just want to spend a little more time with you. We could go back upstairs to Dizzy's Coca Cola Club." She hesitated. "Or, I just live down the street at Forty-Third."

Charley considered her proposal.

"And I have a bottle of Moet & Chandon in my refrigerator. I thought we might need it while we dissect the evening."

Charley laughed. "You did, did you?"

Joanna hailed a cab and directed the driver to Ninth Avenue at Forty-Third Street. Charley leaned in against Joanna as the cab pulled out of Columbus Circle.

"I know your neighborhood pretty well," she said. "Used to spend a lot of time there."

"Really?"

"Mmm." She ran her thumb and finger over the piping on the collar of Joanna's jacket. "Right after college. It was quite the neighborhood, after the Village."

The cab pulled up outside the building. It was right next to the Westway Diner. "How long have you lived here?"

"Twenty years." Joanna paid the driver and leaned over Charley to open the door for her. "Came after nursing school to take care of a very good friend who had AIDS. And because I was chasing a girl who lived here. She got away. He died and I inherited his rent-subsidized apartment, so I stayed."

They made the walk up the five flights of Joanna's brownstone in silence. She led the way to a door at the end of the hallway. A Nantucket basket hung on a hook, a bunch of lilac tulips spilling out of it.

"How do you do that?" Charley marveled.

Joanna took Charley's hand and guided it inside the basket. She felt a deep glass filled with water.

"It's my one extravagance. The tulips don't always last long. But I have flowers in this basket every day." Joanna unlocked the door and opened it. "Frank bought it when we took a trip to Cape Cod that first summer that turned out to be his last trip anywhere. He thought it would look nice on the door, I thought it needed flowers. He made me promise to keep flowers in it in his memory."

Charley looked away, tearing up. "God, I hated those years." She walked into the apartment.

"You lose friends?" Joanna turned on a floor lamp near the door and soft light spilled across a sizable Oriental carpet of woven maroons and cream. Charley looked around the brick-walled room at the mix of dark Bentwood and Mission furniture, antique mirrors and 1920s *Vogue* magazine covers on the walls. A cut-glass vase on the coffee table held more of the tulips. A framed Erté lithograph of a Zeigfeld showgirl wearing nothing more than diamonds hung over the couch, commanding attention. She wondered if it was a reflection of who Frank had been or if this was all Joanna.

Charley turned to her. "About the time you lost Frank, I lost count of the number of funerals I'd been to. But I think it was taking care of and burying my best friend from high school that…well, broke me." She turned away, took off her coat, and draped it over the nearest chair. "I knew after that that I couldn't make any more friends in the gay community." She looked at Joanna again. "I don't know any gay men anymore."

Joanna hugged Charley and kissed her forehead.

"My ex is dying of cancer," Charley said, just managing to stop the tears as they tried to spill out, blinking them back, willing them away. She felt Joanna inhale and slowly let it out.

"This is going to be a bigger debriefing than I thought."

"I just killed the champagne moment, didn't I?"

Joanna led Charley over to a small cabinet and opened it, revealing a bar stocked with bottles of all sorts of liquors. Without a second thought, she picked up the bottle of Laphroaig single malt, Joanna pulled out two snifters, and they sat down on the couch. Joanna pushed her heels off and tucked her feet up beneath her. "Tell me everything."

By the time Charley finished, pearl gray had stolen into the black of the night sky, and the contents of the bottle were significantly lower.

"I should go." Charley stood and put on her heels. "It's far later than I thought."

Joanna retrieved her coat and held it for her. Charley slipped her arms into it, turned around, and kissed her. "I know you said you couldn't do this. I'm not asking you to. That was thank you."

Joanna pulled Charley close and kissed her back, one hand firmly on the small of her back, the other clasping her shoulder. "You're welcome. And it's earlier than you think it is."

Charley looked at her questioningly, lost in the warmth of her emerald eyes.

"We can talk about it the next time we have Monday drinks. But listen, you should have my card so you can help Tricia research private nursing companies. If you google us, everyone else comes up.

We do mostly long-term care, like I told you. But we do occasionally take on short-term clients who just need help pre-hospice. You said you're not really sure what Tricia needs?"

"She hasn't wanted to talk about it, but we need to address it very soon."

"It's a hard thing to confront. It'll be hard for both of you to confront."

"I know…" She leaned in for another slow, sweet kiss. "Thank you for tonight. I think I rather like the 'proceed with caution' zone."

Joanna smiled slightly and walked Charley downstairs. She watched the cab pull away and Charley looked out the back window so she could see her until it turned the corner.

As the taxi made its way up an empty Forty-Second Street, Charley felt a kind of peace she hadn't in a long time, and a turmoil she hadn't felt in an even longer time.

Chapter Twenty-three

The remnants of a headache wreathed Charley's head when she let herself into Tricia's apartment late Sunday afternoon. She hadn't had that much scotch, or that little sleep, in quite a while. Ted was just leaving. "Please tell me you weren't here all day."

"Nope. Came about noon."

"Don't let her work you until you drop."

Tricia appeared in the living room. "May I remind you, you're not his union rep, and Ted and I have an agreement."

"We do," Ted said. "Besides, I love to keep busy, and she's paying me well to do just that. And..." he looked from Tricia to Charley, "she's funny."

"Well, you'd be—"

"No, no, no," Tricia interrupted Charley.

"Among the few to think that about her," Charley whispered, patting Ted on the shoulder.

"Dinner's warming in the oven. I made roasted potatoes and veggies, and there are some slices of meatloaf snugged in with them," Ted said. "See you tomorrow, Trish."

Charley looked at Tricia after he left. "Trish?"

"Come on, let's eat while I'm actually hungry. And I want to hear how last night went."

Over dinner, Charley recounted the evening for Tricia, leaving out everything that happened after Emily and Terry left in their cab.

"A headache, huh? How much did you drink?"

"More than I should have. But I didn't embarrass myself."

"Mmm. Wasn't really worried about that. Just wondering if you mean something to her now. That was a big rescue on her part." Tricia put a second piece of meatloaf on her plate, and Charley added a handful of roasted potatoes to it. "And a Chanel jacket. She's got style."

Charley waited until Tricia fell asleep in her arms in front of the NFL game before carefully pulling her phone out of her pocket to text Joanna.

Hope you're doing okay after last night. So sorry I kept you up so long.

There was no answer for quite a few minutes.

Joanna: *Why are you texting so loud? I have a headache.*

Oh, sweetie, I'm so sorry.

Joanna: *Don't care that you kept me up late. Glad you talked to me. Headache really just a dull roar.*

Okay, well, since we're not seeing each other tom'w, do you want to have lunch Tues? I work from home while E's away. And I understand you're a foodie...

Joanna: *Terry and I spent too much time talking about food, didn't we?*

Charley sent her an emoji face rolling its eyeballs.

Joanna: *Okay, okay, sheesh! Some good places over here. Come over at 1:00.*

❖

Before she'd left the office Friday afternoon, Charley had set her office phone to forward calls to her home phone because that would be her base for the next two weeks while Emily was in Abu Dhabi. With a nine-hour difference, it made more sense for her to work from home.

When the alarm clock went off shortly after midnight Monday morning, Charley felt like she'd been steamrolled; it was half an hour before she needed to be at her computer for Emily, though, so she dragged herself through her morning ritual, and as she was taking a sip of orange juice and reading the emails that had come in over the last few hours, she spotted the red flag from Jenny with a request to

Skype in as soon as possible. Charley dialed her up, wondering what on earth could be so wrong so soon.

"Good morning, bright eyes," Jenny said, smiling.

"If I knew you better," Charley said, "I'd tell you to stuff it."

"I think you just did. So, I guess we're good friends now."

Charley smirked at her. "What's up?"

"It's the presentations."

"Oh, God." Charley sighed. "Let me get the flash drive."

She plugged it into her laptop, smoothed everything out with Jenny, and then asked her to remind Emily she'd be at the doctor with Tricia late in what would be Emily's afternoon. She spent the dawn hours on standby for Jenny, using the time to edit the next set of chapters that Neely had given her some very astute notes for until she could call Tricia at six thirty to make sure she was up and not on the floor of the bathroom again before they met with Dr. Gerard.

She was buried in the Monday music streaming report when the phone rang at half past seven, caller ID announcing her mother. Surprised and a little panicked, she halted her hand above the receiver. Then, chastising herself, she picked up. "Mother? Are you okay?"

"Yes, darling, of course. I just wanted to catch you right away. Irene Palmer passed away early this morning and we're surmising her wake will be Thursday, with the funeral Saturday. I was hoping you could accompany me to the wake. I'll ask Robert to go to the funeral with me, though. I know you don't like those."

Charley tried to concentrate on the rest of her mother's conversation, but all she could think of was Joanna. "Mother," she interrupted, "yes, sure, I'll take you. But I have to dash."

"Of course, dear. I'll call you tonight when I have more information."

Charley sat at her desk, stunned. She picked up her phone and opened a text message.

I'm so, so sorry. She attached an emoji of a dove with an olive branch and hit *Send*. A moment later, the buoy dinged with Joanna's reply.

Joanna: *How did you hear? And thx so much.*

My mother.

Joanna: *Of course.*

Where are you?
Joanna: *At Irene's with her family.*
I hope they're all right... Anything I can do? Take you to dinner tonight? Obviously, lunch tomorrow was out.
Joanna: *I'll be here w/them for a while.*
Okay. Let me know how you are later?
Joanna: *Yes.*

Charley put her phone away and realized she had very little time to get ready and get up to the hospital for Tricia.

Pacing outside the Radiology Department waiting for Tricia to get there, Charley was alarmed when her medical team arrived en masse. Minutes later, Dr. Gerard came down the hall, a depleted Tricia in tow. They examined her, and the team quizzed her about Wednesday's fever. Satisfied with what they heard, they chose a wait-and-see route for the time being. "But if it happens again, you get in here pronto, understand?" Dr. Gerard looked at both Tricia and Charley.

"You should really go home and rest." Charley buttoned Tricia's camel hair coat after the doctors had left the room.

"Don't be ridiculous, I'm going in to work."

"You look like shit."

"I thought I looked like shit warmed over when I looked in the mirror this morning, so I'm going in."

"No fighting you, is there?"

"Was there ever?" Tricia asked.

Charley laughed. "Fuck you." She pulled Tricia's scarf a little higher in her collar. "But call me tonight to let me know how you are."

Charley's mother called her after dinner with the funeral home information. She took it all down and then emailed Emily, letting her know she'd be escorting her mother to a wake Thursday afternoon. Timewise, it wouldn't make a bit of difference to Emily's schedule, but she still kept her apprised of anything out of the ordinary.

Thursday came quickly enough, and Charley pulled her black Givenchy dress out of the closet. She'd bought it years ago, at the height of the AIDS epidemic, when she no longer cared that she showed up at funerals in the same dress. There had been too many services at too many churches, halls, and theatrical venues, and soon enough, no one cared about what they wore to them.

She hadn't heard from Joanna at all, not even after she'd sent her a short text telling her she was thinking about her, adding several hugs at the end.

At the funeral home, she spotted Joanna right away sitting with a group of women who had to be the team that had cared for Irene. She looked almost frail in a one-piece black pantsuit cinched at the waist. Charley saw the pain and sadness etched in her expression and wanted to gather her up and hug her. She realized they'd never really talked about Irene. There must have been quite a bond between them. After she and her mother paid their respects at the casket and she got her mother seated among all her friends, she went over to Joanna.

"No, sit," Charley said, her hand out to prevent Joanna from standing.

"Don't be ridiculous." Joanna stood and hugged Charley, who took in her scent, and hugged her closely. She felt a rigidity that hadn't ever been there before.

"I'm so sorry. This must be so hard for you."

"It's hard for the whole team." Joanna glanced at the six other women sitting with her. She took Charley's hand and led her to the far corner of the room. "Come, I need to speak to you."

Out of the corner of her eye, Charley saw her mother watching her. "Is everything okay? I mean, this—" she swept her hand toward the crowded room, "notwithstanding."

"Yes and no. Irene was like a mother to me. We all knew she couldn't live forever. But it's been devastating." Joanna's eyes teared up, and Charley put her arm around her waist, drawing her to her.

"What will happen now?"

Joanna sighed and leaned into Charley. "The company gives you two weeks off when a patient dies. Then they try to pair you with a relatively easy case for a while."

"Is two weeks going to be enough? Can you take more time?"

"Ever lost anyone close?"

"I have."

"Then you know time really isn't the issue." Joanna shifted and moved out of Charley's embrace. "Charley, I'm going away for a week or so after the funeral. My friends Madeline and Thea have a cabin upstate. I need to...I don't know, collect myself, think about things and just...be."

Charley nodded. "I think that's a really good idea."

"Georgia's coming with me."

If someone had thrown a cold glass of water on her, Charley wouldn't have been more surprised. Or overwhelmed. Or confused. Was this why she'd felt the rigidity in Joanna's hug?

"This doesn't change anything. With you and I," Joanna said. "I just have to figure things out."

Didn't it? But Charley couldn't verbalize that. Every insecurity that had plagued her in the hours after she'd seen Tricia and Reagan in that restaurant, and in the years after as she tried to make sense of what had happened, came flooding back. Intellectually, she knew this wasn't the same situation. At all. But everything in the pit of her stomach told her it was. What if she was one of the "things" Joanna needed to think about? What if she wasn't? Either way, there was nothing she could say in her defense. She had nothing to defend. "Okay."

"Cell phone reception is only good in town up there, and Madeline's cabin is quite a ways outside town. But I can call you from her landline."

"Okay."

"Thank you for understanding." Joanna squeezed Charley's hand and returned to her seat amid the other nurses.

The room suddenly felt cold and empty. She caught her mother looking at her and made her way to where she was sitting. "Time to go?' she asked. Her mother nodded.

CHAPTER TWENTY-FOUR

The phone rang Saturday morning while Charley was standing at her living room window, a cup of coffee in her hand, kicking herself for not having called her brother Robert to tell him she'd take their mother to the funeral. It would be days before she'd see Joanna again. And even though she'd said she'd call, Charley couldn't imagine how those conversations would go with Georgia sitting right there. The caller ID interrupted her angst and had her dashing for the phone immediately. "Hey, Tricia."

Ten minutes later, she was on her way downtown. She found Tricia on her knees in front of the toilet, her white pallor matching the tiles.

"What's wrong?" She reached for Tricia's hair to keep it out of her face as she retched.

"I don't know." Tricia lay down on the floor. "Oh, that's nice and cold."

Charley felt for a temperature, but Tricia's skin was cool to the touch. She frantically searched her mental notes of all the things Dr. Gerard said might suddenly affect Tricia adversely, and finally remembered he'd mentioned hypercalcemia, the cancer tending to produce a substance that removes calcium from the bones, sending it into the bloodstream. *Could that be what this is?* "What time did this start?"

"Around six, I think," Tricia replied.

"And you didn't call me until eleven? How many times have you thrown up? Like, how many times each hour?"

"This is only the third time. I'm all right. It's the rolling nausea I can't handle. Sorry. It unnerved me."

"I'm texting Dr. Gerard. You might not be all right."

"Just help me get back to the bed."

Charley lifted Tricia up and hobbled into the bedroom with her, silently cursing the size of the apartment. After propping her on the bed, she went to the laundry room for the small plastic waste can she had seen there, put two plastic bags in it, and brought it back to the bedroom.

"Here," she said. "If you can't make it to the bathroom, use this." She texted Dr. Gerard. Within minutes, he replied.

Gerard: *Yes, could be hypercalcemia. We'll meet her at radiology tomorrow at 8. Get protein into her in sm amts, & crackers or toast. Also, liquids (non-acidics). If she vomits again, bring her in.*

"Could you eat a soft-boiled egg and toast?" Charley asked Tricia, whose eyes were closed as she rested against the stack of pillows on her bed.

"Yes, that sounds nice."

Waiting for the water to boil for the eggs, Charley was surprised when Tricia appeared in her robe, her hair tied back.

"I brushed my teeth. I feel a lot better. Did I remember to restock my tea supply? I ran out last winter."

Charley found the Earl Grey, filled the kettle, and searched the cupboard for honey. Tricia settled down at the table, watching her work.

"I did two things this past week. One will please you, after the research we did last weekend, and the other will have you rolling your eyes. I've hired a law firm. And I spoke with a private nursing company about sending someone for overnights."

"Oh, thank God."

"That's for the private nurse, I'm sure."

"Yes. I hate to say, I don't care about your law firm."

"I didn't think so."

"When do they start?"

"The law firm Monday. The nurses in two weeks. And before you think I'm being cavalier, I really don't think I need them yet, so I talked it over with Ted, and he can stay nights for the next couple of weeks so you can have your life back. In fact, he's on his way over now. Did you know he was his mother's caretaker when she was sick with breast cancer?"

"Yes, I knew that. Why do you think I wanted you to hire him?" Charley cracked the eggs and scooped them into a bowl, put it in front of Tricia, then plated the dry rye toast for her.

"He's really quite extraordinary. A real Renaissance man."

"I can stay the day. No problem." Charley was, for the first time, afraid for Tricia and wasn't sure she wanted to leave.

"No. Ted's coming over to work, now that I have the law firm lined up." Tricia began eating, and Charley poured her cup of tea.

"Not going to just take it easy today?"

"I don't really have that luxury." Tricia pulled a section of the *New York Times* out and began reading.

"Okay, well, I guess that's my cue. I'm going to put in a load of laundry for you and then prep the roast I saw in the refrigerator for your slow cooker."

"Thank you, Charley. I'm sorry if I get a little grumpy." Tricia took a sip of tea. "Oh, that's good. My throat gets so sore sometimes now."

Charley opened the honey bottle and turned it upside down, squeezing a thick stream into Tricia's tea. She recapped it and headed to the laundry room.

After prepping dinner for the slow cooker, Charley went in search of Tricia and found her in her office, a large shawl of French blue wrapped around her, open law books piled across her desk, her bifocals perched on the end of her nose.

"If you want me to stay, I can." She'd already made that clear, but maybe Tricia would relent.

"I'll be fine with Ted. You go. He has a set of keys now, too."

"You're sure he should have them so soon?"

"He'll be working and staying here. I'm still going into the office until, well, until things change. I'm sure the firm won't be thrilled when they see my lawsuit. So, yes, he needs the keys to get in here every day. Why don't you plan on coming to the hospital tomorrow morning with me? Ted will take care of everything else now. Really, take this whole week for yourself, come next Sunday and watch the game with me."

Charley looked at her hands, threaded together in front of her. "I can't. I'm hosting the NFL dinner that night. Why don't I come down Saturday night? There will be some good college games on."

Tricia thought that sounded like a good idea, and it didn't need to be said that she wouldn't be a welcome addition to the NFL dinner with Charley's friends. It was sad, but that's how it was.

Charley wasn't sure if she felt released or replaced. Or a little of both. She left Tricia to finish cleaning up the kitchen, and when she came back to say good-bye, Tricia was hunched over her books, reading, and making notes, the early afternoon sun suffusing the room with light. Charley stood looking at her, and for the first time, she saw an old woman. Her skin was filigreed with a fine webbing of wrinkles, her hair no longer soft and full despite how well her hairdresser kept her age hidden with the highlights. And of late, that regal bearing had taken quite a hit: the hunch was less about the books, more of a stoop from illness and treatments. Sadness rose in her throat and she stepped back out to control herself.

From the doorway, Charley told her she was leaving, and Tricia waved, not looking up. She rang for the elevator, and when the doors opened, Ted was there peeling off a maroon Harvard hoodie.

"Hey, I thought you'd be gone by now. Glad I caught you."

"Me, too," Charley said. "There's a slow cooker roast going, it'll be done at six. Tricia had a...I don't know what to call it. Hypercalcemic attack, possibly. Keep her hydrated, maybe she won't throw up anymore. But if she does, call me. We'll have to go to the hospital. Chicken soup might be good for lunch."

"Got it."

"Don't let her work you to death."

"I won't."

"And call me if you need anything."

"I will."

Charley gave Ted all her phone numbers. As the elevator descended, she turned the phone over and over in her hand, feeling as though she'd ceded something precious to him, hoping he would be worthy of the job of safekeeping it. An emptiness arose in her. With a tap to the "contact" icon, Joanna's phone numbers appeared. She shook her head and put the phone away. She couldn't torture herself. Although she knew that was exactly what she would be doing all week.

❖

Back in her apartment, too ill at ease to do anything productive, Charley called Brooke.

"The doctor is in. Please deposit five cents," Brooke said. "Who is it today, Tricia, Joanna, or your mother?"

Charley would've laughed, but Brooke was spot-on. "All three?"

"A marathon. Do I need to tell Annie to postpone lunch?"

Charley sat on the floor by her desk and began pulling catalogues out of the large wooden cranberry scoop where she kept them, ripping her name and address off the back covers of the summer and fall catalogues so she could put them out in the recycling room. Might as well make space for the onslaught of holiday catalogues that had already begun to plague her mailbox.

"No. I'll make it quick. I've just come from Tricia's. I think she had an attack of hypercalcemia this morning. At least, that's what I told Dr. Gerard, and he concurred."

"You're getting pretty good at this stuff. You'd probably qualify for an LPN at this point."

"Don't want to, believe me. She was pretty bad, throwing up, wanting to stay on the bathroom floor because it was cold. It was hard to see, Brooke. I was scared."

"I'm sorry, babe. Not pretty. That tile move is usually for migraines and drunks. Were you able to help her?"

"Yeah, I got her into bed, and got some water and food into her at Gerard's request." Charley sighed. "She's just so…fragile. And I feel like I can't do anything for her in moments like this."

"You're *there* for her. That's more than a lot of people would do. Anything from Joanna?"

"No, but she's only going away today, after the funeral."

"Still, I'm kind of surprised she didn't at least text, aren't you?"

"She just lost someone very close. No, I'm not surprised." Charley began stacking the catalogues inside each other until she had four fat piles to take out. It wasn't true. She'd hoped for at least a single reassuring text, but nothing had come.

"Mmm, I suppose. Okay, now the sixty-four-thousand-dollar question. Your mother?"

"I can't get it out of my head, the way she looked at me at the wake. She knows."

"Mothers always know, Charley. It's their job. And anyway, don't you think it'll be the same old same old? You won't say anything about Joanna, she won't ask."

Charley wondered if that finally shouldn't change.

"Listen, Annie's going out with Lindsay tonight," Brooke said. "Jamie's coming over to watch the LSU game. Why don't you join us?"

"What are you serving?" Charley was always leery of what might appear on Brooke's table if Annie wasn't in the kitchen.

"Whatever you're buying us for takeout."

"I'll be there by kickoff."

When Charley walked out of the Hunter Library Tuesday, she pulled her phone out of her pocket and turned it on. She and Neely had decided on a "phones off" policy while they worked, which really helped Charley block out the world for several hours. Now she saw the little number one inside her green phone icon and went to the call log. There was a message from a number she didn't recognize. Probably a spam call, but she hit the voice mail prompt.

"Hey, Charley. I didn't think you went to the pool Tuesday nights. Anyway, just calling to say hi, and…well, hi. I'll try you later, at home."

Charley wondered how much later Joanna might call and considered grabbing a cab. Instead, she ran for the approaching Second Avenue bus.

The message light on her phone was blinking.

"Hey. It's Joanna. Okay, well, ten o'clock is about as late as I call anyone, but you can call me no matter what time you get home." Joanna left a phone number she assumed was Madeline's landline, and Charley called it. The sound of the honeyed voice was like a pair of arms wrapping around her.

"Hi, it's Charley."

"Oh, good, there you are. Is Tuesday night not good? I thought you didn't go to the pool Tuesdays."

"I was with Neely at Hunter Library. We were going over some chapters."

Charley was met with silence.

"Oh, crap. I didn't tell you that I'm not seeing her anymore, did I?"

Joanna chuckled. "Except that you just saw her tonight."

"Yeah, but I...Oh, this is going to sound convoluted."

"Go ahead, try me."

"We *were* dating. But, like I told you, I just didn't see anything there. I mean, she's twenty years younger than I am. I don't know what I was thinking. Sometimes I felt like I was talking to R2D2. But she's an extraordinary writer. And I need that. From her. She's teaching me a lot. And she has amazing editing skills."

"Okay, I think that works for me," Joanna said quietly. "And, maybe she was the bit of fun you didn't think you were looking for?"

The remark stung just a little, reminding her of Joanna telling her she'd been looking for someone fun when she'd met Charley. "I don't think so."

"No?"

"I think...she was a key to open a door I didn't know was locked."

"You do surprise me every once in a while. So, tell me what else you've been up to."

The first thing Charley told her about was Tricia.

"You must've been frightened. And how did you know it was hypercalcemia?"

"I don't know, it was like one of those obscure *Jeopardy* questions you pull the answer out of the hat for at the last nanosecond. I remembered one of the doctors at the very first meeting talking about it."

After telling Joanna about the rest of her thankfully dull week, she nonchalantly inquired about what she and Georgia had been doing, listening with interest to the list of places they were going, the things they were doing, all of them mundane. Toward the end of the conversation, Charley asked her if she was still planning on staying the entire two weeks.

"Hmmm. Do I detect the shallow end of the pool threatening again?"

"You know, I'm sorry God didn't give us the option to turn on sound when we roll our eyes. No, and even though I know you just got up there and you went up there to unwind and think about *things*, well, I should've proffered this invite weeks ago. I feel foolish doing it now, but I'd feel worse if I didn't and then found out you'd have wanted to come."

"That's way more convoluted than the explanation about Neely."

"I'm getting there. I'm having a dinner party on Sunday. It's a weekly get-together a group of us do during football season. We watch the NFL game, eat, swear at the referees, and drink a fair amount. I don't even know if you like football, but I thought if you decided you'd had enough of nature and the small-town life with ex-girlfriends and came back to the city early..."

"Charley, I have four younger brothers, I'm fluent in every sport on earth so that I can talk with them. And yes, I like football. So, I could think about chasing that carrot you're dangling. Georgia's not driving me crazy yet, but I'll see how things feel later in the week."

When they hung up, Charley felt a little better than she had after her conversation with Brooke on Saturday. The thought of being second, of being the woman waiting around to see if the woman she wanted, wanted her in return, was like an itch she couldn't scratch. But she had a feeling Joanna was worth the wait.

Wednesday morning, Jenny ran into an Emily meltdown and called Charley in a panic.

"What happened?" Charley asked.

"I got the time of a meeting wrong in her schedule, so they held it without her."

"Go get the minutes of that meeting."

Jenny was silent a moment. "Okay, and then what?"

"Now. Go get them now. We can figure out from those who she has to see individually to recoup the information she needs, and you'll set up separate meetings for her with those people. I'll wait here until you're back."

After she and Jenny ironed everything out, she picked up the phone to call Tricia but realized that not hearing from her or Ted probably meant she had weathered Tuesday just fine at the office. She decided it might be a good idea to dial back on trying to mother

her, knowing it was futile anyway. Tricia had never cottoned to Charley's maternal instinct, which Charley had decided years ago was borderline anyway.

The next day, she decided to call Joanna after breakfast.

"Prescient timing on your part," Joanna said.

"Oh?" Charley asked.

"Just had a tiff with Georgia."

The wind went right out of her. She should be happy about anything coming between Joanna and Georgia, but she didn't want to see Joanna hurt.

"She doesn't want to come back to the city on Saturday."

Charley wanted to stand up and cheer as though some unknown college freshman quarterback had just connected with his wide receiver on an eighty-yard bomb to the end zone because that admission meant Joanna *did* want to come back "But it's really your decision, isn't it?" Charley asked. "Madeline's lending the cabin to you."

"Mmmm-hmm."

"Oh. Is she there or can you talk?"

"Oh, no, she dramatically slammed out five minutes ago. It snowed last night and the driveway needs shoveling. I told her to go make herself useful."

Charley thought about the handcuff necklace again. "So, you're considering coming back early, then."

"Yes. I think I'd like to come to your dinner."

Charley's breath caught and little fireworks went off in her head. Whatever Joanna and Georgia had, this time Joanna was choosing Charley. "I'm glad. Because I miss seeing you. But I don't want to cause any problems."

"Oh, that ship sailed long before I met you."

When she hung up, Charley sent Brooke a quick text: *Christians, 1. Lions, 0.*

Brooke: *She's coming to dinner Sun?*

One of the things Charley had long loved about Brooke was that she'd always understood her obscure references. *Yes.*

A second later, ten thumbs-up emojis came back, and Charley laughed.

Late Friday night, Charley's phone dinged with the text message buoy tone. She hoped nothing was going wrong for Emily, because who else would text her at this hour? She quickly sat up when she saw Joanna's name.

Joanna: *Compromise. Driving back to the city Sun a.m. Give me your address so I can come over early and help you with the dinner.*

Charley sent it, along with two hugs. As she waited for a reply, she wondered why there was a compromise, and what it might've cost Joanna. And then the thought Charley had been fighting all week strode right in: had Joanna and Georgia been sleeping together this week? It wasn't like she had any ground to stand on in that arena, but the thought still made her stomach churn.

Joanna: *Thanks. I needed those hugs. It's running hot and cold up here. And I don't mean the weather.*

Charley rearranged the stack of pillows behind her and lay back, staring at the little screen. *Sounds like you need some advice.*

Joanna: *?*

For that hot & cold? A cold shoulder and a Teflon heart.

Joanna: *You are too funny. You didn't use those on some poor woman.*

Women. Plural.

Joanna: *Tell me you weren't a player when you were younger.*

Asked the woman who was recently looking for someone to have fun with...

Joanna: *Touche. Hv to turn in now.*

Charley took a chance and sent a kiss. A moment later, a blushing emoji came back to her. She turned out her light and eventually fell asleep after thinking about what it was going to feel like working in her kitchen with Joanna.

Chapter Twenty-five

A fter grabbing a quick lunch on Sunday, Charley vacuumed the living room again even though the apartment had been spotless for a week. Glancing at the TV screen in the living room, she saw the score on the Chiefs-Bills game, and just as Joanna had predicted when she called from the road this morning, the Chiefs were ahead by three points.

She rearranged the pillows on the couch for the tenth time, went to the bedroom to change into her Packers jersey, and got to work in the kitchen. With the ingredients for the guacamole on the butcher block, Charley pulled out the two five-quart enamel pots and got to work on the chili. Minutes later, the vegetables she used for a base were sweating nicely and the beef browning. The doorman called to let her know Joanna was on the way up. She opened the door and bolted the lock to keep it ajar after checking that the cats were asleep on the couch. At the stove, she reached for two jars of spices and shook them into the pots before realizing one of them was paprika, not cumin. The string of words that escaped her caused Bing to sit up. Joanna knocked and opened the door.

"Uh-oh...that didn't sound good."

"Damn spices! I thought I'd picked up the cumin, but it was the paprika."

Joanna took off her fleece vest, peered into the first pot, and then studied Charley's spice shelves. "Please tell me these aren't arranged alphabetically."

Charley looked at her, surprised, and then at the shelves. "The ones I don't use a lot, yes. But the five or six I rely on are right up front."

"You *are* a nerd."

"I am not. I'm acutely organized. Besides, that's how the supermarket does it. Makes it so much easier. How do *you* do it, Julia Child?" Charley noticed the San Francisco 49ers logo on the red V-neck sweater that hugged Joanna's curves. A wave of lust rose right up through her chest. She looked back at her spices to bring it under control.

"I don't have as many as you do, so it's not a problem."

"I thought you were a serious cook, after your discussion with Terry."

"I am. But there are only a handful you really need on a daily basis. So…where are your Cs?"

"Between the Bs and the Ds, where they should be."

"Your mistake is not the crisis you think it is." Joanna found the bottle she was looking for and handed it to Charley.

"Cinnamon?"

"It hides a multitude of sins. You can rebalance the cumin and oregano later."

"I don't use oregano."

Joanna pulled it off the shelf and handed it to her.

"I guess I'm using it now."

"Keep the pots on low over the next hour and the cinnamon will meld into the other tastes. You won't be able to tell the difference."

As Bing slinked into the kitchen and wound his sleek black body along the perimeter, Charley relocked the door, took Joanna's vest from her, and hung it in the small closet by the door. She returned to stirring the pots on the stove. Anything to keep her hands busy so she didn't reach out and touch Joanna. And then kiss her.

Joanna draped her wrist over Charley's shoulder, the cumin still in her hand, her thin silver bracelets sliding down her wrist with a melodic tinkle. There was an ease about her that Charley hadn't heard in her voice all week. The light lemon scent blocked out every other smell rising from the stove, momentarily dizzying Charley's senses.

"You know you can't really screw up chili. Even if this was your mother's copyrighted blue-ribbon recipe. Almost any dish can be rescued from a mistake."

"Not the ones I screw up," Charley snorted.

"I'll teach you. We'll cook together some time."

"Is that a promise?" Charley looked at her and Joanna's eyes seemed to glitter.

Joanna reshelved the cumin. "Oh, who is this?" she asked as Bing leaned up against her. "May I?"

Charley nodded and Joanna picked up the black cat.

"*That* is Bing." Charley tried to keep the note of jealousy out of her voice, watching Bing wrap his paws around Joanna's neck as she hugged and kissed him, his eyes becoming yellow slits reflecting pleasure. "Bob is on the couch." Escaping the love fest, she put the cookbook with the guacamole recipe on the stand that sat on the butcher block table, open to the page she needed.

A very cranky meow greeted Joanna as she peeked over the back of the couch. "Someone's not happy."

"He knows the chili and guacamole mean his space will be invaded tonight by screaming, swearing women. He hates my dinner parties."

"Poor guy." Joanna deposited Bing next to Bob and checked the score on the television. "Or maybe he's a Bills fan. And what do you know, they're losing." Joanna walked back into the kitchen. "Nice jersey, by the way. I'm assuming the Brett Favre signature is real and not machine-made?"

"It is."

"Very nice," Joanna said, running her fingertips over the rise of Charley's breast where the signature had been inked.

Between the bubbly sensation racing through her, and Joanna's emerald eyes catching her, Charley held her breath, trying to keep from reacting, to no avail. The blush was rising of its own accord. A smile ghosted Joanna's lips. "How did you get it?"

"I know the assistant to the Packers' controller."

"That's some serious networking. You *are* acutely organized. So. What can I do? Put me to work. Is this for guacamole?" She pointed to the vegetables on the table.

"You know how to make it?" Charley asked, working to regain her composure. "Recipe's right there."

"Don't need it. You have a lime somewhere? And I'll need your cayenne."

Charley held up the bottle. "Lime is still in the fridge."

As Joanna set to work, Charley leaned against the counter next to the stove and asked her about the week upstate.

"You really want to hear all this?"

"Only if you want to tell me."

Joanna sighed and gave Charley the details of their rather mundane week: the marketing, a local museum, their walks, and long talks. No intimation of sleeping together.

"And the argument?"

Joanna had finished the guacamole by that point and found the plastic wrap to cover the bowl. But she put the bowl down and looked at Charley, her expression inscrutable.

"Okay, none of my business."

Joanna put the bowl in the refrigerator and began washing the dishes. It was an awkward moment.

"You're my guest, you shouldn't do those."

"I came over to help."

Charley nodded and got several heads of lettuce and an array of vegetables out of the salad bin in the refrigerator, mentally kicking herself for crossing a line she should've known better than to cross. A moment later, Joanna stood beside her drying a knife that she'd washed.

"I'm a very good sous chef, too. What do you need chopped?"

They worked in silence for a few minutes.

"I'm sorry, I shouldn't have asked about the argument."

"Look, we're still getting to know each other. How about we allow for mistakes?"

"Hmm. Disclaimer: they freak me out. Because if I make them, the next thing that happens is I get fired."

"I promise I won't fire you." Joanna reached into the refrigerator for the guacamole and unwrapped it.

"Not done yet?" Charley asked.

"Spices usually need adjusting. Might need more heat."

Charley handed her the bottle of cayenne, trying to stifle a smile. "Heat."

Joanna tasted the mix and tossed a generous pinch of cayenne into the guacamole, glancing at Charley.

"You like heat, don't you?" Charley asked.

Joanna stirred the contents thoroughly. "If we're talking about food, I like a lot of things." She tasted the guacamole again. "I think it's done now. Do you want to try it?" The honey in her voice was markedly sweeter. She opened a bag of chips, dragged one through the dip and brought it to Charley's mouth.

Charley felt warmth and color come to her face, equal parts guacamole and Joanna's gaze.

"Oh, too hot for you?"

Charley heard the trace of innocence marking the honey, saw the raised eyebrow. "No...no, that's...great."

Joanna put the back of her hand to Charley's neck. "Hmm. Could be hotter." She leaned in and kissed Charley

"You are so unfair," Charley whispered.

"I believe you were unfair first outside the Palm Too. You know, the orange caution sign?"

"That's before I knew you thought you couldn't do this because you're toxic."

"No, I told you I was toxic before we went out for coffee. You didn't know about Georgia."

"I still don't."

Joanna disengaged herself and sighed softly. "I am being unfair, you're right. Why don't we watch the game for a bit?"

Joanna sat down in front of the TV. Charley tried to control her breathing, which had become ragged under the soft pressure of Joanna's lips. *Why didn't I run with the ball? She handed it right to me. Please, be unfair again...*

"So, how fond of that shirt are you?" Joanna asked when Charley sat down.

"Very. Why?"

"I thought we could put a little wager on tonight's game."

Charley snorted. "You don't have anything that measures up to this."

"How about a Jeter baseball he signed the night he hit three thousand?"

"You do not." Charley wasn't sure she believed Joanna.

"I knew it was going to happen at that game, I had a ticket that night, so I bought a ball and he signed and dated it when I hung over the dugout before the game, batted my eyelashes, and begged. It's already worth a young fortune."

"Get. Out. You wouldn't stake that."

Joanna reached into her pocket and handed Charley a hundred-dollar bill. "I'll stake it with that. On the Colts, because I know you don't like them, but they're winning tonight. Which means I'll win that jersey. I promise to give it the respect it deserves."

Charley couldn't walk away from that kind of arrogance, so she took the money and held out her hand to seal the deal. A moment later, the doorman called. "Brooke and Annie are here."

When the bell buzzed, Joanna walked to the door. "Brooke's your college friend."

"You remembered."

"Yes." Joanna smiled at Charley and opened the door.

It was a raucous evening, the game too close to call until the Colts field goal in the final seconds, but what had been closer was the scrutiny of her friends when it came to Joanna. Brooke had stood at the door until Annie pushed her inside and Charley gave her a kiss on the cheek to wipe the look of surprise off her face. During the first quarter, several women asked Joanna how long she and Charley had been seeing each other, and Joanna patiently explained that they were friends. One even asked Charley, and as she started to answer, Joanna called the infraction on a play before the field judge even reached for his yellow penalty flag.

Charley's friend said, "Well, you *should* be seeing her. She's a keeper. Look at that, beat the ref to the call. We'd like her to come next week."

When she wasn't in hostess mode bussing dishes or refilling glasses, Charley found a spot as close to Joanna as she could to watch the game, content to watch her from time to time as well. During commercial breaks, Joanna joined her in the kitchen and Charley noticed how well they worked together in the small open room, but there was no mistaking the tension between them every time they happened to brush against one another. Just before the end of the game, they were both in the kitchen, Charley leaning on the butcher block table, when a cheer went up for a Colts interception. Joanna put her hand on the back of Charley's neck and slowly ran it down her back, raising goose bumps everywhere on Charley's body. Then Joanna bent over and whispered in her ear, "Someone's going to owe me the shirt on her back." Charley stood and growled at her, and Joanna laughed.

Brooke had spent a fair amount of time talking to Joanna when Charley was busy with other guests. Charley knew she was in interview mode, trying to glean as much information as she could before giving her blessing, something that she'd never granted Tricia.

Joanna stayed to help clean up after the guests left. "Listen, I meant to tell you. I'm starting with a new client on Friday night."

"But it hasn't been two weeks."

"I know. I called and told them I didn't need the entire two. I do better when I'm working. So, I'll be on a different schedule this time because I'm splitting nights and days."

"Oh?"

"I'll be on Friday and Saturday nights, and Tuesdays and Wednesdays."

"That's an odd schedule."

"I wanted more evenings free."

Charley wondered if that was for her benefit, but after the reaction she'd raised with the question about Georgia, she was going to tread carefully now. She really did hate making mistakes. And she found herself right back at Emotional Square One not wanting to get hurt in a relationship she hadn't been looking for, even if this wasn't a relationship yet. "Did they tell you anything about this patient?"

She hesitated and then put several wine glasses away. "Not much. But she's very ill. So I won't have time to bond with her. I didn't want a patient that that could happen with. This will be…" Joanna seemed to search for the right words. "Helping someone get ready to leave. I haven't done that in a long time."

"That must be hard."

"It's really only hard when you're invested in your patient. It's difficult helping the family through it, but I've learned over the years how to divorce myself from the process. The patients always know, and that makes our relationship very clean. It's like we have business to attend to. The family, on the other hand..." Joanna shrugged.

"I don't know if I should say I'm sorry or that's good for you?"

"I'll let you know in a couple of weeks." She got her down vest out of the closet. "I had a lovely time tonight. I'm glad you invited me. Oh, and, I won't be at the pool tomorrow night. I still need time..."

"Of course." Charley was disconsolate.

"But with my new schedule, I'll have almost every night of the week free."

"My God, think of the damage we'll do to this city's bars."

"I'll call you this week." Joanna kissed Charley, a brief, light kiss, and ran her fingers over the Brett Favre signature again, causing Charley to blush. "I won't ask you to hand this over right now. You take a couple days, say good-bye to it, and bring it with you next Monday." Joanna unlocked the door and reached for the handle, but Charley had her hand on it first, opened it and blocked her exit.

"Very funny." She kissed her, took the shirt off, and handed it to her. "Not like we haven't seen a thing or two in the locker room." Charley pushed her out the door as Joanna laughed, slung the shirt over her shoulder, and walked down the hall.

CHAPTER TWENTY-SIX

The week at work went off without a hitch on Jenny's end, which meant Charley spent it standing by at her desk at home from one to nine every morning with nothing to do. For the first time in years, she spent the week writing as though that was her career instead. It felt otherworldly and at the same time exactly what she should be doing. Charley desperately wanted to email or text Emily to find out if she'd been successful, but Emily was an adamantly "no paper or digital trail" executive. She'd learned from a lawsuit at a previous firm, and now conducted all pertinent business face-to-face. Charley would have to wait until Monday morning.

Friday evening, Tricia picked her up in a company car and they rode downtown together. Tricia wanted Charley to meet the three nurses she'd hired, one of whom was starting tonight. And she figured she might as well make dinner for her.

Working through the preparations with Tricia and then sitting down to eat, Charley had the chance to visibly measure the further progression of fatigue since Sunday. Ted's constant presence had absolved her of the need to be there most of the last couple of weeks, though she checked in daily by phone. It had only been twenty-one days since the radiation began, but the effects this week were shocking. Tricia was stiff and unsteady in every way. In the bedroom, she'd dropped her sweatpants several times as she tried to put them on. Charley had spotted peeling skin on her chest when she changed her shirt; in the kitchen, she'd had trouble pulling open the Sub-Zero refrigerator door, and the exertion seemed to leave her short of breath. Charley thought she remembered the doctors at that first meeting talking about lung scarring from treatments that would result in the inability to fully take in air, wondered if that was what this was about, and made a mental note to apprise the new nurse of all these problems. Tricia had also lost some of the patrician bearing that so defined her. And if she hadn't still been going to her hairdresser for highlights, Charley was certain that Tricia's shimmering brown hair would be faded, if not completely gray. She looked lost, and it cut Charley to the quick.

The dinner was a welcome break from all her own distractions. And Tricia stayed put, letting herself be taken care of for once.

"When is this gal coming?" Charley asked. "And do you know anything about her?"

"Eight o'clock. The agency says they match you to nurses whose backgrounds fit your needs. If it works, they keep you together."

"Do you mind if I put on one of the college games while we wait?"

"Of course not."

Charley found the BYU game and pulled the office NFL pool picks out of her pocket, sitting on the couch to review them. The intercom buzzed and she rose to answer it, but Tricia was there first. This nurse was ten minutes early, which was a good sign. Turning her attention back to the game, Charley barely registered the conversation at the door until she became aware that the two women were in the living room and a familiar honeyed tone caught her attention. Not quite believing what she heard, she turned. "Joanna?"

For a moment, she and Joanna stared at each other, Tricia looking from one to the other with surprise and amusement.

"This is *the* Joanna?" Tricia asked.

Dumbfounded, Charley could only answer, "Yes."

Joanna walked down the three steps into the living room, hugged Charley, and said very quietly, "I should've said something to you the other night. I did wonder when I got the assignment, but I thought it had to be a million to one that—"

"You knew who the patient was?" Charley asked just as quietly. She immediately thought of Joanna's description of her new patient being someone she was helping to leave.

"I had a name and an address, yes," Joanna replied. Recovering, she turned to Tricia. "Yes, I'm *the* Joanna, so I can only assume she's talked to you about me, and whatever she said, you can take with a grain of salt because she's certainly said a lot about you to me and I'm going to dismiss all of it so that you and I can forge our own relationship. So, first things first, why don't you show me around. That's the BYU game, isn't it? You like football?"

"That's really her domain. I got into it because she dragged me."

"Well, I understand you dragged her into opera, so maybe you're even."

Tricia laughed. "I like the way you dismiss everything. Okay, so yes, let me show you the place, and then we can watch the game."

Charley sat back down in front of the TV, ignoring Tricia's pointed glance as she and Joanna left of the room. None of the game filtered through the numbness. Instead, what slowly dawned on her was the absence of the lemon that Joanna usually trailed in her wake. And instinctively she knew that she must not wear the perfume when she worked in case it had an adverse effect on a patient. *Helping someone leave.* The finality of it made Charley want to curl into a ball.

When they got back to the living room, Tricia settled into the opposite end of the couch from Charley.

"I have all the charts from your doctors, but I want to take your vital signs so I have a baseline to work from," Joanna said as she took a stethoscope and blood pressure cuff from her canvas bag.

"My living room has become a doctor's office," Tricia noted.

"Nice not to have to leave home to get that kind of service, isn't it?" Joanna replied as she listened to Tricia's heart and put the cuff on her left bicep.

"It's probably the beginning of my world shrinking."

"If you want to think of it that way. Or you could see it as a silver lining, being lucky enough, or perhaps financially savvy enough in your case, to have the wherewithal to bring the world to you."

Tricia looked over at Charley. "I can see why you like her."

Charley blushed and feigned interest in the TV.

"Open," Joanna commanded, a tongue depressor in her hand. Tricia complied. "Sit forward and lift your shirt."

Tricia's eyebrows rose.

"I need to listen to your organs. Takes three seconds. C'mon." Joanna motioned at her shirt.

Tricia complied and Charley watched her thumping in several places around Tricia's back. "Now the front." She pressed around Tricia's abdomen and made notations on the iPad. "Okay, who's winning the game, does anyone want anything from the kitchen because I need a glass of water, and what time do you go to bed?" she asked Tricia.

"I tend to go in around midnight and get up at five thirty."

"Really?"

"She falls asleep out here around nine, Ted takes her in before the news, and I give her a wake-up call at five thirty." Charley amended Tricia's statement.

"That's better. Anything from the kitchen?"

"I'll come with you," Charley said. Leaning on the stove a moment later, she asked Joanna the question that had occurred to her moments after she'd walked in. "What are we going to do?"

"What do you mean?"

"We can pretend that Georgia changes nothing between us, and we can avoid talking about her. But we can't do that here."

Joanna sighed. She took three glasses from the cupboard and filled them with ice. "Probably not. You might not have recognized it when you told me about Tricia the other night, but you're emotionally tethered here in ways you aren't even seeing." She opened the refrigerator, found a filtered water canister on the top shelf, and took it apart to clean it. "Yours is just a different toxicity, Charley. Neither one of us can...we're just going to have to be completely professional about this. I have a literal job here; you have a figurative one."

Charley ran her finger over the marble countertop in a figure eight. "Can we still see each other on Mondays?"

"I'd like to think that we can, but I'm drawing a line in the sand for now. I don't think we should be physically involved with each other while I work for Tricia, and not with your level of emotional investment. Neither one of us is truly free yet." Joanna secured the filter system into the canister, made sure it was tight, and put it under the faucet, watching the water run into the canister.

Charley saw the wisdom in what Joanna said, even as she hated the truth of it, and even as she'd denied her emotions. "All right."

"Now, let's go back to the living room before Tricia wonders what's going on in here." Joanna put the canister in the refrigerator and walked out of the kitchen with two of the glasses.

Charley steadied herself before she followed Joanna, water in hand, and found her standing by the couch, the NFL picks in her hand. "Your office pool?"

"Yes," Charley replied, somewhat surprised. "Why?"

"Are you any good at handicapping?"

"I won the pool the last two weeks."

"Huh. I might have to challenge you on some of these." She sat on the couch and studied the piece of paper before she patted the seat beside her. Charley caught the fascinated expression on Tricia's face.

Turning her attention to the piece of paper, Charley watched Joanna flip her "wins" around three games. "No way!" she said.

Joanna handed the sheet to her. "Put your money where your mouth is."

Charley hesitated.

"Nervous I might be right?" Joanna said.

"Never." She took the folded bills from her pocket, peeled two fifties from the inside, and set them on the coffee table.

"Oh, she's going for it," Joanna said.

"Nervous I might take you to the cleaners?"

Joanna handed one of the fifties back to her. "I can't take you for that much. I'll hold this until Monday."

Tricia laughed out loud. "I do believe, Charley Owens, that you have met your match."

CHAPTER TWENTY-SEVEN

Charley's phone rang Sunday evening. Emily wanted her to set up a team breakfast for eight o'clock in the morning. "I realize how late I'm asking you for this, but I'm counting on those rabbits in your Rolodex," Emily said.

"Never mind the rabbits," she said. "What about getting some of this team into the office at that hour?"

"I've already made those calls."

"Can I assume—" Charley asked excitedly.

"Nothing. Tomorrow. Oh. Get champagne. The good stuff." Emily chuckled and hung up.

Charley called the one caterer she could count on in a pinch like this and hoped she didn't have another job. She had given Leigh, the wife of a former boss, her first break when Leigh launched her personal catering business. Without hesitation, Leigh said yes, and Charley knew she could check that box "done."

When Emily arrived at the office at a quarter to eight, she happened to look over Charley's shoulder at her computer screen.

"You're not working on that online streaming report already, are you? God, I've hardly woken—"

Charley turned to look at Emily when she stopped dead, wondering what happened.

"That's the chairman's conference room schedule," Emily said, horrified. "You're not booking that for us now are you?"

"Yes. It's soundproofed. No one will hear us cheer. And Hans won't be in until ten. I checked his schedule. We just have to go up to the corporate floor one or two at a time so we don't raise any suspicion, and leave that way when we're done."

"You are brazen."

"What better way to announce to the C Levels up there that there's a new sheriff in town than to leave a conference room full of half-eaten omelets, French pastries, and empty bottles of Dom Perignon behind?"

"You ordered Dom?

"My rabbit, my champagne."

The team did, indeed, cheer when Emily announced that the deal would be going through as the first-of-its-kind partnership with their competitor and the new streaming company, and Paul Whitney had leaked it to the *Wall Street Journal* last night with his and Emily's names front and center. "Now," she said, "how many of you think I should still go to the board and put Hans on the hot seat."

"Do you still have the recording of the meeting where he told you to tell Paul the handshake came with our company logo?" Harry asked.

Emily nodded.

Every hand in the room went up.

A week later, Charley and Joanna sat at the bar in Pietro's again.

"We should think about making these Monday nights dinners," Charley said. There was a jumbo shrimp cocktail between them, two pieces left.

"Now you're suggesting dinners when we're supposed to be keeping this relationship professional." Joanna fixed her with a look that took her breath away.

Charley wanted nothing more than to gaze into those emerald eyes for the next hour. "We have to eat."

"Line in the sand. One hour, a drink, like we've *been* doing for weeks. Maybe an appetizer." Joanna dragged a shrimp through the cocktail sauce and bit the end off.

"You should've been an arbitrator."

"I *am* an arbitrator. Getting patients to do things or take meds can be an ordeal. Tricia, by the way, is very ornery."

"Preaching to the choir, sister. And you've only been at this for two weeks, not even."

"How did you deal with her for twenty-five years?"

Charley smiled and raised an eyebrow.

"Oh, no, you can't fix everything with sex."

"*You* might not be able to…"

Joanna laughed. "That ego, my God…"

Charley brushed a piece of nonexistent lint from her shirt. "I think you just might have to get used to it."

"All right, let's get serious for a moment."

"Must we?"

"Tricia gave the nursing staff Thanksgiving weekend off."

"Yes, I knew she was going to do that. We discussed it right after she brought you all on."

"Do you think that's a good idea?"

"No. But I pick my battles with her and this isn't one of them. Ted and I can take care of her for four days. She wants to do it again at Christmas and that's the battle I'm choosing."

"Oh, well, we can shut that right down with a letter from the company telling her she'll be in violation of the contract."

"Then why don't you do that now?" Charley said, surprised.

"Because most of the team would like the time off, so we're not saying anything to Payroll. They won't catch it until afterward, but that's what will generate the letter to her in December."

Charley shook her head. "What will you be doing for Thanksgiving?"

"Going to my brother's in Connecticut."

"You never go back to California to see the rest of your family, do you?" She wanted to ask if Georgia would be going with her, but that part of things was still "hands off," and she wouldn't pry.

Joanna shook her head. "I'm not close to my dad. He has a hard time with…well, with me."

"So does my mother. With me."

"Won't your family want you home for Thanksgiving? Why don't you bring Tricia?"

"Oh, no. My mother and Tricia did *not* get along."

"Ouch. And you had to put up with that for twenty-five years?"

Charley sighed. "My friends didn't like her, either."

Joanna laughed incredulously. "What did you do?"

"Oh, we had plenty of friends, as a couple. It's just that all mine didn't like her, and her friends didn't like me since I'd broken up her relationship with Eleanor. But you and Georgia must've run into a similar problem."

"No." Joanna finished the piece of shrimp. "Our two camps were rooting for us to break up with our then-partners and get together. Lesson learned, never start a relationship by proxy."

"Not something I'd ever considered."

"Good. Don't." Joanna caught the bartender's attention for the bill. "So, will you text me over Thanksgiving to let me know how you're doing?"

"Yes. And we'll have dinner next Monday?"

"Thought you could sneak that through, huh?"

Thanksgiving was far more fun than Charley had thought it was going to be. Ted brought his boyfriend, Ryan, the kitchen became a hive of chefs running amok with no sous chefs among them, and Charley was amazed when a beautiful golden brown turkey showed up on the table stuffed with Ryan's mother's andouille-sausage-and-sage stuffing, along with an enormous variety of side dishes followed by six desserts.

Tricia surveyed the scene before carving the turkey. "I've never seen anything like this," she said.

"You told me you wanted a Thanksgiving you'd never had before," Ted said.

"I think we need to say grace this year," Tricia said.

After dinner, they all settled in to watch *It's a Wonderful Life*, as she and Tricia had done for years, Tricia curled up under Ryan's protective arm. Charley tried not to cry when Tricia lost it, as she had also done for years, when George Bailey begged his guardian angel to take it all back, that he didn't want to die. This year, Charley knew she was crying yet again for George Bailey, and maybe for herself. The bell ringing on the Christmas tree made her wonder where Tricia's guardian angel was.

Turning in that night, Tricia asked Charley to lie down with her. She hesitated.

"Just for a little while. I'm bone-tired, Charley, and I need some comforting."

She stretched out on the bed, and Tricia shifted to put her head on Charley's shoulder; she pulled Tricia close.

"Talk to Joanna today?"

"No."

"Call her. Don't waste time, Charley. It's too precious."

Shortly after that, Tricia was sound asleep, and she slipped off the bed and tucked the quilt around her. Weeks ago, she'd seen the framed picture on the dresser of the two of them, taken at the beach the first summer they were together; now she stopped at the sight of an open mussel shell propped up against the frame, the pearl white interior a startling contrast to the black wings. She knew it couldn't be the one Tricia had picked up that day. Too delicate, it would've dried out and broken long ago. "This is us," Tricia had said, "two halves connected near the top. And, of course, black and white, different as night and day." Who had brought her the shell?

She went to the guest room and got ready for bed, but loneliness hit her in a way that it hadn't in some time. Without allowing herself to think about the ramifications, Charley texted Joanna. *U up?*

Joanna: *Yes.*

How are things at your brother's?

Joanna: *Like being caught in an old episode of Family Ties.*

Then you should be having fun.

Joanna: *Not when you have a nephew as annoying as Alex P. Keaton. How are things there?*

Seinfeld.

Joanna sent a laughing emoticon. *So what's on your mind?*

Charley ran her finger lightly over the keys. *I want you, that's what's on my mind* is what she wanted to send back. *Nothing. Just wanted to see how you are.*

Joanna: *Liar.*

Charley's laughter was momentary, buried right away in pain. *Okay, I'm being eaten alive by mosquitoes of doubt and fear.*

A moment later, her phone rang. "Talk to me."

Charley fought to keep the tears out of her voice. "She cried for George Bailey tonight."

"Everybody cries for George Bailey."

"I don't know if I can keep doing this, coming down here, watching her slowly disappear before my eyes. It hurts."

"Charley, I concluded weeks ago that you are nothing short of titanium to have put up all those years with a woman made of such steel as Tricia. Of course you can do it."

"I'm not. Made of titanium. I feel like every minute I spend with her I'm losing something. Pieces of her. Sand running through the hourglass." Charley sighed. "Pieces of me." Joanna telling her they couldn't get involved because of her own emotional investment came tumbling back to her when all she wanted to do in this moment was find her way into Joanna's arms.

"I'm here to handle this with you. You can call me any time."

"Yeah? And what are *you* made of?"

"I'm a diamond, Charley. There's nothing stronger."

Charley slipped under the covers of the bed and pulled the quilt tight around her. When they finally said good night, Charley felt like even though there were miles between them, Joanna had managed to cradle her in her arms.

Chapter Twenty-eight

Charley was still thinking about Monday night, having drinks with Joanna in the little Spanish restaurant on Forty-First Street after the Thanksgiving weekend, as she walked to work on Friday. There had been quite a bit of shameless flirting, which Charley welcomed, and Joanna had made her laugh with her imitation of her annoying young money-centric nephew.

This morning she decided to follow a lesser-used route to her office building that brought her to the high arched granite underpasses of the Helmsley Building that led to Park Avenue. She hadn't used that option in eons, but she loved the breathtaking view it afforded straight down Park Avenue as far as the eye could see. It could make you feel like you were in a different world, walking up the boulevard with its mix of stately old International Style corporate buildings from the twenties and thirties coupled with the new sparkly glass towers going up on other corners where the city hadn't been smart enough to landmark some of its nineteenth century headquarters of commerce. Set off by flowers and greenery that ran the length of the avenue's median, the walk always brought her peace. A landscaping company changed the flora seasonally, transforming the street, when it happened, as though someone had sprinkled a bit of fairy dust overnight. Charley took in the current riot of maroon and pink dahlias, red and yellow hibiscus scrambling among tall bushes she didn't recognize which bloomed a white flower with bright yellow stamen, and for a moment, everything in life was good.

At Fifty-Sixth Street, Charley decided to stop in at the new Lenny's Bagels shop to get breakfast. As she reached for the door, someone standing in line at the counter caught her eye. It was the unmistakable way the woman moved that arrested her. Joanna. But it was the way she moved around the woman she was with that stopped Charley dead: a tall redhead in a dark brown corporate suit and heels, and it couldn't have been any clearer that the woman was flirting with Joanna. She let the door go and stood transfixed, watching them. At one point, the woman turned to look out the shop's glassed front and Charley inhaled involuntarily. She was quite a beauty, her skin alabaster white against the deep hue of her suit, her light blue eyes searching for something but finding Joanna instead. Charley stood rooted to the spot, and then Joanna glanced out the window, saw her, and walked to the door. Part of her wanted to run. But more of her wanted to know who the redhead was.

"Charley, what are you doing here?"

Joanna hugged her, and Charley was aware of her own rigidity in the moment.

"Picking up breakfast before I go into the office. You?"

"There's an apartment Georgia wants me to see, so we're getting breakfast first."

"That's Georgia?" *Wow.*

Joanna turned to look at her. Georgia, Charley noticed, had been intently studying their exchange. "Yes."

"The apartment's near here?"

"No. In Brooklyn."

"Oh. Good." Charley realized how evident her relief had been when Joanna laughed.

She opened the door and held it for Charley. "Coming in?"

"Uh...no, I'm late, so..." Charley pointed toward Madison Avenue. It was actually her insecurity pointing. She'd had no idea that if Georgia was indeed a foe, she was this formidable.

"Oh. Okay. I'll see you tonight at Tricia's?"

"Yes." Joanna was clearly disappointed, which made Charley feel a tiny bit better, but she knew she couldn't go in there and meet Georgia, so she headed over to the office.

About an hour later, her phone's buoy rang. The text was from Joanna. *Bring your office football pool picks tonight. I could use another hundred dollars.*

Double or nothing, Charley shot back. A second later, a better idea came to her, but she decided to keep it to herself until much later tonight.

The buoy rang again. Joanna had sent a thumbs-up and a slew of dollar signs. Charley laughed. Maybe what they had wasn't romantic just yet, but the friendship they were building was something special.

The picks were tucked into her back pocket when she rang the bell and let herself into Tricia's apartment. She put them on the coffee table for later, wanting to enjoy dinner with Tricia and Joanna without talk of football. She also didn't want Tricia to see or hear the bet she was going to challenge Joanna with. After helping Tricia to bed, Joanna curled up on the couch.

"Your picks, hotshot?" She held out her hand.

Charley gave them to her. She studied the sheet of paper and snorted at several of Charley's choices. "You think the Rams will take the Colts?"

"Have you seen their offensive line lately?" Charley asked.

"Yes, and I disagree. And the Panthers over the Niners?"

"They're overdue."

Joanna raised an eyebrow. "And the Packers? I think you're risking too much this week."

"One of us is about to risk a lot." Charley fixed Joanna with what her friends called her dry ice stare.

"What are you up to?" Joanna asked.

"I'm proposing a new bet. How about a thousand dollars?"

"Are you out of your mind?" Her eyes widened, the familiar flash of shimmering green exciting Charley. "That's serious money. Don't be ridiculous. I'm not betting that."

"Not to be paid all at once or even in cash."

Joanna narrowed her eyes. "I've never heard of a bet like this."

"If you win, I'll pay out the thousand. But if I win, you have to take me out to dinner every Monday until the money is drawn down to zero."

"You little devil!"

Charley laughed.

"You're going to turn our drink dates into dinners come hell or high water, aren't you?"

"I'll give you the option of meeting my thousand, no dinners. So, what'll it be? Hell, the thousand dollars, or high water, the dinners?"

The look Joanna gave her could've melted steel. But Charley reveled in the heat behind it. "Are you doubting your own handicapping?" Charley teased her.

A pink flush rose up Joanna's neck.

"Ah! Or is that blush an admission that my handicapping skills might be better than yours?"

The pink blossomed into red. "Never," Joanna said. She held out her hand. "High water."

Charley shook her hand, secure in the knowledge that Joanna, who could easily pay out that thousand dollars if she lost, wanted the dinners as much as she did. "I love dining out." Charley sighed.

"Oh, my God, are you a spoiled brat about everything?"

"I *am* the baby of the family, with three older brothers. What do *you* think?"

"I'm the oldest with four younger brothers. I think you're going to bug the crap out of me."

"Oh, I think I'll have you wrapped around my little finger in no time. Or maybe I already do…"

Joanna crumpled up the picks and threw them at Charley, who grabbed the pillow next to her and tossed it at her, both of them laughing.

Sunday night, Charley attended the NFL dinner with her friends but paid close attention to the Green Bay game, shutting out all the noise and drinking around her. She and Joanna were dead even in the pool scoring after Sunday afternoon's Chicago Bears loss, and Charley's chances weren't good for a Packer win tonight. Their season had been so bad that she half-expected to receive a "The Packers Regret" card in the mail any day. But if by some miracle they pulled it off, Joanna would be taking her out to dinner next week. And for many weeks after.

Brooke finally sat down next to her on the couch. "Look, I know you love the Packers, but this is ridiculous. You're missing some really good gossip over at the bar."

Charley glanced at her sideways. "Don't care. I have a serious bet on this game."

"A bookie? You never do that."

"Joanna." Charley told Brooke about the bet, and then the two of them were completely engrossed in the game. An hour later, Charley could hardly believe it as the football sailed through the goal posts on a Packer fifty-three-yard field goal, securing the win. She let her head sink back onto the couch as Brooke jumped up cheering. *Game on, Joanna.*

Within five minutes, she had a text from her. *Know any restaurants that serve crow?*

No, but you can bet I'll find them.

Joanna sent back an emoji sticking its tongue out.

When Charley got home, she found a set of printable December, January, and February calendars online, and slotted the names of several restaurants she'd long wanted to try into the Monday blocks, scanned the pages, and sent them off to Joanna. Ten minutes later, her phone rang.

"I so don't care that it's late and you have to get up for the pool in six hours. Mr. Chow's Chinese restaurant? Are you kidding me?"

"Haven't you always wanted to try the most expensive place in town? Wondered why his place is head and shoulders above the little Chinese take-out places all over the city?"

"Honestly, no. I'd rather order from the joint on the corner and watch a movie right here in my living room."

"Okay. I can do that."

"I didn't say that was on the list."

"So take me to Mr. Chow."

"Maybe I'll be adjusting this list later today. It goes against my grain to spend that kind of money on a dinner."

Charley could hear Joanna tapping a pen and figured she must be sitting at the little breakfast bar that separated her kitchen from her living room. "Keep in mind I am not a cheap date, Miss Thang."

"Not dating," Joanna reminded her.

Charley decided she needed to play with a little fire. "You know, I've been meaning to ask you. How was that Brooklyn apartment?"

There was a moment of silence, and Charley trusted for once that she hadn't crossed a line after all the discussions they'd had about both Tricia and Georgia.

"She didn't like it. Or Brooklyn. She thought it might as well be Oklahoma."

"Ah. A fellow snob."

"There is that, yes. You two would get along quite well in that respect."

"So…she's still in the picture."

"Mmm. For now."

"Have you talked to her about me?" Charley asked quietly.

"Didn't have to after the bagel shop. She figured it out."

"And?"

"You were the topic of conversation most of the trip to Brooklyn."

Charley waited for Joanna to elaborate.

"Of course that was threaded throughout a conversation of what's left of our relationship." Joanna sighed. "She thinks she's got both hands wrapped around the reins. She doesn't see that the horse slipped them long ago."

Charley felt a tightening in her chest. Anxiety. It was so hard to control in moments like this. She knew she shouldn't ask the question; it was like watching a train wreck in slow motion. "Did it?"

Joanna cleared her throat. "There's a lot I've wanted out of life, Charley. I've been blessed with the things that have come my way. Other things have eluded me. I've never had that really big romance that defines your life. You had it. I know it doesn't just magically happen, I know you both have to work at it. But you had a quarter century with the same woman, a woman you wanted so much you stole her from someone else."

"Yes, I did," Charley said quietly.

"I want that. I always have. But when I embrace it, her, I need to be free and clear. I don't want to look back with any doubt. And I still have doubts to put away."

"I think I understand."

"I'll take you to Mr. Chow's tomorrow."

A tiny raindrop of her own doubt fell, and she hoped it wouldn't become a deluge. She wasn't sure she could handle that.

CHAPTER TWENTY-NINE

A s the predicted blizzard descended on the city Wednesday morning, Charley kept in touch with Tricia. Thankfully, Ted had talked her into staying home. He had become so adept at managing her that it began to occur to Charley that he might be the conduit to convince her to stay home permanently. She'd been using a cane for a couple of weeks now, and Charley could see that a walker was imminent.

Charley had also been texting with Joanna and thanked the gods that she was on duty today. Aware of her worry, Joanna told Charley they had Christmas carols on in the apartment and the three of them were decorating the tree Ted had brought in. "Tricia's also unpacking the boxes of Christmas decorations," she said when Charley called. "Did this woman lead a hostile takeover of the North Pole at some point in her career? You should see the stuff she's unwrapping."

"I'm familiar with it," Charley deadpanned.

"Look, if you can get through this blizzard, you should come down for dinner. It's kind of a party atmosphere here. I thought I'd make eggnog later, and we're having Moroccan red lentil stew for dinner with a sourdough boule."

"Because nothing says Christmas like a Moroccan stew," Charley replied.

"It's good protein for Tricia. And it's curried, you food snob."

"Oh. I love curry."

"Yes, I know."

"I never told you that." Charley was puzzled.

"You forget where I am four days a week."

"Tricia!"

"There's only so much law I can talk about, Charley. And you're her next favorite topic when I'm here. Try and come tonight. I'm sure a handful of cab drivers will be desperate enough to stay on the roads."

When Charley walked into the apartment that evening, she caught her breath. An eight-foot Christmas tree commanded a corner of the living room, its pine aroma pervasive. Ted had artfully wound a broad candy-cane-striped wire ribbon around it, and among the branches and twinkling lights, she recognized many of the beautiful ornaments she and Tricia had collected over the years, with the glowing star they'd picked up in an outdoor holiday market in Strasbourg atop the tree. Turning slowly, she took in the rest of the room: one of the Metropolitan Museum's Neapolitan angels nestled in the pine swag over the archway (the other three would be in swags over other doors), needlepoint Santa pillows on the couch, and sitting in one of the big windows, the crèche they'd found in the Vatican gift shop one hot July. She knew she'd find the small old-fashioned red sleigh on the dining room table filled with tiny glass ornaments of every hue, a poinsettia runner down the middle of a bright red tablecloth. Tears filled her eyes. She thought she'd never see all this again, and the joy it brought was mixed with the sharp pain of bittersweet nostalgia. Laughter emanated from the kitchen, and she knew she should pull it together and join them. Before she could, Joanna came into the living room.

"Oh, good, you're here."

Charley attempted to answer, but all that came out was a strangled sound awash in the tears she'd been trying to hold back. Joanna had her in her arms as the full force of what she was feeling hit her.

"I've got you, you can let go."

But she couldn't. She knew if she did, capping the bottle again would be next to impossible. So, she did what she was best at: she shut it down as Joanna held her tight. And she struggled to push the door shut against the one thought that had been chasing her since Thanksgiving, since this holiday season loomed on the horizon. But now it stood in front of her, Christmas past, present, and future. Even as the present unfolded, she knew that the possibility of ever spending this holiday that Tricia loved so much with her again was gone. The cruelest irony was that the knowledge demanded her attention as she stood in the arms of the woman with whom she was certain she wanted to spend the rest of her Christmases. That that might not happen, either, was a different kind of difficult. Back in control a few minutes later, she went into the bathroom to douse her face with cold water, and by the time she reached the kitchen, she was able to fake the party spirit the snowstorm had dropped on them. Tricia looked genuinely happy, and that brought a sense of peace. The other sense she felt, of warmth, security, and protection, came from Joanna, who stayed nearer to Charley than she did Tricia all evening.

Charley learned at dinner that Tricia had hired a new legal team, a group of young lawyers who'd thrown all caution to the wind and started their own firm, eager now to cut their teeth on her case. Maybe they'd get Trish what she wanted. It was something for her to focus on, and it was obviously bolstering her spirits.

After dinner, Charley excused herself to the kitchen, then returned with a plate piled with éclairs.

Tricia laughed. "Some things never change."

"I like dessert," Charley said.

"You like éclairs on your birthday," Tricia shot back. "And where the hell did you find those in this storm?"

"It's not my birthday. And there's an adorable bakery at Twenty-Seventh and Third."

"You made some poor driver schlep all the way over there on your way down here," Tricia said.

"It suited his meter and my need for éclairs."

"When *is* your birthday?" Joanna asked.

"I don't celebrate it, so it doesn't matter."

"Next Monday, the seventeenth," Tricia interjected. "So we're close enough tonight."

Joanna got up from the table, a sardonic smile on her face. "You forgot a knife to cut these."

Charley glared at Tricia.

"Will you honestly be okay with Christmas?" Joanna asked after Tricia had gone to bed. Her iPod was on low, the Christmas carols still playing. The fire Charley had built in the large marble fireplace was beginning to die down.

"The ghost of Christmas past caught me off guard, that's all." Charley picked up the poker, moved the screen aside, and shoved a burnt log farther back on the brazier. "I had let Christmas go. I let a lot of things go after we broke up, and I shouldn't have. I robbed myself. And probably my friends, too."

"I think you were healing. Nothing wrong with that."

"Except that it's taken so long. Too long."

"You think there's a time frame on healing? Some universal timetable? Scraped knee, one week. Bruised ego, three days, but symptoms may recur every few weeks. Broken heart, sixteen months."

Charley looked at her skeptically.

"I'm still triaging things from two years ago because they keep breaking open and bleeding. That adage, time heals all wounds, is nonsense. Time just gives us perspective so we can struggle with what we might've done but didn't or couldn't. Genuine healing? That's rare."

"Sort of ironic, coming from someone in the business."

"Someone who knows that even the human body doesn't always heal, Charley."

"Still bleeding from Georgia?"

"Perhaps not as much as you are with the wounds that were opened today."

Charley sat down heavily on the couch.

"Maybe we should find a football game. Some college has to be playing tonight."

"No," Charley said, putting her hand on Joanna's thigh. "I like this, sitting here talking with you in front of a…well, not so roaring fire."

Joanna smiled. "Okay. Then I have to ask two things. Why don't you celebrate your birthday?"

Charley studied Joanna for a moment. "I haven't celebrated *anything* since I left Tricia. I think letting these holidays just be another day of the week was armor. But as Brooke recently pointed out, that's been a little bit selfish of me."

"It probably has been. But we're all allowed to be a little selfish sometimes." Joanna nodded slowly. "I like that you told me, though. You let me in."

Charley sat back and looked at her.

"You know," Joanna said, "Monday was supposed to be our dinner at Dock's."

Her voice, soft, low, intimate, felt like silk being drawn across Charley's skin.

"Was?"

"We're not going out. I'll make a birthday dinner for you at your apartment."

"Are you sure we should do that?"

"Don't worry, I won't skimp. It'll be as nice as if we were going out. Only you'll have to provide the candlelight."

"I'm not talking about the money."

Joanna's gaze pinned her to the couch. "And I'm simply talking about dinner, Charley, nothing more."

Charley nodded. "Noted. What was the second thing you wanted to ask me?"

"Oh, right." Joanna fidgeted with the pillow in her lap. "Christmas we'll be with Tricia." She glanced at Charley. "I don't know what you…how you'll…New Year's Eve…"

Charley cocked her head. "I sense a yawning chasm here. Do you need me to manage this conversation?"

Joana shook her head. "I know you want to spend as much time with her as you can. And I'm not trying to take that away from you. But I wanted to invite you away for New Year's. Madeline and Thea have us all to their cabin for three days. It's a really wonderful and needed break, and I thought…" Joanna looked at her.

"Can I think about it?" Charley knew she wanted to go, but she couldn't fathom not being with Tricia, either. And spending a weekend away with Joanna sounded like heaven, except for all the ambiguity that remained around what they were building. Would it be too risky?

"Of course. Take as long as you like. I've already told Madeline you may or may not come."

Charley curled up on the couch and sighed contentedly when Joanna began to massage her feet. Maybe taking it slow wasn't such a bad thing.

Chapter Thirty

Monday morning, Charley drew her navy suit and white silk shirt from the back of the closet. It was her turn to take the minutes at the board meeting and she had to fit the corporate mold. It would only have briefly registered that it was her birthday if not for the anticipation of having dinner with Joanna tonight right here in the apartment.

The day was busier than she'd anticipated, and although she kept her eye on the clock, she was afraid she might not make it to Anita's class. A cab got her to the Y quickly, and she was steps from the front door when she saw Joanna getting out of a cab with a large canvas carryall that was clearly heavy.

"Are those groceries?" Charley asked, reaching for the bag.

"Oh, hi! No, it's dinner. You didn't think I could start cooking at eight o'clock, did you? We'd never eat." Joanna kissed Charley on the cheek and then stepped back to inspect her, the open camel hair coat revealing her navy blue suit. "Happy birthday, and wow. Do you always dress for your birthday?"

"Board meeting today."

"I like this look on you, almost better than that little black dress you wore to Per Se." Joanna took the bag from her. "Get the door. This is heavy." Joanna greeted the security guard on the front desk. "Can I leave this back here for about two hours?"

He tagged the handle and Charley walked downstairs, Joanna trailing behind. She held the door to the locker room for Joanna.

"Oh, no, you first. I'm enjoying the view."

Charley blinked in astonishment.

"What? You've got great legs and I couldn't exactly ogle you the night we had dinner with your boss and her wife."

Charley laughed as she walked through the door and let it go before Joanna could catch it. She heard her laughing on the other side and walked into one of the first rows to change.

"What are you doing?" Joanna asked when she saw Charley opening a locker right by the door.

"I'm very late for class. I really need to move it." Charley was in her swimsuit in a matter of seconds. If Joanna *was* ogling, she didn't want the first time she really looked at her naked to be in a gym locker room.

An hour later, she was already dressed when Joanna came in from the east pool.

"Someone's eager for dinner."

"Yes, I am. Why don't I meet you upstairs in a few minutes?" Charley picked up her coat.

"Why don't you stay right here where I can keep my eye on you in that suit?"

Charley smiled and leaned on a locker.

Joanna took a bottle of perfume out of her bag and spritzed several pulse points. Charley recognized the familiar black Chanel lettering on the bottle and made a mental note to look up the name of it online later.

Upstairs, they saw a curtain of fat snowflakes floating down outside, the sidewalk already covered.

"Will you be okay in those heels?" Joanna asked.

"I'll be fine, but let's go before any more accumulates." Charley took the canvas bag from the security guard.

A few minutes later, she lowered the canvas bag to the floor in front of the apartment door and searched for the keys in her coat pocket as Joanna brushed the snow from Charley's hair and coat. Then she reached for Charley's necklace.

"Is this a blue diamond?" Joanna's fingers brushed Charley's throat as she moved the necklace's clasp to the back of her neck.

Charley stood stock-still and concentrated on not moving. Joanna was standing so close she was afraid she'd kiss her. "It's zircon. My birthstone."

Neither of them moved, looking into each other's eyes. Then Charley felt the keys in her pocket, pulled them out, and unlocked the door before she did something she'd regret.

She shouldered the door open, picked up Joanna's canvas bag, and swung it inside. Cedar and pine infused the apartment. Charley watched Joanna search for the source, her gaze settling on the small tree in the corner of the living room. "You got a Christmas tree?"

"Such as it is. It's too small for the cats to knock over. No ornaments for them to bat off in the middle of the night, either. Just lights." The tree sat atop a small stool and Charley plugged the lights in. "I decided I couldn't let the past be such an albatross anymore after our talk. So, thank you for that." As if on cue, Bing appeared, sniffing at the bottom branches of the little tree. Charley shooed him away and hung up their coats in the closet.

"And what's this?" A bottle of Dom Perignon sat on the counter, a gift certificate from Charles Tyrwhitt leaning against it.

"Oh. That's from my neighbor Greg. He travels quite a bit, and I take care of his apartment while he's gone."

"What does he have over there that merits these?"

"He raises orchids. Tricky little things."

"Charles Tyrwhitt. Aren't these the guys that make custom shirts?"

"Greg introduced me to them when I told him I couldn't find good shirts for my suits. I was actually kind of hoping he might get me a pair of diamond cuff links for them this year."

"What, you can't afford them, Little Orphan Annie?"

She snorted. "A girl can dream, can't she?"

Joanna unzipped the canvas bag, took out several foil-covered dishes, and turned to the convection oven. "How does this work? I need to warm the cassoulet and the green beans. And get out of that suit. You're driving me a little nuts."

"I am?"

"I'm a sucker for a woman in a well-cut suit and heels with a jewel at her throat." Joanna tapped a manicured nail on the top of the oven.

Charley turned it on and adjusted the temperature. "I think I may stick around and make whisky sours, then. Want one?"

Joanna chuckled and slid the dishes into the oven. "Bitch. Yes, I'll take one. So, tell me what a board meeting is like."

Joanna took a salad and a bottle of dressing out of the bag, and as Charley mixed the drinks, they talked. A splatter of froth hit her shirt when she wrenched the icy top off the shaker.

"Damn it!"

"Serves you right. Go on, I'll take care of this."

Bob scampered into the kitchen and skidded to a stop in front of the food bowl, his fur a post-nap fright wig. Looking into the bowl's emptiness, he pushed it with his nose.

"I might as well feed them, too. Where's the cat food?"

When Charley returned to the kitchen in shorts and a T-shirt, her small kitchen table had been set, and a bottle of open red wine breathed in the middle of it. The cats cleaned their whiskers nearby, keeping an eye on what was happening on the counter. Charley also spotted the small beribboned box next to one of the place settings on the table. Joanna was standing at her desk, Charley's pewter candlesticks in one hand, her other hand on the edge of the desk.

"Is this your novel?" she looked at Charley.

"Yes."

"Are you going to let me read it any time soon?"

It had long been Charley's hard and fast rule to keep whatever she was working on under wraps because she'd always felt revealing anything brought bad luck. But Neely had shown her how much could be gained from sharing. "I could. But you can't be kind. You have to point out any problems."

"You mean typos, punctuation things?"

Charley smirked. "There won't be any of those."

"You want to know if it works."

"I want to know if it makes you forget the world while you're reading."

Joanna nodded. "All right. Can I take it with me tonight?"

Charley collected the dozens of sheets stacked on the corner of the desk, put them in a plastic sleeve, and handed it to Joanna. "Now, what's that?" She pointed to the box at her place setting.

"Here." Joanna handed her the candlesticks. "You promised me candlelight tonight."

"I did no such thing. *You* said I'd have to provide it."

"Same thing."

"It is *not* the same thing, Miss Bossy Pants. And I don't recall either one of us saying birthday presents were in play."

"I decided they are. Candles, please." Joanna walked back to the kitchen. "I promised you a restaurant-like setting. Don't drop the ball on me."

Charley sighed and went to the kitchen for a book of matches, lit the candles, and put them on the table. Joanna turned off the overhead light. With one floor lamp in the living room illuminating the rest of the apartment, the place had become an intimate restaurant for two. Joanna turned to the butcher block island where she'd set up her iPod and pushed the button. The Righteous Brothers' "Unchained Melody" poured softly from the speakers.

Charley put her hands in her pockets and shook her head. "You put Donna Reed to shame."

Joanna raised her eyebrow. "Really? You couldn't maybe liken me to, say, Sophia Loren?"

Charley loved how easy it was, the reference to a star from the 1960s, Joanna getting it and lobbing another one right back at her. Not like the education and research that had gone into being with Neely.

"You've just turned my apartment from the Bailey Savings and Loan into the most romantic, intimate getaway, like Mary did for George Bailey when they couldn't take their honeymoon trip. I thought Donna was a siren." Charley put her hands on Joanna's shoulders and lightly kissed the back of her neck as Joanna dished up dinner. "There is nothing more alluring than a beautiful take-charge woman who can bring a touch of magic to your life. Oh, that smells good," Charley said as Joanna slipped out of her grasp and put the plates on the table. "You really are a good cook."

"You'll have time to prove your culinary skills to me."

"I did that, with my chili."

"As I recall, *I* did that when you had your spice emergency meltdown. Sit down." Joanna pointed to Charley's chair.

Charley sighed. "Fine. How about we do one of these dinners at your apartment, then, and I'll cook. Of course, you're buying the groceries."

Joanna nodded thoughtfully as she poured the wine. "I could do that."

Charley picked up her fork and eyed the little box.

"Are you going to open it tonight?"

"You know you shouldn't have."

"Food's getting cold." Joanna started eating.

Charley tugged the wide ribbon off and saw the familiar black Lord & Taylor script across the red rose on the white box. She opened it and moved the tissue aside. "Wait a minute…how did you do that? I just told you."

"I have an inside source."

Charley took the diamond cuff links out of the box. "Who? And you can't do this. Oh, Jo, they're beautiful. But you can't spend this kind of money."

"You really think you can tell Miss Bossy Pants what to do? Not that it's any of your business, but I went old-school with Lord and Taylor, and I hit a pre-Christmas fire sale. And, I never kiss and tell. Eat. Or I think Bob will swipe it out from under you."

He'd stretched up to put his front paws on the corner of the table and was poking his nose in the direction of Charley's plate.

"I'm going to find out eventually. You might as well tell me who told you."

Joanna shrugged. "You're welcome, birthday girl."

Charley sat back. "Thank you."

"I didn't get you a card. I thought dinner said it better than Hallmark."

Charley smiled. "Okay, you win. For now. So, when is *your* birthday?"

"April nineteenth."

Charley puzzled for a moment. "Aries?"

"Mmm-hmm."

"But right on the cusp of Taurus. You could be scary."

"Aww. Have I scared you so far?"

Charley regarded her silently.

"Have I?" Delight defined Joanna's face.

Charley took a bite of the cassoulet. "Ohhh, this is really good."

"I *do* scare you."

"Almost every day." It was a genuine admission, and it felt good to say it.

"I had no idea."

"Liar."

"But I like that I do."

Charley looked right at her. "So do I."

CHAPTER THIRTY-ONE

Wandering through the tents of the Christmas bazaar at St. Bart's Church with Brooke on the twenty-second of December, Charley found the mere thought of a gift for Tricia depressing and, beyond that, absurd. In her mind, she'd already bought, wrapped, and ribboned dozens of things for Joanna. And that's where they would stay. Despite the birthday gift Joanna had gotten her, she wasn't sure what to do about Christmas. Joanna would be on duty Christmas day, but she'd feel odd putting anything personal or romantic under the tree for her, especially with Tricia there. That would be somewhat Twilight Zone.

Brooke poked Charley. "Look at those bracelets. They're stunning."

Charley followed her into the silversmith's booth, looking at the display cases without registering anything.

"What can I show you?" the jeweler asked.

Brooke pointed to a bracelet in the case in front of Charley. "She'll look at the bracelet with the Gordian knot, and I'd like to see that necklace."

"I don't need to see anything, thanks," Charley begged off.

"The knot is an intractable problem, Charley. It's what you and Joanna seem to have."

The woman put the bracelet on the counter for Charley. She picked it up and examined the delicate braided ropes of white and rose gold coming together into a union that could only be undone by cutting through it. Charley liked the weight of it in her hand. She could imagine it around Joanna's wrist. As she passed the piece back across the counter, a series of thin silver hoop bracelets hanging from the latticework behind the counter caught her eye. A disk with a different initial in beautiful script dangled from each hoop. Charley was mesmerized and asked to see one.

"Which initial would you like?"

"J. Give her the J," Brooke said, examining the necklace the jeweler had given her.

The woman pulled a velvet tablet from beneath the counter and laid the hoop on it. Charley stared at it before finally picking it up.

"It would be the perfect Christmas gift," the jeweler noted. "She'll think of you every time she puts it on."

"While Romeo is trying to figure out what she's doing, I'll take this. Can it be wrapped?"

Charley ran her finger around the hoop and over the disk, the raised J sliding under her fingertip. Brooke moved down the counter to Charley.

"It's simple and understated. And very Joanna."

Charley regarded her with a gimlet eye.

"I paid close attention to her at your dinner. Diamond studs set in silver, gold college pinky ring, silver heart necklace, a bunch of very fine silver bangles. This would be right up her alley."

Charley knew Brooke's inventory was correct. Joanna wore some combination of it every day.

The jeweler handed Brooke a small bag. "Shall I wrap that for you?" she asked Charley.

"Do it," Brooke said as she signed the credit card receipt.

"I can't give this to her in front of Tricia. And I'm not sure I should be giving her anything at all. I mean, I'm not even sure what we have, Brooke. Sometimes it's détente, sometimes it's entente." Charley sighed. "She's still working it through with Georgia and she thinks I have too much on my plate emotionally."

"You do. Give it to her for *her* birthday, then. Get back at her for giving you the cuff links."

Charley continued running her finger over the initial. "Yeah, and who told her I wanted those, I wonder?" She glanced at Brooke.

"Who do you think? Tricia certainly never got 'em for you. You said Joanna likes to cook. Put something fun for her kitchen under the tree. What are you getting for Tricia, by the way?"

"No idea. What do you get for the woman who won't need anything soon?"

"Annie says you can't think like that, sweetie, or you'll jump off the Brooklyn Bridge. Why don't you take her to the opera? Or the *Nutcracker.*"

Charley looked at Brooke as though she was the embodiment of the light bulb going off over one's heads. "My God, that's brilliant. But she just graduated to a wheelchair, and that will be a problem."

"Whoa, that was fast."

"Yeah, she skidded right by the walker to the chair."

"You know about handicapped seating, right? She'll get preferential treatment."

"She'll fight me. She really hates that chair."

"Take Ted, too. He seems to be a wizard at handling her."

Charley extracted her phone from her pocket, handed the jeweler her credit card, and asked for the same Christmas wrapping as Brooke's for the Gordian knot. "And I'll take the J disk bracelet, too, but don't wrap it."

Brooke smiled.

"Ted, it's Charley. What are you doing the night after Christmas?" Charley told him what she wanted, and by the time she finished, Ted, online as they talked, had secured tickets to the New York City Ballet's *Nutcracker.*

As Charley hung up, Brooke suggested a cab ride downtown to Whisk, the kitchen goods store in the Flatiron building. "You need a gift, and I need fresh pasta from Eataly."

Before Charley could respond, Brooke was halfway out to Park Avenue. She grabbed her bag from the jeweler. Within minutes, they were in a cab and downtown, the holiday traffic moving smoothly for once.

In the store, Charley wandered around touching things but not really seeing them, thinking instead of Christmas morning with Joanna. Brooke found several intriguing gadgets, bringing them to her for approval. In a small section marked "International," Charley spotted a tile trivet nearly hidden behind a tower of European cookbooks. It had an artfully rendered color drawing of a cassoulet on it. She carefully extracted it and was studying it when Brooke joined her.

"Okay, I think we're done. What's that?"

Charley dropped the trivet into the basket over Brooke's arm. "It's a cassoulet. That's what she made last week."

"Oh, how utterly romantic," Brooke said flatly. "You should get a bottle of champagne for when you two exchange gifts. And some strawberries."

"Thank you, Cyrano. I can handle this."

"There's a fruit guy at Eataly. We can get the berries there."

Brooke took the basket to the cashier, got them checked out, and guided Charley toward Eataly's double front doors.

"You know I hate brick and mortar stores, right? This is no different than Bloomingdale's for me."

"Suck it up for me. I like spending time with you, and we never get to do enough of that. I'll buy you the pasta of your choice."

"Great. Bribery works."

Brooke shouldered her way through the crowds toward the pasta counter, took a number, and sent Charley to the fruit aisle. "Let's meet at Café Lavazza and get coffees to go. I can't sit in here. It's too noisy."

Out on the sidewalk, they strolled downtown with their coffees.

"I have a dilemma," Charley said.

"Doctor's always in."

"Joanna invited me away for New Year's weekend."

"Really." Brooke stopped.

"With friends. At a cabin. Brooke?" Charley turned around. Brooke was still standing where she'd stopped. "What?"

"That's...man, I'm not sure the doctor is in for this. This is Annie's domain. And I'm sure she won't charge you."

"No, I have to get home and feed the cats. And play with them. I'm afraid they're going to put a sign down in the lobby soon looking for a new owner."

Brooke began walking beside Charley again. "What are you going to do?"

"I want to go."

"Then go."

"And leave Tricia? It's going to be her last…" Charley threw her coffee into the trash and Brooke put her arms around her.

"Don't cry. Why the hell didn't she fight this? Maybe they could've gotten this damn cancer."

"It was bigger than her." Charley took a tissue from her pocket and they continued walking. "And this is the first time you've ever rooted for her."

"I hate what this is doing to you. What did Joanna say? I mean, she must know what a hard decision this could be."

"She does. She was very sensitive to it. But she also told me recently…she alluded to being done with Georgia. Maybe. It's what I've been waiting for. So this could be a place where we could start building."

"Unless it's too soon for her," Brooke said.

"I thought about that. But there's still a lot to build before we get romantically involved."

"Oh, man, you could be walking right into an open manhole."

Charley stopped abruptly and looked at the sidewalk.

"No, I meant with Joanna. Aren't you kind of already romantically involved?"

"We're trying to keep it at arm's length, you know? She's got Georgia, and apparently I've got emotions. Who knew? Honestly, though, if I'm walking into a manhole, it's my choice to fall."

"I think you've already fallen, sweetie."

Brooke was right.

"But here's the only piece of advice I can really give you. And it's not pretty. Tricia's asleep most nights not long after dinner, isn't she?"

Charley nodded.

"And if it wasn't New Year's Eve? If it was some random Monday and Tuesday Joanna invited you away? I mean, I'm not the pope, babe, but I'm absolving you."

They'd arrived in front of Brooke's building. "Here's your pasta. I got you some linguini for that sautéed vegetable dish you do."

Charley dropped the little brown bag into the handled bag with her quart of strawberries. "These berries had better last," she said peering into the bag. "They were expensive."

"It's New York. Everything's expensive. Go, take care of the cats before they call Child Services and report you."

Charley stuck her arm out for a cab. "Thanks for your advice."

"Not sure it was worth much."

"Hey, it's New York," Charley said as she opened the door of the cab that had pulled up. "Everything's expensive."

Chapter Thirty-two

Charley figured Tricia was getting ready for bed and went to say good night to her about an hour after dinner. She found her in her pajamas standing at the window watching the snow drifting down over a Sunday night Manhattan ablaze with holiday parties. The wheelchair was in front of her, and she steadied herself on the back of it, one hand on the wall. The portable oxygen machine stood silently next to the bed, the tube tucked under the pillow. Charley's chest ached at the sight and her eyes burned with tears.

"This is my last Christmas." Tricia turned, catching Charley by surprise. "I saw your reflection."

Charley caught the pain and uncertainty in her eyes.

"I wonder who will be standing here next year?" Tricia asked.

If she concentrated on the floor, Charley knew she'd be able to keep her emotions in check. She wanted to tell Tricia to hush, but she realized shedding light on her fear might be her safety valve. "Why don't you come back and find out?"

Tricia's laugh was gentle. "Come on, you don't believe in that stuff, do you?"

Charley shrugged. "If it turns out to be true, you have to let me know."

"What, give you a sign?"

"Yes."

"You *do* believe." Amused, she gazed out the window again. "Well, maybe I will come back." She sighed. "I love Christmas."

Charley put her hand in her pocket to find the *balance* stone, and remembered she'd given it to Neely.

"Most of us don't get this chance to say good-bye. Or in your case, flag me from the afterlife." Tricia chuckled.

Charley wanted to laugh at Tricia's macabre joke but was afraid if she opened her mouth, she'd cry.

"I'm glad you met Joanna, you know. I'm glad I've been here to see what's happening between the two of you."

"Nothing is happening between the two of us, Trish."

"You can't see it because you're in the middle of it. But despite the distance the two of you are trying to maintain because of me, I can see the bridge going up piling by piling, the main anchor cables, even the suspension cables."

"How can you be so okay with it?"

"Oh, it isn't easy, trust me. But I love you, Charley, and it's time. She's exactly who you need, and she needs someone like you. And I need to know you'll be okay when I'm gone."

"I won't be." She picked up one of the blown glass ornaments Tricia had artfully arranged in a silver bowl on her nightstand and studied it in her hand, tears threatening again.

"Yeah, you will. It'll take a while, but you will be. And she'll be the key to that."

Charley couldn't look at her, fiddling with the ornament instead.

Tricia pushed the lock of hair that had fallen over Charley's eye back into place. "You're going to have to pull her trip wire. You must know that by now."

She didn't want to hear any of this, so she chose to address a problem she and Tricia hadn't resolved some weeks ago. "What are you doing about your brother? And his kids? We never finished that conversation."

"I'll get my lawyer to contact Dennis when I'm gone, just to let the family know."

"That's a little harsh. Don't you want to see them?"

"How many times did I go back home to see any of them?"

"Never."

"They didn't want me. It made turning my back on them much easier." Tricia perched on the window bench. "You know, the day I bought the Modigliani, I thought of them. I wondered if they'd even know what it was, how much it was worth, or what it meant that a farm girl from Nebraska had climbed the kind of pinnacle that put a painting like that within my grasp."

"What are you going to do with it?"

"The Met is getting it."

Charley thought about that for a moment. "Did you buy it with her?"

"No. I bought it when I knew she was leaving me. A lot of money was tied up in paying for it. She wanted it, though, so I gifted it to the Met before she could try and do anything about it."

Charley wanted to ask so much more, but all she could do was watch the snow fall.

"You want to know about Reagan, where she stands in all this."

Charley tried to appear aloof, but Tricia shook her head, amused. "I have marveled at your restraint for so many weeks." She sighed. "There was nothing left of our relationship when Reagan walked. I bought the apartment she wanted, I gave her anything her heart desired, and she still left me." Tricia rearranged a pillow on the bench. "Oh, Lord, I'm beyond tired. Where's Alexandra? I need help getting into bed."

Charley drew back the covers on the bed. "The Modigliani... that's why you need the buyout at your firm, isn't it?"

Tricia's whole body sagged, revealing a defeat Charley had never seen before.

"How are you, financially? Do you have assets you need to deal with?"

"You're standing in them."

"Your co-op?"

"It's almost all I have left."

Charley was so stunned she didn't know what to say. "Does your legal team know?"

Tricia chuckled. "It's why they're fighting so hard for me. They'd like to get paid."

"Is there anything I can do?" Charley helped Tricia shift to the bed.

"You've been doing it for weeks. Good night. Go, and send Alexandra in, would you?"

Charley stood outside Tricia's building looking up at it through the fat, soft flakes of snow wafting down. Then she headed west across Ninth Street toward the Village. It had been a long time since she'd been to that neighborhood, and she was feeling the need to anchor herself in a moment in her life before Tricia had entered it.

At Washington Street, she zigzagged around the neighborhood that had been such a touchstone of identity for her when she was growing up. She looked sadly at the changes gentrification had wrought. Stores sprouted where old haunts used to be, homogeneous bars replaced and erased old dives, and old buildings she recognized from their bones had gotten facelifts that had cost them their charm. The High Line had changed everything down here. She walked farther west, looking for remnants of anything she knew. Waiting for a red light on a corner that could still evoke the far edges of the old Meatpacking District, she finally smiled. This felt more like the old days. A scruffy no-name club across the street announced its existence in the middle of the dark block, strings of white lights outlining the door that an imposing bouncer blocked. She stood looking at it as the light turned green, thinking of all the times years ago that she hadn't had the nerve to enter places like that. A couple walked toward the club, and Charley was about to turn away when she thought she recognized Georgia, that lush red hair swept over one shoulder. The woman with her, dressed head to toe in black leather, was Joanna. The bouncer opened the door to them as though he knew them. Charley was stunned. Did this mean the horse hadn't slipped its knot? And, obviously, that necklace meant what she'd thought it meant the first time she'd seen it.

She didn't even know where to begin with all this information, or what to feel, and she leaned against the lamp post watching the few cabs and delivery trucks whiz by for several minutes. Then, driven by a greater need to know, she crossed the street. The bouncer eyed her stonily as she approached him. "Can I ask what kind of club this is?"

"You need to be a member to get in. Or be with someone who is."

Charley nodded. "Thank you." She walked back across the street no more enlightened, although she knew. She hadn't needed to ask him. Hearing the club's door open, and the bouncer speaking to someone, she glanced back. Joanna stood with the man for a moment, shook his hand, and then headed across the street toward her. If she slinked off or hailed a cab, and she desperately wanted to do one or the other, Joanna might not spot her. But she couldn't have, anyway, because she couldn't take her eyes off Joanna, nor could she say anything when Joanna, approaching, recognized her, and stopped.

"Charley…"

"Hi." A trickle of sweat ran down her back, even though it was that kind of crisp, quiet thirty degrees out brought on by snowfalls. The handcuffs on the necklace were resting just below the hollow of Joanna's neck.

"What are you doing here?"

"I was in the neighborhood." Charley tried to look nonchalant, but she knew by the confused look on Joanna's face that it wasn't working.

"This neighborhood?"

She sighed. "I was at Tricia's for dinner tonight. We had a…very difficult conversation." Over Joanna's shoulder, the lights from the corner bodega pierced the dark. "Just one of many lately." She caught the concern in Joanna's emerald eyes. "Anyway, I needed to take a walk. This is the neighborhood I grew up in. It was where my mother could afford an apartment when we first moved back to the city after my dad died. I guess I came back looking for pieces of me. And then, I saw you. And Georgia. Going into the club."

"Oh." Joanna shifted her stance. "Georgia's had a membership there for years. And I just gave mine up tonight."

"I don't understand."

"She brought me into the lifestyle, but I can't do any of this with her anymore."

"You left her there?"

"Yes. We came down tonight because she needed something. And when we got here, I realized I was no longer willing to let her have it. Not from me, anyway."

"Is that what your relationship was?" Charley nodded toward the club.

"I told you she owned me in so many ways. But that's over. I need to take my life back." She pulled her jacket closer against the cold. "I need to be with someone who…sees me," she said softly.

Charley bit her bottom lip. "So, it's really over with her?"

Joanna nodded.

Charley glanced at the club again.

"If Georgia wasn't in there, I'd take you in."

"Oh, no, I…"

"It can be fun, you know. In the right hands." Joanna arched an eyebrow.

Charley had to stop herself from looking at those hands. "I'm going to take that under advisement. Meantime, I'm going to grab a cab home. Can I drop you anywhere?"

"Forty-Second Street."

Charley stepped into the street with her arm raised. *I'm not sure I'm sharing* this *conversation with Brooke.*

The silence didn't bother Charley as she sat next to Joanna in the cab, watching her as she concentrated on the Tenth Avenue scenery flashing past her window.

"I read your chapters," Joanna finally said, still looking out her window.

"Oh?"

"Started reading them that night."

"Okay…" She held her breath.

Joanna turned to her. "I read way past my bedtime. It's good, Charley."

Charley stifled her sense of elation. "Thanks."

"I do have a couple of observations. Well, and a question."

"Okay."

Joanna put her hand on the seat between them to steady herself as the cab lurched to a stop at a red light. "The second story line that runs concurrently with the first one—that's you and Tricia, isn't it?"

Charley nodded.

"It's a beautiful portrayal. Heartbreaking."

Charley gently ran her thumb over the back of Joanna's hand.

"The younger version of you, though, is she too omniscient? Is there any way to give her the gift of ignorance?"

"I had that note recently from Neely. So, I'm working on changing that."

"I'd like to read more of it, when you have it."

The cab stopped at Ninth Avenue to drop Joanna. "I'm glad we ran into each other. You remember the pool's closed tomorrow, Christmas Eve?" Joanna asked.

Charley nodded. "I'll see you Tuesday at Tricia's."

"You're really making a roast duck?"

"It was our tradition for years. But maybe you should bring your bottle of cinnamon."

Joanna opened the door of the cab and went to step out. "Very funny."

Charley reached for her arm. "Joanna."

She turned back.

"I'm glad it's over with Georgia."

"I knew you would be." She smiled sadly. "Good night."

Charley turned to watch her cross the street as the cab pulled away.

CHAPTER THIRTY-THREE

W hy is it that everyone has to be in the kitchen when the cook is working?" Charley asked, wiping her hands on her apron, spent oranges all over the counter.

Ted, in a Santa hat, pulled two beers from the refrigerator and handed one to Ryan. "Because it's warm and inviting and we all want to watch you work on the duck."

"Leave her alone and come back to the Monopoly game," Tricia said, sitting at the kitchen table jiggling the dice in her hand. "I'm winning and I want Boardwalk from you."

"Never! I'll sell everything I have to Ryan first." Ted sat back down at the game.

Joanna began collecting orange rinds and putting them in the trash. "What else do you need for the glaze? Oh, my God, I'm so sick of Christmas carols."

Charley picked up the iPod, scrolled through the list, and hit a song. Mariah Carey's "All I Want for Christmas" filled the room. She looked at Joanna. "Are you now. And all I need is the Grand Marnier. It's way in the back of the liquor cabinet."

Joanna left the room and Charley tied the ducks, put them in the roasting pan, and turned on the oven. She watched the Monopoly game, took her phone out of her pocket, and surreptitiously snapped a picture of the three of them arguing over the Luxury Tax Tricia had landed on.

"You've got more money than God, of course you have to triple it!" Ted exclaimed.

"Show me where it says that in the rules, you money-grubbing cockroach."

Charley shielded the phone as she looked at the picture, not wanting Tricia to see her or know she'd taken what would be one of the last photos she'd ever have of her, the sun pouring in the window behind her as she laughed at Ted, the blue shawl over her shoulders, the now ever-present oxygen tube in her nose. Joanna handed Charley the bottle, saw the tears in her eyes, and picked up the spatula. "I'm going to encourage her to take a nap now."

Charley nodded and went back to work on the orange glaze.

After dinner, Ted set up the puzzle he'd put under the Christmas tree for Tricia on a card table near the fireplace. Charley quietly approached him.

"Are you kidding? I can't believe you got it for her. That's gonna take weeks…"

"I think that's why Tricia asked Santa for it."

Charley deflated, struck by the meaning of what Tricia was really asking, and that Ted had fulfilled her wish without judgment.

"Oh, good!" Tricia said as Joanna rolled her chair up to the table. "I hate these. A million pieces of blue sky and one small colorful hot air balloon sailing over all these mountains." She picked up the box cover and pointed at the greenery. "I swear, the guys who ran the Spanish Inquisition should've used these to torture people. It'll take me forever just to fit two pieces together."

Ted looked at Charley as Joanna sat down at the table with Tricia. "One hour. And don't blow a gasket trying to find those two pieces."

"I don't have many gaskets left to blow," Tricia said.

Hours later, Ted and Ryan gone and Tricia in bed, Joanna sat in front of the fire. Charley brought out a cold bottle of Dom Perignon, a bowl of strawberries, and two wide-bowled etched art deco glasses from the kitchen.

"What are you doing? Is that the bottle your neighbor gave you for Christmas?"

"Yes." Charley put several pieces of strawberries into the bowls of the glasses. The firelight caught the delicate filigree, and they reflected the prismed light back. She popped the cork on the bottle, corralling the froth into the glasses, then handing one to Joanna.

"You still haven't told me what you're doing."

Charley reached over the back of the couch and took a wrapped box from behind one of the Provincetown buildings where she'd hidden it earlier and handed it to her. "Merry Christmas."

"You already got me something."

"That was the public gift. This is the one from my heart."

Joanna looked at her warily.

"Consider it payback for the cuff links."

"Not fair."

"Oh, so you can spring a gift, but I can't?"

Joanna lifted the glass, breathed in the bubbles, and touched her glass to Charley's. She took a sip, dropped three more strawberry pieces into her glass, and drank them in. "I like these." She shook the box. "I don't think I hear diamonds."

"You won't know that until you open it."

Joanna pulled the ribbon and carefully unwrapped the paper. The lid of the box stuck a little, but when she got it off, she looked at the bracelet and then at Charley, who thought her eyes almost glittered. When Joanna didn't move, she lifted the bracelet from the box and slipped it onto her wrist.

Joanna ran her thumb over the white and rose braids of the Gordian knot. "The golds are beautiful, Charley, and so perfectly woven. You think this is us, don't you?"

Charley's answer was to lean in and kiss her. Joanna didn't pull away, not at first. When she did, she picked up the champagne bottle and refilled their glasses, not meeting her eyes as she dropped more berries into both glasses.

"You're making this hard," Joanna finally said. "There's still so much I need to work out. And that you'll need to process."

"I know that." Charley drained her glass, tucking one berry piece into her cheek. "So let me make it as simple as I can." She reached for Joanna and gave her the kind of kiss that would've buckled her knees had they been standing, Charley's tongue still cold from the champagne, the strawberry on it finding its way into Joanna's mouth. She felt the sigh, Joanna's hand tangling in her hair, then letting go and pushing her away. "Think of this as a promise," Charley said, running her fingers over the bracelet.

"And that kiss?"

"A promissory note. You can hold on to it while you work things out. And if you decide you don't want it…" Charley looked down at her hands. "Just…give it back to me."

Joanna sighed, sat back, and took Charley's hand. "Can we put on something other than Christmas carols now?"

CHAPTER THIRTY-FOUR

It had snowed heavily on New Year's Eve. Charley wondered if she and Joanna would be able to get out of the city, but when she looked out her window, it was evident that the plows had managed to get through. Brownish muck that twelve hours before had been a pristine white blanket on all the roads was now mounded up and down the avenues.

Within two hours, they were driving through countryside frosted in white and dusted with drifts, the occasional barn still bearing a Christmas wreath over its double doors. Charley's gaze was pulled to Joanna's hands on the wheel of the car. She loved contemplating those hands that looked so delicate but were so strong. The nails were polished an opaque white that had bits of glitter in it, mimicking the sunlight glinting off the snow. She still allowed herself to think of how those hands might feel as they learned her body and wondered how Joanna would respond to her touch. She sighed and found a country radio station to listen to as they talked.

They stopped for lunch in an adorable little town that had an antique shop Joanna wanted to explore, and then Charley spotted the local hardware store and dragged Joanna into it, much to her amusement.

"I don't think I knew this side of you existed," Joanna said as they got back on the road.

"My dad's influence. He taught us all how to fix things, so we spent a lot of time in hardware stores when I was a kid. I still love the feel of the old ones, lumber sawdust and tools, the smell of leather and oils. There's magic in those little Norman Rockwell places."

"We had such different childhoods," Joanna said.

"Tell me more about yours. I really only know what you talked about at dinner that night with Emily and Terry."

Joanna glanced at her. "I could give you the list of all the countries we lived in, all the bases here in the States. But you want the full scope, don't you?"

"I want to hear about everything and imagine little Joanna in Germany or Texas or..."

"The Philippines. I was born on the Subic Bay naval base there."

"Oh." Charley settled in for the story of Joanna's life. A while later, looking out the window, she said, "Do you realize that we've been living in the same city just nine blocks from each other for twenty years? And that we lived in the same city in England thirty years ago while your dad got his master's and I did my junior year abroad? What are the chances?"

"I wonder how many times we passed each other on the streets and never knew it?"

Joanna put her blinker on as they approached a bend in the road that looked as Godforsaken as the last twenty miles. Charley saw nothing that indicated humanity until she spotted smoke from a chimney curling up through the trees.

The cabin appeared small, and she wondered how eight women would manage there all weekend without blood being spilled, no matter how well they all knew each other. There were two cars parked at an angle by the side of the garage in a patch that had been shoveled out to accommodate one more. As Joanna maneuvered into the slot left for her, Charley saw a large addition on the back of the house and relaxed a little. Until she realized she was about to meet the most important women in Joanna's life.

Turning off the engine, Joanna interrupted Charley's momentary panic attack. "I promise you it'll be a good weekend."

"You figured out that I'm nervous..."

Joanna popped the trunk. "Don't be."

Charley grabbed her suitcase and Joanna's quilted overnight bag.

The front door of the house opened, and a tall, elegant woman walked out to greet them.

"You made good time, Jo! Let me take that," she said to Charley, reaching for Joanna's bag. "I'm Madeline, by the way, and welcome to Six Pines."

Charley had seen the marker at the bottom of the driveway. Looking quickly around the property that seemed to sit in the middle of a forest, she realized that there were six enormous Douglas firs anchoring the sloping grounds by the street.

Joanna snorted. "Six Pines! I remember planting those things when they were the size of Charlie Brown's pitiful Christmas tree."

Madeline laughed. "*That* was the longest day. And you spent all of it complaining."

"That's because you kept moving the damn things!" Joanna turned to Charley. "I dug at least twelve holes before she was satisfied with where they were going to sit."

"You put those in?" Charley asked, surprised.

"This girl gets things done. I'm afraid if it wasn't for her, those trees would still be sitting in their burlap sacks in my side yard," Madeline said. "Come on in and meet the others. Of course, we started the cocktail hour without you."

"It's three o'clock, you lush." Joanna gave Madeline's shoulder a gentle push.

"Hey, it'll be dark soon, close enough for me." Madeline held the door open and Charley walked in, met immediately by the sound and smell of a crackling fire across the great main room, three women rising to greet them. Two other women were at work in the open kitchen. Several aromas emanating from that direction teased her nose and set her mouth to watering. Charley stowed her suitcase by the front door.

"Are you baking a cherry pie?" she asked.

"Joanna said it was your favorite." An olive-skinned woman with a weathered face and jet-black hair caught up in a ponytail came out from behind the marble counters that set the kitchen apart from the rest of the room. "The standing rib roast goes in when the pie comes out. I understand you have an unusual recipe for Yorkshire pudding." She held out her hand and Charley took it, her skin as warm as the welcome in the woman's eyes. "I'm Thea, Madeline's wife. We're so glad you came."

Standing behind her was a handsome female version of Tom Cruise. Charley knew from Joanna's description that this was Hayden Pierce. Her impish smile caught Charley off-guard. "Nice to meet you. What can I get you to drink?" She had already poured a glass of red wine and handed it to Joanna, who'd walked in right behind Charley.

"Jo, I'm taking your bags and Charley's up to the loft," Madeline called from the front door.

Charley looked at Joanna. They'd be sharing a room? Joanna discreetly shook her head, but Charley wasn't sure what she meant.

"What's the array of scotch here? Charley's a scotch drinker," Joanna said.

One of the women in the living room walked over to a glass-fronted cabinet in a bookcase-lined wall and opened it. "Come on over, pick your poison. Madeline stocks everything. Are you a single malt woman?"

"I do like a good one, yes."

"I'm Meg Houlihan," she said, shaking Charley's hand. Charley liked her eyes, a deep brown dusted with gold that seemed to reflect the fire that highlighted the reds in her hair. Her smile revealed fine crinkles. "This is Dana Evans." Meg turned to a tall lean woman with curly black hair and dark caramel skin tones. "And this is Shelley Roberts." Charley shook Shelley's hand, taking in her thin frame and the gray stubble on her head.

"Ovarian cancer. Finished chemo a little while ago, hair's finally deciding to make a comeback." Shelley patted her head in response to Charley's gaze.

"Oh, right." She wondered why Joanna hadn't mentioned this to her.

"Top-notch surgeon, they got it. I asked Jo not to say anything. No need to start a good party off on a weird note."

"Well, if they got it, I'd say that calls for a Johnnie Walker, if you've got it," Charley said.

Meg moved the bottles around, peering at each label. "We've got black, green, and gold."

"Green," Joanna said, coming over with a tumbler of ice. "It's supposed to be like 'buttah,' according to Charley."

"It is, and I'll take another one, too," Madeline said, returning to the room. She gave Joanna her glass, put her hand on Charley's shoulder, and pointed to an open space above the fireplace. "I put you and Joanna in the loft this weekend. It's the warmest. I wasn't sure if you're a heat-seeker or if you prefer the cold. Up there, you can sleep without the quilt and still be fine."

"Charley, did you bring the recipe for the Yorkshire pudding or do you know it by heart?" Thea asked.

"I don't use it often enough to know it that well. Let me go get it."

Charley stood in the doorway of the loft marveling at the simple luxury. Madeline, a cardiothoracic surgeon, could well afford the best, and that's exactly what she was looking at. Every piece of furniture in the cozy room was Americana antique, but it was meant to be used: a highboy polished to a dark sheen, the old writing desk in front of a window that looked out on a large pond in the back yard, matching Quaker chairs that sat in front of the fireplace wall, their navy blue seat pillows accenting the braided navy blue rug. A large framed work of embroidery, a Colonial girl's ABCs, hung above the bed, and though faded by time, it was still stunning. On the bed, a white wedding ring quilt sewn with patches of navy blues and browns echoed the motif, tying everything together. Charley fished the recipe out of the front pocket of her suitcase and headed back downstairs.

Thea took the recipe card and they read it together. Joanna brought Charley's scotch to her and joined them.

"This is really quite simple, isn't it?" Thea said. "And you don't do it in muffin tins?"

"No. It's done in a baking dish. That's the secret," Charley replied. "Sift the flour and salt, beat the eggs, milk, and water together, mix that into the dry ingredients, and pour it right on top of the quarter cup of hot fat from the roast beef. Do not under any circumstance open that oven until the timer goes off or the pudding will fall. This isn't anything like those muffins. It's like rich and juicy French toast soufflé."

"Maybe you'd better do this with us," Hayden said.

"Happy to. Let me know about fifteen minutes before the roast is done," Charley replied. Wandering over to the conversation by the fire, she listened to the debate about the effect Detroit's bankruptcy might have on the future of New York's various civil service pension funds. Shelley and Meg, both teachers, were worried about what the ramifications might eventually mean for them. Joanna signaled Charley to sit down next to her.

"There's an inflatable mattress and a sleeping bag in the loft closet. That's why Madeline put us up there," Joanna said quietly.

"But it's a king-size bed."

"We can argue that later."

"No. Neither one of us is sleeping on that floor. Period." Charley hoped her face reflected her no-nonsense attitude.

Dinner was a four-hour affair, the conversation and laughter revealing more about each woman than any description Joanna ever could've offered Charley. It was like being at Brooke's, and Charley wondered at one point, looking around the table, if the rest of her friends would make Joanna feel as welcome and at home when they finally met her.

"Oh my God." Dana moaned as she inhaled the Yorkshire pudding. "Who needs dessert? Charley, this is magnificent. How did you come across this recipe?"

"It was my great-grandmother's. She had a farm in Pennsylvania. She served this to the farm hands before the roast beef dinner on Sundays so they wouldn't eat as much meat."

"It's a slice of heaven," Meg said.

Charley automatically got up to help with the cleanup when she saw Joanna take charge. They were done in no time. Back in front of the fireplace, one lamp and the firelight illuminated them, and the conversation took on a decidedly quieter tone. Charley sat on the fireplace ledge next to Joanna and listened to Madeline describing a recent groundbreaking surgery she'd performed on a Syrian child born with a defective heart who'd been brought to her attention by Doctors Without Borders. Joanna absently ran her fingertips up and down Charley's shoulder blades, and she had to stifle the moan that nearly escaped. *I might have to sleep on the damn floor after all.*

The grandfather clock in the hall chiming eleven seemed to signal the witching hour, and everyone made their way upstairs. Charley wanted to sit in front of the fire with her scotch a little bit longer to give Joanna enough time to get ready for bed. "I hope I'm not keeping you," Charley said to Madeline. "I appreciate it if you're in hostess mode, but you don't have to stay down here on my account. I can tamp the fire and turn out the light."

"I am in hostess mode, yes, but I'm enjoying it. I like when the house is full. And I've had a good time getting to know you tonight. You're very funny." Madeline studied her. "Joanna needs someone like you in her life."

Charley started to reply, but Madeline waved it off.

"I know what the party line is," Madeline said gently. "Forgive me, here…Jo told me about what you're going through with your ex, and I'm truly sorry. It all makes for an awfully hard balancing act."

Charley had figured from everything Joanna had told her about Madeline that she was her Brooke.

"Of course, she asked me not to share it with the group." Madeline looked into the fire. "I don't mean to step where I don't belong in this equation, but we can all see that there are obviously feelings between you two, and I've heard it in her voice in all our phone calls since she met you. Now that I've met you, I understand why." Madeline shifted in her seat. "You know, I was skeptical of her taking on a patient like Tricia so soon after losing Irene. But I think the two of you have been very good for each other. I hope you can hang on to that." Madeline appeared to be struggling with something, and then put it away. "There's a sleeping bag and an air mattress in the closet in your room. She knows they're there. I would never have played that kind of roulette with you." Madeline went over to the fireplace to bank what was left of the flames.

"Joanna told me."

Madeline put the poker back in the hod. "You're the best thing that's happened to her in a long time. And something tells me she's the best thing that's happened to you, too."

Charley couldn't look at Madeline. She wasn't sure what she'd see reflected in her eyes, or what Madeline would be able to read in hers. "She is. And you're right, it's difficult right now."

Madeline drew in a deep breath and sighed. "Try to get some sleep."

A few minutes later, Charley turned off the light and went upstairs. Joanna seemed to be asleep but had turned on the light on Charley's side of the bed for her. She brushed her teeth and changed in the bathroom, turned off the light, and slid under the covers, leaving an appropriately wide chasm between them, one she felt keenly. As she was settling in, Joanna's pillow inched closer to hers. For a second, Charley wasn't sure what to do, but she turned over, her pulse thudding, to see Joanna leaning up on her elbow.

"I think tonight went well, don't you?"

Not sure where the moment might be going, Charley wanted to be careful. "I like your friends."

"And they like you. May I reserve this space for a while?" She tapped Charley's shoulder.

Charley hesitated. "There's a slight fee."

"Is there?" In the dark, Joanna leaned down to kiss her. It was soft and sweet and Charley's whole body reacted to it. She wanted to pull Joanna on top of her. "Will that cover it?"

Charley hesitated. "You know what I want," she whispered.

Joanna ran her fingers through Charley's hair. "You have no idea how much I want to give it to you. I don't know what to do…"

In the dark, Charley took Joanna's hand and kissed her fingers, then pressed them to her breast. For a moment, neither of them moved. Charley inhaled Joanna's scent and something she'd never picked up before, reminiscent of cotton candy, threaded throughout the faint lemon. Charley instinctively knew it was the essence of Joanna's arousal, and the fire that her kiss had started deep within built; she wasn't sure she could control it anymore, and she didn't want to. Knowing what the handcuff necklace had meant and taking a chance, Charley moved astride Joanna and pinned her arms above her head, leaning down to kiss her. Joanna arched up into her, and Charley moved her mouth down one side of her neck, kissed and pulled at her nipples through the thin tank top she was wearing. Joanna moaned in response, and Charley worked her way back up the other side of her neck, kissing her again, softly, her tongue finding its way inside and to Joanna's. She felt Joanna's rib cage and breasts moving against her erratically; she was breathing hard. Charley set up a measured, languid pace, decelerating, kissing Joanna as if nothing else in the world existed but this moment, her mouth. Joanna pushed against her, whimpered, and it emboldened Charley. She sat up, pulled off her T-shirt, and Joanna reached for her breasts with both hands. Charley groaned at her touch and sought the hem of Joanna's tank top, pulling the shirt off, and then took Joanna's nipples between her thumbs and forefingers. Joanna inhaled audibly. She moved higher on Joanna's hips and leaned down, her breasts right at Joanna's mouth, and she was rewarded with the double sensation of Joanna sucking one into her mouth while her fingers teased the other. She attempted to move back down, but Joanna put both hands firmly on her waist.

"You're not going anywhere."

Minutes later, Charley found herself shaking with an orgasm she'd never felt before, Joanna's hand on her back, the other still playing with whichever nipple her mouth wasn't. Joanna wouldn't let her pull away until she'd stopped trembling, both of her hands still on Joanna's breasts.

"You've never had a nipple orgasm before, have you?" Joanna asked, pulling Charley to her.

"Oh, my God..." Charley moved her hand between Joanna's legs but felt Joanna stopping her.

"I just want you to lie here in my arms."

"I'll fall asleep if I do that." Charley felt herself floating, falling, and the last thing she heard was Joanna whispering "Happy New Year" to her.

Charley awoke as the midnight blue of pre-dawn seeped across the sky. Her arm was asleep; she ever so slowly rolled onto her side, rubbing her shoulder. Joanna woke up.

"Everything okay?"

"My arm fell asleep."

Joanna shifted up against Charley's back and took over the massage. "I'm sorry, you should've woken me up or moved me," she said as she expertly kneaded Charley's arm.

"That feels good...so did what you did before."

Joanna sighed. "I love nipple orgasms. Love getting them, love watching other women have them."

"Filing that away." Charley turned toward her, and Joanna put a finger on her lips.

"Red light. Nothing more tonight than sleeping in each other's arms."

Charley reached for her T-shirt, but Joanna took it from her and tossed it on the floor. "Hold me."

Charley obeyed. The next thing she knew, the sun was up, and Madeline was knocking on their door. The aroma of bacon and coffee wafted up to the loft.

"Are you two awake? Everyone's downstairs having breakfast. Come on down. We're all still in our pajamas, so grab your robes. We're deciding what to do today."

CHAPTER THIRTY-FIVE

I don't have a robe."

"What about a sweater?"

Charley took a navy blue Henley out of her suitcase.

"Good. Go on down. I'll be down in a minute. I have to put on something a little more presentable."

Charley giggled "Well, you have to put *something* on." The heat of a blush rose at the sight of Joanna in the light of day.

"Oh, God," Joanna said, "there's that beautiful blush. I think I fell in love with you the first time I saw that."

"Say what?" Charley asked.

Joanna balled up her tank top and threw it at her. "Go on, downstairs with you."

Charley reluctantly headed to the kitchen. "Thank you for last night" was on the tip of her tongue, along with "can we do it again tonight?" But they felt flat and didn't nearly convey the elation and peace running through her. Did Joanna mean it, what she'd said about love? She didn't seem like the flippant remark type. Charley floated downstairs on the words.

Madeline had made pancakes, and there was a platter mounded with bacon and sausage sitting on the middle of the table surrounded by pitchers of maple syrup and little ramekins of butter.

"Cardiothoracic surgeon, huh? You trolling for patients here?"

Madeline laughed. "I know, horrible. Roast beef last night, bacon today, and potato leek soup tonight."

"With grilled salmon, that's healthy," Shelley said. "They're trying to fatten me up again."

"Let's talk about what we're doing today," Madeline said. "I need some help in town, and I'd really like to get out on the ice for our annual game of hockey this afternoon."

Madeline's list of errands didn't take long to put together, and then they turned to the hockey game.

"Oh, but I don't skate," Charley said when she was chosen immediately for Team Madeline. "I could referee. From the sideline. Where's the rink? In town?"

Shelley started laughing before Charley even finished her sentence.

"It's broom hockey, on the pond out back. You don't need skates. You just need to be able to stay upright," Dana said.

Shelley was still giggling. "And I'm the referee because I can't play."

"No, you just play favorites," Dana said.

They argued the merits of lunch at the Bluebird Cafe so they could get right to the hockey game when they got home, and by mid-morning, they were headed into town. Charley found herself in the small IGA supermarket with Dana and Hayden. Afterward, she parted ways with them, having no interest in the art gallery they were going to visit. She wanted to walk around the village square. There was a hardware store there. A bell over the door tinkled when she opened it, and as she'd suspected, it was like stepping into that Norman Rockwell painting she'd described to Joanna. Once the proprietor realized she was a junkie getting a fix, he left her alone.

Joanna texted from the antique shop she'd gone to with Meg and Shelley, asking her to save the seat next to her in the restaurant. The request made Charley smile, and in response to Joanna's query about where she was, she sent back: *In a museum of my own—hardware store.*

She got a laughing emoji back and made her way to the restaurant, calling Tricia on the way to check on her. The report wasn't a good one: she was struggling with simple tasks and getting frustrated, so she wasn't cooperating with either Ted or the nurse, had stayed in bed, and decided she didn't want to eat anything. When Joanna slid into the chair beside her at the table, Charley asked her to call Tricia. She left the restaurant, phone in hand, Charley trailing behind her to eavesdrop and as she suspected would happen, Tricia came around after Joanna leveled with her. She handed the phone to Charley and went back inside.

"Are you having a good time?" Tricia asked.

Charley could hear the weariness in her voice. "We're in the middle of East Bumfuck. What do you think?"

"Oh, c'mon, it must be a quaint upstate town."

Charley told her about the hardware store but otherwise grumbled about small towns. It felt wrong to admit she was having a great time.

"You've become a city snob. All right, get back to Nurse Ratched. She read me the riot acts. I'll behave now."

Charley stood outside the café for a minute gathering herself. It felt as though Tricia's health had reached the top of a roller coaster and she was poised for that harrowing descent. Charley was well aware of the ticking clock. That she couldn't see the time left on it infuriated her. She couldn't fight something invisible, and she felt helpless. There was a mound of snow piled near the sidewalk, and Charley grabbed a handful of it. The hard snow was easily packable, and she made a snowball and fired it across the street into the alley between two buildings. She wanted to make twenty more and hurl them right after that first one like an automatic pitching arm set on "Angry." Instead, she returned to the table and slipped the phone into Joanna's back pocket, leaving her hand in the pocket just long enough that Joanna gave her a warning look. Which was exactly what Charley wanted, that flash of emerald green that set her on fire. *Please promise me you'll shake up my world like that every day.*

"Who wants to wager on today's game?" Madeline asked as the waiter brought drinks to the table. "You must be pretty competitive, Charley. We saw you pitch that snowball right over the home plate strike zone out there like you were Noah Syndergaard."

She didn't realize they'd all been watching, and no explanation swam through the mix of pain and desire fogging her brain.

"Stay out of her way. She'd knock your grandmother down to score a goal," Joanna replied.

"You were a jock in school, weren't you?" Dana asked.

Charley nodded. "Guilty. But spoiler alert, I haven't been on the ice since I was seven. I don't know if I can stay upright."

"Well, then, look out. Jo will make sure you spend as much time as possible on your back." Hayden said. "She takes no prisoners."

"Oh, she's familiar with my hardball tactics. I took an autographed Brett Favre jersey from her on a bet a couple of months ago." Joanna smirked.

"Ouch. That's harsh," Meg remarked.

"Why don't we try to win that back for Charley?" Madeline suggested.

"You'd better put up something worthwhile against it, then," Joanna said, nudging Charley, "like that Charles Tyrwhitt gift certificate your neighbor gave you."

"I'm not giving that to you! You already have my favorite shirt, I'm not giving you the custom-made ones, too!"

"But I rather enjoy taking the shirt off your back." Joanna taunted her with an innocent girl next-door smile.

"Really?" Charley said, her mood turning. "Well, then," she leaned forward, invading Joanna's space, and channeled Margaret Hamilton. "How about a little fire, Scarecrow? We'll take you, and your little teammates, too!"

A cheer went up from the table.

"I will make you pay for that," Joanna said, her nose an inch from Charley's.

"Go ahead. Try and melt me, Dorothy."

Joanna's eyes opened wide in surprise. "What makes you think I'll take my revenge on the ice?"

It was Charley's turn to be surprised, and desire shot straight through her.

The game was bruising. Charley's face met the ice more times than she could count, but Madeline scored a hat trick for them, on top of Charley's goal, winning her Favre jersey back, and Charley found out that Dana was right. Shelley played favorites as the referee, calling numerous infractions on her and throwing her into the penalty box, sometimes when it wasn't even her fault.

She crawled into bed that night with a heating pad on one elbow and an ice pack on her knee. Joanna emerged from the bathroom with a glass of water and several Advil in her hand. Desire heated every corner of Charley's body as she looked at her in the tank top and snug boi shorts, obliterating the pain for a moment. She wanted to slip the straps off those shoulders and kiss her from her lips down to her breasts again.

"Here, take these and tell me where it hurts."

For a nanosecond, Charley wanted to name the body part whose current state of inflammation wasn't a result of the hockey game. Instead, she pointed to her knee.

"Why did I play? I knew this would happen."

Joanna propped Charley's leg across her lap and began gently moving the residual fluid up toward her knee. "Because it was fun, and you knew it would be. I think tomorrow we tell Madeline it has to be a snowball war."

"Oh, sure, I'll throw my back out or dislocate my shoulder hurling snow grenades."

"Actually, that was a darn good pitch outside the restaurant today."

Charley looked away.

"Do you want to tell me what that was about?"

"You know what that was about."

Joanna moved up to sit next to Charley on the bed and draped her arm around her. "You can't stop the tide."

"I just wish I knew when it was coming in. I don't want to drown."

"I won't let you."

"You can't save me. I have to figure out how to do that myself." Impulsively, she kissed her, making sure it was as soft and sweet as Joanna's opening foray had been the night before.

"You're in no shape for any shenanigans tonight."

"I'll move slowly."

"You'll lie in my arms again. I like having you there." Joanna continued kneading her inflamed knee.

"Can I ask you something?"

"Hmm. This sound serious."

"No, I think it's…more clarification. The handcuff necklace…"

Joanna looked up at her.

"You were the submissive in that relationship."

Joanna nodded. "For the most part."

"Meaning?"

"I'm a switch. I can fulfill either role."

Charley thought about this.

"Why? Worried about my bossing you around last night and tonight?" Joanna raised an eyebrow.

"I don't think so…"

"Good. It was a problem for Georgia. And…you and Tricia?"

"She initiated, although quite frankly, I teased her into it more often than not. I was always the closer, though."

Joanna ran the back of her hand up Charley's neck and pulled her in for a kiss. "Well, tonight, no teasing and no closing. I want you in my arms. We can talk about the necklace and what it means. And just to be clear, I still have the promissory note in my possession. Especially after last night." Joanna's hand wandered down Charley's chest to her breasts and she shook her head. "I love these."

Charley looked down at her body. "Nothing's where it used to be…"

"You're a voluptuous tease." Joanna pointed to the bed. "In."

When Charley came to in the morning, everything hurt. Joanna stood at the side of the bed with a glass of water and a handful of Tylenol. She handed them to Charley. "Sit up, let me see that knee."

"I can't look at it. I'll scream."

Joanna gently massaged the whole area. "It doesn't look bad, actually. The ice helped."

Her fingers slowly made their way up Charley's thigh until her breath caught and her leg flexed under Joanna's fingers, causing her to look up.

Joanna took in a deep breath and swallowed. "Breakfast?"

Charley dished up oatmeal and fruit salad for both her and Joanna as discussion of the day's plans took hold around the table. Thea proposed a Scrabble tournament for the evening. Joanna suggested a hike to the lake for lunch. Over protests that it was too cold, she pointed out that it would be fifty degrees out by noon, windless and perfect for sitting in the sun in their beach chairs like fat little birds bunched on a telephone wire. "I'll even make the lunches and the thermoses of soup," Joanna said.

A couple of hours later, they made their way through snow drifts and frozen crunching leaves along a barely marked path, toting chairs, and canvas bags. They all settled into their chairs up by the beach grass. Charley turned her face to the sun. She'd forgotten the particular pleasure of that kind of warmth against the cold. Mixed with the company of these women, the conversation and laughter, it was a day she wished she could bottle and pull out years from now to look at and relive.

As the group headed back to the cabin afterward, Joanna pulled Charley aside. "We'll join you guys in a few minutes. I want to show Charley something off the trail."

"Don't be too long," Shelley said. "It's going to be dark soon."

Joanna took Charley's gloved hand in hers and they made their way along a path that only she seemed to know. They came upon a huge white oak in a small clearing. Joanna pointed to the base of the tree. "I hoped it was blooming. I wanted you to see it."

Nestled in a deep protective notch between two giant roots was a small plant sprouting a riot of red heart-shaped blossoms, the ground around it untouched by snow.

"But how?" She looked at Joanna.

"I don't know. We think it's the protection of the tree and the sun at this time of year. See how it slants through the glade, hitting right at the roots? And there's hardly ever any snow in there. It happens in January and February. And then again in spring."

"A bleeding heart at the end of a desire line," Charley said, marveling at the beauty.

"What's a desire line?"

"When a hiker leaves a known trail and forges a new one that's just theirs, searching for something different than what's on that path."

Joanna took her glove off and ran the back of her hand over Charley's cheek. Her touch ignited a yearning in Charley she was unable to deny, and she kissed Joanna. "Thank you for showing this to me. Thank you for the last two nights, for giving us a chance." Joanna's look of surprise pleased Charley. She put Joanna's glove on her hand and let her lead them back out of the glen.

CHAPTER THIRTY-SIX

The drive back to the city on Friday was difficult. Joanna laid out the parameters she needed between them going forward. After last night's frank discussion of her relationship with Georgia that had lasted well into the night, Charley was crestfallen. She understood that Joanna wasn't ready to move in any direction, that she couldn't cap a time frame, that this burgeoning relationship deserved the best possible chance they could give it by allowing for breathing room. She also understood that Tricia's imminent death was going to resonate in her world, possibly for a long time, and in ways she couldn't see now; she was no more ready for anything than Joanna was. She understood it intellectually, even emotionally, but something deep inside her wanted to lie in Joanna's arms every night.

There were several messages on her machine. Two of them were from her mother asking her to pick up items at the market. Charley just shook her head. There was nothing to be done about her mother's marketing lists, now infamous among her brothers and a source of endless amusement at her expense. She was, by now, used to buying each one and dropping it off on her way to work, keeping her mother happy. Another message was from Robert; he'd done the marketing when her mother had complained that Charley wasn't shopping for her on a timely basis lately. Had she forgotten Charley would be away? The fourth message was from Neely telling her she'd been hired by a new online magazine as its editor-in-chief, so she wouldn't be at the Y anymore. And she wanted to have a drink with Charley one night to talk with her about the e-zine. "I might need some stuff from you. To, you know, publish."

The message from Emily reminded her that she and Terry still wanted to go out to dinner with her and Joanna next week. After the dinner at Per Se, Emily told her they'd had such a good time that they hoped to make it a monthly get-together, which had pleasantly surprised both her and Joanna. The last message, from Brooke and Annie, was a raucous moment of everyone at their party counting down the last three seconds of the ball drop in Times Square and then blowing those ridiculous noisemakers into the phone. She rolled her eyes and erased them all.

Thursday morning, Charley called her florist and ordered a flowering peace plant for Madeline and Thea to thank them for the weekend, sending one to Joanna as well. Sometime later, she had a text from her: *It's beautiful! M&T loved theirs, too!*

Friday night, dinner at Tricia's was a sedate affair, with Charley and Joanna falling into their new normal, keeping the friendship that Joanna wanted front and center. Once, when Charley moved around her in the kitchen to pick up the bottle of thyme, she put her hand on Joanna's shoulder and ran it down her back. Joanna caught Charley with her emerald gaze, but instead of a warning shot, it was full of warmth. Charley would have to hang on to things like that to get through what was coming. Tricia, of course, missed nothing between them, but for once, she kept her counsel.

Charley was spending most evenings at Tricia's now and was amazed watching the physical artistry with which the nurses transferred Tricia from her wheelchair to the bed, helped her dress and undress, maneuvered her through what she needed in the bathroom. Of course, Tricia couldn't weigh much more than ninety-five pounds now, and Charley knew from discussions with Joanna weeks ago that that meant Tricia was dangerously close to being unsustainable. She hadn't been a praying person for a long time, but she began to find comfort in turning to God now, often talking to Him as she walked to work.

Tricia and Ted worked tirelessly on the lawsuit, despite her fragile state, and her legal team came to the apartment almost every day.

One day turned into another, into a week, into two. And then came Ted's nearly unintelligible call from the courthouse on Monday:

the suit had been settled out of court, and that evening, Charley finally got to meet the young legal team that had muscled their way to victory after convincing Tricia that her name should remain part of the partnership, not only for the legacy, but also for twice the financial payout.

The next week was a blur getting Emily ready for her trip to the Grammy Awards, until Ted called. He was on the way to the hospital with Tricia. She had collapsed in her bedroom. Charley left immediately.

Within hours, the medical team stabilized her, her creatinine levels having been so high that Dr. Gerard thought her kidneys would shut down. Charley and Ted had sat in the small waiting area until Dr. Gerard came for them.

"I'm sorry, we just don't know what caused the imbalance. Now, we could keep her here," he said, "but I think she needs to be tube-fed because she's not taking in enough nutrition. And the physical waste of her body is such that we'd really like to get her into hospice, and we'd like to do it before the weekend."

Charley was surprised at how swiftly the transition was made, how easily Tricia agreed to it. They had talked about that moment when you leave your home for the last time, not necessarily knowing it *was* your last time, but Tricia knew.

Charley had twenty-four-hour access to Tricia's room, and had asked and been given the same for Ted, Dr. Gerard vouching for the fact that Ted was a close family friend.

That night, Joanna called. "How are you?"

Charley sighed. "I don't know. Everything's happening so fast."

"Please don't think I'm adding fuel to that fire, but with Tricia no longer considered a client, the team's been given the usual time off, and I'm going up to Madeline's cabin again."

"Oh..." Charley was devastated.

"I'll be a phone call away. We can talk every night."

Charley thought she might as well be a million miles away.

Every morning, she arrived at the hospice as the sun rose, when Tricia would be waking up; the pool could wait. And every night she was back to watch the evening news with her. Ted stayed most of the day, making sure the music she wanted to hear was always playing from her iPod, keeping the speakers on low. Tricia simply lay under the covers like a flat doll as things went on around her. Charley concentrated as best she could at work, counting the hours until Emily left for the Grammys later that week.

"You haven't been going to the pool," Tricia said one morning, picking at the covers. Her hands were bony, gnarled. Charley thought about all the times those hands had been entwined with hers.

"No. I'm fine. I don't need it right now."

"I should think now is exactly when you'd need it. Why don't you go over to my apartment and use the pool there at night? It's open until eleven."

It was a good idea, and Charley went the next night. Her neighbor Greg was taking care of the cats, so she decided to stay at Tricia's apartment. The lights were on when she opened the door, classical music floating from the speakers in every room.

"Hello?"

Ted came trotting down the hall from the kitchen. "Hey, sorry, I didn't know you were coming, or I'd have left a note on the door."

"What are you doing here?"

"Tricia and I set up a cleaning schedule for, well, for this eventuality. I'm very quietly taking care of the things she didn't want in her will."

And just like that, Tricia began to disappear. Charley was angry. And grateful. And a million other things she couldn't name.

"You look like you need a drink," Ted said.

That Sunday, Charley watched the Grammy show with Tricia. The nurse had propped her up on her pillows and when she'd left, Tricia patted the bed. Charley very gently eased onto it, afraid she could break something in Tricia's frail state, and stroked her hair, which now lay limp and gray on her pillow. Emily was nowhere in the audience where she knew the record executives sat, or at least, she couldn't spot her. The cameras moved too quickly, the producers focusing instead on rappers and rock stars. Sitting there in a hospice room, Charley thought it might as well have been taking place on another planet.

On Tuesday, Ted called Charley just as she was leaving the office. "Tricia says not to come."

"Why?"

"Dennis and his family are here."

"Oh, shit. Who called them?"

"I did. She asked me to. And maybe don't come tomorrow, either. I think he's staying a couple days."

"No, I can't do that. I won't come tonight, but unless she needs to be alone with him, I'll be there tomorrow night."

Tricia texted her mid-afternoon Wednesday. *Need to be alone with Dennis. He's not handling any of this well.*

For half an instant, Charley felt bad for him, until she remembered that he hadn't called Tricia in all the years she'd been with her.

Even though the dust in her apartment looked like it was an inch thick, Charley couldn't bring herself to do more than play with the cats, who were so glad to see her that they ran after all the little plastic balls with the bells in them that she tossed their way and batted at the many pieces of ribbon she dangled above their heads until Charley herself tired of the games and they settled in a heap on the floor. She rubbed Bing's stomach, and Bob obligingly allowed her to scratch him between his ears. But even he finally swatted at her hand, annoyed, and rolled onto his back to get her to stop. When she awoke on the floor in the middle of the night, she found the cats, more sensible than her, in the bed, Bing with his head on the pillow, Bob curled up next to him, his nose and front paws buried under the covers. She left them and went to the couch.

Early Thursday morning, Charley headed to the hospital. Tricia was still asleep, so she pulled out the Sunday *Times* Style section and turned to her favorite column, Modern Love. Several paragraphs into it, she stopped, blinking, staring at her déjà vu in print. Then she looked at the author's name. Neely Robinson. She had written an homage to their short relationship, a poignant study on falling in love at a time in one's life when it isn't the right time in the other person's life, and never will be. It was difficult for Charley to read, but she read it twice. Then, she carefully excised the page, left it folded on the table next to Tricia's bed and headed to the office. When she came back that evening, Ted told her Tricia had slept most of the day, waking up for one visitor.

"I thought Dennis left yesterday," Charley said.

"He did. Joanna came to see her."

"When?"

"Around two thirty."

"How long did she stay?"

"Half hour. I left them alone."

Had she driven back to the city just to visit Tricia? And not let her know? Incredulously, she checked her phone and saw the text Joanna sent while Charley was in a meeting, the sound on her phone off. Joanna had come back to the city to pick up Thea, who wanted to join her at the cabin for the weekend and stopped to see Tricia. Charley kicked herself.

Tricia was still sleeping when Charley went into her room. She pulled the chair close to her bed and took her hand. It felt as light and delicate as the feathers that periodically escaped her down quilt, and Charley was afraid that if she rubbed the back of it with her thumb, it would bruise. So she sat that way until well into the night, listening to Tricia's uneven breathing.

As she walked home from the hospice, the streets had that ghostly three a.m. emptiness. A taxi swooshed past, the miniscule light from its meter throwing a blue halo around the woman in the back seat; a bus glided by carrying a lone passenger who peered out at the blackness; half a block away, a man hunched against the cold opened a bodega door, the tinkle of the bell above it announcing his arrival, and when Charley passed by a moment later, the customer and the counterman were bent over a newspaper, the store's fluorescent light a bright inviting glow. Charley wanted to grab pieces of light from everywhere and hold on to them, tuck them inside where they would keep her safe and ward off the pain she knew was coming.

Hours later, she was back in Tricia's room, and she didn't want to leave when she awoke.

"You can stay, but it'll be a waste of time watching me sleep. I'm so damn tired. Go. Emily needs you, I'm sure."

"Do we need to talk about anything? Dennis? Should I be helping Ted?"

"Tonight. We'll talk tonight."

"How was Joanna?" Charley blurted it out without thinking.

Tricia's Cheshire Cat smile floated across her face. "She misses you." Tricia stretched. "You know she and I said good-bye to each other before your New Year's trip."

"No, I didn't know that. She didn't say anything."

"She came back to tell me that I don't have to worry, that she'll take good care of you, and cherish you."

Charley couldn't stop tears that spilled. Tricia held out her hand.

Chapter Thirty-seven

When her phone rang late that afternoon, she recognized Ted's cell number. She didn't want to pick up. She knew. Ted's steadfast demeanor cracked only once as he told her. Hanging up, she looked at the calendar. Valentine's Day. The cruelty didn't escape her. She didn't need to go in to Emily to tell her. She simply looked at her through the glass wall. Emily nodded. Charley picked up her coat and canvas bag and walked out.

Through the windy streets of the February dusk, she walked home with her down coat in the crook of her arm. People passing around her walked in pairs, arm in arm, laughing, some of them stopping to kiss, entering restaurants where music and warmth rushed out toward her through the open doors, grabbing at her, but she needed the isolating cold.

It took every last ounce of composure to acknowledge her doorman's "good evening." When she reached her apartment door, she dropped everything on the floor and sank down on top of the pile.

She wasn't sure how long she'd been sitting there crying when someone entered her hall. She wasn't sure she cared, either, and she closed her eyes against the intrusion. The footsteps stopped beside her. A second later, the lemon scent of a certain Chanel perfume overtook her.

When she looked up, Joanna was holding out her hand. "I got in the car as soon as I heard."

"You left Thea up there without a car?"

"She's fine. You're not." Joanna reached down for Charley's hand and lifted her off the floor, picking up her coat and bag. She found the front door keys and unlocked it, propping it open with her foot. Charley walked in and stood by the butcher block. Joanna hung up the coat and took her hand.

Instinctively, Charley wrapped Joanna in her arms and kissed her, and Joanna pressed hard into Charley. Like a woman possessed, she unzipped Joanna's coat and dropped it on the floor, kissing her as she did, stopping only long enough to pull her toward the bedroom. Halfway there, she turned and began undressing her, and Joanna went after the buttons on Charley's shirt, her bra, abandoning both pieces of clothing on the floor with the ones Charley had just taken off her. She pushed Charley toward the bedroom. Charley threw back the covers on the bed and wrenched Joanna's belt open, tore down the zipper on her jeans as Joanna fumbled with Charley's pants. Shoes and socks came off and then they were on the bed, hands and mouths on flesh, as they moved together until Charley felt Joanna slipping inside her. She found her way inside Joanna and they moved to the same rhythm, building to a climax as one, Charley shattering when she reached it, and sobbing in Joanna's arms.

"I've got you," Joanna whispered, the same words she'd said to Charley as she held her so tightly when she'd walked into Tricia's apartment bedecked for Christmas and it had nearly broken her. She let Joanna pull the covers over them, curl around her, and hold her, those same senses of warmth, security, and protection enveloping her like they had that night. "You'll get through this. We'll get through this." Joanna gently rocked her, ran her hand through Charley's hair, and kissed her neck and shoulder. "Why don't you sleep? You must be exhausted. I've got you."

By degrees, Charley relaxed into her arms, knowing Joanna truly did have her.

In the morning, Charley woke bleary eyed, anxiety stealing in when she remembered that Tricia was gone. But when she felt Joanna's arms around her, it receded.

Joanna pulled her close. "Hey. You okay?"

Charley settled in against her. "Maybe. I don't know. How is anyone okay after something like this?"

Joanna kissed the top of her head. "One day at a time. Maybe one hour at a time. We both have to learn how to navigate the world with one less important soul in it."

Charley pulled away so she could look into Joanna's eyes. "You said good-bye to her before we went to Madeline's. She told me."

"I started navigating the night I walked into her apartment. Part of the job. I just didn't expect to become such good friends with her. But yes, we were both ready. And she knew I was taking you away for the weekend."

Charley put her head on Joanna's shoulder. "Thank you for coming last night."

"I got to you as quickly as I could." She gently moved Charley's hair back behind her ear. "And I'm not going anywhere anytime soon. I love you, Charley." Joanna kissed her, gently. "I think I just cashed in the promissory note."

Charley laughed at the surprised look on Joanna's face even as the tears rose. She pulled her closer. "You're my desire line. A path I didn't even know I needed to take, that brought me right where I needed to be. I love you, too." She let her tears fall.

They stayed in bed most of the rest of the day talking, planning, Charley getting caught short with more tears a couple of times, even laughing when she recalled something Tricia had said months ago about her funeral.

"Do you know anything about the funeral?"

"Oh, we planned it right after her diagnosis, while we both still had enough distance." Charley sighed. "Because of her client list, I expect it will be a circus. Ted's working with the funeral home because I knew I couldn't face that."

When Joanna got up to make them something to eat, Charley closed her eyes and whispered a quiet good-bye to Tricia. She'd lost love, grieved, and found love once again. She could begin to let go and embrace what the future held.

Epilogue

Christmas Eve One Year Later

"I like *all* your friends," Joanna said as they came out of Brooke's building. "But I adore Annie. She's so funny."

Charley pulled her close, seeking warmth from the bitter cold by slipping her hands into Joanna's back pants pockets. "Then I have a confession. Would you still adore her, and me, if I admitted we had a fling years ago?"

"She told me at Brooke's birthday party. She told me about you and Brooke, too, and quite frankly, I don't care. Ancient history." Joanna put her arms around Charley's waist. "Mmm. I like this on you." She traced a finger over the little handcuffs on the delicate silver chain around Charley's neck, her smile a tease that Charley wanted to answer.

"You like the *real* ones on my wrists and ankles."

"Yes, I do. I love playing with you when you're naked and restrained. Playing with you in every way, actually."

Charley kissed her. "Are you flirting with me?"

"I'm freezing is what I am, and I want to give you your Christmas present tonight. Your place or mine?"

"Depends on who's got the better stocked refrigerator."

"Oh, that'll be my place until we close on the co-op. Bottle of champagne in my refrigerator," she said, leading Charley toward the street. "And a quart of strawberries."

Charley felt for the little box in her pocket that held a diamond bracelet for Joanna. Maybe she'd hear the diamonds when she shook the box this year. As she always did when she left Brooke's now, she looked downtown the few blocks to the top of Tricia's building. The penthouse was all lit up. She wondered who lived there now.

She missed Tricia, more than she thought she could miss anyone. But with Joanna in her life, the past seemed a little easier to let go. The biggest surprise had been Tricia's will. She'd had far more to her name than she'd told Charley, and she'd left it all to her, with bequests to Ted and two charities. The note she'd left Charley simply said, "Live well together. And love her."

She had taken the note to heart and quit her job to write full time. Emily was beyond sorry to lose her, but the friendship had deepened as she and Joanna went out with Emily and Terry more frequently now. With Neely's unerring eye, she'd finished the novel, secured an agent, and he was in the middle of negotiating both a book and a movie deal, much to her astonishment.

Working from home, she discovered, gave her more time with her mother, something she couldn't appreciate when she was a harried assistant. She'd come to love her mother's one-item shopping lists; they were excuses to visit almost every day which, considering what her relationship had long been with her mother, dumbfounded her brothers. The visits brought her closer to Robert, too, who was also at her mother's apartment almost every day. In those last months, Tricia had taught her by default how valuable these hours and such relationships could be.

As she looked up at the clear, cold winter sky, she gave silent thanks for a life so full of friends, unexpected joy, and now love.

Joanna flagged a cab, opened the door, and Charley slid in. The driver flipped on his meter and she saw the Neapolitan angel hanging from his rearview mirror. It looked just like Tricia's and her breath stopped as Joanna gave the driver her address.

"Is that angel from the Met?" she asked him when she recovered.

"Says so on the bottom, yeah. Got it last year from a woman goin' to Lincoln Center the night after Christmas. Nice lady. Said I should have an angel on my shoulder."

Charley smiled and slipped her hand into Joanna's.

About the Author

Mary Burns is a long-time resident of New York City. She received a master of fine arts in playwriting from Columbia University in 1991, after which the muses departed for points unknown, leaving no forwarding address. So she carved out a career as an executive assistant for the next twenty years until happenstance left her with the opportunity for some major time off, and, with the blessing of her partner of nineteen years, she sharpened her pencils and sat down to write. The muses knocked on her door a short time later, she hasn't stopped writing since, and was lucky enough to have this first novel accepted by Bold Strokes Books.

She also recently had a short story published in *Sinclair Sexsmith's Best Lesbian Erotica vol. 4* (Dec. 2019), with another one coming out in *Sinclair's vol. 5* in Dec. 2020. And she is working on her next novel for Bold Strokes.

When not writing (which is rare, now), she and her partner enjoy bingeing Netflix, she sees her therapist once a week, and emails friends and family. You can reach her at maryburns11C@gmail.com.

Books Available from Bold Strokes Books

Everyday People by Louis Barr. When Film star Diana Danning hires private eye Clint Steele to find her son, Clint turns to his former West Point barracks mate, and ex-buddy with benefits, Mars Hauser to lend his cyber espionage and digital black ops skills to the case. (978-1-63555-698-8)

Forging a Desire Line by Mary P. Burns. When Charley's ex-wife, Tricia, is diagnosed with inoperable cancer, the private duty nurse Tricia hires turns out to be the handsome and aloof Joanna, who ignites something inside Charley she isn't ready to face. (978-1-63555-665-0)

Love on the Night Shift by Radclyffe. Between ruling the night shift in the ER at the Rivers and raising her teenage daughter, Blaise Richilieu has all the drama she needs in her life, until a dashing young attending appears on the scene and relentlessly pursues her. (978-1-63555-668-1)

Olivia's Awakening by Ronica Black. When the daring and dangerously gorgeous Eve Monroe is hired to get Olivia Savage into shape, a fierce passion ignites, causing both to question everything they've ever known about love. (978-1-63555-613-1)

The Duchess and the Dreamer by Jenny Frame. Clementine Fitzroy has lost her faith and love of life. Can dreamer Evan Fox make her believe in life and dream again? (978-1-63555-601-8)

The Road Home by Erin Zak. Hollywood actress Gwendolyn Carter is about to discover that losing someone you love sometimes means gaining someone to fall for. (978-1-63555-633-9)

Waiting for You by Elle Spencer. When passionate past-life lovers meet again in the present day, one remembers it vividly and the other isn't so sure. (978-1-63555-635-3)

While My Heart Beats by Erin McKenzie. Can a love born amidst the horrors of the Great War survive? (978-1-63555-589-9)

Face the Music by Ali Vali. Sweet music is the last thing that happens when Nashville music producer Mason Liner, and daughter of country royalty Victoria Roddy are thrown together in an effort to save country star Sophie Roddy's career. (978-1-63555-532-5)

Flavor of the Month by Georgia Beers. What happens when baker Charlie and chef Emma realize their differing paths have led them right back to each other? (978-1-63555-616-2)

Mending Fences by Angie Williams. Rancher Bobbie Del Rey and veterinarian Grace Hammond are about to discover if heartbreaks of the past can ever truly be mended. (978-1-63555-708-4)

Silk and Leather: Lesbian Erotica with an Edge edited by Victoria Villasenor. This collection of stories by award winning authors offers fantasies as soft as silk and tough as leather. The only question is: How far will you go to make your deepest desires come true? (978-1-63555-587-5)

The Last Place You Look by Aurora Rey. Dumped by her wife and looking for anything but love, Julia Pierce retreats to her hometown, only to rediscover high school friend Taylor Winslow, who's secretly crushed on her for years. (978-1-63555-574-5)

The Mortician's Daughter by Nan Higgins. A singer on the verge of stardom discovers she must give up her dreams to live a life in service to ghosts. (978-1-63555-594-3)

The Real Thing by Laney Webber. When passion flares between actress Virginia Green and masseuse Allison McDonald, can they be sure it's the real thing? (978-1-63555-478-6)

What the Heart Remembers Most by M. Ullrich. For college sweethearts Jax Levine and Gretchen Mills, could an accident be the second chance neither knew they wanted? (978-1-63555-401-4)

White Horse Point by Andrews & Austin. Mystery writer Taylor James finds herself falling for the mysterious woman on White Horse Point who lives alone, protecting a secret she can't share about a murderer who walks among them. (978-1-63555-695-7)

Femme Tales by Anne Shade. Six women find themselves in their own real-life fairy tales when true love finds them in the most unexpected ways. (978-1-63555-657-5)

Jellicle Girl by Stevie Mikayne. One dark summer night, Beth and Jackie go out to the canoe dock. Two years later, Beth is still carrying the weight of what happened to Jackie. (978-1-63555-691-9)

Le Berceau by Julius Eks. If only Ben could tear his heart in two, then he wouldn't have to choose between the love of his life and the most beautiful boy he has ever seen. (978-1-63555-688-9)

My Date with a Wendigo by Genevieve McCluer. Elizabeth Rosseau finds her long lost love and the secret community of fiends she's now a part of. (978-1-63555-679-7)

On the Run by Charlotte Greene. Even when they're cute blondes, it's stupid to pick up hitchhikers, especially when they've just broken out of prison, but doing so is about to change Gwen's life forever. (978-1-63555-682-7)

Perfect Timing by Dena Blake. The choice between love and family has never been so difficult, and Lynn's and Maggie's different visions of the future may end their romance before it's begun. (978-1-63555-466-3)

The Mail Order Bride by R Kent. When a mail order bride is thrust on Austin, he must choose between the bride he never wanted or the dream he lives for. (978-1-63555-678-0)

Through Love's Eyes by C.A. Popovich. When fate reunites Brittany Yardin and Amy Jansons, can they move beyond the pain of their past to find love? (978-1-63555-629-2)

To the Moon and Back by Melissa Brayden. Film actress Carly Daniel thinks that stage work is boring and unexciting, but when she accepts a lead role in a new play, stage manager Lauren Prescott tests both her heart and her ability to share the limelight. (978-1-63555-618-6)

Tokyo Love by Diana Jean. When Kathleen Schmitt is given the opportunity to be on the cutting edge of AI technology, she never thought a failed robotic love companion would bring her closer to her neighbor, Yuriko Velucci, and finding love in unexpected places. (978-1-63555-681-0)

Brooklyn Summer by Maggie Cummings. When opposites attract, can a summer of passion and adventure lead to a lifetime of love? (978-1-63555-578-3)

City Kitty and Country Mouse by Alyssa Linn Palmer. Pulled in two different directions, can a city kitty and country mouse fall in love and make it work? (978-1-63555-553-0)

Elimination by Jackie D. When a dangerous homegrown terrorist seeks refuge with the Russian mafia, the team will be put to the ultimate test. (978-1-63555-570-7)

In the Shadow of Darkness by Nicole Stiling. Angeline Vallencourt is a reluctant vampire who must decide what she wants more—obscurity, revenge, or the woman who makes her feel alive. (978-1-63555-624-7)

On Second Thought by C. Spencer. Madisen is falling hard for Rae. Even single life and co-parenting are beginning to click. At least, that is, until her ex-wife begins to have second thoughts. (978-1-63555-415-1)

Out of Practice by Carsen Taite. When attorney Abby Keane discovers the wedding blogger tormenting her client is the woman she had a passionate, anonymous vacation fling with, sparks and subpoenas fly. Legal Affairs: one law firm, three best friends, three chances to fall in love. (978-1-63555-359-8)

Providence by Leigh Hays. With every click of the shutter, photographer Rebekiah Kearns finds it harder and harder to keep Lindsey Blackwell in focus without getting too close. (978-1-63555-620-9)

Taking a Shot at Love by KC Richardson. When academic and athletic worlds collide, will English professor Celeste Bouchard and basketball coach Lisa Tobias ignore their attraction to achieve their professional goals? (978-1-63555-549-3)

Flight to the Horizon by Julie Tizard. Airline captain Kerri Sullivan and flight attendant Janine Case struggle to survive an emergency water landing and overcome dark secrets to give love a chance to fly. (978-1-63555-331-4)

In Helen's Hands by Nanisi Barrett D'Arnuk. As her mistress, Helen pushes Mickey to her sensual limits, delivering the pleasure only a BDSM lifestyle can provide her. (978-1-63555-639-1)

Jamis Bachman, Ghost Hunter by Jen Jensen. In Sage Creek, Utah, a poltergeist stirs to life and past secrets emerge.(978-1-63555-605-6)

Moon Shadow by Suzie Clarke. Add betrayal, season with survival, then serve revenge smokin' hot with a sharp knife. (978-1-63555-584-4)

Spellbound by Jean Copeland and Jackie D. When the supernatural worlds of good and evil face off, love might be what saves them all. (978-1-63555-564-6)

Temptation by Kris Bryant. Can experienced nanny Cassie Miller deny her growing attraction and keep her relationship with her boss professional? Or will they sidestep propriety and give in to temptation? (978-1-63555-508-0)

The Inheritance by Ali Vali. Family ties bring Tucker Delacroix and Willow Vernon together, but they could also tear them, and any chance they have at love, apart. (978-1-63555-303-1)

Thief of the Heart by MJ Williamz. Kit Hanson makes a living seducing rich women in casinos and relieving them of the expensive jewelry most won't even miss. But her streak ends when she meets beautiful FBI agent Savannah Brown. (978-1-63555-572-1)